SIR GAWAIN AND THE GREEN KNIGHT

broadview editions
series editor: L.W. Conolly

SIR GAWAIN AND THE GREEN KNIGHT

edited by Paul Battles

broadview editions

Library and Archives Canada Cataloguing in Publication

Gawain and the Grene Knight
    Sir Gawain and the Green Knight / edited by Paul Battles.

Includes bibliographical references.
ISBN 978-1-55481-019-2

    1. Gawain (Legendary character)—Romances. 2. Knights and knighthood—Poetry. 3. Arthurian romances. I. Battles, Paul, 1968- II. Title.

PR2065.G3A329 2012   821'.1   C2012-904323-0

Broadview Editions
The Broadview Editions series represents the ever-changing canon of literature in English by bringing together texts long regarded as classics with valuable lesser-known works.

Advisory editor for this volume: Martin Boyne

Broadview Press is an independent, international publishing house, incorporated in 1985.

We welcome comments and suggestions regarding any aspect of our publications—please feel free to contact us at the addresses below or at broadview@broadviewpress.com.

North America
Post Office Box 1243, Peterborough, Ontario, Canada K9J 7H5
2215 Kenmore Avenue, Buffalo, NY, USA 14207
Tel: (705) 743-8990; Fax: (705) 743-8353
email: customerservice@broadviewpress.com

UK, Europe, Central Asia, Middle East, Africa, India, and Southeast Asia
Eurospan Group, 3 Henrietta St., London WC2E 8LU, United Kingdom
Tel: 44 (0) 1767 604972; Fax: 44 (0) 1767 601640
email: eurospan@turpin-distribution.com

Australia and New Zealand
NewSouth Books
c/o TL Distribution, 15-23 Helles Ave., Moorebank, NSW, Australia 2170
Tel: (02) 8778 9999; Fax: (02) 8778 9944
email: orders@tldistribution.com.au

www.broadviewpress.com

This book is printed on paper containing 100% post-consumer fibre.

Typesetting and assembly: True to Type Inc., Claremont, Canada.

PRINTED IN CANADA

To Dominique and Perry

Contents

Acknowledgements

This edition was born of a desire to help students read *Sir Gawain and the Green Knight* in Middle English. I would therefore like to thank all of my students who, over the years, have given both general and specific feedback for improving it. Thanks especially to Rob Allega, Tyler Blaker, Chris Brewer, Jessica Burris, Emma Copeland, Samantha Cornett, Sarah Cramer, Cara Dreher, Liz Gorrell, Kylie Miller, and Jenaba Waggy. Erin Chandler served as my research assistant for two years and worked on many aspects of the project.

I would also like to thank the fellow members of the Middle English reading group at Urbana, especially Rebecca Lartigue, Rebecca Brackman, and Dominique Battles; the germ for the edition came from the group's close reading and discussion of the poem.

Hanover College's Dean of Academic Affairs and Faculty Development Committee provided two grants that funded a research assistant. I am also deeply grateful to the staff of Duggan Library for their sheer inexhaustible diligence in obtaining sources.

I am grateful to the following for granting permission to reprint various texts:

The British Library, for the text of the poem from MS Cotton Nero A. X., f. 95-128.

The Orion Publishing Group, London, for the excerpts from *Caradoc* and *The Knight with the Sword*.

The Taylor and Francis Group, LLC, for the excerpts from *The Story of Merlin* and *Lancelot Part III*.

Above all, I would like to thank Dominique Battles for her unflagging encouragement, can-do attitude, and good cheer. She also read two successive drafts in their entirety and offered many valuable suggestions on both. I couldn't have done it without you!

Introduction

Sir Gawain and the Green Knight is a masterpiece of medieval English literature and one of the finest Arthurian tales in any language. It is primarily a chivalric romance—the story of a knight's perilous quest—but it is also an exemplum, a tale of mystery and betrayal, and a sympathetic but honest character study of a man facing his death. Most unusually for a romance, *Sir Gawain and the Green Knight* describes no jousting, no slaying of monsters, no rescuing of damsels in distress, and no fight to the death against a treacherous adversary. Some of these romance staples do take place, but off-stage. Instead, the poem dwells on descriptions of court life: feasting, hunting, castles, armor, and, perhaps most memorably, the sparkling rapport between a lady and the most courteous of courtiers.

Sir Gawain and the Green Knight affords new insights on every rereading. Nothing is as it first seems, and the poem's apparently simple surfaces hide layers of nuance and subtlety. To use one of the poet's own favorite images, *Sir Gawain and the Green Knight* is like an exquisitely cut jewel: its intricate structure, its highly wrought verbal art, its symbolism, and its numerological patterns dazzle the reader no matter from which vantage the poem is considered, encouraging and rewarding examination from various perspectives.

Time and Place of Composition

Despite the poem's excellence, little is known about its creator. Our sole source of information is the work itself, as well as the unique manuscript in which it survives: London, British Library MS Cotton Nero A. X. This contains three other poems—*Pearl*, *Patience*, and *Cleanness* (or *Purity*)—very similar to *Sir Gawain* in meter, diction, and theme. The four poems were written down in the late fourteenth century and share dialectal characteristics of the north-west Midlands; most editors and critics agree that they are by the same author (Andrew 1997). The language of *Sir Gawain* has been localized to the border of south-east Cheshire and north-west Staffordshire (McIntosh, Samuels, and Benskin 1986; Putter and Stokes 2007), though this may reflect the scribe's rather than the poet's language (Duggan 1997).

Attempts to identify the *Gawain* poet have revolved mostly around the names Hugh and John Massey—variously spelled Massi, Masse, or Mascy—which some scholars believe to be hidden in several locations throughout the Cotton Nero A. X manuscript (e.g., Nolan and Farley-Hills 1971; Vantuono 1975, 1981). However, these conclusions have not been widely accepted.

A different and more fruitful strategy has been to associate the poems with the period in which they were written. *Sir Gawain and the Green*

Knight has often been read as a Ricardian work. This era takes its name from Richard II, who ruled from 1377 to 1399. Broadly speaking, there are two kinds of Ricardian readings. The first compares the poem with the works of notable contemporary authors, especially Geoffrey Chaucer (c. 1343-1400), John Gower (c. 1330-1408), and William Langland (c. 1332-c. 1386) (Burrow 1971). Its focus is literary and comparative, using Richard's name as a convenient label for the later fourteenth century. The second type of Ricardian reading is political and historical. It connects *Sir Gawain and the Green Knight* with specific movements, controversies, events, or figures. Because the manuscript was written in or close to Cheshire, that county has played a prominent role in such criticism (Bennett 1983, 1997; Barrett 2009). Richard was Earl of Chester, and, throughout his reign, the county formed the base of his military power. He came to depend more and more upon his Cheshire subjects, feeling that he could trust only them. In reward for their unflagging loyalty, Richard bestowed great favors upon Cheshire, in the process alienating the rest of the country. Toward the end of his reign, he even elevated it to a principality, a status that it promptly lost upon Richard's deposition. Certain details in *Sir Gawain and the Green Knight* do seem suggestive when read in this light. One of the few localities specifically named in Gawain's journey, the Forest of Wirral, is in Cheshire. The poem's strikingly young King Arthur may allude to the fact that Richard ascended the throne at age ten. Moreover, Richard's concern with sexual purity may well find reflection in the nature of Gawain's test at Castle Hautdesert (Bowers 2001). The heraldic arms of Robert de Vere, Richard's favorite, feature a five-pointed star (Astell 1999; Mann 2009).

Other scholars, however, date the poem to the reign of Richard's predecessor, Edward III (Ingledew 2006; Cooke 1989; Cooke and Boulton 1999). The fashions in clothing, armor, and architecture in *Sir Gawain and the Green Knight* seem to point to the period between 1330 and 1360 (Cooke 1989), though the poem cannot have been written before 1347, the earliest possible time for the founding of the Order of the Garter (Boulton 1987: 103), whose motto is found at the end of the manuscript. Any dating prior to 1377, when Richard ascended to the throne, would obviously negate the Ricardian hypothesis. Moreover, various scholars continue to propose different patrons, and also different pertinent political contexts, for *Sir Gawain and the Green Knight* (Carruthers 2001; Meyer 2001; Stephens 2006; Hill 2009). Until the question of the poem's date of composition has been settled, it is impossible to make definitive pronouncements about these matters.

Meter, Style, and Structure

In *The Parson's Prologue* in Geoffrey Chaucer's *The Canterbury Tales*, the narrator avers, "But trusteth wel, I am a Southren man; I kan nat geeste [compose] 'rum, ram, ruff,' by lettre" (X.42-43). This appears to mock the alliterative style of poems like *Sir Gawain and the Green Knight*. The fourteenth century witnessed a remarkable flourishing of such poetry, a phenomenon known as the "Alliterative Revival." Chaucer, influenced by French verse, wrote his earliest poetry in iambic tetrameter and later established iambic pentameter as the medium of choice for English poetry. By contrast, the *Gawain*-poet uses a poetic form directly descended from Anglo-Saxon verse (Bredehoft 2005; Russom 2004). The differences between these meters have a linguistic origin. Old English, a Germanic language, places stress chiefly on word-beginnings, whereas French, a romance language, stresses word-endings. Consequently, the earliest English poetry "rhymes" on word-beginnings (that is, it employs alliteration), while French verse rhymes on word-endings. The meter favored by Chaucer came to dominate the mainstream of the poetic tradition, while the works of the *Gawain*-poet and his contemporary, William Langland, proved the last great flowering of medieval English alliterative verse.

Since the meter of *Sir Gawain and the Green Knight* may be unfamiliar, it is worth examining its nature and origins in more detail. In Old English poetry, each line is composed of an a-verse (or on-verse) and a b-verse (or off-verse), with an intervening caesura. Each verse has two strongly stressed syllables (or staves) that are linked through alliteration in the manner illustrated below (with *a* marking the alliterating staves, *x* the non-alliterating ones, and / the caesura):

$$a\ a\ /\ a\ x$$
$$a\ x\ /\ a\ x$$
$$x\ a\ /\ a\ x$$

The meter of *Sir Gawain* is quite similar, with the *a a / a x* pattern being very common. The main difference between the Old and Middle English alliterative meters is that the latter is somewhat looser. When compared with the Old English epic poem *Beowulf*, *Sir Gawain and the Green Knight* allows more weakly stressed syllables, often introduces a third stave in the a-verse, and permits alliteration on the second stave of the b-verse. These differences derive from changes in the language itself; late Old English verse already shows some of the "loosening" observable in Middle English alliterative poetry (Lehmann 1956). Using the same notations as above, the primary verse-types in *Sir Gawain* can be represented as follows (Duggan 1997):

$$a\ a\ /\ a\ x \qquad\qquad x\ a\ a\ /\ a\ x$$
$$a\ a\ /\ a\ a \qquad\qquad a\ a\ x\ /\ a\ x$$
$$a\ a\ a\ /\ a\ x \qquad\qquad a\ x\ a\ /\ a\ x$$
$$a\ a\ a\ /\ a\ a$$

The opening sentence of *Sir Gawain and the Green Knight* illustrates two very common types, *a a / a x* and *a a a / a x*:

Sithen (a) the sege (a) and the assaut (a) / was sesed (a) at Troye (x),
The borgh (a) brittened (a) and brent (a) / to brondes (a) and askes (x),
The tulk (a) that the trammes (a) / of tresoun (a) ther wroght (x)
Was tried (a) for his tricherie (a), / the trewest (a) on erthe (x).

The next line shows one further wrinkle, namely that all vowels and initial *h-* alliterate: *Hit (a) was Ennias (a) the athel (a), / and his highe (a) kynde (x).*

The alliterative meter encouraged the development of a poetic "word-hoard," a stock of synonyms that poets could employ when alliterating on a given letter. For example, some Old English poetic synonyms for "man, warrior" include *beorn, freca, guma, leod, rinc, secg,* and *wiga.* Each begins with a different sound and can thus be employed in various metrical environments. These terms also occur in *Sir Gawain and the Green Knight,* as *burn, freke, gome, lede, renk, segge,* and *wyy,* respectively. The utility of these and similar inherited words is shown by the fact they alliterate in over 99 per cent of their occurrences in the poem. Chaucer and other London poets studiously avoid these terms, and they have since vanished from the English language. All of this shows that the inherited epithets for "man, warrior" were poetic and, from the perspective of an urbane Southerner like Chaucer, old-fashioned and dialectal. By contrast, the words Chaucer did employ, such as *man, knyght, lorde,* and *kyng,* had no association with alliterative verse; while they do occur in *Sir Gawain and the Green Knight,* they frequently do not alliterate, and of course they have also survived into Modern English (Borroff 1962).

Unlike most alliterative poems, *Sir Gawain and the Green Knight* employs stanzas. These are of varying length, but each concludes with a *bob and wheel.* The bob consists of a single iambic foot and the wheel of four lines of irregular iambic trimeter, the whole rhyming *ababa.* The idiosyncratic combination of alliterative and rhymed iambic meters may be the poet's attempt to combine the native English and French poetic traditions (though rhyme appears sporadically in late Old English verse as well). The bob and wheel is a surprisingly useful narrative device (Chickering 1997). It often summarizes the main idea of the preceding stanza in a pithy and memorable way, but it can also spring a surprise on the reader. For example, the fact that the Green Knight is in fact completely green—not just in clothes and gear, but in his skin and hair as well—is introduced in the last line of the seventh stanza. Similarly, the fifteenth stanza describes how Arthur is about to strike at the knight, when suddenly, in the bob and wheel, Gawain asks to be given the "game."

The significance of the bob and wheel goes beyond its utility as a poetic device, for its five lines reflect the hero's celebrated "five fives," the set of virtues represented in Gawain's pentangle (see below). The number five is, in various permutations (5, 25, 25 + 5, and so on), woven into the poem's entire fabric. For instance, the stanza that describes Gawain's pentangle contains twenty-five alliterative lines and a five-line bob and wheel. The poem contains 2530 (2525 + 5) lines. Though the individual stanzas are of differing lengths, the total number of lines divided by the total number of stanzas (101) equals twenty-five with a remainder of five. Such patterning may seem contrived, but medieval poets employ numerology to represent essential truths. Some medieval treatises discuss five as the "human" number, for human beings have five wits (or senses), five limbs, five fingers on each hand, five toes on each foot, and so on. In *Sir Gawain and the Green Knight*, the number seems to represent Gawain's human perfection: he is the best knight of the foremost court in Christendom, the idealized representative of an ideal society.

Other aspects of the poem reveal a similarly intricate structure. Large illuminated initials divide the poem into four parts or *fitts*. (*Fitt* is a Middle English term for a poem's divisions, and, although it does not occur in *Sir Gawain and the Green Knight*, the word is traditionally applied to the poem's four sections.) The third fitt features three hunts, three bedroom scenes, three exchanges of winnings, and the triple temptation of Gawain. The last, recalling various biblical "three temptations," probably reveals the fundamental significance of the number.

Sir Gawain and the Green Knight as an Arthurian Poem

Sir Gawain and the Green Knight reveals an intimate knowledge of earlier Arthurian writings. The inspiration for the beheading game, whose ultimate origins seem to have been Celtic (E. Brewer 1997; text in E. Brewer 1992), in all likelihood came to the English poet from the *Livre de Caradoc* (Benson 1961; see Appendix A); this is part of the anonymous *First Continuation* (c. 1200) of Chrétien de Troyes's unfinished poem *Perceval*. In this brief tale—its fullest version is less than one-tenth as long as *Sir Gawain*—a finely dressed knight rides into Arthur's palace during a feast at Pentecost, accuses the knights of cowardice, and demands that someone behead him with the sword he is carrying, in return for which he will deliver a blow in a year's time. The challenge is accepted by Caradoc—a new knight and Arthur's nephew—who cuts off the knight's head. Unperturbed, the stranger reattaches it and bids Caradoc to prepare for the return blow in a year. Next Pentecost, when the knight reappears, Caradoc willingly presents his neck for the cut, but the stranger merely feints a blow and then gives him a tap. He finally reveals himself to be Caradoc's father. Other motifs, such as a beautiful temptress, the hunts, and the exchange of winnings all have parallels in different Arthurian stories, as do the descriptions of feasts, Bertilak's castle, and Gawain's welcome at Hautdesert (E. Brewer 1997; Putter 1995). The French Vulgate cycle (c. 1215-35), a group of five anonymous prose romances very influential in the development of Arthur's "biography," supplies the characters of Bertilak and his wife (see Appendix B), as well as certain details about Morgan le Fay.

However, though inspired by previous Arthurian writings in some aspects, *Sir Gawain and the Green Knight* remains original in others. The figure of the Green Knight has no obvious parallel in any medieval narrative—Arthurian or otherwise—and indeed the whole plot after the challenger's departure follows a different trajectory than the one in the *Livre de Caradoc*. Gawain's quest for the Green Chapel, the juxtaposed scenes of hunting and sexual temptation, and the surprising revelation of just how Gawain has been tested (and found wanting) transform the bare outline of the beheading game into something else entirely. In comparing *Sir Gawain and the Green Knight* to its analogues, one is reminded of Shakespeare reworking stories from Saxo's *Gesta Danorum* (late 12th/early 13th century) and Geoffrey of Monmouth's *History of the Kings of Britain* (c. 1136) into *Hamlet* and *King Lear*. The poet is not afraid to make use of existing plot lines, but he reshapes and enriches them according to his artistic vision. In *Sir Gawain*, this vision entails a close study of human nature as exemplified in the very best of knights (who nevertheless remains merely human), of the psychology of sin and temptation, and of the strengths and limitations of chivalry as an ethical and practical system.

A similarly original treatment of traditional elements can be seen in the poem's depiction of its hero, Sir Gawain. Gawain's rise to fame as Arthurian hero begins with Geoffrey of Monmouth's *History of the Kings of Britain*, where he is Arthur's nephew and best knight. Chrétien de Troyes adds other traits to his character, especially courtesy and wisdom, which resolve many difficult situations. Because he is recognized as Arthur's pre-eminent knight, he is both a role model and foil for heroes such as Erec and Yvain, and, to a lesser extent, Lancelot and Perceval. In his later poems, Chrétien's portrayal of Gawain can be tongue-in-cheek: in *Knight of the Cart*, he gets trapped in the Underwater Bridge while Lancelot succeeds in crossing the more formidable Sword Bridge and Gawain must, humiliatingly, be rescued. Still, he remains an admirable figure. If he fails to compare to Lancelot, this says less about Gawain than it does about Lancelot. In subsequent French Arthurian works, however, Gawain's character deteriorates markedly. This culminates in the thirteenth-century prose *Tristan* and in the Vulgate cycle, where he becomes the antithesis of the ideal knight. In the Vulgate *Quest for the Holy Grail*, he kills no less than eighteen fellow Knights of the Round Table while trying to find the Grail, and he repeatedly rebuffs hermits who advise him to repent and do penance. Throughout most of the Vulgate cycle, Gawain is an irascible and irreligious figure.

Gawain's decline in French Arthurian literature is linked with the rise of French knights such as Lancelot and Galahad, but in England Gawain's character does not undergo a similar pejoration. Gawain remains Arthur's chief knight and the most popular protagonist of knightly tales. This changes only with Sir Thomas Malory's (c. 1405-71) rendering of French Arthurian tales into English (and, in the sections of *Le Morte Darthur* [or *d'Arthur*] drawn from English sources, Gawain is noticeably less debased). But popular though he remains in England, he is not associated with an ideal especially highlighted by *Sir Gawain and the Green Knight*, namely moral purity (*clannes*, 653). In fact, to a reader familiar with the tradition, this is a decidedly unusual trait to associate with him, for one's of Gawain's most enduring attributes is his amorousness (Whiting 2006). The whole catalogue of Gawain's virtues contains few echoes of his more pronounced traits in earlier stories; even his courtesy is mentioned only as the twenty-fourth of twenty-five virtues. Gawain's special devotion to the Virgin Mary is also difficult to parallel.

Again, this allows some insights into the poem's artistic concerns. Gawain's achievements in *Sir Gawain and the Green Knight* can be enumerated as follows: he is not intimidated by the Green Knight and rescues Arthur from an embarrassing situation; he is determined to redeem his word, even if it means his death; and he resists the sexual advances of a stunningly beautiful woman. His major *physical* accomplishment is to travel through a perilous landscape, and—despite being inundated by rain, sleet, and snow—to find the Green Chapel. Gawain's fabulous exploits, such as fighting dragons and *wodwos*, are mentioned only parenthetically. The effect, in a poem otherwise replete with men who give speeches with severed heads and castles that materialize out of nowhere, is to make Gawain a thoroughly believable, realistic hero. He becomes an Everyman whose testing takes the form of a series of ethical dilemmas to which most readers could relate: Would I give my life to honor my word? Could I resist the sexual temptation of a blatant invitation proffered by a beautiful woman? Because Gawain meets these and other ethical challenges, the Green Knight memorably asserts that Gawain surpasses other knights as a pearl exceeds a white pea (2364-65). Gawain judges himself more harshly, and the audience is invited to reach its own conclusions, which brings the matter even closer to home. It is impossible to evaluate Gawain's success or failure without asking what standard applies, and it follows that the reader is urged to ponder whether he or she would be able to meet that same standard.

Themes

Literary criticism has brought to light many important themes in *Sir Gawain and the Green Knight*. Some are explicitly stated in the poem, while others can be inferred. Four of the most important are discussed below.

Trawthe

As noted above, one of the poem's main themes concerns fidelity to one's pledged word, a virtue the poem calls *trawthe* (Burrow 1965; Barron 1980). Gawain seeks out the Green Knight because he has given his word that he will, even if this means certain death. He is given every excuse for not going. When Gawain is about to leave, the courtiers are shocked that Arthur does not try to dissuade him; for them, the agreement amounts to no more than a game that should not be taken too seriously. This is only the first of many temptations that Gawain faces; right up to the very moment when he arrives at the Green Chapel, various characters try to turn him aside from his quest.

The centrality of *trawthe* to Gawain's character and to the poem's action is indicated by its pride of place in the description of Gawain's heraldic device. The significance of this device, the pentangle, is carefully explained by the poet: *Hit is a syngne that Salamon set sumwhyle / In bytoknyng of trawthe* (625-26, "It is a symbol that Solomon devised long ago to signify *trawthe*"). He further asserts that Gawain is entitled to wear the pentangle because he is *tulk of tale most true / And gentylest knyght of lote* (638-39, "the man who is most true to his word and the noblest knight in bearing").

Gawain's *trawthe* is tested in several ways. The first and most obvious test lies in meeting the Green Knight at the appointed time to receive the promised blow. The other challenges lie in the Lady of Hautdesert's seduction and in her offer of the green girdle. Gawain passes all of these tests but the last, which the Green Knight judges a minor transgression. Gawain disagrees, and in the ensuing discussion, as well as in his confession at Camelot, the concept of *trawthe* figures prominently once more (2348-49, 2354, 2383, 2509).

Chivalry

Trawthe is closely connected to the chivalric ethos. One important chivalric virtue, *leuté* ("loyalty"), is in some passages used virtually synonymously with *trawthe* (2366, 2381, 2499). More importantly, the test of Gawain's *trawthe* unfolds through a challenge to the integrity of chivalry as an ideal (Clein 1987).

By the later Middle Ages, chivalry had evolved to include three main components. These can described as "feudal" (serving one's lord), "courtly" (serving one's lady), and "religious" (serving God). That is, a knight was expected to be not only fearless and strong, but also courteous—a quality learned chiefly through *the lel layk of luf* (1513, "the faithful practice of love")—and pious. It is not difficult to see the potential conflicts inherent in this system, and medieval authors were quick to exploit them. Already in Chrétien's chivalric romances, the main challenge for the hero lies less in overcoming external obstacles than in balancing the competing obligations to lord, lady, and God. Erec and Yvain struggle with reconciling their roles as warrior-knights and lover-husbands, and this conflict is even more pronounced for Lancelot. Adulterous love obviously sharpens the conflict of the courtly aspect of chivalry with the feudal and religious ones. Lancelot's relationship with Guinevere necessitates betraying his lord as well as transgressing against the sacrament of marriage.

A similar dynamic obtains in *Sir Gawain and the Green Knight*. If Gawain were to give in to sexual temptation, he would be committing a grave offense against *leuté*, repaying his host's (apparent) trust with betrayal. Also, Gawain would then be false to his own ethos, which involves *clannes* ("purity") and devotion to the Virgin Mary. The poet makes this explicit in several passages, both during (1549-50, 1768-69, 1774-75) and after (2338-68) Gawain's temptation by the chatelaine. In her conversations with Gawain, the Lady lures him not only with her obvious physical charms and barely veiled invitations, but also by arguing that love is the quintessence of chivalry. How could Gawain, with his reputation for courtliness, not be a lover? Gawain resists these advances, but he is eventually betrayed by his courtesy. When at several points she presses the issue, Gawain is tempted to reject the lady firmly. He does not do so because *he cared for his cortaysye* (1773), and courtesy mandates politeness to women. This allows her to continue probing for an area of weakness, and she finally discovers one.

Though Gawain is very nearly impervious to temptation, even an apparently minor weakness threatens to undermine the whole edifice on which his character is built. Because he is too careful of his reputation and therefore loath to reject the chatelaine outright, Gawain allows her to continue tempting him. She finally discovers that although he can resist her romantic overtures, the lure of the green girdle—which promises to protect him from the Green Knight's blow—proves too much for him. When Sir Bertilak says as much to him, Gawain acknowledges the truth of the accusation and, in rather harsh language, calls himself a coward (2374, 2379, 2508). Furthermore, cowardice leads him to conceal the belt from the host, since he would otherwise have to explain just how he came into possession of this piece of intimate apparel, and furthermore, under the terms of the exchange-of-winnings game, he would have had to give it up as well. Sir Bertilak finds that Gawain's failure to return the belt shows a want of *leuté* (2366), and both Gawain himself (2381) and the narrator (2499) concur. Both cowardice and a failure of *leuté* can be interpreted as weaknesses in the feudal aspect of chivalry.

Sir Gawain and the Green Knight emphasizes the integrity of the chivalric ideal. A weakness in any single aspect undermines the soundness of the whole. The poem also shows that it is exceedingly difficult—perhaps impossible—to reconcile the competing obligations that the feudal, courtly, and religious aspects of chivalry make of knights.

The Role of Women

The Lady's temptation of Sir Gawain is only one manifestation of the crucial role women play in *Sir Gawain and the Green Knight*. As the hero learns at the end of the quest, his ordeal was masterminded by the enchantress Morgan le Fay, Arthur's half-sister and Gawain's aunt; the Green Knight acts on her behalf. This surprising revelation inverts the importance of gender to the plot. From the perspective of Gawain—and the audience—the adventure up until Sir Bertilak's explanation can be summarized as follows: when the Green Knight tests the bravery of Arthur's knights, Gawain takes up the challenge and, after a difficult journey, reaches a castle whose lord offers to show Gawain the way to the green chapel; on the appointed day, Gawain redeems his pledged word and thereby upholds both his own honor and that of his lord, King Arthur. But Sir Bertilak's revelation implies that the narrative has a very different trajectory, one that looks more like this: when Morgan le Fay sends an emissary to Camelot to test its pride and to harm her rival, Queen Guinevere, Sir Gawain takes up the game and reaches the site of his real test, the chatelaine's sexual temptations; the Virgin Mary intercedes for her knight, and Gawain only accepts a belt from the Lady, for which he later receives a cut on the neck (the seat of pride), while his life is spared. In the process of revising our understanding of the poem's plot, the female characters go from marginal accessories to planning and shaping its every twist (Heng 1991).

Many editors and critics have found this difficult to accept, even going so far as to change the text to lessen women's agency. They see Morgan le Fay as a *dea ex machina* through which the poet brings the poem to an (unsatisfactory) close, viewing Sir Bertilak as Gawain's real opponent (Friedman 1960). However, efforts to downplay women's importance to the poem are misguided from both thematic (Fisher 1996) and editorial (Rowley 2003; P. Battles 2010a) perspectives. Besides Morgan le Fay, other female characters—especially the Lady—also play key roles, and the audience is invited to reflect on the nature of those roles. Just as the poem offers different perspectives about Gawain's failure, it also presents competing views about Morgan and the Lady. Gawain, after acknowledging his own fault in taking the belt, bitterly casts them in the role of the eternal Eve (2411-26). Yet these comments are made not by the narrator, but by a character whose fallibility and limited perspective have just been exposed. Gawain's obvious anger and disappointment, as well as his exaggeration—he has not, after all, been expelled from Paradise, suffered blindness, or lost his life, like the figures to whom he compares himself— here suggest a certain narratorial distance, if not outright irony. Moreover, by the terms of the beheading game, Morgan would have been within her rights to have the Green Knight kill Gawain regardless of whether he resisted the chatelaine's advances. Thus Morgan is interested not in harming Gawain but in testing him (Williams 1985; Woods 2002). And, insofar as these tests teach him a lesson and thus make him into a better person, Morgan le Fay and the Lady help the hero grow.

Green and Gold

A distinctive characteristic of *Sir Gawain and the Green Knight* is its use of symmetry and antithesis. The poem depicts two New Years, two courts, two feasts, two surpassingly beautiful ladies, and two extensive descriptions of men (and horses) in armor; it also contrasts Camelot's youth with the Green Knight's experience, the intruder's rudeness with Gawain's courtesy, pleasant summers with harsh winters, a beautiful young woman with an ugly crone, and *trawthe* with *unleuté*.

One recurrent contrast lies in the use of two colors, green and gold (Goldhurst 1958). Green is obviously important because of the Green Knight, who is not just clothed in green but green all over; the only part of his body that is not green is his red eyes. He also carries a holly bob, which, as the poet says, is *grattest in grene when graves ar bare* (207, "most vividly green when trees are bare"). Since this plant also has red berries, the poem invites us to associate the Green Knight and the holly that he carries. The intruder is also described as having a beard *much ... as a busk* (182, "as great as that of a bush") and is compared with other natural phenomena; the hue of both knight and horse is likened to green grass (235). The link between the Green Knight and nature is so pronounced that some critics have seen him as a vestigial fertility deity whose ritual slaughter-and-resurrection at the year's end/beginning recalls pagan rituals (Speirs 1957). Of course, we later learn that the Green Knight was really Sir Bertilak, disguised and protected by Morgan le Fay's magic, and the fertility-deity hypothesis remains controversial. However, there does seem to be a fundamental association of the Green Knight with nature, especially since his other persona, Sir Bertilak, is persistently linked with the outdoors and hunting. Meanwhile his opponent, Sir Gawain, is just as persistently associated with civilization: he is justly renowned for his politeness, finds great pleasure in fellowship, and excels in the arts of *luf-talkyng*. Where his antagonist is linked with green, Gawain's color is gold. Not only is Gawain's armor profusely decorated with gold, but more importantly the poet twice mentions—at the beginning and end of the shield's description—that gold is the color of the pentangle (620, 663). The same passage describes how *Gawan was for gode knawen and as golde pured* (633, "Gawain was known for his virtue and as pure as gold"), and this is why he bears the pentangle device (636). Thus gold is important for reasons other than its ornamental or material value: it embodies Gawain's virtues and figures forth the ideals by which he lives.

If the poem suggests an antithesis between "natural" green and "civilized" gold, it also complicates matters by combining green with gold and nature with civilization. The Green Knight wears gold spurs, and his horse is decorated with golden threads and bells; even his axe is green and gold. The juxtaposed hunting and bedroom scenes only superficially represent different poles of the natural-social continuum—Gawain lies comfortably in bed and converses with the Lady while the host braves the bitter cold to kill various animals—for Gawain too is being stalked, even though he does not realize it. The Green Knight turns out to be none other than Gawain's host, who is just as much at home feasting guests as he is at hunting, and whose court is no less sophisticated than Camelot. And finally, the girdle that Gawain receives from the Lady, and which becomes so prominent during and after Gawain's second encounter with the Green Knight, is another green item decorated with gold.

When he takes the girdle, Gawain for the first time mingles green with his native gold. That this is a significant and symbolic action is shown later, when Gawain wears the green girdle as a balderik over his surcoat and calls it the *bende of [his] blame* (2506), where *bende* signifies both "band" but also the heraldic "bend," a diagonal bar that modifies a given device. Because Gawain's surcoat is adorned with his pentangle, the green girdle both visually and heraldically alters Gawain's identity; the gold pentangle is no longer a seamless, unbroken whole (Plummer 1991).

Precisely what the green *bende* signifies is subject to different explanations. The hero understands it as a *token of untrawthe* (2509), the antithesis of the pentangle. Arthur and his court treat the girdle as a badge of distinction; every member of the Round Table wears a green belt, and it was considered a mark of renown and honor (2519-2520). A third explanation is given by Sir Bertilak, who offers the girdle to Gawain as a memento of his adventure; since the girdle reflects his own green hue, and since he emphatically calls it *my wede* (2358, "my garment"), he seems to be giving Gawain part of himself. Perhaps he hopes that his own "natural" green will qualify the excessively "civilized" gold of the hero. Humankind can no more do without nature than it can escape its own imperfect nature. To use a term from analytical psychology, in the poem green is the "shadow" or complementary opposite of gold, just as Sir Bertilak is Gawain's shadow. To grow into a more mature hero, Gawain must accept that both green and gold are part of human nature.

Spelling, Language, and Syntax

To the modern reader, Middle English spelling conventions seem oddly lax. The Cotton Nero A. X. scribe spells "night" *night, nyght, naght,* and *niyght.* However, there is method in this orthographic madness, and bearing in mind a few points will help to minimize confusion.

First, it is always a good idea to sound out any problematic words. When read aloud, it is easier to see that *assaut* is Modern English "assault," that *cogh* is "cough," and so on. Like most Middle English texts, *Sir Gawain and the Green Knight* also does not consistently distinguish the following letter pairs:

> *c* and *s* (cf. *case* and *cace*)
> *c* and *k* (cf. *castel* and *kastel*)
> *i* and *y* (cf. *like* and *lyke*)
> *i* and *é* (cf. *bodi* and *bodé*)[1]
> *a* and *o* (cf. *name* and *nome*)

---

1 In almost all cases, the Modern English equivalent spelling is "y," as in *Maré* (Mary), *jopardé* (jeopardy), or *hevé* (heavy).

Sch stands for "sh," not "sk," in words such as *bischop* and *disch*. Finally, the scribe often doubles consonants after short vowels, so that *bitte* is equivalent to Modern English "bit," *bidde* to "bid," and *hitte* to "hit."

Pronouns

It is a truism of language learning that the "little" words—function words such as prepositions and pronouns—often present the greatest obstacle to fluent comprehension. *Sir Gawain and the Green Knight* is no exception. Though the present edition glosses difficult forms, a familiarity with the personal pronouns, in particular, will make reading the text less onerous. While the first person forms (*I, me, mine—we, us, oure*) will cause few difficulties, it is worth having a closer look at the second and third persons. In the second person, Middle English makes distinction between the singular (*thou, thee, thine*) and plural (*ye, yow, yowre/yowres*):

	Sing./intimate	Pl./polite
Subject	thou	ye
Object	thee	yow
Possessive	thy, thyn	yowre, yowres

As in many modern European languages such as French and German, the plural form is also used when addressing individuals, depending upon the context and intended tone. As a rule, *ye* conveys respect, formality, or distance, while *thou* indicates intimacy, familiarity, or hostility. Rank plays a key role here. As Arthur's inferior, Gawain always addresses the king with *ye* and *yow*, whereas Arthur replies with *thou* and *thee*. When the Green Knight addresses Arthur with *thou* and *thee*, it implies a hostile stance—an unwillingness to show the deference due to a social superior.

The third person forms, with exception of the masculine forms (which are the familiar *he, him, his*), are listed below:

	Fem. sing.	Neut. sing.	Plural (all genders)
Subject	ho, scho	hit	thay
Object	hir, her	hit	hem, hom, him
Possessive	hir, her	his	her, hor, thayr, thayres

Only context can determine whether *him* means "him" or "them," or whether "her" should be understood as "her" or "their."

Morphology and Syntax

Two endings turn a verb into a present participle: the familiar *-ing* (usually spelled *-yng*), but also *-and(e)*. As a rule, the *-ing* forms like *talkyng* ("speech," "conversing") function as nouns (gerunds), while the *-and(e)* forms such as *laghande* ("laughing") function as adjectives or verbs. Similarly, two common adjectival and adverbial suffixes are *-ly* and *-lych*; these, however, are for present purposes identical (*comly* and *comlych* are both used as adjectives meaning "comely," "beautiful": *the comlych quene* 469, *the comly castel* 1366).

Sir Gawain and the Green Knight uses many impersonal constructions. The phrase *me lykes* (390) means "it pleases me," and *him thoght* (49) "it seemed to them."

Middle English has no rule against double negatives, which are often formed with the particle *ne* ("not," "nor"). For example, *Whether hade he no helme ne hawbergh nauther, / Ne no pysan ne no plate* (203-04) means, "Yet he had no helmet, and no coat of mail either, nor breast and neck armor or plate mail."

Inverted syntax occurs frequently in *Sir Gawain and the Green Knight*. For example, the phrase *baret that lofden* (21, literally "battle that loved") can be translated as "who loved battle." Also, prepositions can occur after their object (as postpositions), so that *hem under* (748) means "under them," "beneath them."

Sir Gawain and Twenty-First-Century Readers

In many ways, *Sir Gawain and the Green Knight* is a poem of and for its time. This is true not only of the poem's language, meter, and numero-logical structure, but also of its elaborate descriptions of material culture, which encompass food, drink, castle architecture (from external features such as turrets, to internal ones such as fireplaces), furnishings (tapestries, beds, quilts, cushions, curtains), weapons and armor, jewelry, furs and clothing, heraldry, and horses, to name only a few. This reads exactly like a catalogue of late-fourteenth-century aristocratic concerns (compare Mathew 1968), and no doubt the poem's original audience would have read these descriptions with great interest. The intricate realism with which such items are described would have lent the poem both relevance and verisimilitude. For modern readers, however, just the opposite is true. What does it mean that the Green Knight wears a cloak that is edged with ermine? That Guinevere sits under a canopy made of fabric from Toulouse? That when the hunters kill a deer, the dogs are rewarded with innards and blood-soaked bread placed on the animal's hide? For us such details become part of the poem's "alterity," scarcely less strange than its magic girdle, *wodwos*, and talking severed head.

Yet *Sir Gawain and the Green Knight* also transcends its own time. Since its rediscovery in the early nineteenth century, the poem has never ceased to fascinate readers. Among medieval English literary works, the sheer quantity of editions, translations, and critical monographs and arti-cles devoted to *Sir Gawain and the Green Knight* is rivaled only by those treating *Beowulf* and the works of Geoffrey Chaucer. There are many reasons for this, not least the excellence of the poem's style, plot, and structure. Yet two features, in particular, stand out. The first is the work's ending, which is perfectly in keeping with modern and postmodern sensibilities. *Sir Gawain and the Green Knight* certainly ends, but it provides no closure. We are left with three interpretations of Gawain's performance. If he were to be graded on his quest, these grades would range from something like "A+" (in the judgment of Arthur and his court) to an "almost-F" (in Gawain's own estimation), with the third being somewhere in between, probably "A-/B+" (in the Green Knight's assessment). Which of these is the correct answer? Despite rivers of ink, critics still disagree on this point. Sometimes opinion tilts one way, sometimes another, but it never reaches uniformity. Indeed, today the most widely held view is that the poem deliberately avoids providing the "true" answer (Blanch and Wasserman 1993). The poet refuses to impose a neat moral that wraps up the story, a strategy no doubt chosen to provoke debate and thereby involve the audience more deeply. Since we see the events through Gawain's perspective, he becomes our narrative surrogate, and the question of how harshly we are to judge his failure—if failure it is—forces us to scrutinize our own standards.

This dovetails with the second important factor in the modern reader's engagement with *Sir Gawain and the Green Knight*, namely the protagonist. Gawain is as credible as any character in medieval literature. The delicacy with which the author probes his psyche, making him at once clearly courageous and yet also poignantly afraid of death, reveals a character who is far more real than the stereotypical romance hero. This is not least because his thoughts, feelings, and actions are so thoroughly conflicted. He is both exquisitely humble and not in the least self-conscious about wearing a device that proclaims his perfection. He is obviously attracted to the Lady, yet just as obviously also uncomfortable with her in the bedroom. He is said to place all his faith in the Virgin Mary, but at the crucial moment abandons this for a magical and sexually suggestive girdle. He is so pious that he visits a confessor immediately after committing his sole transgression, but somehow fails to mention that very transgression. He is the master manipulator of language, yet outmaneuvered in conversation not only by the Lady, but also by Bertilak himself (who persuades him to make several questionable decisions). He is faultless in the five senses but fails to recognize his own aunt. Like most of us, Gawain does not see himself clearly, and, when his flaws are exposed in such a way that he has no choice but to acknowledge them, he recoils in anger and self-loathing. This reaction, along with the many other moments in the poem that lend insight into his character—such as his merry dancing after obtaining the green girdle, or his sleepless night before the day of reckoning—make his portrayal a thoroughly convincing one. Gawain's whole adventure is plotted and told in such a way as to make the imaginative gulf between him and us smaller. His fights against dragons and other monsters are barely mentioned, while the several varieties of temptation he experiences—especially the sexual one—are depicted in the utmost detail: appropriately so, for few of the poem's readers are going to kill dragons, but many will encounter some kind of sexual temptation at one time or another. This makes Gawain's tale, though set in a mythical past and embellished with elements of magic, thoroughly real and relevant to the modern reader.

A Note on the Text

Because of its dialect and use of poetic archaisms, *Sir Gawain and the Green Knight* is a work whose language is more difficult than—for instance—Chaucer's. Glosses and explanatory notes are provided to help minimize this difficulty; these are derived, in order of importance, from the *Middle English Dictionary*, scholarly writings, and previous editions of *Sir Gawain and the Green Knight*. Where my interpretation of a particular passage diverges significantly from received opinion, the rationale is explained in a note.

The marginal glosses are intended to create a fluent reading experience. Since these are necessarily brief, they are supplemented by a glossary at the end of this volume, which contains fuller explorations of the meanings of individual words and phrases. Yet even this glossary should not be viewed as the final word on the language of *Sir Gawain and the Green Knight*. As one early scholar noted, "Any attempt to fix or 'freeze' the poet's language into a final and settled form for glossary use is foredoomed to failure. Few other English poets have been as cognizant of the penumbra of other possible meanings into which the chief or unusual meaning of a word might shade off; few others as sensitive to verbal nuances and associations" (Savage 1944: 348). Interested readers are therefore encouraged to consult the *Middle English Dictionary* (*MED*), now available online at <http://quod.lib.umich.edu/m/mec/>, to further explore the poem's language. To make this easier, the glossary references *MED* headwords where these differ significantly in spelling from the forms found in *Sir Gawain and the Green Knight*.

In addition to the poem's language, the scribe's use of unfamiliar graphemes and spelling conventions poses further obstacles for modern readers. Therefore, the following aspects of the text have been normalized: thorn (þ) has been replaced by "th"; initial and medial yogh (ȝ) have been replaced by "y," "gh," or "w," as appropriate; final ȝ and tȝ have been replaced by "s"; the use of "v" and "u," "i" and "j," and "qu-" and "wh-" follows modern conventions; vocalic "w" (that is, where the letter represents a vowel, as in *trwe*, "true," or *nw*, "new") has been regularized;[1] and the objective form of the second person singular pronoun, spelled *the* in the manuscript, is rendered as "thee" throughout. Abbreviations have been silently expanded. The reason for these changes is to make the text as accessible as possible; readers who wish to experience the text as it appears in the manuscript are encouraged to consult the facsimile (London, British Library MS Cotton Nero A. X). In the emendations provided throughout, parentheses denote an illegible space in the manuscript.

---

1 The manuscript already uses such spellings as *newe* (alongside *nwe*), *truly* (as well as *trwly*), and so on.

The notes discuss the poem's language, material culture, customs, iconography, allusions (literary, historical, and religious), and, occasionally, interpretive approaches or problems. I have tried to strike a balance between providing too much and too little information, no doubt occasionally erring in either direction. Notes are intended to convey relevant information, to alert readers to passages whose meaning or import remains disputed, and to provide references for further reading.

Sir Gawain and the Green Knight

Sithen° the sege° and the assaut was sesed° at Troye,[1]	*after / siege / ceased*
The borgh brittened° and brent° to brondes° and askes,°	*citadel smashed / burned / cinders / ashes*
The tulk° that the trammes° of tresoun ther wroght[2]	*man / schemes*
Was tried[3] for his tricherie, the trewest° on erthe.[4]	*most certain*
5 Hit was Ennias° the athel,° and his highe kynde,°	*Aeneas / noble / great descendants*
That sithen depreced provinces,° and patrounes° bicome	*then subjugated nations / lords*
Welneghe° of al the wele° in the west iles:°[5]	*almost / wealth / Europe*
Fro riche° Romulus to Rome ricchis hym swythe° —	*after mighty / proceeds quickly*
With gret bobbaunce° that burghe he biges° upon fyrst,°	*pride / builds / in the beginning*
10 And nevenes hit his aune nome,° as hit now hat°—	*gives it his own name / is still called*
Ticius[6] to Tuskan° and teldes° bigynnes,	*Tuscany / dwellings*
Langaberde in Lumbardie° lyftes° up homes,	*Lombardy / raises*
And fer° over the French flod° Felix Brutus[7]	*far / English channel*
On mony bonkkes° ful brode° Bretayn he settes°	*many banks / very broad / settles*

---

1 The association between Arthurian Britain and Troy, introduced by the ninth-century *History of the Britons* and elaborated by Geoffrey of Monmouth in his *History of the Kings of Britain*, is commonplace in medieval histories. This association was also encouraged by various English kings who were keen to link themselves to Arthur, including Edward III [r. 1327-77] (Boulton 1987: 102-03) and Richard II [r. 1377-99] (Federico 2007: 173).

2 The identity of the Trojan traitor is disputed. Medieval accounts of the fall of Troy identify two co-conspirators, Antenor and Aeneas. Those who favor Antenor argue that he took the lead in planning the betrayal, that only he was actually tried for treason, and that it is unlikely for Aeneas "the athel" to be made an exemplum of treason. Other critics point out that Antenor is here not mentioned, that Aeneas was banished by the Greeks for concealing Polyxena, and that the ambiguity of Aeneas' character resonates well with the illustrious but imperfect Arthurian society that *Sir Gawain and the Green Knight* depicts. See David 1968; Morgan 1991: 41-46; Rutter 2006; Risden 2006; and Scott 2010.

3 Here *tried* probably means "put on trial," but it could also denote "became famous."

4 Some editors prefer a colon or dash at the end of this line; if punctuated this way, the passage definitely marks Aeneas as the traitor. The phrase *the trewest on erthe* probably means "the most certain (treason)," i.e., "an infamous example of treason." Some, however, have argued that it refers to the *tulk* ("man") mentioned in line 3, and that the paradox of calling a traitor "the truest man on earth" is deliberate.

5 Medieval geographical descriptions, following the Bible, often divide the world into three parts: Asia, Africa, and "the Islands of the Gentiles" (*insula gentium*). Each of the regions was settled by one of the sons of Noah after the flood: Shem settled Asia, Ham Africa, and Japhet the *insula gentium* (interpreted by medieval authors as Europe).

6 *Ticius*, a form not recorded elsewhere, may be a corrupt version of *Tuscus* or *Tirius*, both of whom are associated with the founding of Tuscany (Silverstein 1965: 195-96)

7 *Felix*, Lat. "happy," "lucky," "successful," is in Roman tradition associated with imperial lineage and the founding of cities. According to Geoffrey of Monmouth, however, Brutus also commits parricide (Silverstein 1965: 196-202).

15   wyth wynne°[1] —   *joy*

Where werre° and wrake° and wonder°   *war / destruction / marvels*

Bi sythes° has wont° therinne,   *by turns / dwelt*

And oft bothe blysse° and blunder°   *prosperity / strife*

Ful skete° has skyfted synne.°   *very rapidly / alternated since then*

20 Ande when this Bretayn was bigged° bi this burn° rych,°   *settled / man / mighty*

Bolde° bredden° therinne, baret° that lofden,°   *bold men / lived / battle / loved*

In mony turned° tyme tene° that wroghten.   *turbulent / strife*

Mo ferlyes° on this folde° han fallen here oft   *more marvels / in this country*

Then in any other that I wot, syn° that ilk° tyme.   *since / same*

25 Bot of alle that here bult,° of Bretaygne kynges,   *dwelled*

Ay° was Arthur the hendest,° as I haf herde telle.   *always / most courteous*

Forthi° an aunter° in erde° I attle° to schawe,°   *therefore / adventure / earth / intend / tell*

That a selly° in sight summe men hit holden,   *wonder*

And an outtrage° awenture of Arthures wonderes.°   *extraordinary / marvels*

30 If ye wyl lysten this° laye[2] bot on° littel while,   *to this / only a*

I schal telle hit as tit,° as I in toun° herde,[3]   *at once / among people*

    with tonge,

As hit is stad° and stoken°   *set down / fixed*

In stori stif° and stronge,   *bold*

35 With lel° letteres loken,°[4]   *correct / joined*

In londe so° has ben longe.   *as it*

---

1   *Wynne* can denote either "strife," "conflict," or "joy," "happiness." The word probably puns on *Felix Brutus*.

2   A *laye* is "a short narrative poem of love, adventure, etc., to be sung and accompanied on instruments, especially the harp" (*MED*, s.v. "lai," n. 2a). G.V. Smithers argues that this passage evokes the Breton lay genre, since the poem deals "in fayrye and in adventure," is connected with the "matter of Britain," and is "limited to about three main stages in the action" (1953: 91).

3   *As I in toun herde* is unlikely to refer to a specific place (e.g., "at court"), as some have proposed, probably meaning only "as I have heard it told" (*MED*, s.v. "toun," n., 5). *Herde* would suggest an oral source, but *stad and stoken* a written one. The vague source-reference is characteristic of medieval literature.

4   Tolkien and Gordon believe that *with lel letteres loken* is probably a reference to the poem's alliterative style (1930: n. to 35), and indeed various Middle English passages use the term *letter* as a technical term for a line's alliterating sound or "stave" (Putter, Jefferson, and Stokes 2007: 263); thus, "joined in true (correctly alliterating) staves." (On *loken* as "joined," see *MED*, s.v. "louken," v. 1, 4b.) Other interpretations of *lel letteres loken* hold that the poet is "contrasting the power of writing to 'fix' a story in letters with an ephemeral oral retelling that exists only as long as it is being told" (Herman 2010: 313), or that emphasizes the veracity of what is being told, denoting "enclosed in true letters, embodied in truthful words" (Frankis 1961: 330).

This kyng lay° at Camylot upon Krystmasse[1]   *dwelled*

With mony luflych° lorde, ledes° of the best —   *worthy / men*

Rekenly° of the Rounde Table alle tho rich brether° —   *worthily / noble brothers*

40 With rych revel° oryght, and rechles merthes.°   *revelry / carefree entertainments*

Ther tournayed° tulkes° by° tymes ful mony,   *took part in tournaments / men / at*

Justed° ful jolilé° thise gentyle knightes,   *jousted / vigorously*

Sythen kayred° to the court caroles[2] to make.   *then returned*

For ther the fest was ilyche° ful° fiften dayes,   *kept up continuously / fully*

45 With alle the mete° and the mirthe that men couthe avyse;°   *food / devise*

Such glaum° ande gle° glorious to here,   *revelry / mirth*

Dere° dyn upon day, daunsyng° on nyghtes —   *splendid / dancing*

Al was hap° upon heghe° in halles and chambres   *happiness / of the highest degree*

With lordes and ladies, as levest° him thoght.°   *most desirable / to them seemed*

50 With all the wele° of the worlde thay woned° ther samen,°   *joy / dwelt / together*

The most kyd° knyghtes under Krystes selven,°[3]   *famous / below Christ himself*

And the lovelokkest° ladies that ever lif haden,   *loveliest*

And he the comlokest° kyng that the court haldes;°   *most handsome / keeps*

For al was this fayre folk in her° first age,°[4]   *their / young adulthood*

55   on sille,°   *in hall*

The hapnest° under heven,   *happiest*

Kyng hyghest° mon of wylle;°   *noblest / in character*

---

46 glaum ande] glaumande   51 Krystes] Kryste

---

1 Arthur's Christmas feast has a close parallel in the *Alliterative Morte Arthure*; see E. Brewer 1992: 14-15. For a discussion of feasting generally, see D. Brewer 1997c.

2 Not "carols" in the modern sense, but ring-dances accompanied by song (Stevens 1986: 163-71)

3 *Under Krystes selven*, "below Christ Himself," means that they are the best knights on earth.

4 The *MED* glosses this instance of *first age* as "early adulthood" (s.v. "age," n. 1b), but the present passage is the only instance of the phrase with this meaning adduced. Dove argues that "it signifies the early part of youth, after childhood and before full maturity" (1986: 186). Another meaning of *first age* recorded by the *MED* (sense 5b) is "the age of primitive man, the Golden Age." Thus, some critics find that this phrase alludes to the "golden age" of Arthur's court, before its "fall." At any rate, the whole description stresses the youthfulness of Arthur and his court, which is unusual in Arthurian romance. However, in the very influential *History of the Kings of Britain*, Arthur is said to be crowned at 15. Two historical English monarchs with whom the Arthur of this poem has been associated, Edward III and Richard II, were crowned at 14 and 10, respectively. The court of Edward III was especially noted for the youth of its leading figures; see Ingledew 2006: 93-104.

Hit were now gret nye° to neven°   *very difficult / name*

So hardy° a here° on hille.   *bold / company*

60 Wyle New Yer was so yep° that hit was newe cummen,   *young*

That day doubble° on the dece° was the douth° served.   *double portions / dais / company*

Fro° the kyng was cummen with knyghtes into the halle,   *after*

The chauntré° of the chapel cheved° to an ende,   *singing of mass / came*

Loude crye[1] was ther kest of° clerkes and other,   *raised by*

65 "Nowel" nayted onewe,° nevened° ful ofte;   *repeated anew / called out by name*

And sythen riche° forth runnen to reche hondeselle,°[2]   *then nobles / to give gifts*

Yeyed yeres-yiftes° on high, yelde° hem bi hond,   *announced New Year's gifts / gave*

Debated busyly aboute tho° giftes;   *those*

Ladies laghed ful loude, thogh thay lost haden,

70 And he that wan° was not wrothe,° that may ye wel trawe!°   *won / angry / fully believe*

Alle this mirthe thay maden to° the mete° tyme.   *until / meal*

When thay had waschen worthyly,° thay wenten to sete:°   *appropriately / (their) seats*

The best burne° ay abof,° as hit best semed,[3]   *man / always higher*

Quene Guenore,° ful gay, graythed° in the myddes,   *Queen Guinevere / placed*

75 Dressed° on the dere des,° dubbed° al aboute;   *arrayed / noble dais / adorned*

Smal sendal° bisides, a selure° hir over   *fine, precious fabric / canopy*

Of tryed tolouse,° of tars tapites innoghe°[4]   *fine Toulouse fabric / many Tharsian fabrics*

That were enbrawded° and beten° wyth the best gemmes   *embroidered / decorated*

---

58 were] werere

---

1 Savage (1952) argues that the "loud cries" indicate that the poet is referencing the "Feast of Fools," a Saturnalian celebration usually held on the Feast of the Circumcision (1 January).

2 The giving of New Year's gifts was traditional, as are feasting and jousting. (These are the three "January" activities depicted in the famous *Très Riches Heures* of the Duc de Berry [1340-1416].) The hand gifts apparently involve a guessing game; if the lady fails to guess which hand holds the present, she forfeits a kiss.

3 As we learn below, the high table on the dais is reserved for the six most important personages; the other guests eat at *sid-bordes*, "side-tables." Though Arthur's knights are collectively called "the Round Table" in the poem, the table itself is not mentioned. Moorman points out that the seating arrangements probably reflect those with which the poet is familiar (1977: n. to 73).

4 The nature of *tryed tolouse* is discussed by Breeze 1996. *Tars* is a precious fabric (probably silk) from "Tharsia" or "Tartary," that is, the Mongol empire in central Asia (*OED*, s.v. "tars / tarse," n., and "Tartar / Tatar," n.2 and adj.; Hornstein 1941), or possibly Armenia (Ng and Hodges 2010: 280).

That myght be preved° of prys° wyth penyes° to bye,	*proven / worth / money*

80   in daye;

The comlokest° to discrye°	*comeliest woman / see*
Ther glent° with yyen° gray,	*looked / eyes*
A semloker° that ever he syye°	*more beautiful woman / saw*
Soth° moght no mon say!¹	*honestly*

85 Bot Arthure wolde not ete til al were served,	
He was so joly of his joyfnes,° and sumwhat childgered:°	*in his youth / boyish*
His lif liked hym lyght,° he lovied the lasse°	*merry / thus he did not like*
Auther° to longe lye or to longe sitte,	*either*
So bisied him his yonge blod² and his brayn wylde.°³	*unruly*
90 And also an other maner° meved him eke°	*consideration / likewise*
That he thurgh nobelay° had nomen;° he wolde never ete	*as a point of honor / adopted*
Upon such a dere° day er hym devised° were	*great / told*
Of sum aventurus thyng, an uncouthe° tale	*unfamiliar*
Of sum mayn° mervayle that he myght trawe,°	*great / believe*
95 Of alderes,° of armes, of other aventurus;	*princes*
Other° sum segg° hym bisoght of° sum siker° knyght	*or else / man / asked him / stout*
To joyne° wyth hym in justyng,° in jopardé to lay,°	*meet / jousting / hazard*
Lede,° lif for lyf, leve uchon other°	*knight / each to spare the other*
As° fortune wolde fulsun° hom the fayrer° to have.⁴	*since / assist / victory*

88 longe lye] lenge lye   95 of alders] of of alderes

---

1   To paraphrase, "No man could ever say in truth that he had seen a more beautiful woman." Grey eyes were synonymous with feminine beauty.

2   Arthur's *yonge blod* should be understood in the context of the medieval theory of "humors." As Burrow points out, "Of the four 'humours' it was blood which was held to predominate in young people, making them merry and active" (1987: n. 89).

3   The tone of this passage has occasioned much commentary. Are we meant to smile tolerantly at, or to condemn, Arthur's *childgered* nature and *brayn wylde*? Both phrases would permit either reading; see Moody 1976.

4   That is, "Or else some man requested of him to joust against a strong knight, a man to risk life against life, [but] each to spare the other since fortune had granted him the upper hand." The idiom *the fayrer to have* means "to get the better of (someone or something)"; see *MED*, s.v. "fair," adj. 5b. It occurs in this sense in a very similar passage in *The Destruction of Troy*: *It is grauntid of goddis the grekes for to haue / The fairer of þat fight* (4507-08, "it is granted to the Greeks by the gods to have victory in that fight").

100 This was the kynges countenaunce° where he in court were,	*custom*
At uch farand° fest among his fre meny°	*splendid / noble household*
in halle.	
Therfore of face so fere°	*bold*
He stightles stif° in stalle;°	*stands resolute / in place*
105 Ful yep° in that New Yere	*young*
Much mirthe he mas withalle.°	*makes indeed*

Thus ther stondes in stale° the stif° kyng hisselven,°	*place / bold / himself*
Talkkande° bifore the hyghe table of trifles ful hende.°	*talking / courteously*
There gode Gawan° was graythed° Gwenore bisyde,	*good Gawain / placed*
110 And Agravayn a la dure mayn° on that other syde sittes	*of the Hard Hand*
(Bothe the kynges sister-sunes° and ful siker° knightes);[1]	*nephews / stout*
Bischop Bawdewyn abof bigines the table,°	*sits at the place of honor*
And Ywan, Uryn son, ette with hymselven.°[2]	*ate with him*
Thise were dight° on the des° and derworthly° served,	*arrayed / dais / sumptuously*
115 And sithen° mony siker segge° at the sid-bordes.°	*then / trusty men / side-tables*
Then the first cors come with crakkyng° of trumpes°	*blaring / trumpets*
Wyth mony baner ful bryght that ther-bi° henged;	*from them*
Newe° nakryn noyse° with the noble pipes,	*thereafter (came) / sound of kettledrums*
Wylde werbles° and wyght wakned lote,°	*notes / loud rousing noise*

100 the kynges] kynges   113 with] wit

1 Gawain and Agravain are the sons of King Lot of Orkney. According to Geoffrey of Monmouth, their mother Anna is Arthur's sister. In the French Vulgate *Story of Merlin*, their mother is an unnamed half-sister of Arthur (called Morgause by Sir Thomas Malory in his *Le Morte Darthur*). The relationship between uncle and "sister-son" (OE *sweoster-sunu*) is of special importance in Anglo-Saxon literature; see, for example, *The Battle of Maldon* lines 113-21.

2 Thus, the seating arrangement left to right (as seen from the hall) is: Yvain, Baldwin, Arthur, Guenevere, Gawain, and Agravain. In the Welsh triads and *Mabinogion*, Arthur has a Bishop Bedwini (Tolkien and Gordon 1930: n. to 112); no Bishop Baldwin is mentioned in French sources, but he does feature in four other English poems (Kennedy 2007: 145), though none of these is earlier than *Sir Gawain and the Green Knight*. Yvain, the son of King Urien, is a notable Arthurian hero already mentioned by Geoffrey of Monmouth but best known from Chrétien de Troyes's romance about him. In the French Vulgate and Post-Vulgate cycles, he is another "sister-son" of Arthur, which may explain why he sits at the high table.

120 That° mony hert ful highe hef° at her towches.°   *so that / rose / their sound*

      Dayntés dryven° ther-wyth of ful dere metes,°   *dainties were brought in / excellent foods*

      Foysoun° of the fresche,° and on so fele° disches   *abundance / fresh (foods) / many*

      That pine° to fynde the place° the peple biforne   *it was difficult / any space*

      For to sette the sylveren° that sere sewes° halden   *silver dish / various sauces*

125   on clothe.°   *tablecloth*

      Iche lede as he loved hymselve°   *each person as they pleased*

      Ther laght° withouten lothe;°   *took / giving offense*

      Ay two° had disches twelve,   *each pair*

      Good ber° and bryght wyn bothe.   *beer*

130 Now wyl I of hor servise° say yow° no more,   *how they were served / to you*

      For uch wyye° may wel wit° no wont that ther were.°   *everyone / know / nothing was lacking there*

      An other noyse ful newe° neghed bilive,°   *different / drew near quickly*

      That the lude° myght haf leve° liflode° to cach;°   *so that Arthur / permission / nourishment / take*

      For unethe° was the noyce not a whyle sesed,   *scarcely*

135 And the fyrst cource in the court kyndely° served,   *courteously*

      Ther hales° in at the halle dor an aghlich° mayster,°[1]   *rushes / terrifying / huge man*

      On the most° on the molde° on° mesure hyghe;   *the very greatest / earth / in*

      Fro the swyre° to the swange° so sware° and so thik,   *neck / waist / strongly built*

      And his lyndes° and his lymes° so longe and so grete,   *loins / limbs*

140 Half etayn° in erde° I hope° that he were,   *giant / world / believe*

      Bot mon most I algate° mynn° hym to bene,   *nevertheless / declare*

      And that° the myriest° in his muckel° that myght ride: *namely / most handsome / size*

      For° of bak and of brest al were his bodi sturne,°   *because although / massive*

      Both his wombe° and his wast° were worthily smale,°   *stomach / waist / properly slim*

145 And alle his fetures folwande,° in forme that he hade,°   *proportioned / according to his shape*

124 sylveren] sylvener   144 both] bot

---

1 On mayster as "enormous man," see *MED*, "maister," n. 5c.

ful clene;°[1]	*most handsomely*
For wonder of his hue men hade,	
Set in his semblaunt° sene;°	*appearance / visibly*
He ferde° as freke° were fade,°[2]	*came / like a man / fierce*
150 And overal enker-grene.°	*wholly vivid green*

Ande al graythed° in grene, this gome° and his wedes.°	*dressed / man / garments*
A strayt cote° ful streght,° that stek on° his sides;	*tight-fitting tunic / strait / clung to*
A meré mantile° abof, mensked° withinne	*cloak / adorned*
With pelure pured apert,° the pane° ful clene°	*the outside trimmed with fur / edging / bright*
155 With blythe blaunner° ful bryght, and his hod bothe°	*lovely ermine / also*
That was laght° fro his lokkes and layde on his schulderes;	*thrown back*
Heme,° wel-haled hose° of that same grene,	*neat / well pulled up tights*
That spenet° on his sparlyr,° and clene° spures under	*fastened / calf / bright*
Of bryght golde upon silk bordes° barred° ful ryche,[3]	*bands / ornamented with bars*
160 And scholes° under schankes° there the schalk° rides.[4]	*shoe-less / below the legs / man*
And alle his vesture verayly° was clene verdure,°	*clothing truly / bright green*
Bothe the barres° of his belt, and other blythe° stones	*bands / shining*
That were richely rayled° in his aray clene°	*arrayed / elegant*
Aboutte hymself and his sadel, upon silk werkes.°	*embroidery*
165 That were to tor° for to telle of tryfles° the halve	*too difficult / ornamental details*
That were enbrauded abof,° wyth bryddes° and flyyes,°	*embroidered on it / birds / butterflies*

---

1 The primary feature of giants in medieval tradition is their deformity. The poet stresses that there is nothing deformed about the Green Knight. Thus, he is not a giant but a massively huge man (albeit a terrifying one). An important recurring adjective in the following blazon of the Green Knight is *clene*, which is precisely the opposite of "deformed"; in Fitt I, this adjective is used exclusively of the Green Knight.

2 The *MED* notes that *fade* occurs only in Northern texts and almost exclusively in rhymes, and proposes a derivation from *fa*, "foe." It offers two senses for *fade*: "having the character of a foe, an intruder, or a transgressor: inimical, hostile, troublesome" (s.v. "fãd(e), pred. adj., a.) or having the spirit of a warrior: eager for battle, bold, fierce" (b.). However, the ending of *fade* suggests that it is a participial form, and no appropriate verb survives. It has been argued that the word comes from French *fadus*, *fada*, "supernatural being of male (female) sex" (Revard 2001-02: 9). For other interpretations, see Vantuono 1999: n. to 149.

3 The gold spurs indicate knightly rank; the poet describes Gawain's in line 587. Concerning gold spurs see Keen 1984: 65 and Ackerman 1944: 298-99.

4 In this context, the lack of shoes indicates that the Green Knight has come on a peaceful errand. Figures dressed much like the Green Knight appear in the Luttrell Psalter (1320-40) (Cooke and Boulton 1999: 38-39).

With gay gaudi° of grene, the golde ay° inmyddes.	*ornamentation / always*
The pendauntes° of his payttrure,° the proude cropure,°	*ornaments / horse breast-armor / cropper*
His molaynes,° and alle the metail anamayld° was thenne,	*studs on the bit / enameled*
170 The steropes that he stod on stayned° of the same,	*colored*
And his arsouns° al after° and his athel scurtes,°	*saddlebows / likewise / fine saddle-skirts*
That ever glemered° and glent° al of grene stones;	*gleamed / glittered*
The fole° that he ferkkes° on fyn° of that ilke,°	*horse / rides / was completely / same color*
sertayn:°	*indeed*
175 A grene hors gret and thikke° —	*large*
A stede ful stif° to strayne° —	*difficult / restrain*
In brawden° brydel quik,°	*embroidered / lively*
To the gome° he was ful gayn.°	*man / obedient*
Wel gay was this gome gered° in grene,	*dressed*
180 And° the here of his hed of his hors swete.°	*as was / matched (the outfit)*
Fayre fannand fax° umbefoldes° his schulderes;	*flowing hair / encloses*
A much berd° as a busk° over his brest henges,[1]	*great beard / like a bush*
That wyth his highlich° here that of his hed reches°	*splendid / extends from his head*
Was evesed° al umbetorne° abof his elbowes,	*clipped / around*
185 That° half his armes ther-under were halched° in the wyse	*so that / enclosed*
Of a kynges capados° that closes his swyre.°	*hooded cape / neck*
The mane of that mayn° hors much to hit lyke,°	*great / much like the knight's*
Wel cresped° and cemmed,° wyth knottes° ful mony	*curled / combed / tassels*
Folden in wyth fildore° aboute the fayre grene,	*gold thread*
190 Ay a herle° of the here, an other of golde;	*always one strand*
The tayl and his toppyng° twynnen° of a sute,°	*forelock / braided / alike*

168 the proude] þe proude   182 as a] as as

---

1 Similes are comparatively rare in *Sir Gawain and the Green Knight*, averaging less than one per hundred lines (Wade 1986). The three similes in the Green Knight's portrait (182, 199-200, and 233-36), which all compare him to natural phenomena, are therefore noteworthy.

And bounden bothe° wyth a bande of a bryght grene, — *both were bound*

Dubbed° wyth ful dere° stones as the dok lasted,° — *adorned / precious / to the tail's end*

Sythen thrawen° wyth a thwong,° a thwarle° knot alofte,° — *then bound / thong / intricate / on top*

195   Ther mony belles ful bryght of brende° golde rungen. — *pure*

Such a fole° upon folde,° ne freke° that hym rydes, — *horse / earth / the man*

Was never sene in that sale° wyth syght er that tyme, — *hall*

    with yye.° — *eyes*

  He loked as layt° so lyght,° — *lightning / bright*

200   So sayd al that hym syye;° — *see*

  Hit semed as no mon myght

  Under his dynttes dryye.° — *blows endure*

Whether° hade he no helme ne hawbergh° nauther, — *yet / coat of mail*

Ne no pysan° ne no plate° that pented° to armes, — *breast and neck armor / plate armor / pertained*

205   Ne no schafte° ne no schelde° to schuve° ne to smyte; — *spear / shield / shove*

Bot in his on° honde he hade a holyn bobbe,°[1] — *one / holly branch*

That is grattest in grene when greves° ar bare, — *groves*

And an ax in his other, a hoge° and unmete,° — *huge / enormously heavy*

A spetos sparthe° to expoun in spelle,° who-so myght. — *cruel battle-axe / describe in words*

210   The lenkthe of an elnyerde° the large hede hade, — *an ell (45 inches)*

The grayn° al of grene stele and of golde hewen,° — *spike / fashioned*

The bit burnyst° bryght, with a brod egge° — *burnished / edge*

As wel schapen° to schere° as scharp rasores. — *designed / cut*

The stele° of a stif° staf the sturne° hit bi grypte, — *handle / stout / stern man*

215   That was wounden wyth yrn° to the wandes° ende, — *iron / staff's*

And al bigraven° with grene in gracios werkes;° — *engraved / beautiful designs*

A lace lapped° aboute, that louked° at the hede, — *cord wrapped / fastened*

---

203 hawbergh] hawbrgh   210 lenkthe ... hede] hede ... lenkthe   216 gracios] gracons

---

1   The usual symbol of truce would be an olive branch, but holly has appropriate seasonal associations. On the significance and symbolism of the holly bob, see Sadowski 1996: 85-89 and Haydock 2006: 85-89.

And so after° the halme° halched° ful ofte,   *along / handle / looped*

Wyth tryed° tasseles ther-to tacched innoghe°   *fine / many*

220 On botouns° of the bryght grene brayden° ful ryche.   *buttons / embroidered*

This hathel° heldes hym in° and the halle entres,   *man / procedes in*

Drivande° to the heghe dece,° dut he no wothe;°   *pressing / dais / he feared no danger*

Haylsed° he never one, bot heghe he over loked.   *greeted*

The fyrst word that he warp:° "Wher is," he sayd,   *uttered*

225 "The governour° of this gyng?° Gladly I wolde   *lord / band of warriors*

Se that segg° in syght, and with hymself speke   *man*

   raysoun."°   *words*

  To knyghtes he kest his yye,°   *eyes*

  And reled hym up and doun;°[1]   *rolled them back and forth*

230 He stemmed,° and con studie°   *stopped / tried to see*

  Who walt° ther most renoun.   *possessed*

Ther was lokyng on lenthe° the lude° to beholde,   *for a long time / man*

For uch mon had mervayle what hit mene myght

That a hathel° and a horse myght such a hue lach,°   *man / take on*

235 As growe grene as the gres,° and grener hit semed   *as green as grass that grows*

Then grene aumayl° on golde, glowande° bryghter.   *enamel / glowing*

Al studied° that ther stod, and stalked hym nerre°[2]   *were perplexed / moved nearer to him*

Wyth al the wonder of the worlde what he worch schulde.°   *would do*

For fele sellyes° had thay sen, bot such never are;°   *many marvels / before*

240 Forthi° for fantoum° and fayryye° the folk there hit demed.   *thus / an apparition / supernatural*

---

236 glowande] lowande

---

1 Alternatively, this could refer to the Green Knight's movement around the hall: he "swaggered up and down," "turned (rode) to and fro" (Andrew and Waldron 2002: n. to 229). However, a very similar phrase in line 304 specifies that the reference is to the movement of eyes.

2 Since the poet expressly states that the knights have been seated and only Arthur remains standing, this is usually taken to refer to servants. Markus 1974 proposes that this line refers to the Green Knight himself, though *stalken* usually refers to movement on foot (see *MED*, s.v. "stalken," v.), whereas the Green Knight remains on horseback.

Therfore to answare was arwe° mony athel freke,° — *afraid / man*

And al stouned° at his steven° and ston-stil seten° — *were astonished / words / sat stone-still*

In a swoghe° sylence thurgh the sale° riche; — *dead / hall*

As al were slypped upon slepe,° so slaked° hor lotes° — *fallen asleep / grew still / their noise*

245   in hyye° — — *at once*

     I deme° hit not al for doute,° — *believe / because of fear*

     Bot sum for cortaysye,[1]

     Bot let hym[2] that al schulde loute° — *honor*

     Cast° unto that wyye. — *reply*

250 Thenn Arthour bifore the high dece° that aventure byholdes, — *dais*

And rekenly° hym reverenced° — for rad° was he never — — *readily / honored / afraid*

And sayde, "Wyye,° welcum, iwys,° to this place! — *Sir / indeed*

The hede° of this ostel,° Arthour I hat;° — *chief / dwelling / am called*

Light° luflych° adoun and lenge,° I thee praye, — *alight / gracefully / stay*

255 And what-so° thy wylle° is we schal wyt° after." — *whatever / intent / know*

"Nay, as help me," quoth the hathel,° "He that on hyghe syttes, — *man*

To wone° any whyle in this won,° hit was not myn ernde;° — *stay / place / task*

Bot for° the los° of thee, lede,° is lyft up so hyghe, — *because / praise / knight*

And thy burgh and thy burnes° best ar holden,° — *knights / considered*

260 Stifest° under stel-gere° on stedes to ryde, — *boldest / armor*

The wyghtest° and the worthyest° of the worldes kynde, — *most valiant / most honored*

Preve° for to play wyth in other pure laykes,° — *brave / noble sports*

And here is kydde° cortaysye, as I haf herd carp;° — *displayed / said*

And that has wayned° me hider, iwyis,° at this tyme. — *brought / in truth*

---

1 It has been suggested that the poet contradicts himself here, since line 242 states that the knights were quiet out of fear. But there is no contradiction: line 242 merely states that "many" were afraid, and 247-48 add that not all were quiet out of fear, but *sum for cortaysye* ("some out of politeness"); as the poet points out in the next lines, it was Arthur's place to reply. Reading *sum* as "one" here (that is, Gawain), as proposed by J. Martin 1973, runs counter to the poet's normal usage (Metcalf 1976). It is also possible to interpret *sum* and *al* adverbially: "I believe it was not wholly out of fear, but in part because of courtesy." Silverstein explains, "The words are ironic; the guests were scared stiff!" (1984: n. to 246-47).

2 This could also be imperative: "Now let him (Arthur) reply to the Green Knight."

265 Ye may be seker° bi this braunch° that I bere here *sure / branch*

That I passe as in pes,° and no plyght° seche; *peace / fight*

For had I founded in fere°[1] in feghtyng wyse,° *come with an army / equipped for battle*

I have a hauberghe° at home and a helme bothe, *coat of mail*

A schelde° and a scharp spere, schinande° bryght, *shield / shining*

270 Ande other weppenes to welde, I wene° wel, als;° *know how / also*

Bot for° I wolde no were,° my wedes° ar softer. *because / war / clothes*

Bot if thou[2] be so bold as alle burnes tellen,° *men say*

Thou wyl grant me godly° the gomen° that I ask *in good faith / game*

    bi ryght."

275 Arthour con° onsware, *did*

    And sayd, "Sir cortays knyght,

    If thou crave° batayl bare,°[3] *desire / open*

    Here fayles° thou not to fyght." *fail*

"Nay, frayst I° no fyght! In fayth° I thee telle, *I seek / truth*

280 Hit arn° aboute on this bench bot berdles chylder.° *there are / only beardless children*

If I were hasped° in armes on a heghe stede, *enclosed*

Here is no mon me to mach,° for° myghtes so wayke.° *match / because of their / feeble*

Forthy° I crave in this court a Crystemas gomen,° *therefore / sport*

For hit is Yol and Newe Yer, and here ar yep° mony. *young*

285 If any so hardy° in this hous holdes° hymselven, *bold / considers*

Be so bolde in his blod, brayn° in hys hede, *mad*

That dar stifly° strike a strok for an other, *stoutly*

---

282 so] fo   283 gomen] gomne

1   Alternatively, *in fere* could mean "in array (of war)," i.e., armed for battle.

2   Because he is below King Arthur in rank, the Green Knight's use of the informal *thou*, as opposed to the formal *ye*, is insulting. (Compare Gawain's speech in 343-61 below, which contains twelve instances of the polite form.) The use of *thou* and *ye* in the poem is analyzed by Spearing 1964, Clark 1966, and De Roo 1997 (Appendix 2, on pp. 249-50, helpfully lists all uses of *thou* and *ye* by major characters throughout the poem). For examples in other Middle English texts, see Machan 2012.

3   The Green Knight has asked for a *gomen* (273), which can refer to a joust or battle (*MED*, s.v. "game," 3a). Thus, Arthur supposes that he wishes to challenge one of his knights to *batayl bare*, "open combat."

I schal gif hym of° my gyft thys giserne° ryche —   *as / battle-axe*

This ax,[1] that is hevé innogh° — to hondele as hym lykes,°   *very heavy / wield as he wants*

290 And I schal bide the fyrst bur° as bare as I sitte.   *blow*

If any freke° be so felle° to fonde° that I telle,°   *man / bold / test / what I say*

Lepe lyghtly° me to, and lach° this weppen —   *quickly / grasp*

I quit-clayme[2] hit° for ever — kepe hit as his aven,°   *renounce all claim to it / own*

And I schal stonde° hym a strok, stif° on this flet,°   *withstand / unmoving / floor*

295 Elles° thou wyl dight° me the dom° to dele hym an other   *provided / grant / right*

barlay,[3]

And yet gif hym respite,

A twelmonyth and a day;[4]

Now hyye,° and let se tite°   *hurry / see quickly*

300 Dar any° herinne oght° say!"   *if anyone dares / anything*

If he hem stowned° upon fyrst, stiller were thanne   *astonished*

Alle the heredmen° in halle, the hygh and the lowe.   *retainers*

The renk° on his rouncé° hym ruched° in his sadel,   *man / horse / turned*

And runischly° his rede yyen° he reled° aboute,   *fiercely / eyes / rolled*

305 Bende his bresed° browes, blycande° grene,   *shaggy / shining*

Wayved his berde for to wayte who-so wolde ryse.[5]

---

1 Several critics have suggested that the Green Knight's axe may allude to the biblical axe as the instrument that cuts down the bad fruit tree in Matthew 7:18-19 (Longo 1967; Prior 1996: 99-100; and Walls 2003).

2 Here and below, the Green Knight's language is full of legal terminology (Blanch and Wasserman 1984). *Quit-claymen* is legal term meaning "to relinquish entirely (a legal right or claim), relinquish all rights to (property, possessions)" (*MED*, s.v. "quīte-claimen," v.).

3 The meaning of *barlay* is unclear. The *MED* defines it as an interjection "used to confirm a pledge." For various other meanings that have been proposed (and their problems), see Davis 1967: n. to 296 and Van-tuono 1999: n. to 296.

4 Blanch (1983) notes that the "year and a day" period specified by the Green Knight is common in legal agreements "in order to ensure the completion of a full year" (*OED*, s.v. "year," 7b).

5 That is, he turns his head left and right, waiting to see if anyone would rise. According to Benson 1965, the Green Knight's gestures are part of the traditional portrait of the "unmannerly wild men"; they roll their eyes, wave their beards, bend their brows, and generally give violent expression to their emotions. They also exhibit their frenzied energy through fierce movements and loud noises (83-90). Putter 1995 similarly argues that "wild gestures signify rudeness" and points out that they are frequently used by hostile challengers in Arthurian romance (92). According to the *Secreta Secretorum*, red eyes suggest courage, ferocity, and a pre-disposition toward madness (White 1965).

When non wolde kepe° hym with carp,° he coghed ful hyghe,° — *engage / words / loudly*

Ande rimed° hym ful richly,° and ryght° hym to speke: — *drew himself up / lordly / began*

"What, is this Arthures hous," quoth the hathel° thenne, — *man*

310 "That al the rous° rennes of° thurgh ryalmes° so mony? — *fame / runs / realms*

Where is now your sourquydrye° and your conquestes, — *pride*

Your gryndellayk°[1] and your greme,° and your grete wordes? — *fierceness / grimness*

Now is the revel° and the renoun of the Rounde Table — *joy*

Overwalt° wyth a worde of on wyyes° speche, — *overcome / one man's*

315 For al dares° for drede withoute dynt schewed!"° — *tremble / a blow offered*

Wyth this he laghes so loude that the lorde greved;° — *became angry*

The blod schot for scham into his schyre° face — *fair*

and lere;° — *cheek*

He wex° as wroth as wynde,° — *grew / storm*

320 So did alle that ther were.[2]

The kyng as kene bi kynde° — *being brave by nature*

Then stod that stif° mon nere,°[3] — *bold / nearer*

Ande sayde, "Hathel,° by heven, thyn askyng° is nys,° — *fellow / request / foolish*

And as thou foly has frayst,° fynde° thee behoves! — *are looking for folly / to find it*

325 I know no gome° that is gast° of thy grete° wordes; — *no one / afraid / boastful*

Gif me now thy geserne,° upon Godes halve,° — *axe / in God's name*

And I schal baythen° thy bone° that thou boden habbes."° — *grant / boon / have requested*

Lyghtly° lepes he hym to, and laght° at his honde. — *quickly / caught*

Then feersly° that other freke° upon fote lyghtis.° — *fiercely / man / alights*

---

312 gryndellayk] grydel lyk

---

1 The interesting root *grindel* occurs only in *Sir Gawain and the Green Knight* (*gryndellayk* here, *gryndelly* in 2299, and *gryndel* in 2338) and *Patience* (524). It may be related to the name of Beowulf's adversary, Grendel (*MED*, s.v. "grindel," adj.).

2 Arthur's anger has been criticized as intemperate. However, Diamond 1976, citing a very similar passage in the *Morte Arthure*, argues that his reaction is appropriate within the conventions of epic and chronicle (20). It is worth noting that Arthur's courtiers share his anger (Anderson 1990: 342).

3 *Stod nere* implies that Arthur moves toward the Green Knight (*MED*, s.v. "stōnden," v. 4).

330 Now has Arthure his axe, and the halme° grypes,	*handle*
And sturnely stures° hit aboute, that stryke wyth hit thoght.°	*forcefully brandishes / intended*
The stif° mon hym bifore stod upon hyght,	*bold*
Herre° then ani in the hous by the hede and more.	*taller*
Wyth sturne schere° ther° he stod he stroked his berde,	*expression / where*
335 And wyth a countenaunce dryye° he drow doun° his cote,	*impassive / drew down*
No more mate° ne dismayd for hys mayn dintes°	*daunted / forceful swings*
Then° any burne° upon bench hade broght hym to drynk	*than if / man*
of wyne.	
Gawan, that sate bi the quene,	
340 To the kyng he can enclyne:°	*did bow*
"I beseche now with sawes sene°	*in plain words*
This melly° mot° be myne."	*that this battle / might*
"Wolde ye,° worthilych lorde," quoth Wawan[1] to the kyng,	*if you would*
"Bid me bowe° fro this benche, and stonde by yow there,	*depart*
345 That° I wythoute vylanye° myght voyde° this table,	*so that / rudeness / leave*
And that° my legge° lady lyked not ille,°	*if / liege / is not displeased (by this)*
I wolde com to your counseyl° bifore your cort ryche.°	*help / noble*
For me° think hit not semly,° as hit is soth knawen,°	*I / seemly / well known*
Ther° such an askyng is hevened° so hyghe° in your sale° —	*when / uttered / haughtily / hall*
350 Thagh ye yourself be talenttyf° — to take hit to° yourselven,	*eager / upon*
Whil mony so bolde yow aboute upon bench sytten,	
That under heven I hope° non hagherer° of wylle,	*know / readier*
Ne better bodyes on bent ther baret is rered.°	*on a field where battle breaks out*
I am the wakkest,° I wot,° and of wyt feblest,°	*least distinguished person / know / feeblest*
355 And lest lur of° my lyf, who laytes the sothe;°	*least worth if I lose / wants to know the truth*

---

336 hys] hyns   343 Wawan] Gawan

---

1   *Wawan* is an alternate form of *Gawan* used by the poet to alliterate on "w" (as is *Wenore* for *Guenore*). The MS here actually has *Gawan*, but most editors emend to *Wawan*.

Bot for as much as ye ar myn em I am only to prayse,°   *my sole distinction is that you're my uncle*

No bounté° bot your blod I in my bodé knowe;°   *virtue / recognize*

And sythen° this note° is so nys° that noght hit yow falles,°   *as / business / foolish / is fitting for*

And I have frayned° hit at yow fyrst, foldes hit° to me;   *asked / it falls*

360 And if° I carp° not comlyly,° let alle this cort rych°¹   *even if / speak / courteously / noble court*

      bout° blame."   *be without*

      Ryche° togeder con roun,°   *nobles / did confer*

      And sythen° thay redden alle same°   *thereafter / advised unanimously*

      To ryd the kyng wyth croun,°   *crowned king (of the contest)*

365   And gif Gawan the game.

Then comaunded the kyng the knyght for to ryse;

And he ful radly° upros and ruchched hym° fayre,°   *quickly / prepared himself / well*

Kneled doun bifore the kyng and caches° that weppen;   *takes*

And he luflyly° hit hym laft,° and lyfte up his honde,   *Arthur graciously / gave*

370 And gef hym Goddes blessyng, and gladly hym biddes

That his hert and his honde schulde hardi° be bothe.   *fearless*

"Kepe the,° cosyn,"² quoth the kyng, "that thou on kyrf° sette,°   *take care / one blow / inflict*

And if thou redes° hym ryght, redly I trowe°   *deal with / I fully believe*

That thou schal byden° the bur° that he schal bede° after!"³   *endure / blow / offer*

375 Gawan gos° to the gome° with giserne° in honde,   *goes / man / axe*

And he baldly° hym bydes;° he bayst never the helder.°⁴   *bravely / awaits / he was undismayed*

Then carppes° to Sir Gawan the knyght in the grene,   *says*

"Refourme we° oure forwardes,° er we fyrre passe.°   *let us restate / terms / go on*

---

1   Some editors have taken *rych* as a verb, "decide," but this is improbable. Neither the *OED* nor the *MED* gives such a meaning for *richen*.

2   The term "cousin" is appropriate for any blood relation. As the poet states in line 111, Gawain is Arthur's nephew.

3   That is, if Gawain deals a proper blow, he will not have any problems enduring the return blow, since the Green Knight will be dead.

4   "And the Green Knight bravely awaits him; he was dismayed by that (Gawain's approach with the axe) none the more"; that is, the Green Knight was no more afraid of Gawain for the axe than he would have been had Gawain carried no weapon at all.

Fyrst I ethe° thee, hathel,° how that thou hattes,°   *would ask / knight / are called*

380 That thou me telle truly, as I tryst may."°   *so that I may trust in your oath*

"In god fayth," quoth the goode knyght, "Gawan I hatte,

That bede° thee this buffet, what-so° bifalles after,   *offer / whatever*

And at this tyme twelmonyth take at thee° an other   *receive from you*

Wyth what weppen so thou wylt, and wyth° no wyy° elles   *from / man*

385   on lyve."°   *living*

That other onswares agayn,°   *back*

"Sir Gawan, so mot I thryve,°   *upon my life*

As I am ferly fayn°   *I am exceedingly glad*

This dint that thou schal dryve."°   *that it is you who strikes this blow*

390 "Bigog,"° quoth the grene knyght, "Sir Gawan, me lykes°   *by God / it pleases me*

That I schal fange° at thy fust that° I haf frayst° here.   *receive / hand what / sought*

And thou has redily rehersed,° bi resoun ful true,°   *restated / in accurate terms*

Clanly° al the covenaunt[1] that I the kynge asked,   *exactly*

Saf° that thou schal siker° me, segge,° bi thi trawthe,°[2]   *except / assure / knight / honor*

395 That thou schal seche° me thiself, where-so thou hopes°   *seek / believe*

I may be funde upon folde,° and foch° thee such wages   *upon the earth / fetch*

As thou deles me today bifore this douthe ryche."°   *noble company*

"Where schulde I wale° thee," quoth Gavan, "where is thy place?°   *find / home*

I wot never° where thou wonyes,° bi Hym that me wroght,°   *don't know / dwell / created*

400 Ne I know not thee, knyght, thy cort ne° thi name.   *nor*

Bot teche me truly ther-to° and telle me howe thou hates,°   *the way there / are called*

---

384 so] fo

1 *Covenaunt* has legal and religious overtones. In law, it refers to "a formal contract" (*MED*, s.v. "cŏvenaunt," n. 1b); this, in turn, gives rise to the theological denotation, "a covenant between God and man" (1b). For a fuller discussion of the concept of the covenant in *Sir Gawain*, see Blanch and Wasserman 1984 as well as Shoaf 1984: 47-50.

2 Burrow 1965 summarizes the various meanings of *trawthe* as follows: "To praise a man for his 'truth' might mean (a) that he was loyal to people, principles or promises, (b) that he had faith in God, (c) that he was without deceit, or (d) that he was upright and virtuous" (43). According to R.F. Green (1999: 4), *trawthe* is arguably the dominant ideal of fourteenth-century England.

And I schal ware° alle my wyt to wynne° me theder, *use / get*

And that I swere thee for sothe,° and by my seker traweth."° *in truth / firm word of honor*

"That is innogh° in Newe Yer, hit nedes no more,"° *enough / there is no need for more*

405 Quoth the gome° in the grene to Gawan the hende;° *man / courteous*

"Yif° I thee telle truly, when I the tape° have *if / light blow*

And thou me smothely° has smyten, smartly° I thee teche *deftly / quickly*

Of my hous and my home and myn owen nome,

Then may thou frayst my fare° and forwardes holde;° *see what I'll do / keep our agreement*

410 And if I spende no speche, thenne spedes° thou the better, *fare*

For thou may leng° in thy londe and layt° no fyrre. *remain / seek*

    Bot slokes!° *enough*

Ta° now thy grymme tole° to thee, *take / tool*

And let se how thou cnokes."° *deliver a blow*

415 "Gladly, sir, for sothe,"° *indeed*

Quoth Gawan; his ax he strokes.

The grene knyght upon grounde graythely° hym dresses:° *readily / prepares himself*

A littel lut° with the hede, the lere° he discoveres,° *bowed / neck / uncovers*

His longe lovelych lokkes he layd over his croun,° *top of his head*

420 Let the naked nec to the note° schewe. *in readiness*

Gavan gripped to his ax, and gederes hit on hyght,° *lifts it up high*

The kay fot° on the folde° he before sette, *left foot / ground*

Let hit doun lyghtly° lyght° on the naked,° *swiftly / alight / flesh*

That° the scharp° of the schalk° schyndered° the bones, *so that / axe / man / severed*

425 And schrank° thurgh the schyire grece,° and schade° hit in twynne,° *cut / white fat / sliced / in two*

That° the bit of the broun stel° bot° on the grounde. *so that / bright steel / bit*

The fayre hede fro the halce° hit to the erthe, *neck*

That fele° hit foyned° wyth her° fete, there° hit forth roled. *so that many / kicked / their / where*

The blod brayd° fro the body, that blykked° on the grene. *burst / shone*

425 schade] scade

430 And nawther faltered ne fel° the freke never the helder,°	*nor fell / man nevertheless*
Bot stythly° he start forth° upon styf schonkes,°	*forcefully / advanced / firm legs*
And runyschly° he raght° out, there as renkkes° stoden,	*roughly / reached / where men*
Laght to° his lufly° hed, and lyft hit up sone,°	*grabbed / handsome / soon*
And sythen bowes° to his blonk,° the brydel he cachches,°	*then turns / horse / seizes*
435 Steppes into stel-bawe,° and strydes° alofte,	*stirrup / mounts*
And his hede by the here° in his honde haldes;°	*hair / holds*
And as sadly° the segge° hym in his sadel sette	*vigorously / man*
As non unhap° had hym ayled,° thagh hedles he were[1]	*mishap / ailed*
instedde.	
440 He brayde° his bluk° aboute,	*pulled / torso*
That ugly° bodi that bledde;	*dreadful*
Moni on° of hym had doute,°	*many a one / fear*
Bi that his resouns were redde.°	*by the time he had finished talking*
For the hede in his honde he haldes up even,°	*levelly*
445 Toward the derrest° on the dece° he dresses° the face,	*noblest / dais / turns*
And hit lyfte up the yye-lyddes and loked ful brode°	*staringly*
And meled° thus° much with his muthe, as ye may now here:	*said / so*
"Loke, Gawan, thou be graythe° to go as thou hettes,°	*ready / promised*
And layte° as lelly° til thou me, lude,° fynde,	*seek / faithfully / knight*
450 As thou has hette° in this halle, herande° thise knyghtes.	*promised / within hearing of*
To the Grene Chapel thou chose,° I charge thee, to fotte°	*go / come get*
Such a dunt° as thou has dalt; disserved thou habbes°[2]	*blow / have*
To be yederly yolden° on New Yeres morn!	*promptly repaid*
The° knyght of the Grene Chapel, men knowen me mony;	*as the*

---

432 runyschly] ruyschly   438 he were] ho we

---

1 Editors usually emend MS *ho we* to *he were*, as here, or to *now(e)*, "now."
2 It is also possible to punctuate *disserved thou habbes* as a parenthetical expression: "... to fetch such as blow as you have dealt—you deserve it—to be promptly repaid...."

455 Forthi° me for to fynde, if thou fraystes,° fayles thou never.　　*therefore / seek me*

Therfore com, other recreaunt be calde° thee behoves!"　　*or to be called a coward*

With a runisch rout° the raynes° he tornes,　　*violent jerk / reins*

Halled° out at the hal dor, his hed in his hande,　　*hastened*

That the fyr° of the flynt° flawe° fro fole° hoves.　　*fire / cobble-stones / flew / the horse's*

460 To what kyth° he becom° knewe non there,　　*land / went*

Never more then thay wyste° from whethen° he was wonnen.°　　*knew / whence / come*

　　What thenne?

　The kyng and Gawen thare

　At that grene° thay laghe and grenne,°　　*green knight / grin*

465　Yet breved° was hit ful bare°　　*declared / firmly*

　A mervayl among tho° menne.　　*those*

Thagh° Arther the hende° kyng at hert hade wonder,　　*though / courteous*

He let no semblaunt° be sene, bot sayde ful hyghe°　　*sign of this / loudly*

To the comlych° quene wyth cortays° speche,　　*beautiful / courteous*

470 "Dere dame,° today demay yow° never.　　*lady / dismay*

Wel bycommes such craft° upon Cristmasse,　　*events*

Laykyng of enterludes,°[1] to laghe and to syng,　　*playing of interludes*

Among thise kynde caroles° of knyghtes and ladyes.　　*pleasing carols*

Never the lece° to my mete° I may me wel dres,°　　*nevertheless / meal / attend to*

475 For I haf sen a selly° I may not forsake."°　　*marvel / reject*

He glent° upon Sir Gawen, and gaynly° he sayde,　　*glanced / courteously*

"Now, sir, heng up thyn ax,[2] that has innogh hewen."

And hit was don° abof the dece° on doser° to henge,　　*put / dais / wall tapestry*

1　Interludes are dramatic entertainments performed between the courses of a meal; these were frequently extremely elaborate and realistic. Arthur implies that this was a prearranged show; see Weiss 1991. Jonassen 1986 points out some suggestive parallels between this episode and the Mummers' Play, the seasonal visiting of houses in disguise to perform a play. He also entertains the possibility that the beheading is merely staged, on which see Perryman 1978.

2　"Hang up your axe" is meant both literally and figuratively here; it is a proverbial expression that means "Have done with this business."

Ther° alle men for mervayl myght on hit loke,   *where*

480 And bi true tytel° therof to telle the wonder.   *verifiable proof*

Thenne thay bowed° to a borde,° thise burnes° togeder,   *turned / table / men*

The kyng and the gode knyght, and kene° men hem served   *brave*

Of alle dayntyes° double, as derrest° myght falle,°   *delicacies / noblest / be served*

Wyth alle maner of mete° and mynstralcie° bothe.   *food / entertainment*

485 Wyth wele walt thay° that day, til worthed° an ende   *joy they passed / it drew to*

    in londe.

  Now thenk wel,° Sir Gawan,   *be mindful*

  For wothe° that thou ne wonde°   *because of danger / delay*

  This aventure for to frayn°   *attempt*

490   That thou has tan° on honde.   *taken*

II

This hanselle° has Arthur of aventurus on fyrst°	*New Year's gift / at the beginning*
In yonge yer, for he yerned yelpyng°[1] to here.	*a challenge*
Thagh hym wordes were wane° when thay to sete° wenten,	*entirely lacking / sit*
Now ar thay stoken of° sturne° werk, staf-ful her° hond.[2]	*stocked with / serious / stuffed their*
495 Gawan was glad to begynne those gomnes° in halle,	*entertainments*
Bot thagh the ende be hevy,° haf ye no wonder;	*if the ending is unhappy*
For thagh men ben mery in mynde when thay han mayn° drynk,	*strong*
A yere yernes° ful yerne,° and yeldes never lyke,°	*hastens / quickly / no two are the same*
The forme to the fynisment foldes ful selden.°	*beginning and end are very rarely the same*
500 Forthi° this Yol overyede,° and the yere after,	*therefore / passed*
And uche sesoun serlepes° sued° after other:	*separately / followed*
After Crystenmasse com the crabbed Lentoun,°[3]	*disagreeable Lent*
That fraystes° flesch° wyth the fysche° and fode more symple;	*tries / the body / fish*
Bot thenne the weder° of the worlde wyth wynter hit threpes,°	*(Spring) weather / struggles*
505 Colde clenges adoun,° cloudes uplyften,	*shrinks away*
Schyre° schedes° the rayn in schowres ful warme,	*bright / falls*
Falles upon fayre flat,° flowres there schewen,°	*fields / appear*
Bothe groundes and the greves,° grene ar her wedes,°	*groves / their garments*
Bryddes busken° to bylde° and bremlych° syngen	*birds prepare / build (nests) / gloriously*
510 For solace° of the softe somer[4] that sues° therafter	*joy / follows*
bi bonk;°	*on the hills*

---

1 *Yelpyng*, from Old English *gilpan*, generally has a negative connotation ("boasting," "bragging"), but in heroic literature it can also have the more neutral or even positive sense of making a vow or challenge. Conquergood 1981 offers an excellent analysis of this in Old English, and his comments can be applied to the present passage as well.

2 That is, Arthur and his knights had heard no words of challenge (*yelpyng*) when they went to sit, but now they have heard their fill of them.

3 Lent—the forty days before Easter—is a season of penance and fasting; hence the references to fish (as opposed to meat) and "simple" food. It is also a synonym for Spring (*MED*, s.v. "lent(en)," n. 1), being originally connected with the "lengthening" of the day (Holthausen 1974, s.v. "lengten").

4 *Somer* here is "the warm half of the year, the half of the year during which days are long" (*MED*, s.v. "sōmer," n.1, 1b). As Burrow 1987 points out, the poet is actually describing spring, as shown by reference to Zephirus, the mild spring wind, in line 517. Summer proper is described in 518-20.

And blossumes bolne° to blowe°   *swell / bloom*

Bi rawes° rych° and ronk,°   *hedge-rows / flourishing / full*

Then notes noble innoghe°   *many noble notes*

515   Ar herde in wod° so wlonk.°   *woods / beautiful*

After the sesoun of somer wyth the soft wyndes,

When Zeferus° syfles hymself° on sedes and erbes,°   *Zephirus / blows gently / plants*

Wela wynne° is the wort° that waxes° ther-oute,   *very lovely / plant / grows*

When the donkande dewe° dropes of the leves,   *moistening dew*

520   To bide° a blysful blusch° of the bryght sunne.   *abide / joyful gleam*

Bot then hyyes° hervest,° and hardenes hym sone,°   *hastens / harvest (autumn) / them soon*

Warnes hym for° the wynter to wax° ful rype;   *because of / grow*

He dryves° wyth droght° the dust for to ryse,   *causes / dry weather*

Fro the face of the folde° to flyye ful hyghe;   *earth*

525   Wrothe° wynde of the welkyn° wrasteles° with the sunne,   *angry / sky / wrestles*

The leves lancen° fro the lynde° and lyghten on the grounde,   *fly / lime-tree*

And al grayes° the gres° that grene was ere;   *withers / grass*

Thenne al rypes° and rotes° that ros upon fyrst,°   *ripens / rots / grew earlier*

And thus yirnes° the yere in yisterdayes mony,   *passes*

530   And wynter wyndes° ayayn, as the worlde askes,°   *returns / demands*

          no fage,°   *. indeed*

      Til Meghelmas¹ mone°   *Michaelmas moon*

      Was cumen wyth wynter wage;°   *foretaste of winter*

      Then thenkkes Gawan ful sone

535   Of his anious° vyage.   *difficult*

531 fage] sage

---

1   Michaelmas, the Feast of St. Michael and All Angels, is on 29 September. It was also associated with the set-
    tling of accounts; thus, the Michaelmas Moon was a reminder to Gawain of the "payment" owed to the Green
    Knight (Pace 1969).

Yet whyl° Al-hal-day°[1] with Arther he lenges;°	*during / All Saints' Day / remains*
And he made a fare° on that fest° for the frekes° sake,	*feast / feast day / knight's*
With much revel° and ryche° of the Rounde Table.	*revelry / glory*
Knyghtes ful cortays and comlych ladies	
540 Al for luf of that lede° in longynge° thay were,	*knight / distress*
Bot never the lece ne the later° thay nevened bot° merthe;	*nevertheless / talked only about*
Mony joyles for that jentyle° japes° ther maden.	*gentle (knight) / jests*
For aftter mete° with mournyng° he meles° to his eme,°	*meal / sadness / speaks / uncle*
And spekes of his passage,° and pertly° he sayde,	*journey / openly*
545 "Now, lege° lorde of my lyf, leve I yow ask.°	*liege / I ask your leave (to depart)*
Ye knowe the cost of this cace,° kepe I no more°	*conditions of this case / I do not want*
To telle yow tenes° therof never, bot trifel;°	*to go over its difficulties / merely trifling*
Bot I am boun° to the bur° barely° tomorne	*obligated / blow / without fail*
To sech° the gome of the grene, as God wyl me wysse."°	*seek / guide*
550 Thenne the best of the burgh bowed° togeder,	*came*
Aywan,° and Errik,° and other ful mony,	*Yvain / Erec*
Sir Doddinal[2] de Savage,° the Duk of Clarence,	*Dodinel the Wild Man*
Launcelot, and Lyonel, and Lucan the gode,	
Sir Boos,° and Sir Bydver,° big° men bothe,	*Bors / Bedivere / strong*
555 And mony other menskful,° with Mador de la Port.[3]	*noble (knights)*

552 Doddinal] Doddinanal

---

1 All Saints' Day (1 November) is one of the five major feasts that Arthur traditionally celebrates, the others being Easter, Ascension, Pentecost, and Christmas.

2 MS *Doddinanal* (usually read *Doddinaual*) shows duplication of "na" (Silverstein 1984: n. to 552).

3 Lists of important knights of the Round Table present at feasts are traditional in Arthurian romance. Some critics argue that the specific figures mentioned here foreshadow the downfall of Camelot and Arthur's death (Kelley 1982; Gee 1984). In the French Vulgate cycle, Lancelot leaves the Round Table after his adulterous relationship with the Queen is discovered, and Gawain leads Arthur's army against him. Bors and Lionel are Lancelot's cousins and two of his chief supporters, while Yvain is Gawain's cousin. Mador is best known for the episode in which he accuses Guinevere of poisoning an apple—which is one of several events leading up to Arthur's death—and he is not mentioned in English texts prior to the fifteenth century (Kennedy 2007: 153). Lucan, Bedivere, and Dodinal are present at Arthur's last battle. On the other hand, the Duke of Clarence (named Galeschin) and Erec do not feature in these events, and all of these names figure in other stories and lists. Also, the Gawain of the present poem has little in common with his characterization in the latter parts of the Vulgate cycle.

Alle this compayny of court com the kyng nerre

For to counseyl the knyght, with care at her° hert.   *their*

There was much derve doel° driven° in the sale°   *painful grief / voiced / hall*

That so worthé° as Wawan schulde wende° on that ernde,°   *(one) so worthy / go / errand*

560 To dryye° a delful dynt,° and dele no more°   *endure / cruel blow / deal out none*

    wyth bronde.°   *sword*

    The knyght mad ay° god chere,   *always*

    And sayde, "What schuld I wonde?°   *hesitate*

    Of destinés derf° and dere°   *painful / pleasant*

565   What may mon° do, bot fonde?"°   *one / experience (them)*

He dowelles° ther al that day, and dresses on the morn,[1]   *remains*

Askes° erly hys armes, and alle were thay broght.   *calls for*

Fyrst a tulé tapit° tyght over° the flet,°   *red silk carpet / spread on / floor*

And miche was the gyld gere° that glent° ther alofte.°   *gold gear / shone / on it*

570 The stif° mon steppes ther-on, and the stel hondeles,°   *strong / takes hold of*

Dubbed° in a dublet° of a dere tars,°   *clad / doublet / precious Tharsian silk*

And sythen° a crafty capados,° closed aloft,°   *then / well-made hooded cape / at the neck*

That wyth a bryght blaunner° was bounden withinne.   *ermine*

Thenne set thay the sabatouns° upon the segge fotes,°   *steel shoes / man's feet*

575 His leges lapped° in stel with luflych greves,°   *encased / beautiful shin armor*

With polaynes° piched° ther-to, policed° ful clene,°   *knee-plates / attached / polished / brightly*

Aboute his knes knaged° wyth knotes of golde;   *fastened*

Queme quyssewes° then, that coyntlych closed°   *fine thigh-pieces / neatly enclosed*

His thik thrawen thyghes,° with thwonges to tachched;°   *burly thighs / thongs attached*

580 And sythen° the brawden bryné° of bryght stel rynges   *then / linked byrnie*

Umbeweved° that wyy° upon wlonk stuffe,°   *enclosed / man / over rich cloth*

And wel bornyst brace° upon his bothe armes,   *burnished arm-plates*

---

1   Gawain's departure is on All Souls' Day (2 November), "on whose morn the three masses are offered for the souls of the departed and the *Dies Irae* is sung. We are to consider him a dead man, one as good as gone" (Savage 1956: 27).

With gode cowters° and gay, and gloves of plate,°   *elbow-pieces / plate-mail gauntlets*

And alle the godlych gere° that hym gayn° schulde   *gear / benefit*

585   that tyde;°   *at that time*

    Wyth ryche cote-armure,°[1]   *surcoat*

    His gold spores spend° with pryde,°   *fastened / splendidly*

    Gurde° wyth a bront° ful sure°   *girded / sword / trusty*

    With silk sayn° umbe° his syde.   *belt / around*

590 When he was hasped° in armes, his harnays° was ryche: *buckled / armor*

    The lest° lachet over loupe° lemed° of golde.   *even the least / strap or loop / gleamed*

    So harnayst° as he was, he herknes° his masse,   *equipped / hears*

    Offred and honoured° at the heghe auter.°   *worshipped / altar*

    Sythen° he comes to the kyng and to his cort-feres,°   *then / companions at court*

595 Laches lufly° his leve at lordes and ladyes;   *takes gracefully*

    And thay hym kyst and conveyed,° bikende° hym to Kryst.   *accompanied / commended*

    Bi that° was Gryngolet grayth, and gurde with a sadel   *by that time / ready*

    That glemed ful gayly° with mony golde frenges,°   *richly / fringes*

    Aywhere naylet° ful newe, for that note ryched;°   *everywhere decorated with studs / occasion adorned*

600 The brydel barred° aboute, with bryght golde bounden;°   *ornamented with bars / bound*

    The apparayl° of the payttrure° and of the proude skyrtes,°   *adornment / breast-armor / saddle-skirts*

    The cropore° and the covertor° acorded wyth° the arsounes;°   *cropper / cloth / matched / saddle-bows*

    And al° was rayled on red° ryche° golde nayles,   *everywhere / set on red cloth / precious*

    That al glytered and glent° as glem° of the sunne.   *shone / gleam*

605 Thenne hentes° he the helme, and hastily° hit kysses,   *takes / eagerly*

    That was stapled stifly,°[2] and stoffed° wythinne.   *equipped with secure vervelles / padded*

    Hit was hyghe on his hede, hasped° bihynde   *fastened*

---

1 A knight's surcoat was worn over armor and embroidered with his heraldic device.

2 Southwood has shown that Gawain's helmet must be a visor-less basinet, and therefore *stapled stifly* means that the helmet "was equipped with secure staples for the attachment of the aventail. Such staples were known as vervelles, and consisted of rolls or rings of steel attached at the lower neck and either side of the basinet's face-opening" (1997: 165).

Wyth a lyghtly urysoun° over the aventayle,°[1]   *light silk mantling / neck-guard*

Enbrawden° and bounden wyth the best gemmes   *embroidered*

610 On brode sylkyn borde,° and bryddes° on semes,°[2]   *wide silk strip / birds / seams*

As papiayes° paynted pervyng[3] bitwene,°   *parrots / depicted among periwinkles*

Tortors° and tru-lofes°[4] entayled° so thyk   *turtle-doves / true-loves / embroidered*

As mony burde° ther-aboute had ben° seven wynter   *as if many a lady / had worked on it*

    in toune.

615   The cercle° was more o prys°   *gold band / of even greater worth*

That umbeclypped° hys croun,°   *clasped / head*

Of diamauntes° a devys°   *diamonds / of the best*

That bothe were bryght and broun.°[5]   *shining*

Then thay schewed° hym the schelde,° that was of schyr gowles°   *brought / shield / gules*

620 Wyth the pentangel[6] depaynt° of pure golde hewes;   *depicted*

---

1 Since Gawain's helmet is a visor-less war basinet, the *aventayle* is probably a mail neck and shoulder guard that attaches to the helmet. The description of thickly clustering birds and plants plus gem-encrusted border means that the *urysoun* must be of substantial size. W.G. Cooke suggests that "the accessory to a helmet that best suits the description is a mantling or lambrequin, a cloth covering the back and sides of the helm," and that the *cercle* mentioned in 615 "is most naturally understood as the band that held [the mantling] in place" (1989: 43; on other possible interpretations of *aventayle* and *urysoun*, see pp. 42-43).

2 E. Watson 1987 notes that *semes* could refer either to the seams themselves or to "strips of embroidered material laid over the hem as such: a kind of applique" (33). She finds the latter more probable, since "such strips would strengthen the work, and they would be more likely than the most intricate forms of hemming to allow of the detail subsequently described"; also, this would explain the reference to how many ladies contributed to the making of the *urysoun*, because the fashioning and decorating of such strips "could easily be shared out" (33).

3 The periwinkle was traditionally viewed as an amatory herb, and both periwinkle and parrot are also associated with the Virgin Mary (E. Watson 1987: 34).

4 Burrow 1965 points out that the items embroidered on Gawain's *urysoun* belong to the medieval iconography of true, committed love (40-41).

5 *Broun* is generally rendered "brown," and medieval lapidaries do mention brown diamonds. However, *bryght and broun* is a common alliterative doublet that means "bright and shining" (P. Battles 2007).

6 No other poem associates the pentangle with Sir Gawain. Several critics have explored the contemporary connotations of this figure. Some have pointed out that it is often associated with necromancy, while others see it as a symbol of human rationality and perfection; in two sixteenth-century sources, it is associated (as below, 642-43) with the five wounds of Christ. Other critics note that medieval numerology often associates the number five with humankind, just as three is linked with God. See R.H. Green 1962; Lass 1966; Arthur 1987: 18-46; Sadowski 1996: 116-28; Morgan 1979 and 1997; Condren 2002: 39-40 and 117-46; Tracey 2007; and the notes in Davis 1967 and Silverstein 1984. Still other critics believe that the text tells us all we need to know about the pentangle: "The poet elaborates a variety of relationships which the outlined star adumbrates, and these relationships have an explicit, a fixed and 'locked' form which the star bodes ... the poet insists on its status as an openly legible symbol" (Hanna 1983: 289). In addition to scrutinizing its symbolic meaning, scholars have also read the shield as alluding to contemporary figures such as Enguerrand de Coucy [1340-97] (Savage 1956: 158-68) or Robert de Vere [1362-92] (Astell 1999: 125-26; Mann 2009: 240-

He braydes° hit by the bauderyk,° aboute the hals kestes,°	*takes / baldric / neck casts (it)*
That bisemed the segge semlyly fayre.°	*became the knight very well*
And why the pentangel apendes° to that prynce noble	*belongs*
I am in tent yow to telle, thof tary hyt me schulde:°	*though it will delay me a while*
625 Hit is a syngne° that Salamon[1] set° sumwhyle°	*symbol / Solomon devised / in the past*
In bytoknyng of trawthe,° bi tytle that hit habbes,°	*fidelity / as it is entitled to do*
For hit is a figure that haldes° fyve poyntes,[2]	*has*
And uche lyne umbelappes° and loukes in° other,	*overlaps / joins*
And aywhere hit is endeles;° and Englych° hit callen	*never-ending / the English*
630 Overal,° as I here, the endeles knot.[3]	*everywhere*
Forthy hit acordes° to this knyght and to his cler° armes,	*thus it is appropriate / pure*
For ay faythful in fyve,° and sere fyve sythes,°	*five (aspects) / and each in five ways*
Gawan was for gode° knawen and as golde pured,°[4]	*virtue / pure as gold*
Voyded° of uche vylany,° wyth vertues ennourned°	*devoid / kind of baseness / adorned*
635 in mote;°	*among people*
Forthy° the pentangel newe°[5]	*therefore / without precedent*
He ber in schelde and cote,°	*surcoat*

629 endeles] emdeles   634 vertues] verertues

---

1   R.H. Green points out that Solomon was considered both a type of Christ and a deeply flawed figure; he concludes that "the poet could hardly have chosen a more ambiguous patron for Gawain's virtue" (1962: 130). Of course, Solomon was firmly associated with the pentangle before the Gawain-poet.

2   Throughout this passage, the poet puns on two meanings of *poynt*: "one of the angular points of a figure or star" (*MED*, s.v. "pointe," n. 12c) and "a good quality, virtue" (10c), which underscores the symbolism of the pentangle.

3   Scholars have been unable to find evidence for the pentangle being called "the endless knot" among the English. However, as Burrow points out, "The idea that the virtues are interconnected ... is quite common in patristic and medieval writers." He further explains that "the virtues, therefore, stand and fall together ... Courtesy, one might say, is not praised as a virtue without cleanness and loyalty; not loyalty without courtesy and cleanness—and so with the others. Just as a broken pentangle loses its magical power, so 'truth' loses its moral power if it is 'sundered' in any of its parts; for it is an ideal of integrity or oneness" (1965: 50).

4   Silverstein notes that this comparison ("pure as gold") is "an ancient commonplace for the testing and fining of virtue" (1984: n. to 632-33).

5   It is not obvious why the pentangle should be described as *newe* when the poet has just described its currency as a symbol among the English. Some critics believe *newe* means that the pentangle has been "newly painted" on Gawain's shield. However, the next line shows that Gawain bears the *pentangel newe* not merely on his shield, but on his surcoat as well. Evans 1968 proposes that Gawain has just adopted the pentangle as heraldic device, but the poet would surely have mentioned this fact. On balance, it seems preferable to read *newe* adverbially and in the specific sense of "without precedent" (*MED*, s.v. "neue," adv. 4b). That is, Gawain is the first and only "pentangle knight."

As tulk° of tale° most true   *man / word*

And gentylest° knyght of lote.°   *noblest / bearing*

640 Fyrst he was funden fautles in his fyve wyttes,°[1]   *five senses*

And efte° fayled never the freke in his fyve fyngres,[2]   *next*

And alle his afyaunce° upon folde° was in the fyve woundes[3]   *faith / earth*

That Cryst kaght° on the croys, as the crede° telles.°   *received / Creed / states*

And where-so-ever thys mon in melly° was stad,°   *battle / hard-pressed*

645 His thro° thoght was in that, thurgh° alle other thynges,   *steadfast / above*

That alle his forsnes° he feng at° the fyve joyes[4]   *strength / derived from*

That the hende° heven-quene had of hir chylde;   *gracious*

At this cause° the knyght comlyche° hade   *for this reason / beautifully*

In the inore half° of his schelde hir ymage depaynted,°   *inner side / depicted*

650 That when he blusched° ther-to his belde° never payred.°[5]   *looked / courage / failed*

The fyft fyve[6] that I finde that the frek used°   *practiced*

Was fraunchyse° and felawschyp forbe° al thyng,   *generosity / friendship above*

---

1   Traditionally the "five wits" are sight, hearing, taste, smell, and touch, and most critics—following Ackerman 1958—believe that being *fautles in his fyve wyttes* means that Gawain is free from venial sin. However, Whiteford 2004 argues that the poet is not referring to Gawain's "outer" (bodily) senses, but to his "inner" (psychological) ones: will, reason, mind, imagination, and thought; thus, Gawain's mental faculties are set on God. See also Blackwell 2008. For a general overview of the significance of the number five in medieval thought, see Meyer and Suntrup 1987.

2   The five fingers are often linked with sin and virtue. Positively, they are said to represent the virtues of justice, prudence, temperance, fortitude, and obedience (R.H. Green 1962: 134); negatively, they frequently represent the five means by which the devil tempts human beings (*MED*, s.v. "finger," n. 3).

3   The list of Christ's five wounds differs. Tolkien and Gordon (1930: n. to 642) explain them as being in the head (from the crown of thorns), two hands, side, and through the feet; Davis (1967: n. to 642) lists feet, hands, and side; Cherewatuk cites a text that ennumerates five times when Christ sheds blood to save humanity, those being "at his circumcision, in Gethsemane, at the flagellation, during the crucifixion, and at the piercing" (2009: 18). Davis further notes that the five wounds are a favorite topic of medieval devotional writing, and he points out the association of the five wounds with the five senses in the *Ancrene Wisse* (Part One, 127-29).

4   The five joys of Mary—generally Annunciation, Nativity, Resurrection, Ascension, and Assumption—were the focus of much late medieval devotional writing and practice; see Gollancz 1940: n. to 646. For the association between Mary's joys and Gawain's fortitude, see Allen 1992.

5   The shield bearing an image of the Virgin Mary is traditionally associated with Arthur, not Gawain. Gollancz (1940: n. to 649) compares the influential commentary on the Book of Wisdom by Robert Holcot (c. 1290-1349), which in a passage quite similar to the present one explains that the image was painted on the inside of the shield so that Arthur could recover his comfort and hope by looking at her when weary in battle.

6   The final group comprises primarily social virtues and is generally understood as the "chivalric" *fyve* or pentad. As Spearing puts it, these "are the virtues to which any great medieval court would be committed, at least in theory, and this part of the allegorization establishes Gawain as the personal representative of the qualities in the courtly civilization whose reputation he defends" (1970: 197). Derrickson 1980 proposes that this group comprises the virtues tested throughout the poem.

His clannes°[1] and his cortaysye croked° were never,	*purity / crooked*
And pité,° that passes° alle poyntes;°[2] thyse pure fyve	*compassion / surpasses / virtues*
655 Were harder happed on° that hathel° then on any other.	*more firmly attached to / man*
Now alle these fyve sythes,° for sothe,° were fetled° on this knyght,	*five sets / indeed / bestowed*
And uchone halched° in other, that non ende hade,	*each one joined*
And fyched° upon fyve poyntes that fayld° never,	*attached / ended*
Ne samned never° in no syde, ne sundred nouther,°	*came together / either*
660 Withouten ende at any noke° I owhere° fynde,	*point / anywhere*
Where-ever the gomen° bygan or glod° to an ende.	*process / came*
Therfore on his schene° schelde schapen° was the knot	*splendid / depicted*
Ryally° wyth red golde upon red goules,°	*royally / heraldic red*
That is the pure pentaungel wyth° the peple called	*by*
665 with lore.°[3]	*learning*
Now graythed° is Gawan gay,	*prepared*
And laght° his launce ryght thore,°	*took / there*
And gef hem alle goud day,	
He wende° for evermore.	*thought*
670 He sperred° the sted° with the spures and sprong° on his way	*spurred / steed / sprang*
So stif° that the ston-fyr stroke out° therafter.	*forcefully / sparks dashed out*
Al that sey° that semly syked° in hert,	*saw / fair (knight) sighed*
And sayde sothly°[4] al same° segges° til other,	*quietly / all together / men*

659 nouther] nouth( )r   660 owhere] jwhere

1   *Clannes*, literally "cleanness," is often used metaphorically to describe one's condition, here either "moral purity" or, more specifically, "chastity, celibacy" (*MED*, "clennesse," n. 2a and 2b). Another poem in the Cotton Nero A. x. manuscript, variously titled *Cleanness* or *Purity* by editors, closely links the virtues of *clannes* and *cortaysye* as well as *trawth*.

2   *Pité* can mean either "compassion" or "righteousness, piety" (*MED*, s.v. "pite," n., senses 1 and 4). As a chivalric virtue, the former is more likely; compare Chaucer's *pitee runneth soone in gentil herte* (*Knight's Tale*, I.1761; *Merchant's Tale* IV.1986; *Squire's Tale* V.479; etc.).

3   Burrow 1987 notes that this stanza, which explains Gawain's perfection in the "five fives," is itself composed of 25 lines (followed by a five-line bob and wheel).

4   *Sothly* ordinarily means "truly." Gollancz, however, proposes the sense "quietly, softly" (1940: n. to 673). Andrew and Waldron point out that this must be the sense of the word in *Cleanness* 654 (2002: n. to 673).

Carande° for that comly,° "Bi Kryst, hit is scathe° *being anxious / comely (knight) / a pity*

675 That thou, leude,° schal be lost, that art of lyf noble! *knight*

To fynde hys fere° upon folde,° in fayth, is not ethe.° *his equal / earth / easy*

Warloker° to haf wroght° had more wyt bene,° *wiser / acted / would've been smarter*

And haf dyght° yonder dere° a duk° to have worthed;° *appointed / dear (man) / duke / become*

A lowande leder° of ledes° in londe hym wel semes,° *brilliant leader / men / suits*

680 And so had better haf ben° then britned to noght,° *this would have been better / killed*

Hadet wyth° an alvisch° mon, for angardes° pryde. *beheaded by / supernatural / overweening*

Who knew ever any kyng such counsel to take° *accept advice*

As knyghtes' in cavelaciouns on° Crystmasse gomnes?"° *pretend arguments about / games*

Wel° much was the warme water that waltered° of yyen,° *very / welled out / eyes*

685 When that semly syre° soght fro° tho wones° *fair lord / set out from / dwellings*

    thad daye.

    He made non abode,° *did not linger*

    Bot wyghtly° went hys way; *swiftly*

    Mony wylsum° way he rode, *(a) desolate*

690   The bok° as I herde say. *book*

Now rides this renk° thurgh the ryalme° of Logres,[1] *knight / realm*

Sir Gavan, on Godes halve,° thagh hym no gomen thoght.° *name / seemed no game to him*

Oft leudles,° alone, he lenges° on nyghtes *without companion / abides*

Ther° he fonde noght° hym byfore° the fare°[2] that he lyked. *where / not / before him / feasting*

695 Hade he no fere° bot his fole° bi frythes° and dounes,° *companion / horse / woods / hills*

Ne no gome° bot God bi gate° wyth to karp,° *man / on the way / speak*

Til that he neghed° ful neghe° into the Northe Wales.[3] *neared / very close*

683 cavelaciouns] cavelouns   697 neghe] noghe

---

1 Logres is the traditional name for Arthur's realm (Lacy and Ashe 1997: 331).

2 The word *fare* further underscores Gawain's solitude. Its meaning in this context is "provisions (of food, entertain-ment, hospitality)" (*MED*, s.v. "fare," n. (1), 8a), which suggests that Gawain misses not merely good food but also the associated social pleasantries. The word is therefore here glossed as "feasting." Compare Putter 1995: 24-26.

3 Gawain's itinerary is here described in specific and realistic detail, contrasting with its vague beginning and ending. This portion of the journey in all likelihood follows a route well known to the poet and his audience,

Alle the iles° of Anglesay on lyft half° he haldes,° — *isles / left side / keeps*

And fares over the fordes by the forlondes,°[1] — *headlands*

700 Over at the Holy Hede,[2] til he hade eft bonk° — *again reached shore*

In the wyldrenesse of Wyrale:°[3] wonde ther bot lyte° — *Wirral / only few*

That auther God other gome° wyth goud hert lovied.° — *either God or man / loved*

And ay° he frayned,° as he ferde,° at frekes° that he met, — *always / asked / went / of men*

If thay hade herde any karp° of a knyght grene, — *mention*

705 In any grounde° ther-aboute, of the Grene Chapel; — *area*

And al nykked hym° wyth nay, that never in her lyve° — *said not / their lives*

Thay seye° never no segge° that was of suche hues — *had they seen / man*

of grene.

The knyght tok gates° straunge — *ways*

710 In mony a bonk unbene,° — *cheerless hill-side*

His cher° ful oft con° chaunge — *mood / did*

That chapel er° he myght sene.° — *before / see*

Mony klyf he overclambe° in contrayes straunge; — *climbed over*

Fer floten° fro his frendes, fremedly° he rydes. — *having wandered far / as a stranger*

715 At uche warthe other° water ther° the wyye passed — *ford or / where*

He fonde a foo° hym byfore, bot ferly hit were,° — *foe / if not it was a surprise*

And that so foule and so felle° that feght hym byhode.° — *fierce / he was forced to fight*

705 chapel] clapel

---

and takes Gawain into the vicinity of the likely place of composition (see p. 11 above on dialect and place of composition). On landscape and geography in the poem, see Elliott 1997.

1 Elliott 1974 suggests that *forlondes* means "the land between sea and hills" (134).

2 The location of "Holy Head" is disputed. There is a Holyhead on the west side of Anglesey, but editors and critics disagree as to whether this is the place referenced here (see Vantuono 1999: n. to 700). It is possible that this refers to Holywell, named after St. Winifred, who was beheaded; if so, this would be an uncomfortable reminder to Sir Gawain of what is to come (Burrow 1965: 52).

3 Wirral, located in Cheshire, is mentioned as harboring marauding bands of armed men in 1386 and 1392 (Savage 1931; Stewart-Brown 1907: 40). During this time Wirral was a royal forest, a hunting preserve for the aristocracy; forest law prescribed heavy penalties against anyone tampering with game animals such as deer, boars, and hares. The hereditary foresters of Wirral, the Stanley family, have been associated with the poem (Wilson 1979), but they seem to have been resented by the local population (Roberts 2002: 78-80). In 1376, Edward III granted a petition by the citizens of Chester for the abolition of the forest.

So mony mervayl bi mount° ther the mon fyndes,   *in (those) mountains*

Hit were to tore° for to telle of the tenthe dole.°   *too hard / a tenth part*

720 Sumwhyle° wyth wormes° he werres,° and with wolves als,°   *sometimes / dragons / fights / also*

Sumwhyle wyth wodwos°[1] that woned° in the knarres,°   *wild men / lived / crags*

Bothe wyth bulles and beres, and bores° otherwhyle,°   *boars / at other times*

And etaynes° that hym anelede° of the heghe felle.°   *giants / pursued / hill*

Nade he ben dughty° and dryye,° and Dryghtyn° had served,   *had he not been brave / hardy / God*

725 Douteles he hade ben ded and dreped° ful ofte,   *killed*

For werre wrathed° hym not so much that wynter nas° wors;   *fighting vexed / was not*

When the colde cler water fro the cloudes schadde°   *fell*

And fres° er hit falle myght to the fale° erthe,   *froze / pale*

Ner slayn wyth the slete° he sleped° in his yrnes°   *sleet / slept / armor*

730 Mo° nyghtes then innoghe° in naked° rokkes,   *more / many / barren*

Ther-as claterande° fro the crest° the colde borne rennes°   *splashing / mountaintop / stream runs*

And henged° heghe over his hede in hard iisse-ikkles.°[2]   *hung / icicles*

Thus in peryl and payne° and plytes° ful harde°   *suffering / troubles / very difficult*

Bi contray caryes° this knyght, tyl Krystmasse even,°   *through open country travels / eve*

735   al one;°   *alone*

The knyght wel that tyde°   *at that time*

To Mary made his mone°   *prayer*

That ho° hym red° to ryde   *she / would advise*

And wysse° hym to sum wone.°   *guide / dwelling*

---

726 nas] was   727 schadde] schadden

---

1 "Wodwos" and similar wild men of medieval literature are discussed in detail by Bernheimer 1952 and Sprunger 1993.

2 This passage is frequently linked with depictions of winter in Old English poetry (e.g., Christophersen 1971), which are often associated with exile (see D. Battles, forthcoming in 2013). Burrow points out that the action here takes place during the season of Advent, which is "like Lent, a season of penitential preparation" (1965: 55). He further notes that "the best-known of all penitential scenes in Arthurian literature, the Good Friday episode of the Perceval story, opens, in Wolfram's *Parzival*, with the hero riding through a great wood, in bitter cold, with the snow lying on the ground" (54).

740 Bi a mounte° on the morne meryly°[1] he rydes	*mountain / briskly*
Into a forest ful dep° that ferly° was wylde —	*very deep / extremely*
Highe hilles on uche a halve° — and holtwodes under°[2]	*on each side / underneath groves*
Of hore° okes ful hoge,° a hundreth° togeder;[3]	*ancient / huge / countless number*
The hasel° and the hawthorne were harled° al samen,°	*hazel tree / intertwined / together*
745 With roghe, raged° mosse rayled° aywhere,°	*thick, shaggy / strewn / everywhere*
With mony bryddes unblythe° upon bare twyges,	*joyless birds*
That pitosly° ther piped° for pyne° of the colde.	*pitifully / cheeped / affliction*
The gome° upon Gryngolet glydes hem under,°	*man / underneath them*
Thurgh mony misy° and myre, mon al hym one,°	*swamps / all alone*
750 Carande° for his costes° lest he ne kever schulde°	*anxious / situation / wouldn't manage*
To se the servyse° of that Syre° that on that self° nyght	*attend the service / lord / same*
Of a burde° was borne oure baret° to quelle.°	*maid / woes / end*
And therfore sykyng° he sayde, "I beseche thee, Lorde,	*sighing*
And Mary, that is myldest° moder so dere,°	*most gracious / dear*
755 Of sum herber ther° heghly° I myght here masse,	*lodging where / solemnly*
Ande thy matynes tomorne;° mekely° I ask,	*tomorrow / meekly*
And ther-to prestly° I pray my Pater° and Ave°	*eagerly / Pater Noster / Ave Maria*
and Crede."°	*Creed*
He rode in his prayere,	
760 And cryed for° his mysdede,°	*lamented / wrong-doings*
He sayned hym° in sythes sere,°	*crossed himself / many times*
And sayde "Cros Kryst me spede!"°	*may Christ's cross aid me*

---

751 servyse] servy

1 The usual meaning of *meryly*—"cheerfully," "joyfully," etc. —is inappropriate here; Gawain is described as anxious just a few lines below. Davis 1967 and Andrew and Waldron 2002 gloss *meryly* as "handsomely" and "splendidly," respectively (see glossaries), while Silverstein proposes "bravely" (1984: n. to 740). The *MED* suggests "?briskly; quickly; shortly" (s.v. "mirīlī," adv. 3).

2 *Holtwodes under* is usually glossed "forests below," meaning that the forest is below Gawain as he rides through the hillcountry. However, the passage as a whole suggests that Gawain is riding through the forest (cf. 741 *into a forest ful dep*) which looms above him; thus *under* is probably not an adverb, but a preposition that follows the noun phrase (that is, a post-posed preposition). This is also the case six lines below, where birds huddle against the cold upon branches as Gawain *glides hem under* (748). For further details, see P. Battles 2008.

3 In Middle English "hundred" can be short-hand for "an indefinite large number" (*MED*, s.v. "hundred," card. num. 3). It recurs in this sense in ll. 1144 and 1543.

Nade he sayned° hymself, segge,° bot thrye° — *he had not crossed / man / thrice*

Er he was war° in the wod of a won° in a mote,° — *aware / dwelling / moat*

765 Abof a launde° on a lawe° loken° under boghes° — *clearing / mound / enclosed / branches*

Of mony borelych bole° aboute bi the diches° — — *large trees / ditches (of the moat)*

A castel the comlokest° that ever knyght aghte,° — *comliest / owned*

Pyched on a prayere,° a park al aboute,[1] — *built in a meadow*

With a pyked palays° pyned° ful thik,° — *palisade of spiked poles / enclosed / close-set*

770 That umbeteye° mony tre mo° then two myle. — *encircled / for more*

That holde° on that on° syde the hathel avysed,° — *castle / on that one / knight looked at*

As hit schemered and schon° thurgh the schyre° okes.[2] — *shimmered and shone / fair*

Thenne has he hendly of° his helme, and heghly° he thonkes — *quickly takes off / devoutly*

Jesus and Sayn Gilyan° — that gentyle°[3] ar bothe — — *St. Julian / noble*

775 That cortaysly° hade hym kydde°[4] and his cry herkened. — *courteously / revealed themselves*

"Now bone hostel," cothe the burne, "I beseche yow yette!"[5]

Thenne gederes he° to Gryngolet with the gilt heles,° — *put spurs / spurs*

And he ful chauncely° has chosen to° the chef gate,° — *luckily / selected / main road*

That broght bremly° the burne° to the bryge° ende — *speedily / man / drawbridge's*

780   in haste.

The bryge° was breme upbrayde,° — *drawbridge / completely pulled up*

The yates° wer stoken faste,° — *gates / locked up tightly*

774 Sayn] say

1 This is probably the deer park where the first hunt described in part three takes place (M. Thompson 1997: 123).
2 For examples of three motifs in this passage—"the efficacious prayer, the sudden changes in the landscape, and the vision of the castle"—see Putter 1995: 27-41. A very detailed analysis of the castle description is provided by Cockcroft 1978; see also M. Thompson 1997.
3 *Gentyle* means either "of noble rank or birth" (*MED*, s.v. "gentil," adj. 1a) or, in its extended meaning, "kind," "gracious." Silverstein believes that the narrower sense is the one evoked here: Jesus and St. Julian are both "as it were, gentlemen" and "hence respond with understanding to the prayer of a weary fellow knight" (1984: n. to 774). St. Julian the Hospitaller is the patron of travelers. For a detailed analysis of this scene, see Tamplin 1969: 405-07.
4 *Cortaysly hade hym kydde* is usually translated as "had shown him courtesy." However, *cortaysly* is an adverb, not a noun. Therefore the verb *kithen* must be intransitive and reflexive, with the meaning "make oneself known" (*MED*, s.v. "kīthen," v. 2f). Gawain is thanking Jesus and Saint Julian for graciously interceding on his behalf; they make known their presence by revealing the castle to him (P. Battles 2008).
5 "Now for good lodging," said the man, "I beg you once again!"

The walles were wel arayed;°   *built*

Hit dut° no wyndes blaste!¹   *feared*

785 The burne bode° on blonk° that on bonk hoved°   *man remained / the horse / waited*

Of the depe double dich² that drof to° the place.   *enclosed*

The walle wod° in the water wonderly° depe,   *went down into / wondrously*

Ande eft° a ful huge° heght hit haled° upon lofte°³   *then / very great / thrust / aloft*

Of harde hewen ston° up to the tables,°⁴   *shaped stone / cornice*

790 Enbaned° under the abataylment°⁵ in the best lawe;°   *fortified with projections / battlement / manner*

And sythen garytes° ful gaye gered° bitwene,   *watchtowers / placed*

Wyth mony luflych loupe°⁶ that louked° ful clene;°   *loopholes / were closed / neatly*

A better barbican⁷ that burne blusched upon° never.   *beheld*

And innermore° he behelde that halle ful hyghe,   *farther within*

795 Towres telded° bytwene, trochet ful thik,°   *set / embellished with many pinnacles*

Fayre fylyoles° that fyyed,° and ferlyly° long,   *pinnacles / matched in style / wondrously*

With corvon° coprounes° craftyly sleye.°   *carved / capitals / expertly crafted*

Chalkwhyt chymnees ther ches° he innoghe,°   *saw / many*

Upon bastel roves,° that blenked° ful whyte.   *turret roofs / shone*

800 So mony pynakle payntet° was poudred° aywhere,   *painted / scattered*

---

785 blonk ... bonk] bonk ... blonk   795 towres] towre

---

1 Strong winds actually did occasionally wreck wooden and even stone fortifications (Cockcroft 1978: 467).
2 The *double dich* "seems to mean not two moats but one that required a double throw or cast when digging to clear the soil" (M. Thompson 1997: 125). This would make the moat about forty feet wide.
3 Two verbs in this passage, *wod* and *haled*, convey active motion. The description is subjective: from Gawain's perspective, the wall "goes down" deep into the water, and then "rushes back up" to dizzying heights (P. Battles 2008).
4 The following castle description presents several difficulties. Some words occur here for the first (sometimes only) time in Middle English. They seem primarily to be derived from French, but the medieval French word is not always recorded. Some terms may have been coined by the poet. For an analysis of the individual terms, see Clough 1985.
5 *Enbaned under the abataylment* means that the castle is fortified with projecting masonry (machicolations), which would allow defenders to see the base of the wall and drop missiles onto attackers. Michael Thompson reads *enbaued* for *enbaned*, deriving this from the Old English *boga*, "arch" (1997: 121). This is also one of several features in this description which suggests that the poet is describing the very latest in castle architecture; "the poet's interest in [the machicolations] certainly implies a date after about 1360" (121).
6 Slits through which defenders could fire longbows or crossbows.
7 The barbican "could be a pair of parallel walls projecting in front of the gate to confine an enemy's attack but in the fourteenth century it often meant a fortified outer enclosure or bailey" (M. Thompson 1997: 125).

Among the castel carneles° clambred° so thik,° *battlements / clustered / densely*

That pared° out of papure°[1] purely° hit semed! *cut / paper / entirely*

The fre freke° on the fole° hit fayr innoghe thoght,° *noble man / horse / thought it very fair*

If he myght kever° to com the cloyster° wythinne, *manage / enclosure*

805 To herber° in that hostel° whyl halyday° lested, *lodge / dwelling / holiday*

avinant.° *(since it looked) agreeable*

He calde,° and sone ther com *called*

A porter,° pure° plesaunt; *gatekeeper / completely*

On the wal his ernd° he nome,° *request / took in*

810 And haylsed° the knyght erraunt.° *greeted / on a quest*

"Gode sir," quoth Gawan, "woldes thou go myn ernde° *will you take my request*

To the hegh lorde of this hous, herber° to crave?"° *lodging / ask for*

"Ye, Peter,"°[2] quoth the porter, "and purely I trowoe° *Yes, by Peter / I fully expect*

That ye be, wyye,° welcum to won° whyle yow lykes."° *sir / stay / it pleases you*

815 Then yede° the wyye yerne° and com ayayn swythe,° *went / at once / back quickly*

And folke frely° hym wyth, to fonge° the knyght. *courteously / receive*

Thay let doun the grete draght° and derely° out yeden° *drawbridge / courteously / went*

And kneled doun on her° knes upon the colde erthe *their*

To welcum this ilk wyy,° as worthy hom thoght.° *same knight / seemed fitting to them*

820 Thay yolden° hym the brode yate,° yarked° up wyde, *yielded / gate / opened*

And he hem raysed° rekenly° and rod over the brygge. *bid them arise / courteously*

Sere segges° hym sesed by° sadel whel° he lyght,° *several men / held his / while / dismounted*

And sythen stabeled his stede, stif° men innoghe.° *strong / many*

---

803 innoghe] in nghe   815 yerne and com] *supplied*

---

1 Paper was both rare and precious at this time, and not infrequently used for elaborate table ornaments (Acker-man 1957). *Cleanness* 1408 describes food at a feast being served with canopies *pared out of paper and poynted of golde*; see also *The Parson's Tale* (X, 443-44). In both, these are condemned as instances of conspicuous consumption, leading some to see this as a veiled criticism of the castle. It should be noted, however, that this description is not concerned with *pride of the table* (PT 443), but with the fine detail of the castle's decorations.

2 St. Peter is the patron saint of porters; see Tamplin 1969: 403-05.

Knyghtes and swyeres° comen doun thenne	*squires*
825 For to bryng this buurne° wyth blys° into halle.	*man / joy*
When he hef° up his helme, ther hiyed innoghe°	*lifted / hurried many*
For to hent hit at° his honde, the hende° to serven;	*take it from / noble (man)*
His bronde° and his blasoun° bothe thay token.	*sword / shield*
Then haylsed° he ful hendly° tho hatheles° uchone,°	*greeted / courteously / men / each one*
830 And mony proud mon ther presed° that prynce to honour.	*pressed forward*
Alle hasped° in his hegh[1] wede° to halle thay hym wonnen,°	*clad / armor / brought*
Ther° fayre fyre upon flet° fersly brenned.°[2]	*where / on the floor / vigorously burned*
Thenne the lorde of the lede° loutes° fro his chambre	*people / descends*
For to mete wyth menske° the mon on the flor.	*honor*
835 He sayde: "Ye ar welcum to welde° as yow lykes°	*enjoy / desire*
That° here is; al is yowre awen, to have at yowre wylle	*(all) that*
and welde."°	*use*
"Graunt mercy,"° quoth Gawayn,	*many thanks*
"Ther°[3] Kryst hit yow foryelde."°	*in heaven / repay you for this*
840 As frekes° that semed fayn°	*like men / glad (to meet)*
Ayther other° in armes con felde.°	*each the other / did embrace*
Gawayn glyght° on the gome° that godly° hym gret°	*looked / man / courteously / greeted*
And thought hit a bolde burne° that the burgh aghte° —	*knight / owned*
A hoge hathel for the nones,° and of hyghe eldee.°[4]	*huge man indeed / full in years*
845 Brode, bryght, was his berde, and al bever-hued,°	*beaver-colored (reddish brown)*
Sturne,° stif° on the stryththe° on stalworth schonkes,°	*bold / firm / in stance / powerful legs*

---

1 The *MED* gives "full, complete, total" as one meaning of *hegh* (s.v. "heigh," adj. 6b). In other words, Gawain is led into the hall with all the gear he has been wearing. Later he is divested of his armor in a private chamber.

2 At this time, castles featured wall fireplaces only in chambers (cf. 875); they did not become normal in the hall until the fifteenth century (M. Thompson 1997: 128).

3 On *ther* as a reference to heaven when used in conjunction with God or Christ, see *MED*, s.v. "thēr," adv. 1a.

4 The expression *hyghe eldee* is not recorded elsewhere; it is usually glossed as "the prime of life." However, Suzuki (1977, 1981) notes that the very similar expression *hyghe age* means "advanced in age," "old." Dove finds the phrase ambiguous, carrying with it "the twin ideas of full manhood and old age" (1986: 139). Supporting Suzuki's argument is that the host is called the *olde lorde of that leude* in l. 1124. Compare the description in Appendix B on p. 156.

Felle° face as the fyre,° and fre° of hys speche;   *fierce / fire / frank*

And wel hym semed,° for sothe,° as the segge° thught,   *suited / indeed / knight*

To lede a lortschyp in lee° of leudes° ful gode.   *a castle / men*

850   The lorde hym charred° to a chambre, and chesly°[1] cumaundes°   *took / solicitously / commands*

To delyver° hym a leude° hym lowly° to serve;   *bring / man / humbly*

And there were boun° at his bode° burnes innoghe°   *ready / command / many men*

That broght hym to a bryght boure,° ther beddyng° was noble: *chamber / bed-furnishings*

Of cortynes° of clene° sylk wyth cler golde hemmes,°   *bed-curtains / bright / borders*

855   And covertores° ful curious° with comlych panes°   *quilts / excellent / beautiful lining*

Of bryght blaunmer° above, enbrawded bisydes,°   *ermine / embroidered on the sides*

Rudeles° rennande° on ropes,° red golde rynges,   *bed-curtain / running / cords*

Tapytes tyght° to the wowe° of tuly and tars,°   *tapestries hung / walls / fabric of Toulouse and Tharsia*

And under fete,° on the flet,° of folwande sute.°   *underfoot / floor / (carpets) of the same kind*

860   Ther he was dispoyled,° wyth speches of myerthe,°   *undressed / jesting*

The burn of his bruny° and of his bryght wedes.°   *byrnie / clothes*

Ryche robes ful rad° renkkes° hym broghten,   *promptly / men*

For to charge° and to chaunge and chose of the best.[2]   *put on*

Sone as he on hent,° and happed° therinne,   *as soon as received one / clothed*

865   That sete° on hym semly wyth saylande° skyrtes,°   *fitted / flowing / lower part of the robe*

The ver° by his visage° verayly°[3] hit semed   *Spring / appearance / truly*

Welnegh to uche hathel,° alle on hues,°   *to almost every man / in all its colors*

Lowande° and lufly° alle his lymmes° under,   *shining / handsome / limbs*

That° a comloker° knyght never Kryst made,   *so that / more comely*

870   hem° thoght.   *they*

---

850 chesly] clesly   862 hym] hem   865 hym] hyn

---

1   MS *clesly* is generally emended to *chefly*, but Andrew and Waldron show (2002: n. to 850) that *chesly* (a variant of *chysly*) is the more probable reading.

2   Putter 1995 points out that the change of clothes is an important part of the hospitality ritual; refusing to shed one's armor and accept fresh clothes would suggest a distrust of the host (57-58).

3   *The ver by his visage* is a difficult phrase. Some critics have assumed that it refers to a type of fur trimming (*MED*, s.v. "veir," n.) near Gawain's face, but it seems preferable to interpret *ver* as "Spring" (*MED*, s.v. "vēr," n. 1) and *visage* as "appearance" (*MED*, s.v. "visāǧe," n. 1d), since the next lines then make much better sense. According to Astell (1999: 126), *the ver* and *verayly* pun on the name of Richard II's favorite, Robert de Vere.

Whethen° in worlde he were,	*from whatever place*
Hit semed as he myght	
Be prynce withouten pere°	*peer*
In felde° ther felle° men fyght.°	*battle-field / fierce / fight*

875 A cheyer° byfore the chemné° ther charcole brenned°	*chair / fireplace / was burning*
Was graythed° for Sir Gawan graythely° with clothes,°	*prepared / readily / cloth coverings*
Quyssynes° upon queldepoyntes° that koynt° wer bothe;	*cushions / quilted coverlets / well made*
And thenne a meré mantyle° was on that mon cast	*fine sleeveless robe*
Of a broun° bleeaunt,° enbrauded° ful ryche	*bright / costly silk / embroidered*
880 And fayre furred° wythinne with felles° of the best,	*attractively lined with fur / furs*
Alle of ermyn° in erde,° his hode of the same;	*ermine / world*
And he sete° in that settel° semlych° ryche,	*sat / seat / wonderfully*
And achaufed° hym chefly,° and thenne his cher mended.°	*warmed / quickly / mood improved*
Sone was telded up° a tabil on trestes° ful fayre,	*set up / trestles*
885 Clad wyth a clene clothe that cler° whyt schewed,°	*bright / was in color*
Sanap° and salure° and sylverin° spones.	*(on it) a cloth runner / dish for salt / silver*
The wyye wesche° at his wylle and went to his mete.°[1]	*washed (his hands) / food*
Segges° hym served semly° innoghe	*men / decorously*
Wyth sere sewes° and sete,° sesounde of the best.	*various sauces / tasty*
890 Double-felde,° as hit falles,° and fele kyn° fisches,	*two servings / is fitting / many kinds of*
Summe baken in bred,° summe brad° on the gledes,°	*breading / roasted / fire*
Summe sothen,° summe in sewe° savered° with spyces,	*boiled / stew / flavored*
And ay sawes° so sleye° that the segge° lyked.	*sauces / subtly seasoned / knight*
The freke° calde hit a fest° ful frely° and ofte	*knight / feast / freely*
895 Ful hendely,° when alle the hatheles rehayted° hym at ones°	*graciously / men encouraged / in unison*
as hende,°	*equally courteously*

877 that] tha   883 chefly] cefly   884 tabil] tapit   893 sleye] sleyes

---

1   It was an especial honor to be served one's meal in a private chamber (Nicholls 1985: 127).

"This penaunce°[1] now ye take,	*meager meal*
And eft hit schal amende."°	*later the food will improve*
That mon much merthe con° make,	*did*
900 For wyn° in his hed that wende.	*wine*
Thenne was spyed° and spured upon° spare wyse°	*inquired / asked in / tactful manner*
Bi prevé poyntes° of that prynce, put to hymselven,	*discreet questions*
That° he beknew° cortaysly of the court that he were	*so that / revealed*
That athel° Arthure the hende° haldes° hym one,°	*noble / courtly / commands / alone*
905 That is the ryche ryal° kyng of the Rounde Table,	*royal*
And hit was Wawen hymself that in that won° syttes,	*dwelling*
Comen to that Krystmasse, as case hym then lymped.°	*befell*
When the lorde hade lerned that he the leude° hade,	*knight*
Loude laghed he therat, so lef° hit hym thoght,	*wonderful*
910 And alle the men in that mote° maden much joye	*castle*
To apere in his presense° prestly° that tyme,	*to present themselves / promptly*
That°[2] alle prys° and prowes and pured thewes°	*because / honor / refined manners*
Apendes° to hys persoun,° and praysed is ever;	*belongs / himself*
Byfore alle men upon molde° his mensk° is the most.°	*earth / fame / greatest*
915 Uch segge° ful softly sayde to his fere:°	*each man / fellow*
"Now schal we semlych° se sleghtes° of thewes°	*decorous / subtleties / manners*
And the teccheles° termes of talkyng noble;°	*faultless / noble speech*
Wich spede is in speche,° unspurd° may we lerne,	*what power lies in speech / without asking*
Syn we haf fonged° that fyne fader of nurture.°	*welcomed / father of good breeding*
920 God has geven uus his grace godly°[3] for sothe,°	*kindly / indeed*
That such a gest as Gawan grauntes uus to have,	

---

1   Though sumptuously prepared, the meal features fish (rather than meat) so that Gawain can keep the fast, for it is Christmas Eve; hence it is a "penance."

2   Usually *that* is construed as a relative pronoun ("to whom all honor" etc.), but this leaves *to hys persoun* dangling awkwardly. It is preferable to interpret *that* as a subordinate conjuction, "because" (*MED*, s.v. "that," conj. 4); that is, all the residents of the castle "made much joy" *because* their guest is famed for his honor, prowess, and refined manners.

3   This line puns on two senses of *godly*: "goodly" ("graciously," "kindly") and "godly" ("divinely").

When burnes blythe of° His burthe° schal sitte
and synge.

In menyng° of maneres mere°

925   This burne now schal uus bryng,

I hope that may hym here°

Schal lerne of luf-talkyng."°[1]

happy about / birth

understanding / fine

I believe those who may listen to him

love-talking

Bi that° the diner° was done and the dere° up,

Hit was negh at the niyght neghed° the tyme.

930   Chaplaynes to the chapeles[2] chosen the gate,°

Rungen° ful rychely° — ryght as thay schulden —

To the hersum[3] evensong° of the hyghe tyde.°

The lorde loutes° ther-to, and the lady als;°

Into a cumly closet° coyntly ho° entres.

935   Gawan glydes° ful gay° and gos theder sone;°

The lorde laches° hym by the lappe° and ledes hym to sytte,

And couthly° hym knowes° and calles hym his nome,°

And sayde he was the welcomest wyye° of the worlde;

And he hym thonkked throly,° and ayther halched°[4] other

940   And seten soberly samen° the servise whyle.°

Thenne° lyst° the lady to loke on the knyght,

Thenne com ho° of hir closet with mony cler burdes.°

Ho was the fayrest in felle,° of flesche° and of lyre°

by the time that / feast / dear man (Gawain)

nearly drawn near to night

took their way to

rung (the bells) / ceremoniously

devout vespers / festive occasion

descends (from his chamber) / also

a private pew / gracefully she

walks / cheerfully / without delay

catches / sleeve

familiarly / acknowledges / by name

man

warmly / saluted

solmenly together / during the service

when / desired

then she left / beautiful maids

skin / body / face

---

930 chaplaynes] claplaynes

---

1   This phrase can mean either "courtly love talk" or, more generally, "polite conversation" (McCarthy 2008). Gawain's fame for courtesy is proverbial (Whiting 2006). A useful resource for further information about Gawain as a character in Arthurian literature is Thompson and Busby 2006.

2   It was normal for large castles to have a main chapel as well as several smaller ones (M. Thompson 1997: 128).

3   ME *hersum* usually means "obedient," "compliant," but this sense does not fit the context. Many editors, as well as the *MED*, gloss the present instance as "devout." Gollancz (1940: n. to 932) derives the word from OE *her*, as in *herlic*, "noble," "exalted," but this sense does not seem to have survived into the Middle English period, and there is no instance of OE *hyrsum* or ME *hersum* where the root has this meaning.

4   On *halched*, see Gollancz 1940: n. to 939.

And of compas° and colour° and costes,° of alle other, *figure / complexion / manners*

945 And wener° then Wenore,° as the wyye° thoght. *more lovely / Guinevere / knight*

Ho ches° thurgh the chaunsel[1] to cheryche° that hende.° *came / greet / courteous man*

An other lady hir lad° bi the lyft° honde, *led / left*

That was alder° then ho — an auncian° hit semed — *older / person of great age*

And heghly° honowred with hatheles° aboute. *highly / by men*

950 Bot unlyke on to loke tho° ladyes were: *those*

For if the yonge was yep,° yolwe° was that other; *youthful / yellow (of complexion)*

Riche red on that on° rayled° aywhere, *the former / adorned*

Rugh, ronkled° chekes that other on rolled;° *wrinkled / hung in folds on the latter*

Kerchofes° of that on° wyth mony cler° perles, *head-cloths / one / pure*

955 Hir brest[2] and hir bryght throte bare displayed,

Schon schyrer° then snawe that schedes° on hilles; *brighter / falls*

That other wyth a gorger° was gered° over the swyre,° *wimple / clothed / neck*

Chymbled° over hir blake chyn° with chalkwhyte vayles,° *wrapped up / chin / veils*

Hir frount° folden in sylk, enfoubled° aywhere, *forehead / covered*

960 Toret° and treleted° with tryfles° aboute, *edged / interlaced / decorative details*

That° noght was bare of that burde° bot the blake browes,° *so that / woman / brows*

The tweyne yyen° and the nase, the naked lyppes; *eyes*

And those were soure° to se and sellyly blered.° *unpleasant / very bleary*

A mensk° lady on molde° mon° may hir calle, *beautiful / earth / one*

965   for Gode!

Hir body was schort and thik,

Hir buttokes balw° and brode; *big*

---

946 ho] he   956 schedes] scheder   958 chalkwhyte] mylkwhyte   967 balw] bay

---

1   The chancel is "the part of the church containing the altar and the choir seats, set off by a railing or screen from the nave" (*MED*). The Lord and his (male) intimates sit in one private pew, while the Lady and her maids sit in the other.
2   Depending on context, ME *brest* can refer to the throat, breast, or the region in between. On some different ways that this passage could be punctuated and interpreted, see Markus 1974: 628.

More lykkerwys on to lyk°[1]	*tempting to taste*
Was that scho hade on lode.°	*the one she was leading*

970	When Gawayn glyght on° that gay° that graciously loked,	*glanced at / the elegant (lady)*
	Wyth leve laght of° the lorde, he lent hem ayaynes;°	*excusing himself from / approached them*
	The alder° he haylses,° heldande° ful lowe,	*older / salutes / bowing*
	The loveloker° he lappes° a lyttel in armes;	*lovelier one / embraces*
	He kysses hir comlyly,° and knyghtly he meles.°	*courteously / speaks*
975	Thay kallen hym of aquoyntaunce,° and he hit quyk° askes	*ask to get to know him / at once*
	To be her° servaunt sothly,° if hemself lyked.°	*their / truly / it pleased them*
	Thay tan° hym bytwene hem, wyth talkyng hym leden	*take*
	To chambre, to chemné,° and chefly° thay asken	*fireplace / first of all*
	Spyces,° that unsparely° men speded hom to bryng,	*spiced cakes / without stinting*
980	And the wynnelych° wyne ther-with, uche tyme.	*delightful*
	The lorde luflych° aloft lepes° ful ofte,	*cheerfully / leaps*
	Mynned merthe° to be made upon mony sythes,°	*called for mirth / repeatedly*
	Hent heghly of his hode° and on a spere° henged,	*cheerfully took off his hood / spear*
	And wayned° hom to wynne the worchip therof°	*challenged / to win it as a prize*
985	That most myrthe myght meve° that Crystenmas whyle;°	*who could create most mirth / time*
	"And I schal fonde,° bi my fayth, to fylter° wyth the best,	*attempt / contend*
	Er me wont the wede,° with help of my frendes."	*before I lose this garment*
	Thus wyth laghande lotes° the lorde hit tayt makes,°	*words / makes merry*
	For to glade° Sir Gawayn with gomnes° in halle	*gladden / games*
990	that nyght,	
	Til that hit was tyme	
	The lord comaundet lyght;[2]	

971 lent] went   987 wede] wedes   992 lord] kyng

---

1   This line contains both wordplay (*lykkerwys* — *lyk*) and a food metaphor: *lyk* literally means "to lick" and *lykkerwys* fare is "delicious"; see *MED*, s.v. "likerŏus," adj. 3a, and "liken," v. 1. The erotic implications of the metaphor are heightened by the fact that the primary meaning of *lykkerwys* is "inciting to lechery" (*MED*, s.v. "likerŏus," 1c); see Markus 1974: 628.
2   That is, the Lord has servants bring lights so that the guests can find their chambers.

Sir Gawen his leve con nyme°   *did take*

And to his bed hym dight.°   *went*

995 On the morne, as° uch mon mynes° that tyme   *when / is mindful of*

That Dryghtyn° for oure destyné° to deye was borne,   *the Lord / fate*

Wele waxes° in uche a won° in worlde for His sake.   *happiness grows / dwelling*

So did hit there on that day thurgh dayntés° mony;   *delicacies*

Bothe at mes and at mele,° messes° ful quaynt°   *small meals and large / dishes / marvelous*

1000 Derf° men upon dece° drest° of the best.   *noble / dais / served*

The olde auncian wyf,° heghest ho° syttes;   *woman / she*

The lorde lufly° her by lent,° as I trowe.°   *courteously / sat / believe*

Gawan and the gay burde° togeder thay seten,   *lady*

Even inmyddes, as the messe metely come,°   *right in the center, where food was rightly served (first)*

1005 And sythen° thurgh al the sale° — as hem best semed° —   *afterwards / hall / suited*

Bi uche grome° at his degré° graythely° was served.   *to each man / according to his rank / readily*

Ther was mete,° ther was myrthe, ther was much joye,   *food*

That for to telle therof hit me tene° were,   *tedious*

And to poynte hit° yet[1] I pyned me,° paraventure.°   *if to detail it / I took pains / indeed*

1010 Bot yet I wot that Wawen and the wale burde°   *lovely lady*

Such comfort° of her compaynye° caghten° togeder   *delight / each other's company / took*

Thurgh her dere dalyaunce° of her derne° wordes,[2]   *their delightful conversation / intimate*

Wyth clene,° cortays carp° closed fro fylthe,°   *pure / speech / devoid of sordidness*

That hor° play was passande° uche prynce gomen,°   *their / surpassed / prince's pleasure*

---

995 tyme] tyny   1014 that] and

---

1 Anderson 1994, pointing out that *and ... yet* is not attested with the meaning "even if" in Middle English, provides an alternate interpretation of this line: "and as for describing it in detail, I would perhaps still be troubling myself (to do it)"; in other words, "The task of describing the feast in general terms would be difficult enough for him, but the task of describing it in detail would be never-ending" (443). On *poynte*, see *OED*, s.v. "point," v.1, II.5.

2 *Dalyaunce* can have sexual connotations (MED, s.v. "daliaunce," n.), and so can *derne*, for *derne luf* ("hidden love") is a phrase that applies to illicit affairs (Chaucer uses it in parodying the language of courtly love in *The Miller's Tale*).

1015 in vayres.°	*in truth*
Trumpes and nakerys,°	*trumpets and kettledrums*
Much pypyng ther repayres;°	*arrives*
Uche mon tented hys,°	*tended his (business)*
And thay two tented thayres.	

1020 Much dut° was ther dryven° that day and that other,°	*joy / made / the next*
And the thryd° as thro° thronge° in therafter;	*third / delightful / rushed*
The joye of Sayn Jones° Day was gentyle° to here,	*St. John's / delightful*
And was the last of the layk,° leudes° ther thoghten.	*festival / men*
Ther wer gestes to go upon the gray morne;	
1025 Forthy wonderly° thay woke,° and the wyn dronken,	*thus greatly / feasted into the night*
Daunsed ful dreyly° wyth dere° caroles.	*without pause / pleasant*
At the last, when hit was late, thay lachen her° leve,	*take their*
Uchon° to wende on his way that was wyye stronge.°¹	*everyone / who was a guest*
Gawan gef hym god day; the godmon° hym lachches,°	*master of the house / grabs hold of*
1030 Ledes hym to his awen chambre, the chymné° bysyde,	*fireplace*
And there he drawes hym on dryye° and derely° hym thonkkes	*keeps him from leaving / graciously*
Of the wynne worschip° that he hym wayved° hade	*delightful honor / shown*
As to honour his hous on that hyghe tyde°	*holiday season*
And enbelyse° his burgh with his bele chere:°	*adorn / good company*

1030 the chymné] the hymne   1032 that] and

---

1   The timing here and in the following lines is problematic. A day seems to be unaccounted for: the poet describes St. John's Day (27 December) as the last day of festivities; the last three days of the year (29-31 December) are occupied by the hunting and bedroom scenes; and Gawain leaves on 1 January. What has happened to 28 December? Various theories have attempted to account for the so-called "missing day." However, it is actually hidden in plain sight. St. John's Day is indeed the last day of the feast; yet the guests do not leave that evening, but on the morning of the 28th (*upon the gray morne*, 1024). Gawain, too, feasts and says his farewells on the evening of 31 December (1958-97) but only leaves on the morning of 1 January (1998-2068); this is also the case in Fitt II, where Gawain takes his leave on 1 November but leaves on the next day. After the guests have left, Gawain tells the host that he has *bot bare thre dayes* (1066), that is, "only three days," to find the Green Knight. These are the three days of the hunt. In other words, Gawain is not counting the partial days (the remainder of 28 December and the morning of 1 January); if he were, then line 1066 below would have to read *foure dayes*, even if there were a missing day. Compare the somewhat different arguments advanced by M. Watson (1949), who however comes to the same conclusion about 27 and 28 December.

1035 "Iwysse,° sir, whyl I leve,° me worthes the better°	*indeed / live / it increases my honor*
That Gawayn has ben my gest at Goddes awen fest."°	*God's own feast (Christmas)*
"Grant merci,° sir," quoth Gawayn, "in god fayth hit is yowres,	*many thanks*
Al the honour is your awen;°[1] the heghe Kyng yow yelde!°	*own / may God thank you*
And I am wyye° at your wylle to worch° youre hest,°	*man / to carry out / command*
1040 As I am halden ther-to,° in hyghe and in lowe,	*as courtesy demands*
bi right."	
The lorde fast° can hym payne°	*tenaciously / did exert himself*
To holde° lenger the knyght;	*detain*
To hym answres Gawayn	
1045 Bi non way° that he myght.	*there was no way*

Then frayned° the freke° ful fayre° at himselven	*inquired / lord / very politely*
What derve dede° had hym dryven at that dere° tyme	*difficult task / festive*
So kenly° fro the kynges kourt to kayre° al his one,°	*daringly / depart / all alone*
Er the halidayes holly° were halet out of toun.°	*wholly / over and done*
1050 "For sothe,° sir," quoth the segge,° "ye sayn bot° the trawthe,	*indeed / knight / speak only*
A heghe ernde° and a hasty° me hade° fro tho wones,°	*vital mission / urgent / took / that dwelling*
For I am sumned° myselfe to sech to° a place,	*summoned / seek out*
I ne wot° in worlde whederwarde° to wende° hit to fynde.	*don't know / where / to go*
I nolde bot if I hit negh myght° on New Yeres morne	*I would not wish to miss finding it*
1055 For alle the londe inwyth Logres,° so me oure Lorde help!	*within Arthur's kingdom*
Forthy,° sir, this enquest° I require° yow here,	*therefore / question / ask*
That ye me telle with trawthe if ever ye tale herde	
Of the Grene Chapel, where hit on grounde stondes,	
And of the knyght that hit kepes,° of colour of grene.	*defends*
1060 Ther was stabled bi statut° a steven° uus bytwene	*established by contract / meeting*

1037 merci] nerci   1053 ne wot] wot

---

1   Gawain politely denies that his presence bestows honor upon the Lord. To paraphrase the exchange: "You honor me with your presence." "No, the honor is mine."

To mete that mon at that mere,° yif I myght last;°   *landmark / live*

And of that ilk° New Yere bot neked° now wontes,°   *same / only a little / is lacking*

And I wolde loke on that lede — if God me let wolde —

Gladloker,° bi Goddes Sun, then any god welde!°   *more gladly / to have anything*

1065 Forthi, iwysse,° bi yowre wylle,° wende me bihoves;°   *therefore indeed / leave / I must go*

Naf I now° to busy° bot bare° thre dayes,   *I now have no more / get busy / just*

And me als fayn° to falle feye° as fayly° of myyn ernde."°   *I'd just as soon / dead / fail / mission*

Thenne laghande° quoth the lorde, "Now leng thee byhoves,°   *laughing / you must stay*

For I schal teche° yow to that terme° bi the tymes ende.   *show / appointed place*

1070 The Grene Chapayle upon grounde° greve° yow no more!   *at all / (let it) trouble*

Bot ye schal be in yowre bed, burne,° at thyn ese;   *knight*

Whyle forth dayes° and ferk° on the fyrst of the yere,   *while away the days / go*

And cum to that merk° at mydmorn,° to make° what yow likes   *place / mid-morning / do*

in spenne.°   *there*

1075 Dowelles whyle° New Yeres daye,   *remain until*

And rys, and raykes thenne;°   *go there*

Mon schal yow sette in waye,°   *you shall be set on the right path*

Hit is not two myle henne."°   *from here*

Thenne was Gawan ful glad, and gomenly° he laghed: *joyfully*

1080 "Now I thonk yow thryvandely thurgh° alle other thynge!   *heartily beyond*

Now acheved is my chaunce,° I schal at your wylle   *since my purpose is accomplished*

Dowelle° and elles° do what ye demen."°[1]   *remain / also / decree*

Thenne sesed° hym the syre and set hym bysyde,   *seized*

Let the ladies be fette° to lyke hem° the better.   *fetched / please him (Gawain)*

1085 Ther was seme solace° by hemself stille;°   *seemly amusement / in private*

The lorde let° for luf° lotes° so myry,   *let (out) / joy / words*

1069 that terme] tha terme

---

1 *Demen* is another example of legal language; its primary meaning is "to render judgment" (in a trial). The host seizes on Gawain's use of this judicial terminology to propose a bargain whose details are spelled out with legal language (e.g., 1105 *forwarde*, 1112 *bargayn*, and 1123 *covenauntes*).

As wyy° that wolde of his wyte,° ne wyst what he myght.°   *man / going out of his mind / did*

Thenne he carped° to the knyght, criande° loude,   *said / crying*

"Ye han demed° to do the dede° that I bidde;°   *agreed / deed / command*

1090 Wyl ye halde this hes° here at thys ones?"°   *keep this promise / right now*

"Ye, sir, for sothe,"° sayd the segge° true,   *indeed / knight*

"Whyl I byde° in yowre borghe, be bayn° to yowre hest."°   *remain / obedient / command*

"For° ye haf travayled," quoth the tulk,° "towen° fro ferre,°   *since / man / come / afar*

And sythen waked° me wyth, ye arn not wel waryst°   *then feasted / are not fully recovered*

1095 Nauther of sostnaunce° ne of slepe, sothly° I knowe;   *either in nourishment / truly*

Ye schal lenge° in your lofte,° and lyye in your ese   *remain / chamber*

Tomorn whyle the messewhyle,° and to mete° wende   *during Mass / go to (your) meal*

When ye wyl, wyth my wyf, that wyth yow schal sitte

And comfort° yow with compayny, til I to cort torne.°   *amuse / return*

1100   Ye lende°   *you (will) stay*

And I schal erly ryse;

On huntyng wyl I wende."°   *go*

Gavayn grantes alle thyse,°   *these (requests)*

Hym heldande° as the hende.°   *bowing to him / like a courteous (one)*

1105 "Yet firre,"° quoth the freke,° "a forwarde we make:°   *further / lord / let's make an agreement*

What-so-ever I wynne in the wod,° hit worthes to youres;°   *wood / it will become yours*

And what chek so ye acheve,° chaunge me therforne.°   *whatever gains you make / for it*

Swete,° swap°¹ we so, sware° with trawthe,   *dear (man) / (let us) agree / swear*

Whether, leude,° so lymp lere other better."°   *knight / it turns out better or worse*

1110 "Bi God," quoth Gawayn the gode, "I grant ther-tylle,°   *that request*

And that yow lyst for to layke,° lef° hit me thynkes."°   *wish to play / pleasant / seems to me*

1092 yowre hest] yowe hest

---

1   Most editors gloss *swap* with its modern meaning ("exchange," "swap"), but the *OED* records this sense only as of the late sixteenth century (s.v. "swap," "swop" v., 8a.-c.). It seems best to prefer the attested Middle English meaning "strike a bargain, make an agreement" (*MED*, s.v. "swappen," v. 4).

"Who° brynges uus this beverage, this bargayn is maked,"°[1]   *if someone / sealed*

So sayde the lorde of that lede;° thay laghed uchone,°   *people / all of them*

Thay dronken and daylyeden° and dalten untyghtel,°   *had fun / reveled*

1115 Thise lordes and ladyes, whyle that hem lyked;°   *it pleased them*

And sythen° with Frenkysch fare°[2] and fele fayre lotes°   *then / French manners / words*

Thay stoden and stemed° and stylly° speken,   *lingered / quietly*

Kysten° ful comlyly° and kaghten her° leve.   *kissed / courteously / took their*

With mony leude ful lyght° and lemande° torches   *many eager attendants / shining*

1120 Uche burne° to his bed was broght at the laste,   *each one*

ful softe.°   *comfortably*

To bed yet er thay yede,°   *but before they went to bed*

Recorded covenauntes° ofte;   *(they) repeated their agreements*

The olde lorde of that leude°   *people*

1125 Cowthe wel halde layk alofte.°   *knew well how to keep up the sport*

---

1 On the ceremonial role of drink in sealing legal agreements, see Blanch and Wasserman 1984: 603-04.

2 "French manners and words" suggest aristocratic refinement. Moorman (1977: n. to 1116) points out that the phrase is used satirically by Noah's wife in the Chester cycle's *Noah's Flood* (l. 100) in the sense of "elaborate politeness."

Ful erly bifore the day the folk uprysen;°	*arise*
Gestes° that go wolde hor gromes° thay calden,	*guests / grooms*
And thay busken up bilyve° blonkkes° to sadel,	*hurry at once / horses*
Tyffen her takles,° trussen her males,°	*prepare their things / tie up their bags*
1130 Richen hem° the rychest,° to ryde alle arayde,°	*prepared / most nobly / organized*
Lepen up lyghtly,° lachen her° brydeles,	*gracefully / seize their*
Uche wyye° on his way ther° hym wel lyked.	*each one / wherever*
The leve° lorde of the londe was not the last,	*dear*
Arayed for the rydyng, with renkkes° ful mony;	*men*
1135 Ete a sop° hastyly° when he hade herde masse,	*light meal / quickly*
With bugle to bent-felde° he buskes bylyve.°	*hunting-field / hastens eagerly*
By° that any daylyght lemed° upon erthe	*by the time / gleamed*
He with his hatheles° on hyghe horsses weren.	*men*
Thenne this cacheres°[1] that couthe° cowpled hor° houndes,	*hunters / knew how / leashed their*
1140 Unclosed the kenel dore and calde hem ther-oute,	
Blewe bygly° in bugles thre bare mote;°	*vigorously / three long notes*
Braches°[2] bayed therfore and breme° noyse maked;	*small scent hounds / fierce*
And thay chastysed° and charred° on chasyng° that went,[3]	*curbed / turned back / to the hunt*
A hundreth° of hunteres, as I haf herde telle,	*countless*
1145 of the best.	
To trystors° vewters° yod,°	*stations / dog keepers / went*
Couples° huntes° of kest;°	*leashes / hunters / untied*

1129 her takles] he takles   1137 that] that that

---

1 The *cacheres* and *hunteres* (1144) are professional huntsmen.
2 *Braches*, as well as *raches* (or *rachches*) are running dogs that hunt by scent.
3 Because the *thre bare mote* signal the beginning of the hunt, the dogs begin baying, so the hunters restrain them; the animals must learn to howl only once they have scented their prey. This difficult line is explicated by Putter 2006: 362-63.

Ther ros for blastes° gode	*because of (bugle) blasts*
Gret rurd° in that forest.[1]	*noise*

1150 At the fyrst quethe° of the quest° quaked the wylde;°	*sound / cry of hounds / game*
Der drof° in the dale, doted° for drede,	*deer rushed / crazed*
Hiyed° to the hyghe,° bot heterly° thay were	*hurried / high ground / fiercely*
Restayed with° the stablye,° that stoutly ascryed.°	*turned back by / huntsmen / shouted*
Thay let the herttes° haf the gate,° with the hyghe hedes,	*harts / pass freely*
1155 The breme bukkes° also with hor brode paumes;°	*big bucks / antlers*
For the fre° lorde hade defende° in fermysoun° tyme	*noble / prohibited / closed season*
That ther schulde no mon meve to° the male dere.	*hunt*
The hindes were halden in° with "Hay!" and "War!,"	*prevented from escaping*
The does dryven with gret dyn° to the depe slades.°[2]	*din / valleys*
1160 Ther myght mon° se, as thay slypte,° slentyng° of arwes° —	*one / slipped / shooting / arrows*
At uche wende under wande° wapped° a flone° —	*at every turn under a tree / flew / arrow*
That bigly bote° on the broun° with ful brode hedes.	*fiercely bit / brown hide*
What! Thay brayen° and bleden,° bi bonkkes° thay deyen,°	*bray / bleed / banks / die*
And ay rachches° in a res° radly° hem folwes,	*always scent hounds / rush / quickly*
1165 Hunteres wyth hyghe horne° hasted hem after	*loud horns*
Wyth such a crakkande kry° as klyffes° haden brusten.°	*thundering noise / as if cliffs / burst*
What wylde so atwaped° wyyes that schotten°	*whatever game escaped / men that shot*

1 The deer hunt presumably takes place in a deer park attached to the castle. First the deer are flushed from cover; as they try to escape, the female animals—being in season—are turned back at the *stablyes* (stations of huntsmen and dogs, located throughout the park). The latter direct the deer toward the Lord and other hunters, located at the *trystors*, who shoot them with arrows; the *trystors* also have dogs that chase down and kill any game that escapes.

2 Harts and hinds are "red" deer (*Cervus elaphus*). The red deer, native to England, is a large animal, standing some four feet at the shoulder; the male (hart) has long and high antlers, explaining the reference to their *hyghe hedes*. Bucks and does are "fallow" deer (*Dama dama*), originating in the Mediterranean region and in Asia; they were introduced to England by the Normans in the twelfth century. These are smaller, standing only three feet at the shoulders. The buck's antlers are broad and flattened; hence their *brode paumes*. As the following lines explain, the male deer (of both species) are not in season and are therefore allowed to escape. For further details about the two types of deer, see Ong 1950 and Sykes 2007.

Chasse au cerf. Manuscrits occidentaux - FR 616, FOL 111v. Bibliothèque national de France.

Was al toraced° and rent° at the resayt,°[1] *mutilated / torn apart / receiving station*

Bi° thay were tened° at the hyghe° and taysed° to the wattres — *after / beset / high ground / driven*

1170 The ledes° were so lerned° at the lowe trysteres,° *men / skilled / stations*

And the grehoundes so grete° that geten hem bylyve° *large / got them quickly*

And hem tofylched° as fast as frekes° myght loke, *seized / men*

ther-ryght.° *right there*

The lorde for blys° abloy° *joy / was carried away*

1175 Ful oft con launce° and light,° *did gallop / dismount*

And drof° that day wyth joy *passed*

Thus to the derk nyght.

Thus laykes° this lorde by lynde-wodes eves,° *plays / forest's borders*

And Gawayn the god mon in gay bed lyges,° *lies*

1180 Lurkkes°[2] whyl the daylyght lemed° on the wowes° *lies concealed / shone / walls*

Under covertour° ful clere,° cortyned aboute.° *blanket / fair / surrounded by curtains*

And as in° slomeryng he slode,° sleyly° he herde *from / was emerging / a furtive (noise)*

A littel dyn° at his dor, and derfly[3] upon;° *slight noise / promptly open*

And he heves° up his hed out of the clothes,° *lifts / covers*

1185 A corner of the cortyn he caght up° a lyttel, *lifted up*

And waytes° warly° thiderwarde,° what hit be myght. *looks / warily / in that direction*

Hit was the ladi loflyest to beholde,

---

1 *The Master of Game* mentions two special types of dogs used in a deer drive: "teasers" and "receivers" (198). The former are small hounds that "tease forth" game (189), while the latter are larger dogs that "receive" it, pulling it down after it has been chased. It is likely, therefore, that *resayt* has the specialized meaning of the station where "receiving" dogs are kept.

2 Most editors gloss *lurkkes* with some variant of "lies comfortably": Gawain "stay[s] snug in bed" (Andrew and Waldron 2002: glossary), "lies snug" (Vantuono 1999: 67), "lie[s] at ease" (Burrow 1987: glossary), and so on. Shaw (1980), however, points out that ME *lurken* does not connote comfort, snugness, or ease; it often involves skulking or some related ignoble activity. Yet the larger context makes it unlikely we are meant to picture Gawain as "skulking" or "cowering." *Lurkes* not only varies *lyges*, but this intransitive verb is also modified by *under covertour ful clere* and *cortyned aboute*. The scene is most likely meant to compare Gawain to an animal lying concealed in its sheltering den (*MED*, s.v. "lurken," v., and "lurkinge," ger.); *lurken* is used in this sense again in line 1195 ("covered," "concealed"). This comparison affects a transition between forest and bedroom, which is also emphasized by the alliterating second-person verb forms (*laykes*, *lyges*, *lurkkes*) that describe the Lord and Gawain.

3 It is possible that MS *derfly* is a mistake for *dernly* (Davis 1967: n. to 1183), a word also found in line 1188.

That drow° the dor after hir ful dernly° and stylle, *closed / secretly*

And bowed° towarde the bed; and the burne schamed,° *moved / was embarassed*

1190 And layde hym doun lystyly° and let as° he slepte. *craftily / pretended that*

And ho stepped stilly° and stel° to his bedde, *silently / stole*

Kest° up the cortyn and creped withinne, *held*

And set hir ful softly° on the bed-syde, *quietly*

And lenged° there selly° longe to loke when he wakened. *remained / quite*

1195 The lede lay lurked° a ful longe whyle, *covered*

Compast° in his concience° to what that cace° myght *considered / mind / situation*

Meve° other amount;° to mervayle hym thoght.° *mean / result in / it seemed strange*

Bot yet he sayde in hymself, "More semly hit were

To aspye° wyth my spelle° in space° what ho wolde." *find out / speech / shortly*

1200 Then he wakenede and wroth,° and to hir warde torned, *stretched*

And unlouked° his yye-lyddes and let as hym wondered,° *opened / pretended surprise*

And sayned° hym, as bi his sawe° the saver to worthe,° *crossed / prayer / to be protected*

with hande.

Wyth chynne and cheke ful swete,

1205 Bothe whit and red in blande,° *side-by-side*

Ful lufly con ho lete° *she behaved very attractively*

Wyth lyppes smal laghande.° *smiling*

"God moroun, Sir Gawayn," sayde that gay lady,

"Ye ar a sleper unslyye,° that mon° may slyde° hider; *unwary / one / enter*

1210 Now ar ye tan° as tyt!° Bot true uus may schape,° *taken / quickly / we arrange a truce*

I schal bynde yow in your bedde, that° be ye trayst."°[1] *of that / assured*

Al laghande the lady lanced tho bourdes.° *uttered these jests*

1199 in] *supplied*   1208 gay] fayr

---

1   The language here suggests that Gawain has been defeated in combat. He must yield and ask for grace (or else be killed); he is then taken captive. If he does not arrange for his release via a truce, he will be imprisoned. The "prison of love" is a common motif in medieval literature.

"Goud moroun, gay," quoth Gawayn the blythe,°	*happy*
"Me schal worthe° at your wille, and that me wel lykes,°	*I shall be / pleases*
1215 For I yelde me yederly° and yeye after grace,°	*yield myself promptly / ask for mercy*
And that is the best, be my dome,° for me byhoves nede."°	*judgment / out of necessity*
And thus he bourded ayayn° with mony a blythe laghter.	*jested back*
"Bot wolde ye, lady lovely, then leve° me grante,	*permission*
And deprece° your prysoun° and pray hym to ryse,	*release / prisoner*
1220 I wolde bowe° of this bed, and busk° me better;	*get out / dress*
I schulde kever° the more comfort° to karp° yow wyth."	*obtain / assurance / speak*
"Nay for sothe,° beau° sir," sayd that swete,	*indeed / good*
"Ye schal not rise of your bedde; I rych° yow better —	*will arrange*
I schal happe yow here that other half als,°	*I'll tuck you in on the other side, too*
1225 And sythen karp° wyth my knyght that I kaght° have;	*then speak / captured*
For I wene° wel, iwysse,° Sir Wowen ye are,	*know / in fact*
That alle the worlde worchipes° where-so ye ride;	*honors*
Your honour, your hendelayk° is hendely° praysed	*courtesy / freely*
With° lordes, wyth ladyes, with alle that lyf bere.°	*among / are alive*
1230 And now ye ar here, iwysse,° and we bot oure one;°	*indeed / are all alone*
My lorde and his ledes° ar on lenthe faren,°	*men / gone far away*
Other burnes in her° bedde, and my burdes° als,	*their / maids*
The dor drawen° and dit° with a derf haspe;°	*drawn shut / locked / strong latch*
And sythen° I have in this hous hym that al lykes,°	*since / whom everyone loves*
1235 I schal ware my whyle° wel, whyl hit lastes,	*use my opportunity*
with tale.°1	*in conversation*
Ye ar welcum to my cors,°2	*person*

1213 gay] g( )   1214 your] yourr   1216 be] he

---

1   Seductions that take place during the absence of a hunting father or husband occur frequently in medieval literature; see Rooney 1993: 186. For one such story involving Gawain, see Appendix C.
2   Literally, "You are welcome to my body." However, Davis notes that *cors* here is an idiom for "person," meaning that the line should be read as "You are welcome to me," "I am glad you are here" (1967: n. to 1237). Still, the next line ("your own pleasure to take") underscores the double meaning of *cors*. For an analysis of possible sexual innuendos in the Lady's speech, see Mills 1968: 614-16.

Yowre awen won° to wale,°   *pleasure / take*

Me behoves of fyne force°   *sheer necessity*

1240   Your servaunt be, and schale."°   *to be your servant, and I will*

"In god fayth," quoth Gawayn, "gayn hit me thynkkes,°   *that seems pleasing*

Thagh I be not now he that ye of speken;

To reche to° such reverence° as ye reherce° here   *merit / honor / describe*

I am wyye° unworthy, I wot wel myselven.   *man*

1245   Bi God, I were glad — and yow god thoght° —   *if it seemed good to you*

At sawe° other at servyce° that I sette° myght   *in speech / action / attain*

To the plesaunce° of your prys;° hit were a pure joye."   *pleasure / praise*

"In god fayth, Sir Gawayn," quoth the gay lady,

"The prys° and the prowes° that pleses al other,   *honor / prowess*

1250   If I hit lakked other set at lyght,° hit were littel daynté;°   *scorned or undervalued / honor (to me)*

Bot hit ar ladyes innoghe that lever wer° nowthe°   *whom it would please more / now*

Haf° thee, hende,° in hor holde° as I thee habbe here —   *to have / courteous (man) / possession*

To daly°[1] with derely° your daynté° wordes,   *converse / pleasantly / agreeable*

Kever hem comfort° and colen her° cares —   *obtain pleasure / relieve their*

1255   Then much of the garysoun other° golde that thay haven.   *treasure or*

Bot I louve° that ilk° Lorde that the lyfte haldes,°   *praise / same / who rules the heavens*

I haf hit holly° in my honde that al° desyres,   *that I have wholly / what everyone*

    thurghe grace."

Scho made hym so gret chere,°   *showed such great affection for him*

1260   That° was so fayr of face;   *who*

The knyght with speches skere°[2]   *faultless words*

Answered to uche a cace.°   *every suggestion*

1255 that] that that   1262 answered] aswared

---

1 *Daly* can simply mean "converse politely," but also "flirt."

2 *Skere* has a range of possible meanings, both neutral ("sincere") and morally pointed ("innocent," "fault-less"); see *MED*, s.v. "skēre," adj.

"Madame," quoth the myry mon, "Mary yow yelde,° *may Mary reward you*

For I haf founden, in god fayth, yowre fraunchis° nobele, *generosity*

1265 And other ful much of other folk fongen° bi hor dedes,°[1] *have received much from others / deeds*

Bot the daynté° that thay delen,° for my disert nys ever,°[2] *praise / accord me / as I don't deserve it*

Hit is the worchyp of yourself,° that noght bot wel connes."° *the honor belongs to yourself / does*

"Bi Mary," quoth the menskful,° "me thynk hit an other!° *noble woman / I see it differently*

For were I worth al the wone° of wymmen alyve, *sum total*

1270 And al the wele° of the worlde were in my honde, *wealth*

And° I schulde chepen° and chose to cheve° me a lorde, *if / obtain / get*

For the costes° that I haf knowen upon° thee, knyght, here, *qualities / discovered within*

Of bewté° and debonerté° and blythe semblaunt,° *beauty / humility / cheerful manner*

And that I haf er herkkened and halde hit here true,° *heard before and consider true*

1275 Ther schulde no freke° upon folde bifore yow be chosen."[3] *man*

"Iwysse, worthy," quoth the wyye, "ye haf waled wel better.[4]

Bot I am proude of the prys°[5] that ye put on me, *worth*

And, soberly° your servaunt, my soverayn I holde° yow *earnestly / consider*

And yowre knyght I becom, and Kryst yow foryelde."° *may Christ reward you*

1280 Thus thay meled° of muchwhat° til mydmorn° paste, *spoke / various things / mid-morning*

And ay° the lady let lyk as° hym loved mych; *always / acted like she*

The freke ferde with defence° and feted° ful fayre, *knight resisted / behaved*

1265 bi] *supplied* 1266 nys ever] nyseu 1281 as hym] a hym

---

1 This is a notoriously problematic line, and there is no agreement on how it should be construed. I follow Davis 1967 and Silverstein 1984 in supplying *bi*. The first *other* is probably adverbial. Rearranging the line may help to clarify its syntax: *And other [haf] fongen ful much of other folk bi hor dedes*, "And also have received very much from others through their deeds." The *much* that Gawain receives is evidently *daynté*, "praise."

2 The manuscript has *nysen* or *nyseu*. Andrew and Waldron 2002 plausibly read this as *nys euer* with an omitted "er" abbreviation.

3 Analyzing this and other speeches by the Lady, Clark notes its similarities to Gawain's language. Both tend to present their main points only after outlining all the facts and circumstances that come to bear on it. However, whereas "in Gawain's usage such delaying of a conclusion usually serves to attenuate and muffle the main point," the Lady employs the same tactic "to make of it an arresting and emphatic climax" (1966: 370-71). Clark further notes that other characters in the poem employ more straightforward syntax.

4 "Indeed, noble [lady]," said the knight, "you have chosen far better!"

5 Literally, "I am proud of the value at which you assess me." Gawain is responding to the language of commerce in the Lady's speech, including *worth* (1269), *wele* (1270), *chepen* (1271), and *costes* (1272, punning on "qualities" and "value"). See Shoaf 1984, Mann 1986, and Aers 2000: 76-86.

"Thagh I were burde bryghtest,"° the burde[1] in mynde hade,   *most beautiful woman*

"The lasse luf in his lode° for lur° that he soght   *he brought with him / because of the harm*

1285   boute hone° —   *without delay*

The dunte that schulde hym deve,°   *the blow that would strike him down*

And nedes hit most be done."

The lady thenn spek of leve,°   *departing*

He granted hir ful sone.

1290 Thenne ho gef hym god day, and wyth a glent° laghed,   *glance*

And, as ho stod, ho stonyed° hym wyth ful stor° wordes: *surprised / very reproving*

"Now He that spedes° uche spech this disport yelde yow!°   *blesses / may he requite your conduct*

Bot that ye be Gawan, hit gos not[2] in mynde."°   *it is impossible to believe*

"Wherfore?"° quoth the freke,° and freschly° he askes,   *why / knight / quickly*

1295 Ferde° lest he hade fayled in fourme° of his castes.°   *fearing / conduct / manners*

Bot the burde hym blessed, and "Bi this skyl"° sayde: *for this reason*

"So god as Gawayn gaynly° is halden,°   *properly / considered to be*

And cortaysye is closed so clene° in hymselven,   *flawlessly*

Couth° not lyghtly° haf lenged° so long wyth a lady,   *(he) could / easily / remained*

1300 Bot he had craved a cosse° bi his courtaysye,   *craved a kiss*

Bi sum towch° of summe tryfle° at sum tales ende."   *hint / playful reference*

Then quoth Wowen: "Iwysse,° worthe° as yow lykes;   *indeed / let it be*

I schal kysse at your comaundement, as a knyght falles;°   *is fitting for*

1286 schulde] sculde   1293 not] *supplied*

---

1 Most editors introduce two changes here so that the line would read *thagh <u>ho</u> were <u>burde</u> bryghtest, the burne in mynde hade*. The thought would therefore be Gawain's, not the Lady's; for arguments against these changes, and on how they distort the meaning of the passage, see Sanderlin 1973, Rowley 2003, and P. Battles 2010a.

2 I follow Gollancz 1940, Burrow 1987, and Anderson 1996 in supplying *not* to MS *hit gos in mynde*. Otherwise it is difficult to make sense of the Lady's comment—which would be "I believe that you are Gawain"—since the remark is introduced as one that astonishes him. By supplying *not*, her comment becomes, "It is impossible that you are Gawain," which would explain both his astonishment and also his anxiety that he has *fayled in fourme of his castes* (1295). Whiting (2006: 76-82) cites numerous similar passages in French romance, always spoken by ladies who want to be wooed by Gawain.

And fire — lest he displese yow — so plede hit no more."[1]

1305 Ho comes nerre with that and caches° hym in armes, *takes*

 Loutes° luflych° adoun and the leude° kysses. *bows / gracefully / man*

 Thay comly bykennen to Kryst ayther other;° *gracefully commend each other to Christ*

 Ho dos hir forth° at the dore withouten dyn° more, *goes out / noise*

 And he ryches hym° to ryse and rapes° hym sone, *prepares / hurries*

1310 Clepes° to his chamberlayn, choses his wede,° *calls to / clothes*

 Bowes° forth, when he was boun,° blythely° to masse; *goes / prepared / cheerfully*

 And thenne he meved° to his mete° that menskly° hym keped,° *went / meal / fittingly / was waiting*

 And made myry al day, til the mone° rysed, *moon*

  with game.° *entertainment*

1315 Was never freke fayrer fonge° *man better received*

  Bitwene two so dyngne° dame, *noble*

  The alder° and the yonge; *older*

  Much solace set thay same.° *pleasure they had together*

 And ay the lorde of the londe is lent on° his gamnes,° *engaged in / sport*

1320 To hunt in holtes and hethe° at hyndes barayne.° *woods and heath / barren hinds*

 Such a sowme° he ther slowe° bi that° the sunne heldet,° *number / slew / by the time / set*

 Of dos° and of other dere, to deme° were wonder. *does / describe (it all)*

 Thenne fersly° thay flokked in, folk at the laste,° *boldly / finally*

 And quykly of the quelled° dere a querré° thay maked. *killed / collection*

1325 The best bowed° ther-to with burnes innoghe,° *came / many men*

 Gedered° the grattest° of gres° that ther were, *collected / most ample / fat*

 And didden hem derely° undo,° as the dede askes.°[2] *in courtly fashion / carve up / task requires*

1304 so] fo 1315 was] with

---

1 That is: "But [and] do not argue [plede] your case [hit] further [fire] in this way [so], lest he displese you." Burrow explains, "If the lady does claim more than kisses, he will be forced to incur her displeasure by refusing" (1972: 44).

2 The detailed description of the breaking of the deer (excoriation) follows the rules laid out in hunting manuals with remarkable fidelity, and is a sign of the courtly accomplishments of the hunters; see Rooney 1993: 169-71 and Sykes 2007. See also Appendix D.

Serched° hem at the asay°[1] summe that ther were;   *examined / test*

Two fyngeres[2] thay fonde of the fowlest° of alle.   *found even in the poorest*

1330 Sythen thay slyt the slot,° sesed the erber°   *hollow at base of throat / esophagus*

Schaved° wyth a scharp knyf, and the schyre° knitten.°   *scraped it / fair flesh / knotted*

Sythen rytte° thay the foure lymmes° and rent° of the hyde;   *cut off / limbs / stripped*

Then brek° thay the bale,° the boweles out token   *cut open / belly*

Lystily° for laucyng° the lere° of the knot.   *carefully / to not undo / binding*

1335 Thay gryped to° the gargulun,° and graythely° departed°   *took / throat / properly / separated*

The wesaunt° fro the wynt-hole,° and walt° out the guttes;   *esophagus / wind-pipe / cast*

Then scher° thay out the schulderes° with her° scharp knyves,   *cut / shoulder joints / their*

Haled hem by° a lyttel hole, to have hole° sydes.   *pulled them through / whole*

Sithen britned° thay the brest and brayden° hit in twynne,°   *then divided / pulled / two*

1340 And eft° at the gargulun° bigynes on° thenne,   *once more / throat / one*

Ryves° hit up radly° ryght to the byght,°   *cuts / quickly / fork of the hind legs*

Voydes out° the avanters,° and verayly therafter   *removes / entrails in neck*

Alle the rymes° by the rybbes radly° thay lance;°   *membranes / swiftly / detach*

So ryde thay of,° by resound,° bi the rygge° bones,   *cleared out organs / correctly / back*

1345 Evenden°[3] to the haunche, that henged° alle samen,°   *trimmed it / hung / all together*

And heven° hit up al hole,° and hewen° hit of there,   *lifted / intact / cut*

And that thay neme for° the "noumbles"° bi nome, as I trowe,°   *name / numbles / believe*

    bi kynde;°   *properly*

Bi the byght° al of° the thyghes   *fork / of all*

1350 The lappes° thay lance° bihynde;   *flaps of flesh / loosened*

To hewe hit in two thay hyyes,°   *hurry*

Bi the bak-bon° to unbynde.°   *back-bone / cut apart*

Bothe the hede and the hals° thay hewen of thenne,   *neck*

And sythen sunder° thay the sydes swyft fro the chyne,°   *separate / backbone*

1333 boweles] bales   1334 the lere] and lere   1344 so] fo

---

1   In the "assay," a trial cut of the brisket (chest meat) determines the quality of the meat.

2   That is, the flesh is "two fingers" thick.

3   *Evenden* can also be read adverbially, as a form of *even-doun* "right down," "straight down."

1355 And the corbeles fee°[1] thay kest in a greve.° — *raven's portion / thicket*

Thenn thurled° thay ayther° thik side thurgh bi the rybbe,° — *pierced / both / rib*

And henged thenne ayther° bi hoghes° of the fourches,° — *both / hocks / forks of the legs*

Uche freke° for his fee° as falles° for to have. — *each man / portion / was fitting*

Upon a felle° of the fayre best° fede thay thayr houndes — *skin / beast*

1360 Wyth the lyver and the lyghtes,° the lether° of the paunches,° — *lungs / lining / stomachs*

And bred bathed° in blod blende ther-amonges.°[2] — *soaked / mixed in with it*

Baldely° thay blew prys,°[3] bayed thayr rachches;° — *vigorously / prize / scent-hounds*

Sythen fonge° thay her° flesche, folden° to home, — *then took / their / turned back*

Strakande°[4] ful stoutly° mony stif motes.° — *blowing / vigorously / loud notes*

1365 Bi that° the daylyght was done, the douthe° was al wonen° — *by the time that / company / returned*

Into the comly castel ther° the knyght bides° — *where / remains*

    ful stille,

Wyth blys and bryght fyr bette.° — *kindled*

The lorde is comen ther-tylle;° — *to that place*

1370 When Gawayn wyth hym mette,

Ther was bot wele° at wylle.° — *only joy / as they liked*

Thenne comaunded the lorde in that sale° to samen° alle the meny,° — *hall / gather / household*

Bothe the ladyes on loghe° to lyght° with her burdes;° — *downstairs / come / their maids*

Bifore alle the folk on the flette,° frekes° he beddes° — *floor of the hall / men / bids*

1375 Verayly° his venysoun to fech° hym byforne;° — *indeed / bring / before him*

And al godly° in gomen° Gawayn he called, — *graciously / in fun*

Teches hym to° the tayles of ful tayt° bestes, — *showed him / well grown*

1357 ayther] ather   1376 Gawayn] Gaway

---

1 Tolkien and Gordon (1930: n. to 1355) explain that the "raven's bone" was a piece of gristle at the end of the
   breast bone, thrown into a tree to the crows and ravens that followed the hunters in expectation of carrion.

2 The "rewarding" of the dogs is an important element of the hunt, and varies according to the type of game
   that has been killed. Compare lines 1609-10 and 1918.

3 On *blew prys*, which here signifies the call blown when game has been killed, see Putter 2006: 363-68.

4 *Strakande* has the technical meaning of "blow[ing] one of several prolonged hunting calls on a horn, involv-
   ing the repetition of notes in various combinations of frequency and length, after the death of a quarry, at the
   end of a hunt, or on the journey home" (*MED*, s.v. "strāken," v.2, 1a).

Schewes hym the schyree grece°¹ schorne upon° rybbes.   *white fat / cut from the*

"How payes° yow this play? Haf I prys wonnen?"°²   *pleases / taken the prize*

1380 Have I thryvandely° thonk° thurgh my craft° served?"°   *abundantly / thanks / skill / deserved*

"Ye, iwysse,"° quoth that other wyye,° "here is wayth° fayrest   *certainly / man / spoils of a hunt*

That I sey this° seven yere, in sesoun of wynter."   *have seen in*

"And al° I gif yow, Gawayn," quoth the gome° thenne,   *all this / man*

"For by acorde of covenaunt° ye crave° hit as your awen."   *terms of our agreement / may claim*

1385 "This is soth,"° quoth the segge,° "I say yow that ilke° —   *true / man / the same*

That° I haf worthyly° wonnen this wones° wythinne,   *that which / honorably / dwelling*

Iwysse,° with as god wylle, hit worthes to youres."°   *certainly / it shall be yours*

He hasppes° his fayre hals° his armes wythinne,   *embraces / neck*

And kysses hym as comlyly° as he couthe awyse.°   *gracefully / could contrive*

1390 "Tas° yow there my chevicaunce,° I cheved° no more;   *take / winnings / won*

I wowche hit saf° fynly,° thagh feler° hit were."   *give it to you / fully / even if more*

"Hit is god," quoth the godmon,° "grant mercy° therfore.   *master of the house / many thanks*

Hit may be such° hit is the better — and° ye me breve° wolde   *perhaps / if / tell*

Where ye wan this ilk wele,° bi wytte of yorselven."°³   *these same riches / your own wits*

1395 "That was not forward,"° quoth he. "Frayst° me no more,   *the agreement / ask*

For ye haf tan that yow tydes;° trawe ye° non other   *gotten your due / expect*

ye mowe!"°   *may*

Thay laghed, and made hem blythe°   *made merry*

Wyth lotes° that were to lowe;°   *words / to be praised*

1400 To soper thay yede as-swythe,°   *went at once*

Wyth dayntés° newe innowe.°   *delicious dishes / quite novel*

1386 that] and   wonnen] *supplied*   1389 he] ho   1394 yorselven] horselven

---

1 Game was hunted during its "fat" season; ample fat means that the animal is healthy and that its meat will be tender when cooked.

2 This line puns on *paien*, which in this context has the primary meaning "to please," but also suggests the idea of payment (since Gawain and his host pledge to exchange "winnings"). This metaphor is also used in ll. 1941 and 1945. On *prys wonnen* (usually glossed as "deserved thanks") as meaning "win victory, have dominance," see *MED*, s.v. "prīs," n.1, 8c. In both of the other exchanges with Gawain, his host similarly compares the relative value of their winnings (1646-47, 1938-47). This is also the case when the bargain is first proposed (1108-09).

3 To paraphrase, "It is possible that this kiss is worth more than my gifts to you—if you will tell me where you got it."

And sythen° by the chymné° in chamber thay seten;　　*afterwards / fireplace*

Wyyes° the walle° wyn weghed° to hem oft,　　*servants / excellent / brought*

And efte° in her bourdyng° thay baythen° in the morn　　*again / their jesting / agreed*

1405　To fylle° the same forwardes° that thay byfore maden,　　*keep / terms of agreement*

What chaunce so bytides, hor chevysaunce to chaunge[1] —

What newes° so thay nome° — at naght° when thay metten.　　*whatever new spoils / took / night*

Thay acorded of° the covenauntes byfore the court alle;　　*agreed to*

The beverage was broght forth in bourde° at that tyme,　　*in a jesting manner*

1410　Thenne thay lovelych° leghten leve° at the last;　　*courteously / took leave of each other*

Uche burne° to his bedde busked bylyve.°　　*each one / hurried quickly*

Bi that° the coke hade crowen and cakled bot° thryse,　　*by the time that / clucked no more than*

The lorde was lopen° of his bedde, the leudes uchone,°　　*had leapt / each of his men also*

So that the mete° and the masse was metely° delyvered.°　　*meal / fittingly / completed*

1415　The douthe dressed° to the wod er any day sprenged,°　　*company went / daylight appeared*

　　to chace.°　　*hunt*

　　Hegh° with hunte° and hornes　　*loudly / hunters*

　　Thurgh playnes° thay passe in space,°　　*fields / shortly*

　　Uncoupled° among tho° thornes　　*unleashed / the*

1420　Raches° that ran on race.　　*scent-hounds*

Sone thay calle of a quest° in a ker syde;°[2]　　*bay for a chase / side of a marsh*

The hunt rehayted° the houndes that hit fyrst mynged,°　　*hunters urged on / called out*

Wylde° wordes hym warp° wyth a wrast noyce.°　　*fierce / shouted to them / loud clamor*

The howndes that hit herde hastid thider swythe,°　　*quickly*

1425　And fellen as fast to the fuyt,° fourty at ones;　　*trail*

1406 what] that　　　1412 crowen] crowes

1　"Whatever would happen, their winnings to exchange."

2　The mention of thorns, as well as a marsh, suggests that the intended quarry for this hunt is a wild boar (Rooney 1993: 172). Boar-hunting was a traditional December pastime. For a description of boars and boar-hunting, see Appendix D, pp. 175-78. The word *ker(re)*—as well as *flosche* (1430), *cragge* (1430), and *rasse* (1570)—is rare and of Old Norse origin. The poet may have used such words when describing familiar local landscape features (Elliott 1974).

Thenne such a glaver° ande glam° of gedered rachches°	*noise / din / scent-hounts*
Ros, that the rocheres° rungen aboute.	*rocky hillsides*
Hunteres hem hardened° with horne and wyth muthe.°	*encouraged them / voice*
Then al in a semblé° sweyed° togeder,	*throng / rushed*
1430 Bitwene a flosche° in that fryth° and a foo° cragge.	*pool / wood / perilous*
In a knot° bi a clyffe, at the kerre syde,°	*thicket / side of a marsh*
Ther as the rogh rocher° unrydely° was fallen,	*rugged rock / disorderly*
Thay ferden to the fyndyng,°¹ and frekes hem after.°	*trailed the game / men after them*
Thay umbekesten° the knarre° and the knot° bothe,	*searched / crag / thicket*
1435 Wyyes,° whyl° thay wysten° wel wythinne hem hit were,	*men / until / knew*
The best° that ther breved was wyth° the blodhoundes.	*beast / who was announced by*
Thenne thay beten° on the buskes,° and bede hym upryse:°	*beat / bushes / come out*
And he unsoundyly° out soght segges° overthwert° —	*in deadly fashion / sought out men / angrily*
On the sellokest swyn° swenged° out there,	*one of the hugest boars / rushed*
1440 Long sythen° fro the sounder,° that wight° ful° olde;²	*since departed / herd / creature / very*
For he was breme,°³ bor alther-grattest,°	*fierce / very largest*
Ful grymme when he gronyed.° Thenne greved° mony,	*grunted / were troubled*
For thre at the fyrst thrast° he thryght° to the erthe,	*thrust / threw*
And sparred forth good sped° boute spyt° more.	*rushed away quickly / without injuring*
1445 Thise other hallowed,° "Hyghe!" ful hyghe,° and "Hay!" "Hay!" cryed,⁴	*called out / loudly*

1426 glaver ande] glaverande   1433 thay] ( )   1435 wythinne] wytinne   1440 fro the] for the
1441 breme] ( )   1442 ful grymme] f( )me   1443 thre at] ( )   1444 and sparred forth] ( )th
1445 thise other halowed] ( )ise ( )wed

1   *Fyndyng* is here used in the specialized sense of "the action of trailing game with dogs for the purpose of starting or rousing it" (*MED*, s.v. "finding," ger. 2).

2   Mature boars separate from the herd (*sounder*) and live alone. The penultimate word in the line is difficult to read; most editors render it *for*, but the facsimile suggests *ful*. Vantuono (1999: n. to 1440) reads *fol*, a variant spelling of *ful*.

3   The word between *was* and *bor* is illegible, though the first letter seems to be "b." Editors variously read *breme*, as here, or *brode* ("large"), *bronde* ("brawny"), or *bige*.

4   The first words in lines 1442-45 cannot be read. However, because the MS leaf was placed against the preceding one before it was completely dry, a mirror image of some letters from the words in question appear on the opposite page, folio 109b as numbered in the facsimile (Tolkien and Gordon 1930: n. to 1442). However, the readings are still largely conjectural, and various editions supply different words here.

	Haden° hornes to mouthe, heterly rechated.°[1]	*held / vigorously blew a recheat*
	Mony was the miyry mouthe° of men and of houndes	*voice*
	That buskkes° after this bor with bost° and wyth noyse	*hurries / clamor*
	to quelle;°	*kill*
1450	Ful oft he bydes° the baye,°	*stands / at bay*
	And maymes° the mute° inn melle;°	*maims / pack / completely*
	He hurtes of°[2] the houndes, and thay	*drives off*
	Ful yomerly yaule° and yelle.°	*pitifully yowl / cry out*

	Schalkes° to schote° at hym schowen to° thenne,	*men / shoot / pressed forward*
1455	Haled to hym° of her° arewes, hitten hym oft,	*loosed at / their*
	Bot the poyntes payred at the pyth, that pyght in his scheldes,[3]	
	And the barbes of his browe° bite° non wolde;	*brows / pierce*
	Thagh the schaven° schaft schyndered° in peces,	*smoothed / shattered*
	The hede hypped ayayn° were-so-ever hit hitte.	*rebounded*
1460	Bot when the dyntes° hym dered,° of her dryye° strokes,	*blows / hurt / their heavy*
	Then — braynwod° for bate° — on burnes he rases,°	*maddened / battle / charges the men*
	Hurtes hem ful heterly ther° he forth hyyes,°	*viciously where / hurries*
	And mony arwed° ther-at, and on lyte drowen.°	*grew frightened / hesitated*
	Bot the lorde on a lyght° horce launces° hym after;	*swift / gallops*
1465	As burne° bolde upon bent° his bugle he blowes,	*man / battle-field*
	He rechated,° and rydes thurgh rones° ful thyk,	*blew a recheat / thickets*
	Suande° this wylde swyn til the sunne schafted.°	*pursuing / set*
	This day wyth this ilk dede° thay dryven° on this wyse,	*same pursuit / pass*
	Whyle oure luflych° lede lys in his bedde,	*excellent*
1470	Gawayn graythely° at home, in geres° ful ryche	*pleasantly / bed-clothes*

1466 rydes] ry( )

---

1   The recheat calls back and summons together the hounds. The various calls blown on the horn—an important element in the proper conduct of the hunt—are discussed by Feinstein 2001.
2   On *hurten of* as "drive off," "thrust away," see *MED*, s.v. "hurten," v. 5a.
3   "But the points that struck [*pyght*] his neck-skin [*scheldes*] failed [*payred*] at its toughness [*pyth*]."

of hue.

The lady noght foryate,°	*forgot*
Com to hym to salue;°	*greet*
Ful erly ho was hym ate°	*at him*
1475 His mode for to remewe.°	*to change his mind*

Ho commes to the cortyn and at the knyght totes.°	*peers*
Sir Wawen her welcumed worthy on fyrst,°	*courteously right away*
And ho hym yeldes ayayn° ful yerne° of hir wordes,	*answers back / eagerly*
Settes hir softly by his syde, and swythely° ho laghes,	*quickly*
1480 And wyth a luflych loke° ho layde° hym thyse wordes:	*attractive look / spoke*
"Sir, yif ye be Wawen, wonder me thynkkes,°	*it seems a marvel to me*
Wyye° that is so wel wrast° alway to god,	*(how a) man / disposed*
And connes not of compaynye the costes undertake,°	*doesn't know how to act in company*
And if mon kennes° yow hom to knowe, ye kest° hom of your mynde;	*anyone teaches / cast*
1485 Thou has foryeten yederly° that° yisterday I taghtte	*forgotten quickly / what*
Bi alder-truest° token° of talk that I cowthe."°	*most true / lesson / could devise*
"What is that?" quoth the wyghe, "Iwysse,° I wot never;°	*certainly / don't know*
If hit be sothe that ye breve,° the blame is myn awen."	*true what you say*
"Yet I kende yow of° kyssyng," quoth the clere° thenne,	*taught you this concerning / beauty*
1490 "Where-so countenaunce° is couthe,° quikly to clayme;	*a favorable expression / shown*
That bicumes uche a° knyght that cortaysy uses."°	*every / practices*
"Do way,"° quoth that derf° mon, "my dere, that speche,	*cease / noble*
For that durst I not do, lest I devayed were;°	*were refused*
If I were werned,° I were wrang,° iwysse, yif I profered."°	*refused / in the wrong / asked*
1495 "Ma fay,"° quoth the meré° wyf, "ye may not be werned,	*by my faith / merry*
Ye ar stif° innoghe to constrayne° wyth strenkthe, yif yow lykes,	*strong / compel*
Yif any were so vilanous° that yow devaye° wolde."[1]	*ill-bred / refuse*

1479 softly] sofly

---

1 Ovid infamously counsels the use of force to overcome a would-be lover's reluctance in Book 1 of the *Art of Love* (c. 2 CE), and Andreas Capellanus in *The Art of Courtly Love* (late 12th century) approves of this

"Ye, be° God," quoth Gawayn, "good is your speche,   *by*

Bot threte is unthryvande in thede ther I lende,°   *force is thought ignoble where I live*

1500 And uche° gift that is geven not with goud wylle.   *as is every*

I am at your comaundement, to kysse when yow lykes;

Ye may lach° when yow lyst, and leve° when yow thynkkes,°   *take the kiss / leave off / like*

    in space."°   *time*

    The lady loutes° adoun,   *bows*

1505 And comlyly° kysses his face,   *graciously*

    Much speche thay ther expoun°   *many conversations they have there*

    Of druryes greme° and grace.   *love's grief*

"I woled wyt at° yow, wyye," that worthy ther sayde,   *would like to know from*

"And yow wrathed not ther-wyth,° what were the skylle°   *if it doesn't anger you / reason*

1510 That so yong and so yepe° as ye at this tyme,   *dashing*

So cortayse, so knyghtyly, as ye ar knowen oute° —   *far and wide*

And of alle chevalry to chose,° the chef° thyng alosed°   *select / chief / esteemed*

Is the lel layk° of luf, the lettrure° of armes;°[1]   *true practice / essence / knighthood*

For to telle of this tevelyng° of this true knyghtes,   *such toiling*

1515 Hit is the tytelet token° and tyxt° of her werkkes:°[2]   *inscribed title / text / their works*

How ledes° for her lele° luf hor lyves han auntered,°   *knights / their true / ventured*

    Endured for her drury° dulful stoundes,°   *their love / grievous hardships*

1514 for] f( )   1516 ledes for] l( ) fo( )

---

approach when it comes to peasant women (Book 1, ch. 11). Burrow explains that "the lady's argument is that anyone who fails to appreciate Gawain must have the dull soul of a villain, or churl, and may be treated accordingly" (1987: n. to 1496-97).

1 *Lettrure of armes* is ambiguous. The operative senses of ME "letter" are "something written," "an alphabetic character" (*MED*, s.v. "lettrūre," n. 1a and b) and "knowledge," "learning" (2a). Moreover, "arms" can refer to "weapons" (*MED*, s.v. "armes," n. pl. 1a) but also to "fighting" or "chivalry." The *MED* glosses *lettrure of armes* in a literal fashion, "knowledge of warfare" (s.v. "lettrūre," n. 2a). However, since the *lettrure of armes* varies *lel layk of luf*, which according to the Lady is the quality most esteemed about knights, it is unlikely that she would switch abruptly from "love" to "knowledge of warfare." Most editors therefore interpret the phrase as referring to knightly conduct. Davis (1967: n. to 1508 ff.) translates it as "the learning of the knightly profession," Burrow (1987: n. to 1513) "the doctrinal essence of chivalry," and Andrew and Waldron (2002: n. to 1512-13) "the (very) doctrine of knighthood."

2 One might say that love is the sum (title) and substance (text) of chivalry (works). Gollancz points out that the metaphor compares knighthood with a book, particularly with a romance (1940: n. to 1515).

And after wenged° with her walour° and voyded° her care,   *avenged / their valor / removed*

And broght blysse into boure° with bountees hor awen° —   *chambers / their own merits*

1520 And ye ar knyght comlokest kyd° of your elde,°   *known / generation*

Your worde° and your worchip walkes° aywhere,   *fame / is known*

And I haf seten by yourself here sere twyes,°   *two times*

Yet herde I never of your hed° helde° no wordes   *from your head / come*

That ever longed° to luf, lasse ne more;   *pertained*

1525 And ye, that ar so cortays and coynt° of your hetes,°   *exact / vows*

Oghe° to a yonke thynk° yern° to schewe   *ought / young thing / be eager*

And teche sum tokenes° of true-luf craftes.°[1]   *lessons / ways*

Why! Ar ye lewed,° that alle the los weldes?°   *ignorant / possess all renown*

Other° elles ye demen me to dille° your dalyaunce° to herken?   *or / stupid / conversation*

1530   For schame!

I com hider sengel,° and sitte   *alone*

To lerne at yow sum game;°   *to learn some lessons from you*

Dos,° teches me of your wytte,°   *do / wit*

Whil my lorde is fro hame."

1535 "In goud faythe," quoth Gawayn, "God yow foryelde!°   *may God requite you*

Gret is the gode gle,° and gomen° to me huge,   *joy / pleasure*

That so worthy as ye wolde wynne° hidere,   *come*

And pyne yow° with so pover° a mon, as play wyth your knyght   *take pains / poor*

With anyskynnes countenaunce,° hit keveres me ese;°   *any kind of countenance / gives me joy*

1540 Bot to take the torvayle° to myself to tru-luf expoun,°   *trouble / expound*

---

1   The upshot of the Lady's speech is, "Why is it that, since true love is the essence of chivalry, you are not talking more about love?" The long sentence begins as a question (1508-11), moves on to an intricately developed general assertion about love (1512-19), poses a specific observation about Gawain's behavior (1522-24), and finally concludes with an injunction about what Gawain should do (1525-27). It is not until lines 1528-30 that the Lady finally completes the question begun in 1509. Commenting on this passage, Clark notes, "Here, just as in Gawain's most typical speeches, the main point is held back until all the conditions and qualifications bearing on it have been rehearsed; but here, as is never the case with Gawain's speeches, the conclusion (if such it can be called) is not what the beginning implied and required" (1966: 370). Clark identifies this rhetorical device, anacoluthon (an abrupt change of grammatical structure in mid-sentence), as characteristic of the Lady's speeches.

And towche° the temes° of tyxt° and tales of armes° — *describe / themes / text / knighthood*

To yow that — I wot wel — weldes° more slyght° — *wield / skill*

Of that art, bi the half, or a hundreth of seche° — *than a hundred of such*

As I am, other° ever schal, in erde ther I leve,° — *or / where I live*

1545 Hit were a folé felefolde,° my fre,° by my trawthe.° — *a great folly / noble (lady) / honor*

I wolde yowre wylnyng° worche° at my myght, — *request / carry out*

As I am hyghly bihalden,° and evermore wylle — *strictly obligated*

Be servaunt to yourselven, so save me Dryghtyn!"° — *as God may save me*

Thus hym frayned° that fre,° and fondet° hym ofte, — *questioned / lady / tested*

1550 For to haf wonnen hym to woghe,°[1] what-so scho thoght elles;° — *sin / whatever else she intended*

Bot he defended hym so fayr° that no faut semed,° — *well / flaw was apparent*

Ne non evel on nawther halve, nawther thay wysten° — *nor did they experience anything*

    bot blysse.

Thay laghed and layked° longe; — *played*

1555 At the last scho con° hym kysse, — *did*

Hir leve fayre con scho fonge° — *graciously did take*

And went hir waye, iwysse.° — *indeed*

Then ruthes hym° the renk° and ryses to the masse, — *gets up / knight*

And sithen° hor diner° was dyght° and derely° served. — *then / breakfast / prepared / splendidly*

1560 The lede with the ladyes layked° alle day; — *amused himself with*

Bot the lorde over the londes launced° ful ofte, — *galloped*

Sues° his uncely swyn° that swynges° bi the bonkkes° — *pursues / vicious boar / rushes / hills*

And bote° the best of his braches° the bakkes° in sunder° — *bit / hounds / backs / asunder*

Ther he bode in his bay,° tel bawemen hit breken° — *where he waited at bay / forced him on*

1565 And madee hym mawgref his hed° for to mewe° utter,° — *despite his resistence / move / out*

So felle flones° ther flete° when the folk gedered. — *such deadly arrows / fell*

---

1 Davis (1967: n. to 1550) derives *woghe* from *wouen*, "to woo, court," but the *MED* adduces no corresponding noun form, only the gerund form, *wouinge*. The most likely meaning of *woghe* is "sin"; see *MED*, s.v. "wough," n. 2, 2a, which lists several examples, including a similar passage in *Pearl*. Compare also Andrew and Waldron 2002: n. to 1550.

Bot yet° the styffest° to start° bi stoundes° he made,   *even / bravest / draw back / in turn*

Til at the last he was so mat° he myght no more renne,   *tired*

Bot in the hast that he myght° he to a hole wynnes°   *as fast as he could / makes his way*

1570 Of a rasse° bi a rokk ther° rennes the boerne.°   *ledge / where / stream*

He gete° the bonk° at his bak, bigynes to scrape;°   *got / bank / paw the ground*

The frothe femed° at his mouth unfayre° bi the wykes,°   *foamed / profusely / corners*

Whettes his whyte tusches.° With° hym then irked°   *tusks / of / grew weary*

Alle the burnes° so bolde that hym by stoden,   *men*

1575 To nye° hym on-ferum,° bot neghe° hym non durst   *injure / from afar / draw near him*

    for wothe;°   *danger*

    He hade hurt so mony byforne

    That al thught° thenne ful lothe°   *thought it / very unpleasant*

    Be° more wyth his tusches° torne,   *to be / tusks*

1580   That breme was° and braynwod° bothe,   *who was fierce / raging*

Til the knyght com hymself, kachande° his blonk,°   *urging on / horse*

Syy° hym byde at the bay, his burnes° bysyde.   *saw / men*

He lyghtes luflych adoun,° leves his corsour,°   *dismounts gracefully / steed*

Braydes° out a bryght bront,° and bigly° forth strydes,   *draws / sword / vigorously*

1585 Foundes° fast thurgh the forth ther° the felle° bydes.   *proceeds / ford to where / ferocious boar*

The wylde° was war° of the wyye° with weppen in honde,   *wild boar / aware / knight*

Hef hyghly the here;° so hetterly° he fnast°   *raised high his bristles / violently / snorted*

That fele ferde° for the freke,° lest felle[1] hym the worre.°   *many feared / lord / the worst befall him*

The swyn settes hym out° on the segge even,°   *rushes out / straight towards the man*

1590 That° the burne° and the bor were bothe upon hepes°   *so that / man / both came together*

In the wyghtest° of the water; the worre° hade that other,   *swiftest part / worse of it*

For the mon merkkes° hym wel as thay mette fyrst,   *marks*

1580 and] *supplied*   1583 luflych] luslych   1588 freke] frekes

---

1   Alternatively, *felle* could derive from *fellen*, "to fell," so that the phrase would mean "they feared that the worse (= more wicked combatant) would throw him (= their Lord) down."

Chasse au sanglier: chasse à la laie à l'épée.
Manuscrits occidentaux - FR 12399 - FOL 26. Bibliothèque national de France.

Set sadly° the scharp° in the slot° even,°	*firmly / sword / base of throat / directly*
Hit hym up to the hult,° that° the hert schyndered,°	*hilt / so that / burst*
1595 And he yarrande° hym yelde,° and yedoun° the water	*snarling / surrendered / went down*
ful tyt.°	*quickly*
A hundreth° houndes hym hent,°	*countless / caught*
That bremely° con° hym bite;	*fiercely / did*
Burnes him broght to bent,°[1]	*bay*
1600 And dogges to dethe endite.°	*consigned him*
There was blawyng of prys° in mony breme° horne,	*prize / loud*
Heghe halowing° on highe with hatheles° that myght;°	*loud shouting / men / could*

---

1 *Bent* is problematic. Most editors gloss it as "bank," but the *MED* does not adduce such a meaning, which elsewhere—including in several other passages in *Sir Gawain*—always means "field," "battlefield." The *MED* instead suggests that *bringen to bent* is an idiom meaning "bring to bay," and this is the reading followed here.

Brachetes° bayed¹ that best,° as bidden the maysteres	*hounds / at that beast*
Of that chargeaunt chace° that were chef huntes.°	*troublesome hunt / chief hunters*
1605 Thenne a wyye° that was wys upon wodcraftes°	*man / art of hunting*
To unlace° this bor lufly° bigynnes.	*carve up / skillfully*
Fyrst he hewes of° his hed and on highe° settes,	*cuts off / high (on a stake)*
And sythen rendes° him al roghe°² bi the rygge° after,	*then cuts apart / unflayed / back*
Braydes° out the boweles, brennes° hom on glede;°	*pulls / cooks / fire*
1610 With bred blent ther-with his braches rewardes.	
Sythen he britnes° out the brawen° in bryght brode cheldes,°	*cuts / flesh / broad slabs*
And has° out the hastlettes,°³ as hightly bisemes;°	*cuts / choice pieces / is entirely fitting*
And yet° hem halches° al hole° the halves togeder,	*then / fastens / whole*
And sythen on a stif stange° stoutly° hem henges.	*sturdy pole / securely*
1615 Now with this ilk° swyn thay swengen to° home;	*same / hurried*
The bores hed was borne bifore the burnes selven°	*himself*
That him forferde° in the forthe° thurgh forse° of his honde	*killed / ford / force*
so stronge.	
Til he sey° Sir Gawayne	*saw*
1620 In halle, hym thoght ful longe;°	*a very long time*
He calde, and he° com gayn°	*Sir Gawain / directly*
His fees° ther for to fonge.°	*payment / receive*
The lorde ful lowde° with lote° and laghter myry,°	*loud / cries / merry*
When he seye Sir Gawayn, with solace° he spekes.	*mirth*
1625 The goude ladyes were geten,° and gedered° the meyny;°	*fetched / gathered / household*
He schewes hem the scheldes,° and schapes° hem the tale	*slabs of meat / tells*
Of the largesse° and the lenthe,° the lithernes° also	*bulk / length / ferocity*

1620 thoght] poght   1623 laghter] laghed

---

1   When used transitively, *baien* denotes "bring (a quarry) to bay, hold at bay" (*MED*, "baien," v. 2). Since the boar is already dead, the intended image is probably of the hounds surrounding it at a short distance.
2   On *al roghe* as "unflayed," see Rooney (1993: 181).
3   *Hastlettes* are choice pieces of boar, probably meant to be roasted on a spit (Kropp 1992; Scott-Macnab 2010).

Of the were° of the wylde swyn, in wod ther° he fled.　　　*fight / where*

That other knyght ful comly° comended his dedes,　　　*courteously*

1630　And praysed hit as gret prys° that he proved° hade,　　　*prowess / shown*

For suche a brawne° of a best,° the bolde burne° sayde,　　　*(large amount of) flesh / beast / man*

Ne such sydes of a swyn segh° he never are.°　　　*saw / before*

Thenne hondeled° thay the hoge° hed, the hende° mon hit praysed　　　*touched / huge / courteous*

And let lodly° ther-at, the lorde for to here.　　　*pretended fright*

1635　"Now, Gawayn," quoth the godmon,° "this gomen° is your awen°　　　*master of the house / prize / own*

Bi fyn forwarde° and faste,° faythely° ye knowe."　　　*binding agreement / firm / truly*

"Hit is sothe,"° quoth the segge,° "and as siker° true　　　*that is correct / knight / completely*

Alle my get° I schal yow gif agayn,° bi my trawthe."°　　　*gains / in return / honor*

He hent° the hathel° aboute the halse,° and hendely° hym kysses,　　　*caught / host / neck / courteously*

1640　And eftersones° of the same he served hym there.　　　*immediately*

"Now ar we even," quoth the hathel,° "in this eventide°　　　*knight / evening*

Of alle the covenauntes° that we knyt,° sythen I com hider,　　　*agreements / made*

　　bi lawe."

The lorde sayde, "Bi saynt Gile,°¹　　　*St. Giles*

1645　Ye ar the best that I knowe!

Ye ben° ryche in a whyle,　　　*will be*

Such chaffer° and° ye drowe."°　　　*trading / if / do*

Thenne thay teldet° tables trestes alofte,°　　　*set up / upon trestles*

Kesten clothen° upon; clere lyght° thenne　　　*tablecloths / bright lights*

1650　Wakned° bi wowes,° waxen torches;　　　*sprang up / on the walls*

Segges sette° and served in sale° al aboute;　　　*men set the tables / hall*

Much glam° and gle° glent up° therinne　　　*noise / joyous din / arose*

1639　hent] *supplied*

1　St. Giles was a seventh-century hermit and later abbot. Gollancz argues that because St. Giles is often depicted with a hind, this would make him an appropriate patron for the Lord (1940: n. to 1644); however, Silverstein notes that this association is not found in contemporary French or English romances, nor in Chaucer (1984: n. to 1644). Tamplin 1969 finds the Lord's oath ironic: "St. Giles was notably unworldly, becoming a hermit because he dreaded prosperity and fame and resisting offers of money and even medical care" (408).

Aboute the fyre upon flet,° and on fele° wyse — *floor of the hall / many*

At the soper and after: mony athel° songes, — *noble*

1655 As coundutes° of Krystmasse and caroles newe, — *songs*

With alle the manerly merthe° that mon° may of telle, — *seemly mirth / one*

And ever oure luflych° knyght the lady bisyde. — *worthy*

Such semblaunt° to that segge semly° ho made° — *looks / virtuous knight / she gave*

Wyth stille stollen countenaunce° — that stalworth° to plese — — *furtive glances / valiant man*

1660 That al forwondered° was the wyye,° and wroth° with hymselven,[1] — *astonished / knight / vexed*

Bot he nolde° not for his nurture° nurne hir ayaynes,° — *would / good manners / rebuke her*

Bot dalt with hir al in daynté,° how-se-ever the dede° turned — *politely / this behavior*

towrast.° — *awry*

When thay hade played in halle

1665 As longe as hor wylle hom° last, — *their desire did*

To chambre he con° hym calle,° — *(the host) did / invite*

And to the chemné° thay past. — *fireplace*

Ande ther thay dronken and dalten,° and demed eft newe° — *conversed / decided then anew*

To norne° on the same note° on Newe Yeres even;° — *propose / the same conditions / eve*

1670 Bot the knyght craved leve to kayre° on the morn, — *depart*

For hit was negh at the terme° that he to° schulde.° — *appointed time / leave / must*

The lorde hym letted° of that, to lenge hym resteyed,° — *dissuaded / insisted he stay longer*

And sayde, "As I am true segge,° I siker° my trawthe° — *knight / pledge / word*

Thou schal cheve to° the Grene Chapel thy charres° to make,° — *reach / tasks / perform*

1675 Leude,° on New Yeres lyght,° longe bifore pryme!°[2] — *sir / dawn / prime is over*

Forthy° thow lye in thy loft° and lach thyn ese,° — *therefore / chamber / take it easy*

And I schal hunt in this holt,° and halde° the towches,° — *wood / keep / covenant*

---

1 This could mean either that Gawain was angry *at* himself, or *within* himself (that is, he did not let his anger show).

2 Prime, the first canonical "hour," would last from about 6 to 9 a.m. It can also be used synonymously with "dawn," but the host tells Gawain that he will be underway "at dawn, long before prime." Since during late December and early January the sun rises around 8 a.m. in England, the host must mean that Gawain will be underway long before prime is over.

Chaunge° wyth thee chevisaunce,° bi that° I charre° hider. *exchange / winnings / when / return*

For I haf fraysted° thee twys,° and faythful I fynde thee: *tested / twice*

1680 Now 'thrid tyme throwe best'°[1] thenk on the morne. *third time's the charm*

Make we mery whyl we may and mynne upon joye,° *be joyful*

For the lur° may mon°[2] lach° when-so mon lykes!" *sorrow / one / find*

This was graythely° graunted, and Gawayn is lenged.° *readily / remains*

Blithe° broght was hym drynk, and thay to bedde yeden° *graciously / went*

1685   with light.

   Sir Gawayn lis and slepes

   Ful stille and softe° al night; *comfortably*

   The lorde that his craftes° kepes,° *purpose / pursues*

   Ful erly he was dight.° *dressed*

1690 After messe° a morsel he and his men token; *mass*

Miry was the mornyng, his mounture° he askes.° *mount / calls for*

Alle the hatheles° that on horse schulde helden° hym after *men / follow*

Were boun,° busked° on hor blonkkes° bifore the halle yates.° *set / ready / their horses / gates*

Ferly° fayre was the folde,° for the forst clenged,° *wondrously / ground / frost clung*

1695 In rede,° rudede° upon rak,° rises the sunne, *red / fiery / clouds*

And ful clere° costes° the clowdes of the welkyn.° *bright / drifted / sky*

Hunteres unhardeled° bi a holt° syde, *unleashed the dogs / wood's*

Rocheres roungen° bi rys° for rurde° of her° hornes. *hillsides rang / thicket / clamor / their*

Summe fel in° the fute° ther° the fox bade, *picked up / trail / to where*

1700 Trayles° ofte a trayteres° bi traunt° of her wyles.°[3] *crossing / by tricks / cunning / cleverness*

1690 morsel] nnorsel   1693 bifore] biforere

---

1   On this proverb, see *MED*, s.v. "throuen," v. 1, 11.
2   Here *mon* is the indefinite pronoun "one," "anyone." To paraphrase, "Let's make an effort to be merry and joyful while we can, for one can find sorrow anytime with no trouble at all."
3   Editors are divided on whether this line refers to the fox or hounds. The emphasis on cunning would suggest the fox, but the use of the plural (*her wyles*) the hounds. For a contemporary description of fox-hunting, see Appendix D, pp. 178-79. MS *a trayteres* is normally emended to *a traveres*, but Silverstein (1984: n. to 1700) points out the Old French *a trestors*, meaning "by tricks or turns."

A kenet° kryes° therof, the hunt on hym calles; *small hunting dog / gives tongue*

His felawes fallen hym to, that fnasted° ful thike,° *panted / hard*

Runnen forth in a rabel° in his ryght fare,° *pack / track*

And he fyskes° hem byfore; thay founden hym sone, *scampers*

1705 And when thay seghe° hym with syght, thay sued° hym fast, *saw / pursued*

Wreyande hym° ful weterly° with a wroth° noyse; *revealing his location / clearly / loud*

And he trantes and tornayees° thurgh mony tene greve,° *doubles back / dense thicket*

Havilounes,° and herkenes° bi hegges ful ofte. *doubles back / listens*

At the last, bi a littel dich° he lepes over a spenne,° *ditch / fence*

1710 Steles out ful stilly° bi a strothe rande,° *quietly / strip of marshy land*

Went haf wylt° of the wode with wyles° fro the houndes; *thought to steal away / tricks*

Thenne was he went,° er he wyst,° to a wale tryster,° *come / knew it / good hunting station*

Ther thre° thro° at a thrich thrat° hym at ones, *where three / bold (dogs) / in a rush attacked*

al graye.° *grey*

1715 He blenched ayayn° bilyve° *turned around / quickly*

And stifly° start on-stray,° *swiftly / ran away*

With alle the wo on lyve° *woe in the world*

To the wod he went away.

Thenne was hit lof upon list°[1] to lythen° the houndes, *pleasing to the ear / hear*

1720 When alle the mute° hade hym met,° menged° togeder: *pack / encountered / joined*

Suche a sorwe° at that syght thay sette on his hede *(loud) curse*

As° alle the clamberande° clyffes hade clatered° on hepes. *as if / clustering / crashed down*

Here he was halawed,° when hatheles° hym metten, *shouted at / men*

Loude he was yayned° with yarande° speche; *greeted / raucous*

1725 Ther he was threted° and ofte thef° called, *cursed / thief*

And ay° the titleres° at his tayl, that° tary he ne myght; *always / hounds / so that*

1706 hym] h( )   weterly] ( )eterly   1712 to a] to to a

---

1 Most editors read *lif upon list* and emend to *list upon lif*. However, the facsimile suggests that the vowel in the first word is a partly faded "o" rather than an "i," yielding *lof upon list*; compare Vantuono 1999: n. to. 1719.

Ofte he was runnen at when he out rayked,°   *rushed from cover*

And ofte reled in° ayayn, so Reniarde°[1] was wylé.°   *doubled back / Reynard / wily*

And ye° he lad hem bi lagmon,°[2] the lorde and his meyny,°   *indeed / them astray / company*

1730 On° this maner bi the mountes° whyle myd-over-under,°[3] *in / hills / during mid-afternoon*

Whyle the hende° knyght at home holsumly° slepes   *courteous / soundly*

Withinne the comly° cortynes, on the colde morne.   *elegant*

Bot the lady for luf let not° to slepe,   *did not allow herself*

Ne the purpose to payre° that pyght° in hir hert,   *weaken / was fixed*

1735 Bot ros hir up radly,° rayked hir° theder   *quickly / betook herself*

In a mery mantyle,° mete° to the erthe,   *mantle / which extended*

That was furred° ful fyne with felles° wel pured,°   *lined with fur / skins / trimmed*

No howe°[4] goud on hir hede bot° the hagher stones°   *coif / except / noble gems*

Trased°[5] aboute hir tressour° be twenty in clusteres;°   *entwined / hair-net / in clusters of twenty*

1740 Hir thryven° face and hir throte throwen° al naked,   *lovely / laid*

Hir brest bare bifore,° and bihinde eke.°[6]   *in front / likewise*

Ho comes withinne the chambre dore, and closes hit hir after,

Wayves up° a wyndow, and on the wyye° calles,   *swings open / knight*

And radly° thus rehayted° hym with hir riche° wordes,   *quickly / greeted cheerfully / noble*

1745   with chere:°   *cheer*

   "A! Mon, how may thou slepe?

   This morning is so clere!"°   *beautiful*

1738 howe] hwes

---

1   "Reynard" is a generic name for "fox."
2   *Bi lagmon* is notoriously difficult. Its most likely meanings are either "led astray" or "led to come out last." Context suggests the former. The various proposed meanings are reviewed by Matthews 1975.
3   *Myd-over-under* means "middle of the period after undern." Originally, *undern* would have referred to the third hour after sunrise, approximately 9 a.m. However, in the fourteenth and fifteenth centuries *undern* was also used for noon, and this is the more likely meaning here. (For the two senses, see *MED*, s.v. "undern," n. 1 and 2).
4   MS *hwez* (i.e., "hues") does not make much sense in the present context. Gollancz (1940: n. to 1738) argues that the intended word is "head-dress," Middle English *houve*, which also has the variant spellings *how* and *howe*. The lack of head-dress would imply that the Lady, as a married woman, is not dressed very chastely, an impression confirmed by the rest of her description.
5   On *trased*, see *OED* s.v. "trace," v3.
6   This recalls the Lady's dress in the chapel scene of Fitt 2 (955, *Hir brest and hir bryght throte bare displayed*). As A.V.C. Schmidt explains, "[T]he Lady is to be understood as wearing a décolleté dress under her sleeveless overgarment" (1987: 158).

He was in drowping° depe,   *uneasy sleep*

Bot thenne he con° hir here.   *did*

1750 In drey° droupyng° of dreme draveled° that noble,   *heavy / uneasy sleep / muttered*

As mon that was in mornyng of° mony thro° thoghtes,   *troubled with / oppressive*

How that destiné schulde that day[1] dele hym his wyrde°   *fate*

At the Grene Chapel, when he the gome° metes,   *knight*

And bihoves° his buffet° abide withoute debate° more;   *must / blow / resistance*

1755 Bot when that comly° com, he kevered° his wyttes,   *beautiful lady / recovered*

Swenges° out of the swevenes,° and swares° with hast.   *started / dreams / answers*

The lady luflych com laghande swete,

Felle° over his fayre face, and fetly° hym kyssed;   *leaned / elegantly*

He welcumes hir worthily with a wale chere.°   *pleasant demeanor*

1760 He sey° hir so glorious and gayly atyred,°   *saw / beautifully attired*

So fautles° of hir fetures and of so fyne hues,°   *flawless / excellent complexion*

Wight wallande° joye warmed his hert.   *swiftly surging*

With smothe° smylyng and smolt° thay smeten° into merthe,   *pleasant / gentle (smiles) / fell*

That al was blis and bonchef° that breke° hem bitwene,   *cheerfulness / passed*

1765   and wynne.°   *joy*

Thay lanced° wordes gode,   *spoke*

Much wele° then was therinne;   *delight*

Gret perile°[2] bitwene hem stod,°   *danger / loomed*

Nif Maré of hir knyght mynne.°   *if Mary was not mindful of her knight*

1770 For that prynces of pris° depresed° hym so thikke,°   *noble princess / pressed / hard*

Nurned° hym so neghe° the thred,°[3] that nede hym bihoved°   *pushed / near / limit / that he must*

1752 dele hym] *supplied*   1755 com] *supplied*   1770 prynces] prynce

---

1 As Andrew and Waldron note, "Since he is not to meet the Green Knight until next day, we must construe: 'on that day when he meets the man at the Green Chapel'" (2002: n. to 1752-53).
2 *Peril* can mean not only "danger," "peril," etc., but also "spiritual peril, danger to the soul from sin" (*MED*, s.v. "peril," 2a).
3 *Thred*, literally "thread," is here used in the sense of "a (fine) dividing line or boundary line" (*OED*, s.v. "thread," n. 10). The use of embroidery images in the poem is discussed by Myer 1995.

Other lach° ther hir luf, other lodly° refuse. — *either accept / or harshly*

He cared for his cortaysye,° lest crathayn° he were, — *courtesy / a boor*

And more° for his meschef° yif he schulde make° synne — *even more / wickedness / commit*

1775 And be traytor to that tolke° that that telde aght.° — *man / owned that house*

"God schylde,"° quoth the schalk,° "that schal not befalle!" — *forbid / knight*

With luf-laghyng a lyt° he layd hym bysyde° — *brief, friendly laughter / turned aside*

Alle the speches of specialté° that sprange° of her mouthe. — *words of love / issued*

Quoth that burde° to the burne,° "Blame ye disserve, — *lady / knight*

1780 Yif ye luf not that lyf° that ye lye nexte,° — *person / lie next to*

Bifore alle the wyyes° in the worlde wounded in hert,°[1] — *more than anyone else / heart*

Bot if° ye haf a lemman,° a lever,° that yow lykes° better — *unless / sweetheart / dearer / you love*

And folden° fayth to that fre,° festned° so harde° — *pledged / noble (lady) / committed / firmly*

That yow lausen ne lyst° — and that I leve nouthe,° — *don't wish to loosen (the bond) / believe now*

1785 And° that ye telle me that now, truly I pray yow: — *unless*

For alle the lufes upon lyve,° layne° not the sothe° — *lovers that are alive / hide / truth*

for gile."° — *guile*

The knyght sayde, "Be Sayn Jon,"°[2] — *Saint John*

And smethely con° he smyle, — *politely did*

1790 "In fayth I welde° right non,° — *have / none at all*

Ne non wil welde the while."° — *for the time being*

"That is a worde," quoth that wyght,° "that worst is of alle, — *lady*

Bot I am swared° for sothe,° that sore° me thinkkes.° — *answered / truly / grievous / seems to me*

Kysse me now comly,° and I schal cach hethen,° — *gracefully / depart from here*

1795 I may bot mourne° upon molde,° as may° that much lovyes." — *grieve / earth / like a woman*

Sykande° ho sweye° doun and semly° hym kyssed, — *sighing / leaned / pleasantly*

And sithen ho severes° hym fro, and says as ho stondes, — *then she departs*

---

1 "The one lying next to you, more wounded in the heart than anyone else in the world" is of course the Lady herself.

2 St. John is "an exemplar of chastity and ... often associated in Christian thought and art with the Virgin [Mary]" (Tamplin 1969: 411).

"Now, dere,° at this departyng° do me this ese,°   *dear / parting / give me this comfort*

Gif me sumwhat of° thy gifte, thi glove if hit were,°   *something as / if only your glove*

1800 That I may mynne on° thee, mon, my mournyng to lassen."°   *remember / lessen*

"Now, iwysse,"° quoth that wyye, "I wolde° I hade here   *indeed / wished*

The levest° thing, for thy luf, that I in londe welde,°   *dearest / own*

For ye haf deserved, for sothe,° sellyly ofte°   *in truth / many times over*

More rewarde, bi resoun,° then I reche° myght;   *by rights / give*

1805 Bot to dele° yow for drurye° that dawed bot neked,°   *give / love / was worth but little*

Hit is not your honour° to haf at this tyme   *it is below your honor*

A glove for a garysoun° of Gawaynes giftes,   *keepsake*

And I am here an erande in erdes° uncouthe,°   *lands / foreign*

And have no men wyth no males° with menskful° thinges;   *bags / beautiful*

1810 That mislykes° me, ladé,° for luf at this tyme;   *displeases / lady*

Iche tolke° mon° do as he is tan,° tas to non ille°   *everyone / must / circumstanced / take it not ill*

ne pine."°   *or grieve*

"Nay, hende° of hyghe° honours,"   *courteous (knight) / great*

Quoth that lufsum° under lyne.°1   *lovely one / dressed in linen*

1815 "Thagh I hade noght of youres,

Yet schulde ye have of° myne."   *(something) of*

Ho raght° hym a riche rynk° of red golde werkes,°   *offered / precious ring / made of red gold*

Wyth a starande° ston stondande alofte°   *glittering / mounted prominently*

That bere° blusschande bemes° as the bryght sunne;   *cast / shining beams*

1820 Wyt ye wel,° hit was worth wele ful hoge.°2   *be assured / worth a great deal*

Bot the renk° hit renayed,° and redyly he sayde,   *man / refused*

"I wil no giftes, for Gode, my gay,° at this tyme;   *cheerful (lady)*

1799 glove if] glove of   1810 tyme] tyne   1815 noght] oght

---

1   Literally, "that lovely one under linen." Tolkien and Gordon (1930: n. to 1814) point out that the formula "fair under garment" is conventional in Middle English poetry.

2   In romance, rings given by ladies to knights frequently have protective properties and are given as love-tokens (J. Cooke 1998: 4-5 and n. 23).

I haf none yow to norne,° ne noght wyl I take."   *offer in return*

Ho bede° hit hym ful bysily,° and he hir bode wernes,°   *offered / zealously / offer rejects*

1825 And swere° swyfte by his sothe° that he hit sese° nolde,   *swore / honor / take*

And ho soré° that he forsoke,° and sayde therafter,   *she was sad / refused*

"If ye renay° my rynk,° to ryche for hit semes,°   *reject / ring / because it seems too precious*

Ye wolde not so hyghly halden be° to me,   *don't want to be so greatly indebted*

I schal gif yow my girdel,° that gaynes° yow lasse."°   *belt / profits / less*

1830 Ho laght° a lace° lyghtly that leke umbe° hir sydes,°   *took / belt / was fastened around / waist*

Knit° upon hir kyrtel° under the clere mantyle,°   *tied / gown / beautiful mantle*

Gered° hit was with grene sylke and with golde schaped,°   *made / adorned*

Noght bot° arounde° brayden,° beten° with fyngres;   *only / at the edges / embroidered / worked*

And that ho bede° to the burne,° and blythely bisoght,°   *offered / knight / cheerfully asked*

1835 Thagh hit unworthi° were, that he hit take wolde.   *of little worth*

And he nay° that he nolde neghe° in no wyse   *refused / would touch*

Nauther golde ne garysoun,° er God hym grace sende   *treasure*

To acheve to the chaunce° that he hade chosen° there.   *finish the adventure / ventured*

"And therfore, I pray yow, displese yow noght,

1840 And lettes be° your bisinesse,° for I baythe° hit yow never   *let be / insistence / agree*

to graunte;

I am derely to yow biholde°   *indebted*

Bicause of your sembelaunt,°   *behavior*

And ever in hot and colde°   *whatever the circumstance*

1845 To be your true servaunt."

"Now forsake° ye this silke," sayde the burde° thenne,   *reject / lady*

"For° hit is symple° in hitself? And so hit wel° semes.   *because / modest / indeed*

Lo,° so hit is littel° — and lasse hit is worthy° —   *see / though it is small / worth*

Bot who-so knew the costes° that knit° ar therinne,   *virtues / fixed*

1850 He wolde hit prayse° at more prys,° paraventure;°   *value / more highly / indeed*

1825 swyfte by] swyftel   1830 that] that that

For what gome so is gorde° with this grene lace,° — *whoever is girded / belt*

While he hit hade hemely° halched° aboute, — *neatly / fastened*

Ther is no hathel° under heven tohewe° hym that myght, — *man / cut down*

For he myght not be slayn for slyght° upon erthe."[1] — *by any means*

1855 Then kest° the knyght, and hit come to his hert — *considered*

Hit were a juel° for the jopardé° that hym jugged° were: — *treasure / danger / ordained*

When he acheved to° the chapel his chek° for to fech,° — *reached / blow / receive*

Myght he haf slypped to be unslayn,° the sleght° were noble. — *if he could escape alive / trick*

Thenne he thulged with° hir threpe° and tholed° hir to speke, — *bore / insistence / allowed*

1860 And ho bere° on hym the belt and bede° hit hym swythe° — — *she urged / offered / eagerly*

And he granted and hym gafe° with a goud wylle — — *gave in*

And bisoght hym, for hir sake, discever° hit never, — *reveal*

Bot to lelly layne° fro hir lorde; the leude hym acordes° — *loyally hide it / knight agrees*

That never wyye° schulde hit wyt,° iwysse,° bot thay twayne — *anyone / know / indeed*

1865 for noghte;° — *for anything*

He thonkked hir oft ful swythe,° — *earnestly*

Ful thro° with hert and thoght; — *eagerly*

Bi that, on thrynne sythe° — *with that, for the third time*

Ho has kyst the knyght so toght.° — *strong*

1870 Thenne lachches ho° hir leve, and leves hym there, — *she takes*

For more myrthe° of that mon moght ho not gete. — *pleasure*

When ho was gon, Sir Gawayn geres° hym sone,° — *dresses / at once*

Rises and riches hym° in araye° noble, — *dresses himself / garments*

Lays up° the luf-lace the lady hym raght,° — *puts away / had given*

1875 Hid hit ful holdely,° ther° he hit eft fonde.° — *carefully / where / later might find*

Sythen chevely° to the chapel choses° he the waye, — *then promptly / takes*

1858 myght] mygh   1863 fro] for   1872 ho] he

---

1   On the girdle and its association with women and protective magic, see Friedman and Osberg 1977, as well as Hardman 1999.

Prevély° aproched to a prest, and prayed hym there — *privately*

That he wolde lyste° his lyf° and lern° hym better — *would hear / confession / instruct*

How his sawle° schulde be saved when he schuld seye hethen.° — *soul / go hence*

1880 There he schrof° hym schyrly° and schewed° his mysdedes, — *confessed / entirely / revealed*

Of the more° and the mynne,° and merci beseches, — *greater / lesser*

And of° absolucioun he on the segge° calles; — *for / priest*

And he asoyled° hym surely° and sette hym so clene° — *absolved / completely / pure*

As domesday° schulde haf ben dight° on the morn.[1] — *as if the Last Judgment / decreed*

1885 And sythen° he mace° hym as mery among the fre° ladyes, — *then / makes / noble*

With comlych° caroles and alle kynnes° joye — *beautiful / kinds of*

— As never he did bot° that daye — to the derk nyght, — *apart from*

with blys.

Uche° mon hade daynté° thare — *each / admired*

1890 Of hym,[2] and sayde, "Iwysse,° — *indeed*

Thus myry° he was never are,° — *merry / before*

Syn° he com hider,° er this." — *since / hither*

Now hym lenge° in that lee,° ther luf hym bityde.° — *let him remain / shelter / love came his way*

Yet is the lorde on the launde° ledande his gomnes;° — *forest / leading his men*

1895 He has forfaren°[3] this fox that he folwed longe. — *intercepted*

As he sprent° over a spenne° to spye° the schrewe,° — *sprang / fence / find / villain*

Ther as° he herd the howndes that hasted hym° swythe,° — *there where / were hurrying / greatly*

1878 lyste] lyfte

---

1   Gawain has taken the belt and intends to keep it from the Lord, despite their bargain, and there is no sign that he reveals this during confession. Some critics feel that this invalidates the confession: see Gollancz 1940: n. to 1880; Burrow 1959; and Blanch and Wasserman 1986: 124. However, other critics object that Gawain would be obliged to confess only mortal not venial sins: see Davis 1967: n. to 1882; Silverstein 1984: 12; Field 1971; and Morgan 1985. The narrator does explicitly state that Gawain's confession is as complete as if the priest had known that Judgment Day were imminent (1883-84). Also, the adverb *surely* probably has legal overtones in this context: the priest's absolution is given "with legally binding assurance" (*MED*, s.v. "seurlī," adv. c).

2   *Hade daynté ... of hym* means "have regard or affection for (sth.), take pleasure in, set store by, admire, like, respect" (MED, s.v. "deintē," n. 1c).

3   *Forfaren* could also mean "killed" (*MED*, s.v. "forfāran," v. 1, 1b), as in line 1617.

Renaud com richchande° thurgh a roghe greve,° — *making his way / dense thicket*

And alle the rabel° in a res,° ryght at his heles. — *pack / rush*

1900 The wyye° was war° of the wylde,° and warly° abides, — *man / aware / animal / stealthily*

And braydes° out the bryght bronde,° and at the best castes;° — *pulls / sword / beast strikes*

And he schunt° for the scharp,° and schulde° haf arered.° — *the fox dodged / sword / would / fled*

A rach° rapes° hym to, ryght er° he myght, — *scent-hound / rushes / just before*

And ryght bifore the hors fete,° thay fel on hym alle, — *feet*

1905 And woried me°[1] this wyly° wyth a wroth° noyse. — *worried / wily (fox) / angry*

The lorde lyghtes bilyve,° and laches° hym sone,° — *dismounts quickly / seizes / at once*

Rased° hym ful radly° out of the rach° mouthes, — *snatched / swiftly / hounds'*

Haldes° heghe over his hede, halowes faste,° — *holds him / calls out loudly*

And ther bayen hym° mony brath° houndes. — *bayed at him / fierce*

1910 Huntes° hyyed hem° theder° with hornes ful mony, — *hunters / hurried / to that place*

Ay rechatande° aryght° til thay the renk° seyen. — *always blowing a recheat / properly / man*

Bi that° was comen his compeyny noble; — *by this time*

Alle that ever ber° bugle blowed at ones,° — *bore / once*

And alle thise other halowed,° that hade no hornes; — *called out*

1915 Hit was the myriest mute° that ever men herde, — *baying of a pack*

The rich rurd° that ther was raysed for Renaude saule° — *great clamor / soul*

    with lote.° — *din*

    Hor° houndes thay ther rewarde, — *their*

    Her hedes° thay fawne° and frote,° — *heads / pat / caress*

1920   And sythen° thay tan° Reynarde, — *then / take*

    And tyrven of° his cote.° — *strip off / coat*

And thenne thay helden to° home, for hit was niegh° nyght, — *made for / almost*

Strakande° ful stoutly° in hor store° hornes. — *blowing / vigorously / their loud*

1906 laches hym] chaches by   1909 brath] bray   1919 her] her her

---

1   *Woried* here means "to seize by the throat with the teeth and tear or lacerate; to kill or injure by biting and shaking" (*OED*, s.v. "worry," v. 3a). As Andrew and Waldron note, the ethic dative *me* is untranslatable, but "conveys a colloquial or ironic tone, suggesting the involvement of the narrator" (2002: n. to 1905). Other instances occur in lines 1932, 2014, and 2144.

Poursuite au renard.
Manuscrits occidentaux - FR 12399 - FOL 26. Bibliothèque national de France.

	The lorde is lyght° at the laste at hys lef° home,	*dismounted / dear*
1925	Fyndes fire upon flet,° the freke° ther-byside,	*floor of the hall / knight*
	Sir Gawayn the gode, that glad was withalle;°	*indeed*
	Among the ladies for° luf he ladde° much joye.	*because of / made*
	He were a bleaunt° of blue[1] that bradde° to the erthe,	*costly tunic of silk / reached*
	His surkot° semed° hym wel that softe was forred,°	*surcoat / suited / lined with soft fur*
1930	And his hode° of that ilke° henged° on his schulder;	*hood / same material /hung*
	Blande° al of blaunner° were bothe al aboute.	*adorned / ermine*
	He metes me° this godmon° inmyddes the flore,	*meets / master of the house*
	And al with gomen° he hym gret, and goudly° he sayde,[2]	*good cheer / graciously*
	"I schal fylle° upon fyrst° oure forwardes nouthe,°	*fulfill / first of all / agreement right now*
1935	That° we spedly° han spoken ther° spared was no drynk."	*which / readily / when*

---

1 Burrow points out that blue is traditionally associated with faithfulness; the color is mentioned only here, where ironically Gawain commits "his single act of duplicity" (1987: n. to 1928).

2 This is the only time that Gawain initiates the exchange of winnings.

Then acoles° he the knyght and kysses hym thryes,° *embraces / thrice*

As saverly°[1] and sadly° as he hem° sette° couthe. *confidently / firmly / them / give*

"Bi Kryst," quoth that other knyght, "ye cach° much sele° *get / good fortune*

In chevisaunce° of this chaffer,° yif° ye hade goud chepes."°[2] *fulfillment / deal / if / good price*

1940 "Ye,° of° the chepe no charg,"° quoth chefly° that other, *Indeed / about / never mind / promptly*

"As° is pertly° payed the chepes° that I aghte."° *since / clearly / goods / received*

"Mary,"° quoth that other mon, "myn is bihynde,° *By Mary / my (goods) are worse*

For I haf hunted al this day, and noght° haf I geten° *nothing / gotten*

Bot this foule[3] fox felle;° the fende° haf the godes!° *skin / may the devil / goods*

1945 And that is ful pore° for to pay for suche prys° thinges *poor reward / valuable*

As ye haf thryght° me here thro,° suche thre cosses° *pressed / firmly / kisses*

    so gode."

   "Inogh," quoth Sir Gawayn,

   "I thonk yow, bi the rode,"° *Christ's cross*

1950 And how the fox was slayn

   He tolde hym as thay stode.

With merthe and mynstralsye,° wyth metes° at hor wylle,° *entertainment / foods / their desire*

Thay maden as mery as any men moghten° — *could*

With laghyng° of ladies, with lotes° of bordes° — *laughing / merry words / ladies*

1955 Gawayn and the godemon° so glad° were thay bothe, *master of the house / joyful*

Bot if[4] the douthe had doted other dronken ben other.° *unless the company were dazed or drunk*

Bothe the mon and the meyny° maden mony japes,° *the company / jests*

1936 the knyght] knyght

---

1   Or, possibly, "with as much relish" (*MED*, s.v. "sāverlī" and "sāvǒurlī").

2   In other words, "You will come out ahead here, provided you did not pay too much for the three kisses." Here the host is again asking Gawain to divulge information about where he got his "winnings."

3   *The Master of Game* notes that fox fur stinks if it is not properly treated; see Appendix D, p. 179. Because of its guile, the fox was also often associated with the devil, as for example in the bestiary tradition. Compare Chaucer's tongue-in-cheek harangue of the fox in The Nun's Priest's Tale: *O false murdrour, lurkynge in thy den! / O newe Scariot, newe Genylon, / False dissymulour, O Greek Synon, / That broghtest Troye al outrely to sorwe* (3226-29). Judas Iscariot, Ganelon, and Sinon are archetypal traitors.

4   The following clause complements *moghten*: they made as merry as any men might who were not out of control or drunk. See Andrew and Waldron 2002: n. to 1956.

Til the sesoun° was seyen° that thay sever° moste.   *time / come / part*

Burnes to hor° bedde behoved° at the laste.   *men to their / must (go)*

1960 Thenne lowly° his leve at° the lorde fyrst   *humbly / from*

Fochches° this fre° mon, and fayre° he hym thonkkes: *takes / noble / graciously*

"Of° such a selly sojorne° as I haf hade here,   *for / wonderful stay*

Your honour° at this hyghe fest, the° hyghe Kyng yow yelde!°   *noble conduct / (may) the / reward*

I yef° yow me° for on° of youres, if yowreself lykes,°[1]   *will give / myself / a (man) / it pleases*

1965 For I mot° nedes° — as ye wot° — meve° tomorne,   *must / of necessity / know / set out*

And° ye me take° sum tolke° to teche,° as ye hyght,°   *if / assign / man / show / promised*

The gate° to the Grene Chapel, as° God wyl me suffer°   *way / for / allow me*

To dele° on New Yeres Day the dome° of my wyrdes."°   *receive / judgment / fate*

"In god faythe," quoth the godmon,° "wyth a goud wylle   *master of the house*

1970 Al that ever I yow hyght,° halde° schal I redé."°   *promised / carry out / readily*

Ther asyngnes he a servaunt to sett° hym in° the waye,   *guide / on*

And coundue hym by the downes, that he no drechch had[2]

For to ferk° thurgh the fryth° and fare° at the gaynest°   *travel / woods / journey / most quickly*

     bi greve.°   *through the woods*

1975 The lorde Gawayn con° thonk,   *did*

Such worchip° he wolde hym weve.°   *honor / show*

Then at° tho ladyes wlonk°   *from / noble*

The knyght has tan° his leve.   *taken*

With care° and wyth kyssyng he carppes° hem tille,   *sadness / speaks*

1980 And fele thryvande° thonkkes he thrat° hom to have,   *many hearty / urged*

And thay yelden hym ayayn° yeply° that ilk;°   *returned to him / at once / same*

Thay bikende° hym to Kryst with ful colde sykynges.°   *commended / disconsolate sighing*

Sythen° fro the meyny° he menskly° departes;   *then / company / courteously*

1962 selly] sellyly   1973 ferk] frk   1981 ayayn] ayay

---

1   In other words, "I will be your servant if you give me one of yours."

2   "And lead him by the hills [downes], so that he would have no trouble [drechch]."

Uche° mon that he mette, he made° hem a thonke°   *each / gave / thanks*

1985 For his servyse and his solace° and his sere pyne,°   *assistance / various troubles*

That thay wyth busynes° had ben aboute° hym, to serve;   *solicitude / attendant upon*

And uche segge° as soré° to sever° with hym there   *each man (was) / sorry / part*

As° thay hade wonde° worthyly with that wlonk° ever.°   *as if / lived / noble man / always*

Then with ledes° and lyght he was ladde to his chambre   *men*

1990 And blythely° broght to his bedde, to be at his rest.   *splendidly*

Yif he ne slepe soundyly,° say ne dar° I;   *soundly / can*

For he hade muche on the morn° to mynne,° yif he wolde,   *morrow / consider*

    in thoght.

    Let hym lyye there stille,

1995 He has nere° that° he soght;   *(drawn) near / to that which*

And° ye wyl a whyle be stylle,[1]   *if*

I schal telle yow how thay wroght.°   *conducted themselves*

---

1 Chickering points out the three senses of *stille* on which lines 1994 and 1996 play: "yet," "motionless," and "quiet" (1997: 20).

Now neghes° the New Yere, and the nyght passes,   *draws near*

The day dryves to° the derk, as Dryghtyn° biddes;   *away / the Lord*

2000 Bot wylde wederes° of the worlde wakned° ther-oute,°   *weather / awakened / outside*

Clowdes kesten° kenly the colde to the erthe,   *cast*

Wyth nyye innoghe° of the northe, the naked to tene;°   *much wrath / distress*

The snawe snitered° ful snart,° that snayped° the wylde;°   *fell / bitterly / nipped / wild beasts*

The werbelande° wynde wapped° fro the hyghe,°   *whistling / rushed / heights*

2005 And drof uche dale° ful of dryftes° ful grete.   *every valley / snow drifts*

The leude° lystened ful wel that ley in his bedde;   *knight*

Thagh he lowkes° his liddes,° ful lyttel he slepes.   *shuts / eye-lids*

Bi uch kok that crue° he knewe wel the steven.°[1]   *crowed / time*

Deliverly° he dressed° up, er the day sprenged,°   *quickly / got / broke*

2010 For there was lyght of a lampe that lemed° in his chambre;   *shone*

He called to his chamberlayn, that cofly° hym swared,°   *quickly / answered*

And bede hym bryng hym his bruny° and his blonk° sadel;   *byrnie / horse's*

That other ferkes hym up° and feches hym his wedes,°   *gets up / clothes*

And graythes me° Sir Gawayn upon a grett wyse.°   *dresses / splendid manner*

2015 Fyrst he clad hym in his clothes the colde for to were,°   *resist*

And sythen° his other harnays,° that holdely° was keped,°   *then / gear / faithfully / had been tended*

Bothe his paunce° and his plates,[2] piked° ful clene,°   *stomach armor / burnished / bright*

The rynges° rokked of the roust°[3] of his riche bruny;   *byrnie rings / cleansed of rust*

2010 lampe] laupe

---

1   Anderson (1996: n. to 2008) notes that during the Middle Ages, cocks were thought to crow at midnight, 3 a.m., and dawn.

2   Gawain's *paunce* and *plates* are not mentioned in the first arming scene, but they are standard knightly equipment. *Plate* can denote any type of plate armor, but the context and also the use of the plural (*plates*) suggests paired chest and back pieces; see *MED*, s.v. "plāt(e)," n. 3. Lacy speculates that Gawain may consider "the protection of his mail and coat armour sufficient for the hazards of the road" but "chooses full battle-armour for the inevitable conflict with the Green Knight" (1997: 169).

3   Armor was burnished by rolling it back and forth, probably by placing it in a barrel of sand which was then rocked.

And al was fresch° as upon fyrst, and he was fayn° thenne   *new / glad*

2020   to thonk;°   *thank (the attendants)*

     He hade upon° uche pece,°   *put on / each piece*

     Wypped° ful wel and wlonk;°   *burnished / splendid*

     The gayest into Grece,°   *best attired from here to Greece*

     The burne bede° bryng his blonk.°   *knight commanded / horse*

2025 Whyle the wlonkest wedes° he warp° on hymselven —   *most splendid clothes / threw*

     His cote° wyth the conysaunce° of the clere werkes°   *surcoat / heraldic device / fair workmanship*

     Ennurned° upon velvet, vertuus[1] stones°   *worked / gems with beneficial properties*

     Aboute beten° and bounden,° enbrauded° semes,   *everywhere inlaid / fastened / embroidered*

     And fayre furred° withinne wyth fayre pelures° —   *lined with furs / furs*

2030 Yet laft° he not the lace,° the ladies gifte,   *left / belt*

     That forgat not Gawayn for gode of hymselven.°   *for his own good*

     Bi° he hade belted the bronde° upon his balwe haunches,°   *when / sword / strong hips*

     Thenn dressed° he his drurye° double° hym aboute,   *wrapped / love-token / twice*

     Swythe swethled umbe° his swange° swetely° that knyght   *diligently wound around / waist / eagerly*

2035 The gordel° of the grene silke, that gay wel bisemed,°[2]   *belt / appeared*

     Upon that ryol° red clothe that ryche° was to schewe.°[3]   *royal / precious / look upon*

     Bot wered not this ilk wyye° for wele° this gordel,°   *very man / because of its value / belt*

     For pryde of° the pendauntes,°[4] thagh polyst° thay were,   *in / the belt-ends / polished*

     And thagh the glyterande° golde glent° upon endes,°   *glittering / gleamed / the ends*

2040 Bot for to saven hymself, when suffer[5] hym byhoved°   *he was compelled*

2027 vertuus] vertuuus

---

1   The supposed beneficial properties of gems—such as protecting the wearer from physical or mental harm— are catalogued in medieval lapidaries.

2   *That gay wel bisemed*, usually glossed "which suited that noble (man) well," more likely means "which appeared very splendid" (*MED*, s.v. "bisēmen," 1a).

3   Friedman and Osberg note that the most common way to activate an amulet's power is to display it prominently (1977: 313).

4   A *pendaunt* is "the hanging end of a belt, girdle, or garter, often richly ornamented" (*MED*, 1a).

5   This expression is best construed as *suffren* + *inf.* (see *MED*, s.v. "suffren," v. 3b), "to bear (something)," so that the whole would mean "he was compelled (*him byhoved*) to bear abiding his death (*suffer to byde bale*)."

To byde bale° withoute dabate° of bronde° hym to were° — *await death / defense / sword / protect*

    other knyffe.° — *or knife*

    Bi that° the bolde mon boun° — *when / (thus) prepared*

    Wynnes° ther-oute bilyve,° — *goes / quickly*

2045 Alle the meyny of renoun° — *esteemed members of the household*

    He thonkkes ofte ful ryve.° — *amply*

Thenne was Gryngolet graythe,° that gret was and huge, — *ready*

And hade ben sojourned saverly° and in a siker wyse,° — *had been stabled safely / securely*

Hym lyst prik° for poynt,° that proude hors thenne. — *wanted to gallop / good condition*

2050 The wyye° wynnes hym to° and wytes on° his lyre,° — *knight / goes to him / examines / coat*

And sayde soberly° hymself, and by his soth° sweres: — *earnestly / honor*

"Here is a meyny° in this mote° that on menske thenkkes,° — *household / castle / practices courtesy*

The mon hem maynteines,° joy mot° he have; — *the man who commands them / may*

The leve° lady on lyve,° luf hir bityde;° — *dear / all of her life / may she have love*

2055 Yif thay for charyté cherysen° a gest, — *entertain*

And halden honour in her honde,° the Hathel hem yelde° — *maintain honor / may He requite them*

That haldes the heven upon hyghe,° and also yow alle! — *who holds the heavens on high*

And yif I myght lyf upon londe, lede,° any whyle,° — *sir / any space of time (longer)*

I schuld rech° yow sum rewarde redyly, if I myght." — *give*

2060 Thenn steppes he into stirop and strydes° alofte; — *mounts*

His schalk° schewed° hym his schelde, on schulder he hit laght,° — *servant / brought / slung*

Gordes to° Gryngolet with his gilt heles,° — *put his spurs to / spurs*

And he startes° on the ston,° stod he no lenger — *bounded forward / stone pavement*

    to praunce.° — *prance*

2065 His hathel° on hors was thenne, — *servant*

    That bere° his spere and launce. — *who carried*

    "This kastel to Kryst I kenne":° — *commend*

    He gef° hit ay° god chaunce.° — *wished / always / fortune*

2053 he] thay

The brygge° was brayde doun,° and the brode yates   *drawbridge / lowered*

2070 Unbarred and born° open upon bothe halve.°   *swung / sides*

The burne blessed hym bilyve,° and the bredes° passed —   *crossed himself quickly / planks*

Prayses the porter° bifore the prynce kneled,   *gate-keeper (who)*

Gef hym God and° goud day,[1] that Gawayn he save —   *commended him to God and gave him*

And went on his way with his wyye one,°   *servant alone*

2075 That schulde teche hym to tourne to° that tene° place   *guide him in reaching / perilous*

Ther the ruful race° he schulde resayve.°   *dreadful stroke / receive*

Thay bowen° bi bonkkes° ther boghes° ar bare,   *travel / hills / where boughs*

Thay clomben bi clyffes ther clenges° the colde.   *remains*

The heven° was uphalt,° bot ugly° ther-under   *clouds / high / threateningly*

2080 Mist muged° on the mor,° malt° on the mountes;°   *drizzled / moor / melted / mountains*

Uch° hille hade a hatte,° a myst-hakel° huge.   *each / hat / misty mantle*

Brokes° byled° and breke° bi bonkkes aboute,   *streams / boiled / foamed*

Schyre schaterande° on schores, ther° thay doun schowved.°   *brightly breaking / where / flowed*

Wela wylle° was the way ther° thay bi wod schulden,°   *very wild / where / had to (go)*

2085 Til hit was sone sesoun° that the sunne ryses   *the time*

    that tyde.°   *during that season*

Thay were on a hille ful hyghe,

The whyte snaw lay bisyde;

The burne° that rod hym by   *servant*

2090 Bede° his mayster abide.°   *asked / stop*

"For I haf wonnen° yow hider, wyye,° at this tyme,   *led / sir*

And now nar° ye not fer fro that note° place   *are not / notorious*

That ye han spied° and spuryed° so specially° after;   *inquired / asked / particularly*

Bot I schal say yow for sothe,° sythen° I yow knowe,   *in earnest / since*

2095 And ye ar a lede upon lyve that I wel lovy:°   *admire*

---

1   I follow Davis 1970 in construing *Gef hym God and goud day* "as commended him to God and wished him good day."

Wolde ye worch bi my wytte,° ye worthed° the better.   *do as I suggest / it would turn out*

The place that ye prece to° ful perelous is halden;°   *hasten toward / considered*

Ther wones° a wyye° in that waste,° the worst upon erthe,   *dwells / man / wasteland*

For he is stiffe° and sturne,° and to strike lovies,   *fierce / cruel*

2100 And more° he is then any mon upon myddel-erde,°   *larger / earth*

And his body bigger then the best fowre°   *four (knights)*

That ar in Arthures hous, Hestor,°¹ other other.°   *Hector / or anyone else*

He cheves that chaunce° at the Chapel Grene,   *brings it about (that ...)*

Ther passes non bi that place so proude in his armes

2105 That he ne dynges hym to dethe° with dynt° of his honde;   *kills him / blow*

For he is a mon methles,° and mercy non uses,°   *violent / gives*

For be hit chorle other chaplayn° that bi the chapel rydes,   *peasant or chaplain*

Monk other masse-prest,° other° any mon elles,   *priest / or*

Hym thynk° as queme° hym to quelle° as quyk go° hymselven.   *he finds it / fine / kill / as to be alive*

2110 Forthy° I say thee,² as sothe° as ye in sadel sitte,   *therefore / surely*

Com ye° there, ye be kylled, may the knyght rede°³ —   *if you come / if the knight spots you*

Trawe° ye me that truely, thagh ye had twenty lyves   *believe*

   to spende!

He has wonyd° here ful yore,°   *lived / long time*

2115 On bent° much baret bende,°   *in battle / strife caused*

Ayayn° his dyntes° sore°   *against / blows / grievous*

Ye may not yow defende.°   *protect*

2105 dynges] dynnes

---

1   Presumably this refers to the Trojan hero Hector, one of the "Nine Worthies," who was renowned for his size and strength in the Middle Ages. Lancelot's brother (H)ector de Maris could also be meant, but Tolkien and Gordon rightly point out that the latter was not so great a warrior that Gawain would be afraid to encounter a knight like him (1930: n. to 2102).

2   Note the use of the familiar second person pronoun, which the guide uses no less than thirteen times in addressing Gawain; this is a breach of decorum, probably meant to give his words a quality of sincerity and trustworthiness (Delany 1965). Compare also the note to line 272 above.

3   Editors disagree about the meaning of *may the knyght rede*, but it most likely means "if the knight catches sight of you"; for details, see P. Battles 2010b.

"Forthy,° goude Sir Gawayn, let the gome one,°   *therefore / man alone*

And gos away sum other gate,° upon Goddes halve!°   *way / for God's sake*

2120 Cayres bi° sum other kyth,° ther° Kryst mot yow spede,°   *go to / place / where / help*

And I schal hyy° me hom ayayn, and hete° yow fyrre°   *hasten / promise / also*

That I schal swere bi God and alle his gode halwes,°   *saints*

As help me God and the halydam,° and othes innoghe,°   *sacred relics / many oaths*

That I schal lelly° yow layne,° and lance° never tale   *faithfully / keep your secret / tell*

2125 That ever ye fondet° to fle for freke,° that I wyst."°   *tried / (any) man / knew of*

"Grant merci,"° quoth Gawayn, and gruchyng° he sayde: *thank you / annoyed*

"Wel worth thee,° wyye,° that woldes° my gode;   *I wish you well / fellow / desire*

And that lelly° me layne,° I leve° wel thou woldes.   *faithfully / keep my secret / believe*

Bot helde° thou hit never so holde,° and° I here passed,°   *conceal / faithfully / if / departed*

2130 Founded° for ferde° for to fle, in fourme° that thou telles,   *tried / fear / such a way*

I were a knyght kowarde; I myght not be excused.

Bot I wyl to the chapel, for chaunce° that may falle,   *whatever*

And talk wyth that ilk tulk° the tale° that me lyste,   *man / words*

Worthe hit wele other wo,° as the wyrde°[1] lykes   *for better or worse / Fate*

2135   hit hafe.

    Thaghe he be a sturn knape°   *tough fellow*

    To stightel,° and stad° with stave,°[2]   *fight / equipped / club*

    Ful wel con Dryghtyn° schape°   *the Lord / bring it about*

    His servauntes for to save."

2140 "Mary!" quoth that other mon, "now thou so much spelles,°   *now that you say as much*

That thou wylt thyn awen nye° nyme° to thyselven,   *harm / bring*

2131 not] mot   2137 and] and and

---

1   *The wyrde* is an interesting construction, recalling Old English and early Middle English *seo wyrd*, that is, Fate (*seo* is the feminine definite article, equivalent to "the"). Most Middle English authors, particularly in the fourteenth century, equate *wyrde* with the classical Fates and thus prefer the plural form (*wyrdes*) and/or drop the article. *The wyrde* appears to reflect an older, native conception of Fate.

2   The guide's description makes the Green Knight sound like one of the stock giants of medieval romance who prey upon passers-by. This explains Gawain's suggestion that the Green Knight may be armed with a *stave* or club, for this is the favorite weapon of such giants.

And thee lyst° lese thy lyf, thee lette I ne kepe.°   *you desire / don't care to prevent you*

Haf here thi helme on thy hede, thi spere in thi honde,

And ryde me doun this ilk rake° bi yon rokke syde,°   *same path / cliff-side*

2145 Til thou be broght to the bothem° of the brem° valay;   *bottom / rugged*

Thenne loke a littel on the launde,° on thi lyfte° honde,   *clearing / left*

And thou schal se in that slade° the self° chapel,   *glade /same*

And the borelych burne on bent° that hit kepes.°   *man stout in battle / guards*

Now fares wel,° on Godes half,° Gawayn the noble!   *farewell / name*

2150 For alle the golde upon grounde° I nolde° go wyth thee,   *earth / would not*

Ne bere thee felawschyp thurgh this fryth° on° fote fyrre."°   *wood / one / further*

Bi° that, the wyye in° the wod wendes° his brydel,   *with / man toward / turns*

Hit the hors with the heles° as harde as he myght,   *heels*

Lepes hym over the launde,° and leves the knyght there   *clearing*

2155   al one.°   *alone*

    "Bi Goddes self,"° quoth Gawayn,   *God himself*

    "I wyl nauther grete° ne grone;°   *weep / groan*

    To Goddes wylle I am ful bayn,°   *obedient*

    And to hym I haf me tone."°   *committed*

2160 Thenne gyrdes he to° Gryngolet, and gederes the rake,°[1]   *he spurred on / follows the path*

Schowves in° bi a schore° at a schawe syde,°   *presses forward / cliff / forest's edge*

Rides thurgh the roghe bonk° ryght to the dale;   *hill-side*

And thenne he wayted hym° aboute, and wylde hit hym thoght,°   *looked / seemed to him*

And seye no syngne of resette° bisydes nowhere,°   *dwelling / anywhere around*

2165 Bot hyghe bonkkes and brent° upon bothe halve,°   *steep (hill-sides) / sides*

And rughe knokled knarres° with knorned° stones;   *rugged crags / gnarled*

2150 go] ge

---

1   The description of both the Green Chapel and its surroundings is detailed, replete with rare words that describe specific landscape features, and full of realistic imagery; none of this fits the pattern of conventional landscape descriptions in Arthurian romance. It is therefore not unreasonable to assume that the poet is describing a real place, and there have been several attempts to identify it (see especially Elliott 1984 and 1997, as well as Hill 2009). On Gawain's psychological reactions to the landscape, see Renoir 1960 and Veldhoen 1990.

The skewes of° the scowtes° skayned,° hym thoght.   *clouds by / crags / were grazed*

Thenne he hoved,° and wythhylde° his hors at that tyde,°   *halted / stopped / time*

And ofte chaunged his cher° the chapel to seche:°   *position / find*

2170 He sey non suche in no syde,° and selly° hym thoght,   *place / a marvel*

Save,° a lyttel° on a launde,° a lawe° as hit were,   *except / little ways off / clearing / hill*

A balw berw°[1] bi a bonke° the brymme° bysyde,   *rounded mound / bank / water*

Bi a forw° of a flode° that ferked° thare;   *course / stream / flowed*

The borne blubred° therinne as hit° boyled hade.   *stream seethed / as if it*

2175 The knyght kaches° his caple,° and com to the lawe,   *urges on / horse*

Lightes doun luflyly,° and at a lynde taches°   *gracefully / tree fastens*

The rayne° and his riche with° a roghe° braunche.   *rein / noble (steed) to / rough*

Thenne he bowes° to the berwe,° aboute hit he walkes,   *goes / mound*

Debatande° with hymself what hit be myght.   *debating*

2180 Hit hade a hole on the ende and on ayther° syde,   *either*

And overgrowen with gresse in glodes aywhere,°   *patches everywhere*

And al was holw inwith,° nobot° an olde cave,   *hollow within / nothing but*

Or a crevisse° of an olde cragge; he couthe hit noght deme°   *hollow / describe*

    with spelle.°   *in words*

2185   "We!° Lorde," quoth the gentyle knyght,   *alas*

    "Whether° this be the Grene Chapelle?   *can*

    Here myght aboute mydnyght

    The dele° his matynnes telle!"°   *devil / say*

"Now, iwysse,"° quoth Wowayn, "wysty° is here;   *indeed / desolate*

2190 This oritore° is ugly,° with erbes° overgrowen;   *oratory / loathsome / vegetation*

2171 were] we   2178 thenne] then( )e   2179 debatande] d( )batande   2180 hade] ( )ade
2181 overgrowen] o( )growen   2187 here] he

---

1 *Berw* (*berg, bergh*) can denote either a natural structure or an artificial one, such as a barrow. The word is not common in Middle English, but has interesting antecedents in Old English poetry; as Silverstein (1984: n. to 2163-84) points out, both Beowulf and Guthlac confront monsters at barrows that are described in similar terms (Beowulf a dragon, Guthlac a band of demons). In pre-conquest England, especially in the West Midlands (where the poem was composed; see Introduction, p. 11), barrows could also serve as places of judgment; on this, see D. Battles, forthcoming in 2013.

Wel bisemes° the wyye wruxled° in grene	*is fitting for / knight clad*
Dele° here his devocioun° on the develes wyse.	*hold / worship*
Now I fele° hit is the fende,°[1] in my fyve wyttes,	*perceive / fiend*
That has stoken° me this steven° to strye° me here.	*set / appointment / kill*

2195 This is a chapel of meschaunce,° that chekke hit bytyde!°   *ill fortune / may ruin overtake it*

Hit is the corsedest kyrk° that ever I com inne!"   *most accursed church*

With heghe helme on his hede, his launce in his honde,

He romes° up to the roffe° of tho rogh wones.°   *walks / roof / dwelling*

Thene herde he of° that hyghe hil, in a harde roche°   *from / rough crag*

2200 Biyonde the broke,° in a bonk,° a wonder breme° noyse: *brook / cliff / extraordinarily fierce*

What! Hit clatered in the clyff, as hit cleve schulde,°   *as if it would crack*

As° one upon a gryndelston° hade grounden° a sythe.°   *as if / grind-stone / ground / scythe*

What! Hit wharred° and whette,° as water at a mulne;°   *whirred / made a grinding noise / mill*

What! Hit rusched° and ronge,° rawthe° to here.   *made a rushing noise / rang / horrible*

2205 Thenne "Bi Godde," quoth Gawayn, "that gere,° as I trowe,°   *equipment / believe*

Is rryched° at the reverence° me, renk,° to mete   *being prepared / to honor / (a) knight*

    bi rote.°[2]   *from habit*

Let God worche!° 'We loo'° —   *exercise His power / to cry "Woe, alas!"*

Hit helppes me not a mote.°   *not a jot*

2210 My lif thagh I forgoo,°   *lose*

Drede dos me no lote."°   *no noise makes me afraid*

Thenne the knyght con° calle ful hyghe:°   *did / loudly*

"Who stightles° in this sted,° me steven° to holde?   *governs / place / appointment*

2205 as] at

---

1   Medieval iconography associates the devil with the color green (Robertson 1954). Gawain's belief that the Green Knight is the *fende* turns out to be incorrect, but the suggestion here may encourage the audience to see the Green Knight as "acting the role of the 'adversarial' Devil" familiar from the Book of Job, who is "ultimately an instrument of God for trying and proving the simplicity, uprightness, piety, and innocence of his servant Sir Gawain" (Schmidt 1987: 162).

2   In other words, the Green Knight greets all strangers by preparing to fight them (?). The *MED* tentatively suggests the meaning "in due order, with ceremony," but adduces only this line with that meaning. Davis notes that "*bi rote* does not occur elsewhere in a sense that seems appropriate" (1967: n. to 2205ff.). There is considerable disagreement over the meaning of this line.

For now is gode Gawayn goande° ryght here. *going*

2215 If any wyye oght wyl,° wynne° hider fast, *anyone wants anything / come*

Other° now other° never, his nedes° to spede."° *either / or / desires / fulfill*

"Abyde," quoth on° on the bonke° aboven over his hede, *one / hill*

"And thou schal haf al, in hast,° that I thee hyght° ones."° *haste / promised / before*

Yet he rusched on° that rurde° rapely° a throwe,° *kept up / clamor / urgently / while*

2220 And wyth° whettyng awharf,° er he wolde lyght;° *to / turned back / come down*

And sythen° he keveres° bi a cragge, and comes of° a hole, *then / proceeds / out of*

Whyrlande° out of a wro° wyth a felle° weppen, *whirling / nook / terrible*

A denes° ax¹ newe dyght,° the dynt° with to yelde,° *Danish / made ready / blow / return*

With a borelych bytte° bende° by the halme,° *huge blade / bent / along the handle*

2225 Fyled° in a fylor,° fowre fote° large — *sharpened / grindstone / four foot*

Hit was no lasse° bi that lace° that lemed° ful bryght² — *no smaller / for the lace / shone*

And the gome° in the grene gered° as fyrst,° *knight / dressed / before*

Bothe the lyre° and the legges, lokkes and berde, *face*

Save° that fayre° on his fote he foundes° on the erthe,³ *except / deliberately / walks*

2230 Sette the stele° to the stone, and stalked° bysyde. *handle / walked*

When he wan° to the watter, ther he wade nolde,° *came / where he didn't want to wade*

He hypped° over on hys ax, and orpedly° strydes, *hopped / boldly*

Bremly brothe,° on a bent° that brode was aboute,° *fiercely eager / field / in circumference*

on snawe.

2235 Sir Gawayn the knyght con° mete, *did*

He ne lutte hym nothyng lowe;° *did not bow low to him*

That other sayde, "Now, sir swete,

2223 to] o

---

1 A Danish axe is a "battle-axe with a very long blade, and usually without a spike on the back" (*OED*, s.v. "Danish," a. and n.).

2 The axe that the Green Knight brings to (and leaves at) Arthur's court is said to have a richly decorated lace wrapped about its haft, and this axe might be similarly equipped. Alternatively, as Gollancz suggests (1940: n. to 2226), it could refer to the belt Gawain is wearing. Malarkey and Toelken argue for the latter, translating the line, "It was no smaller by reason of that girdle that gleamed so brightly" (1964: 16).

3 That is, the Green Knight's appearance is exactly the same as at Camelot, except that he goes on foot. He evidently uses the handle of the axe like a walking stick.

Of steven° mon° may thee trowe."°   *keeping appointments / one / trust*

"Gawayn," quoth that grene gome,° "God thee mot loke!°   *knight / may God protect you*

2240 Iwysse,° thou art welcom, wyye,° to my place,°   *certainly / sir / home*

And thou has tymed thi travayl° as truee° mon schulde,   *journey / (a) true*

And thou knowes the covenauntes kest° uus bytwene: *established*

At this tyme twelmonyth° thou toke that thee falled,°   *a year ago / took what was allotted you*

And I schulde at this Newe Yere yeply° thee quyte.°   *quickly / requite*

2245 And we ar in this valay verayly° oure one;°   *truly / all alone*

Here ar no renkes° us to rydde,° rele° as uus likes.   *men / part / we may do*

Haf° thy helme of thy hede, and haf here thy pay.   *remove*

Busk° no more debate° then I thee bede thenne°   *make / defense / offered then*

When thou wypped° of my hede at a wap° one."   *struck / blow*

2250 "Nay, bi God," quoth Gawayn, "that me gost lante,°   *who gave me my life*

I schal gruch° thee no grue° for grem° that falles.°   *resist / whit / harm / happens*

Bot styghtel thee° upon on° strok, and I schal stonde stylle   *limit yourself / one*

And warp° thee no wernyng° to worch° as thee lykes,   *offer / resistance / do*

nowhare."°   *none at all*

2255 He lened with° the nek, and lutte,°   *stuck out / bowed*

And schewed° that schyre° al bare,   *revealed / white flesh*

And lette as° he noght dutte;°   *acted as if / was not afraid*

For drede° he wolde not dare.°   *fear / tremble*

Then the gome° in the grene graythed hym° swythe,°   *knight / prepared / quickly*

2260 Gederes° up hys grymme tole° Gawayn to smyte;   *lifts / tool*

With alle the bur° in his body he ber° hit on lofte,   *strength / raised*

Munt° as maghtyly° as marre° hym he wolde;   *took aim / mightily / kill*

Hade hit dryven adoun° as drey° as he atled,°   *come driving down / fiercely / aimed*

2240 welcom] welcon   2247 haf thy] haf thy thy

Ther hade ben ded of his dynt° that° doghty° was ever.[1] *blow / he who / brave*

2265 Bot Gawayn on that giserne° glyfte° hym bysyde, *axe / glanced*

As hit com glydande° adoun on glode° hym to schende,° *falling / in the clearing / kill*

And schranke a lytel with the schulderes for the scharp yrne.° *iron*

That other schalk° wyth a schunt° the schene wythhaldes,° *man / jerk / bright axe restrains*

And thenne repreved he the prynce with mony prowde° wordes: *proud*

2270 "Thou art not Gawayn," quoth the gome,° "that is so goud halden,° *man / considered*

That never arwed° for no here° by hylle ne be vale, *grew frightened / army*

And now thou fles° for ferde° er thou fele° harmes! *flinch / fear / feel*

Such cowardise of that knyght cowthe I never here.° *have I never heard of*

Nawther fyked° I ne flaghe,° freke,° when thou myntest,° *flinched / fled / knight / struck*

2275 Ne kest no kavelacion° in kynges hous Arthor. *made no objection*

My hede flaw° to my fote, and yet flagh° I never; *flew / fled*

And thou, er any harme hent,° arwes° in hert; *receive / grow frightened*

Wherfore the better burne° me burde° be called *man / I deserve*

therfore."

2280 Quoth Gawayn, "I schunt° ones, *flinched*

And so wyl I no more;

Bot thagh° my hede falle on the stones, *if*

I con not hit restore.° *revive*

"Bot busk,° burne, bi thi fayth, and bryng me° to the poynt. *hurry / get*

2285 Dele to me my destiné,° and do hit out of honde,° *fate / at once*

For I schal stonde° thee a strok, and start no more *withstand*

Til thyn ax have me hitte; haf here my trawthe!"° *word*

"Haf at thee thenne!" quoth that other, and heves° hit alofte, *raises*

And waytes° as wrothely° as he wode° were. *looks / enraged / insane*

2269 prowde wordes] prowd( )   2270 so goud halden] s( )

---

1 Unless the narrator has forgotten about the belt, this statement would indicate that the green girdle does not have the efficacy ascribed to it earlier.

2290 He myntes° at hym maghtyly,° bot not the mon rynes,°	*swung / mightily / touches*
Withhelde heterly° his honde er hit hurt myght.	*checked quickly*
Gawayn graythely° hit bydes,° and glent° with no membre,°	*willingly / awaits / moved / limb*
Bot stode stylle as the ston, other a stubbe° auther	*tree stump*
That ratheled° is in roché° grounde with rotes° a hundreth.°	*rooted / rocky / roots / hundred*
2295 Then muryly efte° con° he mele,° the mon in the grene:	*cheerfully thereafter / did / speak*
"So, now° thou has thi hert holle,° hitte me bihovs.°	*now that / intact / I must strike*
Halde° thee now the hyghe hode° that Arthur thee raght,°	*may it preserve / order of knighthood / gave*
And kepe° thy kanel at° this kest,° yif hit kever° may."	*protect / neck from / blow / shield you*
Gawayn ful gryndelly° with greme° thenne sayde:	*fiercely / anger*
2300 "Wy,° thresch° on, thou thro° mon, thou thretes to° longe;	*well / strike / savage / threaten too*
I hope° that thi hert arwe° wyth° thyn awen selven."	*believe / grows fearful / of*
"For sothe," quoth that other freke,° "so felly° thou spekes,	*man / fiercely*
I wyl no lenger on lyte° lette° thin ernde°	*through delay / hinder ending / mission*
right nowe."	
2305 Thenne tas° he hym strythe° to stryke,	*takes up / stance*
And frounses bothe lyppe and browe;°	*purses his lips and wrinkles his brow*
No mervayle thagh hym myslyke°	*no surprise if he was perturbed*
That hoped of° no rescowe!	*who expected*
He lyftes lyghtly° his lome,° and let hit doun fayre°	*easily / weapon / precisely*
2310 With the barbe° of the bitte° bi the bare nek;	*edge / blade*
Thagh he homered heterly,° hurt hym no more	*struck quickly*
Bot snyrt° hym on that on syde, that severed° the hyde.°	*than nicking / cut / skin*
The scharp schrank° to the flesche thurgh the schyre grece,°	*sharp blade cut / white fat*
That the schene° blod over his schulderes schot to the erthe;	*bright*
2315 And when the burne° sey the blode blenk° on the snawe,	*knight / glisten*
He sprit° forth spenne-fote° more then a spere° lenthe,	*leaped / feet together / spear's*
Hent° heterly° his helme, and on his hed cast,	*seized / quickly*

2291 his] hs   2305 he] he he   2307 no] ( )

Schot with° his schulderes his fayre schelde under,°   *tossed from / down*

Braydes° out a bryght sworde, and bremely° he spekes —   *pulls / fiercely*

2320 Never syn that he was burne borne° of his moder   *since he was born*

Was he never in this worlde wyye half so blythe° —   *happy*

"Blynne,° burne,° of thy bur,° bede° me no mo!   *cease / sir / with your blow / offer*

I haf a stroke in this sted° withoute stryf hent,°   *place / received*

And if thow reches° me any mo, I redyly schal quyte,°   *offer / requite*

2325 And yelde yederly ayayn° — and ther-to ye tryst° —   *repay you quickly / may count on it*

and foo.°   *fiercely*

Bot on° stroke here me falles° —   *only one / falls to my lot*

The covenaunt schop ryght so,°   *agreement specified exactly this*

Fermed°1 in Arthures halles —   *made*

2330 And therfore, hende,° now hoo!"°   *noble (knight) / cease*

The hathel° heldet hym fro,° and on his ax rested,   *knight / kept back from him*

Sette the schaft upon schore,° and to the scharp° lened,   *ground / on the blade*

And loked to the leude° that on the launde° yede,°   *man / clearing / went*

How that doghty,° dredles,° dervely° ther stondes   *doughty knight / fearless / boldly*

2335 Armed, ful awles:° in hert hit hym lykes.°   *fearless / pleases*

Thenn he meles° muryly° wyth a much steven,°   *speaks / merrily / great voice*

And wyth a rynkande rurde° he to the renk° sayde: *ringing voice / knight*

"Bolde burne,° on this bent° be not so gryndel.°   *knight / field / fierce*

No mon here unmanerly thee mysboden° habbes,°   *mistreated / has*

2340 Ne kyd° bot° as covenaunde at kynges kort schaped.°   *treated you / except / agreed upon*

I hyght° thee a strok and thou hit has; halde° thee wel payed!   *promised / consider*

I relece thee of the remnaunt of ryghtes° alle other.2   *claims*

2329 fermed in] ( )   2337 rynkande] rykande   2339 habbes] habbe

1   The beginning of this line is illegible, and editors variously read *fermed in* (as here), *festned in*, or *fettled in*. All three phrases roughly mean "concluded in," "agreed in."

2   More legal language. Gawain is obliged to repay the Green Knight fully by receiving a decapitating stroke from him; since he receives only a nick, it is necessary for the Green Knight to release him from the remainder of the payment (Shoaf 1984: 52-53).

Iif I deliver had bene,° a boffet,° paraunter,°   *had exerted myself / blow / as it happens*

I couthe wrotheloker° haf waret,° to thee haf wroght anger.°   *more harshly / dealt / harm*

2345 Fyrst I mansed° thee muryly° with a mynt one,°   *menaced / in jest / single feint*

And rove° thee wyth no rof-sore,° with ryght° I thee profered   *cut / gash / by rights*

For the forwarde° that we fest° in the fyrst nyght,   *agreement / made*

And thou trystyly° the trawthe° and truly° me haldes:°   *faithfully / word / sincerely / keep*

Al the gayne° thow me gef, as god mon schulde.   *gains*

2350 That other munt° for the morne, mon, I thee profered,   *feint*

Thou° kyssedes my clere° wyf, the cosses me raghtes.°   *when you / beautiful / gave*

For bothe two here, I thee bede° bot° two bare myntes°   *offered you / only / feints*

   boute scathe.°   *without harm*

   True mon true restore,°   *true person must make true restoration*

2355 Thenne thar mon drede° no wathe.°   *one need fear / danger*

At the thrid° thou fayled thore,°   *third day / there*

And therfor that tappe° ta thee.°[1]   *tap / you must take*

"For hit is my wede° that thou weres, that ilke° woven girdel,°   *garment / same / belt*

Myn owen wyf hit thee weved,° I wot° wel for sothe.°   *weaved / know / for certain*

2360 Now know I wel thy cosses,° and thy costes als,°   *kisses / conduct also*

And the wowyng of° my wyf: I wroght° hit myselven.   *seduction by / brought it about*

I sende hir to asay° thee, and sothly° me thynkkes°   *test / truly / it seems to me*

On the fautlest freke° that ever on fote yede° —   *the most faultless man / went*

As perle° bi° the white pese° is of prys° more,   *pearl / next to / pea / value*

2365 So is Gawayn, in god fayth, bi other gay knyghtes.

Bot here yow lakked° a lyttel, sir, and lewté° yow wonted;°   *were lacking / loyalty / lacked*

Bot that was for no wylyde werke,°[2] ne wowyng° nauther,   *precious object / love-making*

2344 anger] ang(　)

---

1 Weiss 1977 points out parallels between this scene, especially in the "tap" Gawain receives, and the ritual in which squires are knighted; see also Cherewatuk 1993.

2 Literally, "a thing of skillful workmanship." That is, Gawain does not take the girdle because it is precious; see Gollancz 1940: n. to 2367.

Bot for° ye lufed your lyf; the lasse I yow blame."   *because*

That other stif° mon in study° stod a gret whyle,   *bold / lost in thought*

2370 So agreved° for greme° he gryed° withinne;   *aggrieved / shame / shuddered*

Alle the blode of his brest blende in° his face,   *rushed to*

That al he schrank for schome° that the schalk talked.°   *shame / at what the knight said*

The forme° worde upon folde that the freke meled:°   *first / man spoke*

"Corsed worth° cowarddyse and covetyse°¹ bothe!   *be / covetousness*

2375 In yow is vylany° and vyse° that vertue disstryes."°   *sinfulness / vice / destroys*

Thenne he kaght to° the knot, and the kest lawses,°   *caught hold of / belt loosens*

Brayde brothely° the belt to the burne° selven: *threw angrily / man*

"Lo° ther the falssyng,° foule mot hit falle!°   *see / deceitful thing / may evil befall it*

For care° of thy knokke,° cowardyse me taght   *fear / blow*

2380 To acorde me° with covetyse, my kynde° to forsake,   *make common cause with / nature*

That is larges° and lewté° that longes to° knyghtes.   *generosity / loyalty / is fitting for*

Now am I fawty° and falce,° and ferde° haf ben ever   *faulty / false / afraid*

Of trecherye° and untrawthe:° bothe bityde sorwe°   *duplicity / dishonesty / may both have sorrow*

and care!

2385 I biknowe° yow,² knyght, here stylle,°   *confess to / meekly*

Al fawty° is my fare;°   *flawed / conduct*

Letes° me overtake your° wylle³   *let / regain your good*

And efte° I schal be ware."°   *thereafter / on guard*

2382 ferde] fererde

---

1 The poem states explicitly that Gawain takes the green girdle not because of its value, but because it will protect his life (1856-59, 2037-42, 2368). Therefore, some critics have found it inconsistent that Gawain should accuse himself of *covetyse*; see especially Burrow 1959: 78-79. However, as Davis points out (1967: n. to 2374), the medieval understanding of covetousness was quite broad, and would have covered Gawain's failure to turn over the belt as part of his winnings. Others have argued that the operative sense of coveting here involves an inordinate fondness for one's own life; see especially Newhauser 1990 and Farley-Hills 1996. In favor of the former view, both the Green Knight and Gawain specifically connect keeping the belt with a lack of *lewté* (2366, 2381), a term that encompasses both loyalty to one's oath (*MED*, s.v. "leauté," n. 1c) and, more generally, moral uprightness (1a). The latter position finds support in 2379, where Gawain connects taking the belt with fear of the Green Knight's blow.

2 Note the language of confession here and in the following passage. Gawain performs the three acts of penance (contrition, confession, and satisfaction), and the Green Knight grants Gawain his forgiveness (Burrow 1959 and Morgan 1985: 14-18).

3 *Letes me overtake your wylle* could also mean "Let me understand your will (as to the penance I should do)" (Barron 1998: n. to 2387).

Thenn loghe° that other leude° and luflyly° sayde,   *laughed / knight / amiably*

2390 "I halde° hit hardily hole,° the harme that I hade.   *consider / fully redressed*

Thou art confessed so clene,° beknowen of° thy mysses,°   *fully / absolved from / errors*

And has the penaunce apert of° the poynt of myn egge,°   *obvious from / blade*

I halde° thee polysed° of that plyght,° and pured° as clene°   *hold / cleansed / sin / purified / wholly*

As° thou hades never forfeted° sythen° thou was fyrst borne;   *as if / transgressed / since*

2395 And I gif thee, sir, the gurdel that is golde-hemmed.°   *fringed with gold*

For° hit is grene as my goune,° Sir Gawayn, ye maye   *since / garment*

Thenk upon this ilke threpe,° ther° thou forth thrynges°   *same contest / when / go*

Among prynces of prys,° and this° a pure° token   *renown / this will be / true*

Of the chaunce° of the Grene Chapel at° chevalrous knyghtes.[1]   *adventure / among*

2400 And ye schal in this Newe Yer ayayn° to my wones,°   *(come) again / dwelling*

And we schyn revel° the remnaunt° of this ryche fest   *shall make merry / the remainder*

ful bene."°   *very pleasantly*

Ther lathed° hym fast° the lorde   *invited / earnestly*

And sayde: "With my wyf, I wene,°   *believe*

2405 We schal yow wel acorde,°   *reconcile*

That was your enmy kene."°   *fierce*

"Nay, for sothe,"° quoth the segge,° and sesed° hys helme,   *indeed / knight / grasped*

And has hit of hendely,° and the hathel° thonkkes.   *takes it off courteously / man*

"I haf sojorned sadly;° sele yow bytyde,°   *stayed long enough / good fortune to you*

2410 And he yelde hit° yow yare° that yarkkes° al menskes!°   *may he bestow it / fully / gives / favors*

And comaundes° me to that cortays,° your comlych fere° —   *commend / courteous (lady) / wife*

Bothe that on° and that other, myn honoured ladyes,   *one*

That thus hor° knyght wyth hor kest° han koyntly bigyled.°   *their / scheme / cunningly led astray*

Bot hit is no ferly° thagh° a fole madde,°   *marvel / if / fool behaves madly*

2415 And thurgh wyles° of wymmen be wonen° to sorwe,°   *tricks / brought / sorrow*

2390 hardily] hardilyly

---

1   On the syntax and punctuation of this passage, see Andrew and Waldron 2002: n. to 2396-99.

For so was Adam in erde° with° one bygyled,   *on earth / by*

And Salamon with fele sere,° and Samson eftsones° —   *many various ones / thereafter*

Dalyda° dalt hym hys wyrde° — and Davyth° therafter   *Delilah / fate / David*

Was blended wyth° Barsabe,°[1] that much bale tholed.°   *blinded by / Bathsheba / sorrow suffered*

2420 Now° these were wrathed wyth her° wyles, hit were a wynne° huge   *since / harmed by their / gain*

To luf hom wel and leve° hem not, a leude° that couthe.°   *trust / any man / were able*

For thes wer forne° the freest° that folwed alle the sele°[2]   *of old / best / enjoyed all good fortune*

Exellently,° of alle thyse other under heven-ryche°   *without equal / heaven*

    that mused;°   *lived*

2425 And alle thay were biwyled°   *deluded*

    With wymmen that thay used.°[3]   *had dealings with*

    Thagh I be now bigyled,

    Me think° me burde° be excused."[4]   *I believe / I should*

"Bot your gordel," quoth Gawayn, "— God yow foryelde!° —   *belt / may God reward you*

2430 That wyl I welde° wyth guod wylle, not for the wynne° golde,   *wear / precious*

Ne° the saynt,° ne the sylk, ne the syde pendaundes,°   *nor / girdle / long pendants*

For wele° ne for worchyp,° ne for the wlonk werkkes,°   *riches / honor / fine workmanship*

Bot in syngne° of my surfet° I schal se° hit ofte,   *token / fault / see*

When I ride in renoun,[5] remorde° to myselven   *recall with remorse*

2435 The faut° and the fayntyse° of the flesche crabbed,°   *flaw / frailty / wicked*

2426 with] with wyth

---

1 In 2 Kings, David sees Bathsheba from the roof of his house as she is bathing (11.2), but medieval anti-femi-
  nist writings nevertheless cast her in the role of seductress. Both the biblical account and later commentaries
  stress the importance of sight in David's temptation. The Gawain poet is probably playing on this by stating
  that David was *blended with* Bathsheba, which literally means that he "was blinded by" her; *blenden* also has
  the secondary, figurative meaning of destroying someone's "insight, discernment, moral sense, or natural
  feeling" (*MED*, s.v. "blēnden," v. 2).
2 *That folwed alle the sele* could also be read as "to whom all prosperity came."
3 The topos of great men ruined by women is conventional; on the significance of the allusion, see Cox 2001.
4 Critics have interpreted the tone of this passage in various ways: some see Gawain's speech as factually accu-
  rate (he is, in fact, *bigyled* by the Lady); others consider it an embittered misogynistic rant that predictably
  pins the blame for his shortcomings on "the eternal Eve"; and still others consider it an expression of the
  hero's disillusionment. The various possibilities are usefully surveyed by Chickering 1997: 22-23. For spe-
  cific interpretations, see, among others, Lucas 1968, Eadie 1981, Batt 1992, and Morgan 2002.
5 The *MED* glosses *riden in renoun* as "to be honored wherever one travels" (s.v. "renoun," n. 1c).

How tender° hit is to entyse teches° of fylthe;°   *eager / attract blemish / corruption*

And thus, when pryde schal me pryk° for prowes of armes,   *tempt*

The loke° to this luf-lace schal lethe° my hert.   *glance / humble*

Bot on° I wolde yow pray, displeses° yow never: *one thing / if it offends*

2440 Syn ye be lorde of the yonder londe that° I haf lent° inne   *where / stayed*

Wyth yow wyth worschyp° — the Wyye hit yow yelde°   *honor / may the One reward you*

That uphaldes° the heven and on hygh sittes! —   *holds up*

How norne° ye yowre ryght nome° (and thenne no more°)?"   *call / true name / more questions*

"That schal I telle thee truly," quoth that other thenne,   *truly*

2445 "Bertilak de Hautdesert[1] I hat° in this londe,[2]   *am called*

Thurgh myght of Morgne la Faye,[3] that in my hous lenges,°   *resides*

And koyntyse° of clergye,° bi craftes° wel lerned.   *knowledge / occult learning / arts*

The maystres° of Merlyn[4] mony has taken,°   *mistress / overcome*

For ho has dalt drury° ful dere° sumtyme°   *had a love-affair / pleasurable / in the past*

2448 has] ho

---

1   On purely paleographical grounds, it is difficult to determine whether the name reads "Bercilak" or "Berti-lak"; MS "ci" and "ti" are very similar. "Bernlak" has also been proposed, but the characters are clearly "ci" or "ti," not "n." The Old French Vulgate cycle features a "Bertholai" who shares a number of characteristics with the Green Knight's alter ego; see Appendix B. In the Middle English *Prose Merlin*, this name is ren-dered "Bertelak." The problem and its accompanying literature are ably reviewed by Kitson 1998; see also the relevant notes by Gollancz 1940, Davis 1967, and Vantuono 1999. For a discussion of the parallels between "Bertholais" and Sir Bertilak, see Griffith 1978. The second element, *de Hautdesert*, is most plausi-bly interpreted as OFr. *haut* "high" + *desert* "deserted or solitary place, wasteland," and refers to the remote location of Bertilak's castle; see the note in Davis 1967. Burrow points out that there are two medieval English castles named Beaudesert (1965: 125, n. 17), one of these being in Staffordshire, near the area where the poem's dialect places its probable origin (Silverstein 1984: n. to 2445); on the poem's connection with this area, see the Introduction, p. 11. For a different perspective on Hautdesert, see Breeze 2007.

2   Most editors place a period after this line, but this makes the syntax unnecessarily convoluted and muddles the Green Knight's point about Morgan; see P. Battles 2010a.

3   The Middle English poet casts Bertilak as Morgan's feudal vassal, holding castle Hautdesert from her; hence, he owes his name—de Hautdesert—to her (Twomey 2001). In the Vulgate *Story of Merlin*, Arthur exiles Bertholai and deprives him of his property; see Appendix B, pp. 152-53.

4   The word *maystres* most often refers to a woman who has power or control (over a nation, family, household, etc.), but, as in modern English, it can also refer to a man's sexual partner (see esp. *OED*, "mistress," n. and adj. I.7, as well as I.5); the second sense presumably grew out of the first. In Arthurian tradition, Morgan is often described as Merlin's "mistress" in both senses of the word, as in the Post-Vulgate *Merlin Continuation*: "Then Morgan made Merlin's acquaintance and begged him to teach her what he knew, on her promise that she would do for him whatever he dared ask of her.... He taught her so much [magic] in a short time, because she was clever and ingenious and eager to learn, that she knew a great part of what she wanted, and the science and art of necromancy pleased her greatly.... When she had learned as much of the art of necromancy as she wanted, she drove Merlin away from her, because she saw that he loved her excessively, and she told him she would have him killed if he came near her again" (ch. 15, p. 200).

2450 With that conable klerk,° that knowes° alle your knyghtes	*excellent master / as know*
at hame;°	*home*
Morgne the goddes,[1]	
Therfore, hit is hir name.	
Weldes non° so hyghe hawtesse°	*no one has / great haughtiness*
2455 That ho ne con° make ful tame.	*can not*

"Ho wayned° me upon this wyse to your wynne° halle	*sent / goodly*
For to assay° the surquidré,° yif hit soth° were	*test / arrogance / true*
That rennes° of the grete renoun of the Rounde Table.	*what travels abroad*
Ho wayned° me this wonder your wyttes° to reve,°	*sent / wits / take away*
2460 For to haf greved° Gaynour° and gart° hir to dye	*frightened / Guinevere / caused*
With glopnyng° of that ilke gome° that gostlych° speked	*fright / same man / like a spirit*
With his hede in his honde bifore the hyghe table.	
That is ho that is at home, the auncian° lady;[2]	*aged*
Ho is even° thyn aunt, Arthures half-suster,	*indeed*
2465 The duches' doghter of Tyntagelle,° that dere Uter after°	*Tintagel / later*
Hade° Arthur upon, that athel° is nowthe.°[3]	*begat / famous / now*

2461 glopnyng] gopnyng   gome] gomen

---

1   Morgan is a goddess in several early texts, but the *therfore* in line 2453, which refers back to the story about how she learned magic from Merlin, indicates that the poet has in mind the later tradition that Morgan's knowledge of the occult arts merely caused some to mistake her for a goddess. As the *Prose Lancelot* explains: "The truth is that Morgan, the sister of King Arthur, knew more about witchcraft and spells than any other woman; and because of her keen interest in such things, she gave up and forsook all dealings with people and lived day and night in far-off forests, so that many people (there was no dearth of fools at that time through the country-side) never spoke of her as a woman but rather called her Morgan the Goddess" (Part III, ch. 93, p. 305). On the pejoration of Morgan's character, see Fries 1994.

2   Thus the mysterious old woman in whose company the Lady first appears in lines 947-69 was Morgan (she is called an *auncian*, "ancient person," both here and in line 948). In hindsight, this explains why she sits in the place of honor at the feast (line 1001). It seems odd that Arthur is described as extremely young while his half-sister has the appearance of a very old woman, but the reason for this is given in the Post-Vulgate *Merlin Continuation*: "Unquestionably [Morgan] was a beautiful girl up to the time she began to learn enchantments and magic charms; but once the enemy entered her and she was inspired with sensuality and the devil, she lost her beauty so completely that she became very ugly, nor did anyone think her beautiful after that, unless he was under a spell" (ch. 3, p. 172).

3   According to the Vulgate *Story of Merlin*, Morgan is the younger daughter of Igraine, Duchess of Tintagel; the older daughter is Gawain's mother. Arthur is conceived when King Uther Pendragon impersonates Ygraine's husband; after the latter is killed, Uther marries Igraine. Hence, Morgan is both Gawain's aunt and Arthur's half-sister.

Therfore I ethe° thee, hathel,° to com to thyn aunt,   *entreat / knight*

Make myry° in my hous; my meny° thee lovies,   *merry / household*

And I wol° thee as wel, wyye,° bi my faythe,   *esteem / sir*

2470 As any gome° under God for thy grete trauthe."°   *man / constancy*

And he nikked hym naye,° he nolde° bi no wayes.°   *refused / would not / means*

Thay acolen° and kyssen and kennen° ayther° other   *embrace / commend / each*

To the Prynce of paradise, and parten ryght there

    on coolde.°   *the cold (ground)*

2475 Gawayn on blonk° ful bene°   *horse / very good*

To the kynges burgh buskes° bolde,°   *sets out for / boldly*

And the knyght in the enker-grene°   *vivid green*

Whiderwarde-so-ever° he wolde.°   *in whatever direction / wished*

Wylde wayes° in the worlde Wowen° now rydes   *paths / Gawain*

2480 On Gryngolet, that the grace° hade geten° of his lyve.   *gift / received*

Ofte he herbered° in house and ofte al ther-oute,°   *took shelter / out in the open*

And mony aventure in vale,° and venquyst° ofte,   *valleys / defeated foes*

That I ne tyght° at this tyme in tale to remene.°   *intend / recount*

The hurt was hole° that he hade hent° in his nek,   *healed / received*

2485 And the blykkande° belt he bere ther-aboute,°   *shining / wore near it*

Abelef° as a bauderyk,° bounden° bi his syde,   *obliquely / baldric / tied*

Loken° under his lyfte° arme, the lace,° with a knot,[1]   *fastened / left / belt*

In tokenyng° he was tane,° in tech[2] of a faute;°   *signifying / defeated / token / blemish*

2472 and kennen] *supplied*

---

1 The detailed description of how the belt is worn, and the emphasis on its *tokenyng*, seem significant. Since Gawain wears the pentangle on his cote-armure, the belt becomes part of his heraldic emblem, which, as Schmidt 1987 explains, would now be "a *bend vert* athwart the pentangle (*or*, on a ground *gules*)" (149). Plummer (1991: 205) notes that *abelef* has a specifically heraldic meaning in this context. Clein 1987 points out that changes in heraldic emblems were not uncommon; such changes "testify to the ongoing chivalric practices of the bearers" (28).

2 These parallel *in ... in ...* phrases are best read as standing in apposition; *in tech of a faute* varies *in tokenyng he was tane*. There are other instances of this in the surrounding verses (*loken under his lyfte arme* (*continued*)

And thus he commes to the court, knyght al in sounde.° — *good health*

2490 Ther wakned wele° in that wone,° when wyst° the grete° — *arose joy / dwelling / saw / great king*

That gode Gawayn was commen; gayn° hit hym thoght.° — *pleasing / seemed to him*

The kyng kysses the knyght, and the quene° alce,° — *queen / also*

And sythen mony syker° knyght that soght hym to haylce,° — *trusty / greet*

Of his fare° that hym frayned;° and ferlyly° he telles: — *journey / asked / of the marvels*

2495 Biknowes° alle the costes of care° that he hade, — *reveals / hardships*

The chaunce° of the chapel, the chere° of the knyght, — *adventure / behavior*

The luf of the ladi, the lace° at the last.° — *belt / last of all*

The nirt° in the nek[1] he naked° hem schewed — *scar / plainly*

That he laght° for his unleuté° at the leudes° hondes — *received / dishonesty / man's*

2500   for blame.° — *as reproof*

He tened° when he schulde° telle, — *grew vexed / had to*

He groned° for gref and grame;° — *groaned / remorse*

The blod in° his face con melle° — *to / did rush*

When he hit schulde schewe,° for schame. — *had to reveal*

2505 "Lo,° lorde!" quoth the leude,° and the lace° hondeled, — *see / man / belt*

"This is the bende°[2] of this blame° I bere in my nek; — *band / offense*

This is the lathe° and the losse that I laght° have — *harm / received*

2506 in] *supplied*

---

varies *bounden bi his syde*; *the lace* varies *belt*; and *knyght al in sounde* varies *he*). Alternatively, *in tokenyng he was tane in tech of a faute* would mean something like "in order to signify that he had been found guilty of a fault" (Andrew and Waldron 2002: n. to 2488). See *MED*, s.v. "tach(e)," n. 3. On *tan*, compare line 2509 below.

1 Reichardt (1984: 157) points out that the back of the neck, where Gawain receives his blow, is in biblical tradition and in medieval zoology associated with stiff-necked pride. Furthermore, Neaman 1976 notes an allusion to Psalm 128.4, which was recited as part of the Feast of the Circumcision of Jesus on 1 January, the same day Gawain receives his wound: "The Lord who is just will cut the necks of sinners."

2 *Bende* can also refer to a heraldic device, namely a diagonal stripe that usually runs from dexter chief (top right) to sinister base (bottom left). Gawain's belt rests on his right shoulder and is tied beneath his left arm. Thus, *bende of this blame* puns on the dual meaning of "band." Friedman and Osberg 1977 speculate that the wearing of the bend in this manner "represents the heraldic differencing of illegitimacy, the bend or bar sinister of nineteenth century novels" (313), but Plummer (1991: 206) points out that Gawain's bend is dexter not sinister. Compare also the note to lines 2485-88 above.

Of covardise and covetyse,° that I haf caght°[1] thare;   *covetousness / caught*

This is the token of untrawthe° that I am tan° inne,   *dishonesty / discovered*

2510 And I mot nedes° hit were wyle° I may last.°   *must / wear while / live*

For mon may hyden° his harme,° bot unhap°[2] ne may hit,   *hide / wrong-doing / come undone*

For ther° hit ones° is tachched,° twynne° wil hit never."   *where / once / attached / depart*

The kyng comfortes the knyght, and alle the court als°   *likewise*

Laghen loude ther-at, and luflyly acorden°   *graciously agree*

2515 That lordes and ladis[3] that longed° to the Table,   *who belonged*

— Uche burne° of the brotherhede — a bauderyk° schulde have,   *every member / baldric*

A bende° abelef hym aboute° of a bryght grene,   *band / obliquely around them*

And that, for sake of that segge,° in swete° to were.°[4]   *knight / together / wear*

For that was acorded° the renoun° of the Rounde Table,   *considered / distinction*

2520 And he honoured that hit hade,° evermore after,   *who had (received) it*

As hit is breved° in the best boke of romaunce.°   *recorded / romance*

Thus in Arthurus day this aunter bitidde;°   *adventure befell*

The Brutus bokes°[5] therof beres° wyttenesse.   *chronicles / bear*

2511 mon] non

---

1 "Catching" cowardice and covetousness compares these sins to a disease, a common analogy in the Middle Ages.

2 *Unhap* puns on at least two meanings of *happen*, "befall" and "fasten": one can hide one's transgressions, but they will still have happened; and one can hide one's transgressions, but they cannot be "untied"—an appropriate image given the belt—or separated from one's self. In addition, *unhap* means "mishap," "bad fortune," though the syntax obviously does not permit a noun here. See *MED*, s.v. "happen," v. 1, "happen," v. 2, and "unhap," n.

3 Some editors emend *ladis* to *ledes* ("knights"), arguing that ladies could not belong to the Round Table. For a counter-argument, see P. Battles 2010a.

4 The decision to wear a green belt to memorialize Gawain's adventure parallels the practice of fourteenth-century chivalric orders, which adopted articles of clothing as distinctive devices. The *Greene Knight*, a poem probably based on *Sir Gawain and the Green Knight*, features a scene much like the present one and states that *That is the matter and the case / Why Knights of the Bathe weare the lace* (501-02). The latter society is mentioned as early as 1399—although it was not a formally constituted order at that time—when Henry IV created forty-six Knights of the Bath at his coronation. The best-known chivalric order, the Order of the Garter, was founded by Edward III around 1348 in conscious imitation of the Round Table. Its motto appears at the end of the poem. Thus there have been attempts to connect this scene with the Order of the Garter; see, most recently, Ingledew 2006. The Garter was not green, nor worn like a baldric, but instead took the form of "a miniature belt with a metal buckle and pendant, and was invariably made of cloth dyed in the light blue colour officially known as *bleu* or *bluetus*" (Boulton 1987: 152).

5 "Brutus books" are chronicles or histories that take their name from Brutus, the legendary founder of Britain. The two most famous are Wace's *Roman de Brut* (c. 1155) and Lawman's *Brut* (c. 1190); both derive from Geoffrey of Monmouth's *History of the Kings of Britain* (c. 1136).

Sythen Brutus, the bolde burne,° bowed° hider fyrst,   *warrior / traveled*

2525 After the segge° and the asaute was sesed at Troye,[1]   *siege*

Iwysse,°   *indeed*

Mony aunteres° here biforne°   *adventures / earlier*

Haf fallen° suche, er this.   *happened*

Now that° bere° the croun° of thorne,   *(may he) who / bears / crown*

2530 He bryng uus to his blysse!   AMEN.

HONY SOYT QUI MAL [Y] PENCE[2]

---

1 Except for the substitution of *after* for *siththen*, this line is identical to the poem's opening verse. It is also the poem's last long line. Given the emphasis in Fitt 2 upon the "five fives," the number 2525 (plus five in the concluding bob and wheel) is symbolically significant.

2 This literally translates as "shame be to him who thinks evil of it" and is the motto of the Order of the Garter. It is set off from the text of the poem; authorities disagree over whether it was written by the original scribe or added somewhat later; cf. Gollancz 1940: n. to 2530, as well as Condren 2002: 19-20 and Ingledew 2006: 224, n. 10.

Appendix A: From Caradoc[1]

[Chrétien de Troyes left his verse romance *Perceval* unfinished. After his death in about 1190, several continuations were written. One of these, known simply as the First Continuation (c. 1200), focuses largely on the adventures of Gawain while also introducing a new character, Caradoc. Because the story of Caradoc is of substantial length and largely self-contained, it is often called the *Livre* (or *Roman*) *de Caradoc*. There are three versions of the First Continuation, known as the short, long, and mixed redactions; there is also a later retelling in prose. In each, the narrative varies slightly. Most critics agree that the *Gawain* poet based the beheading game on an episode in the story of Caradoc; the long redaction seems the most likely source, although a number of significant parallels are found only in the prose version. The episode below, excerpted from the long redaction, takes place immediately after Caradoc has been knighted along with fifty other prominent young men.]

And so my story continues. They went to the church to hear the divine service. The Archbishop of Canterbury began to celebrate the mass of the Holy Spirit for them. The service was glorious and marvellous and there were many people in attendance. The King wore his crown that day, and he looked magnificent. When the service was complete, they returned to the hall, and the servants prepared the cloths and spread the tables with bread, wine, precious knives, and gold and silver cups and chalices. I couldn't describe all the wealth of plate even if someone threatened to cut off my nose! The tables were elegantly spread indeed. The brave knights passed the time agreeably with the King, and every one of them honoured him. Sir Kay, wearing no mantle, came out of a room and crossed the hall towards the King, holding a small baton in his hand. "My lord," he said, "when it pleases you, it will be time for you to take the water."

"Kay," replied the King, "don't be in such a hurry! By all God's saints, you know very well that as long as I have been holding royal court I have never eaten, and water will never be distributed before some cause for wonder has been seen. I do not want to begin now!"

Even as they spoke, a knight on a grey horse came through the door. His horse was carrying him quickly and he rode along singing a little song. He was wearing a hat because of the great heat and an ermine robe, and over it he had girded on a sword with a fine silk strap, which soon would have cut off his head! He rode right up to the King and said: "May God protect you, Your Majesty, the best and the greatest king on earth! I have come to ask you for a gift, if it pleases you to give it to me."

"Welcome, my friend," said the King, "I greet you in return. When I have heard what gift you want to ask of me, you may be sure it won't be refused."

---

1 From *Three Arthurian Romances: Poems from Medieval France*, trans. Ross G. Arthur, Everyman Library (London: J.M. Dent; Vermont: C.E. Tuttle, 1996), pp. 11-15. Reprinted with permission of The Orion Publishing Group, London.

"I do not want to deceive you, Your Majesty. The gift that I ask for is to receive a blow to the neck in exchange for another."

"What? You'll have to explain that to me."

"I will tell you, Your Majesty: here in your presence, I will give this sword to a knight. If he can cut off my head with a single stroke, let him strike away. If I can recover from this blow, let him accept one from me in turn, a year from now, here in your presence."

"By Saint John," said Kay, "I wouldn't do that for all the wealth in Normandy! Sir Knight, a man would be a fool to strike you on those terms!"

The knight dismounted. "Your Majesty," he said, "I seek the gift from you. If you refuse it to me, it will be reported throughout the world. I will surely know how to reveal that at your court I failed to find a little gift I was seeking— and I have come a long way to obtain it from you."

He drew his sword from the scabbard. The King looked pensive, and everyone, great and small, was amazed. They wondered in their hearts what honour they could win by striking him. Caradoc, who had just become a knight, could bear it no more; he threw off his mantle at once, rushed towards the knight, and took the steel blade in his hand. The other man asked him one of his questions: "Have you been chosen as the best knight?"

"Certainly not, just the biggest fool!"

The knight placed his head on a table and stretched out his neck. You may be sure that the King and all the nobles of the court were very disturbed. Sir Yvain almost ran up to grab the sword from his hands: but nothing came from that, he won't take it from him! Caradoc raised the sword and delivered such a blow that the sword plunged into the table. The knight's head flew off, no small distance, but the body followed it so closely that before anyone was aware of it, the body had retrieved its head and placed it back in its proper place. The knight leaped up in their midst in front of the King, perfectly safe and sound. "Your Majesty," he said, "do not be false now! Since I have received a neck-blow, another must be received in turn from me, at your court a year from today."

The King did not delay: he ordered all his lords from all over the kingdom to be present again at his court the next year, in that same place and on exactly the same day. "Caradoc," said the knight, "you have given a hard blow to my neck in the presence of the King: one year from today, you will receive mine in return."

Then the knight set out on his way and departed from the court, and the King remained in sad and troubled thought. No one could describe the sorrow of the ladies and the knights: they hardly laughed at all during their meal and all the court was dumbfounded. Caradoc was not upset, but said: "Give up your sorrow, uncle; it now depends entirely on God."

Many eyes shed tears for Caradoc. The court was announced for Cardueil the next year, at Pentecost. Caradoc the King of Vannes and his wife Lady Ysave[1] heard this painful news, and felt such great sorrow for their beloved child

---

1 King Caradoc and Lady Ysave are Caradoc's parents.

that no one could recount or describe the despair and torment they suffered all that year. Caradoc stayed at the court of his uncle the King, caring little for his life, but going out in search of adventures. Never in all your life have you heard of any one knight performing as many acts of prowess as he did during that one year. He was spoken about in many places; everyone who saw him mourned and wept for him. The end of the year did not delay, and they had to reassemble at the court. Everyone who had heard about it came there by land and sea to witness these marvels, but many maidens and ladies, and even King Caradoc and his wife, were so sorrowful that they didn't dare come. You may be sure, however, that they were far from idle: on that day they performed many acts of charity and good deeds on Caradoc's behalf so that God, who surpasses all good things, would preserve him from all shame that day.

It was the day of Pentecost, and Caradoc was very troubled and disturbed by the adventure which was threatening his life. The whole court was assembled and the processions were completed; the masses had been sung in the churches and the water was distributed for the meal. The knight arrived on a horse, with his sword at his side; his face was not fresh-coloured, but red with the heat. "Your Majesty," he said, "may God protect you."

"My friend, may God bless you as well."

"Caradoc, I can't see you: come forward, and you'll get your reward! Present your head to me at once. Just as I offered you mine before, now it's proper for people to see how I can strike with my sword, and so you will receive your neck-blow!"

Caradoc understood that his task was awaiting him. He removed his mantle, leapt forward, and offered his head to the knight at once, saying, "Dear lord, now you have me; do the best you can."

"Sir Knight," said the King, "do not be so uncourtly as to refuse to take ransom for him."

"Ransom? Name the gift to me."

"I will do so gladly. I will give you a large ransom. Without a lie, I will give you all the plate to be found in my court, no matter who brought it, and a knight's full equipment, because he is my nephew and I hold him very dear."

"I will certainly not accept that! I will take his head at once, and nothing else will happen."

"I will say more to you. I will give you all the treasures, whether precious stones, silver or gold, to be found in my land, in Brittany or England or in all my kingdom!"

"I will certainly not accept that. Rather I will cut off his head. You may think me cruel, but I will take his head at once; he cannot escape me. Nothing else will happen!"

"And yet I will add something more still ..."

The knight raised his hand and prepared to strike. The King saw this and fainted with sorrow. Caradoc shouted angrily, "Why do you not strike, dear lord? You are making me die twice, by taking so long to strike. Now I believe that you are a great coward!"

For her part, the Queen came out of her room with a hundred ladies and maidens of great beauty to entreat the knight. "Sir Knight," she said, "do not touch him. It would be a sin and a great pity if he were killed. In God's name, have mercy on him! If you spare his life for me, you will be well rewarded. Take my advice and you will profit from it! Will you do something for me? Grant me this much: release the King's nephew Caradoc from this neck-blow. A large ransom will be paid for it! You see here many young ladies with pleasing bodies and many beautiful maidens: you can have them all! Let him go, and you'll be acting wisely."

"My lady," the knight replied, "I will not take all the ladies in the world or any other payment but his life! If you do not dare to watch, go back and stay in your room."

The Queen covered her head and began her lamentations again. She went back to her room with the ladies of the country. They all felt such extreme sorrow that they almost died. Neither the King nor any of his knights knew what to do, but displayed such grief that no mortal man could describe it.

Caradoc approached a table and laid his head on top of it; the knight raised his sword, and struck him with the flat of it without doing him the least harm! "Caradoc," he said, "get up now. It would be a great pity and an outrage if I killed you. Come and talk with me alone; I want to have a few words with you."

He spoke to him privately: "Do you know why I didn't kill you? You are my son and I am your father."

"I will certainly defend my mother," said Caradoc. "She is not and never has been your lover and she never did anything she shouldn't!"

The knight told him to be quiet. He recounted all the story to him just as it happened, about how he lay with Ysave for three nights.[1] It would be too tiresome to tell it to you all over again. Caradoc wanted to fight with him, for the words he heard caused him uncommon sorrow. "Knight," he said, "you are boasting about a lie: you never deceived my father, you never lay with my mother, and you never did anything to her so that she bore me or anyone else! If you dare to say it again, I will make you regret it!" The knight paid no attention to him; he mounted his horse at once, took his leave, and went on his way.

The court was left in great joy. The trumpet was sounded, the King asked for water, and it was given to him. The ladies and the knights washed and then took their places to eat. King Arthur sat down at the dais. I do not want to describe all the dishes to you, for even when I was wearied by it myself, I would not have said enough! When the court broke up, many presents of great value and inestimable beauty were given out: gold, silver, horses, and birds. No matter how poor they were, everyone who came to that court went home rich. Each one returned to his own country, but the King preferred to stay there with his closest companions.

---

1 As the story relates earlier, Caradoc's mother was bewitched and tricked into sleeping with the knight Eliavrés, a great enchanter, on her wedding night and the next two evenings.

Appendix B: The Story of the False Guenevere and Bertelay[1]

[Between 1215 and 1235, an anonymous group of authors composed the Vulgate cycle, five Old French prose romances that trace the rise and fall of King Arthur and the knights of the Round Table. Two of these works, the prose *Lancelot* (1215-20) and *The Story of Merlin* (after 1230), narrate the story of the "False Guenevere" and Bertelay. The latter name is rendered "Bertelak" in a Middle English translation of *The Story of Merlin*. Several allusions to the Vulgate cycle, particularly to the prose *Lancelot*, suggest that the *Gawain* poet was intimately familiar with this work. It therefore seems likely that the mysterious Bertilak de Hautdesert and his wife are modeled on Bertelay and the false Guenevere.

As the story opens, we learn that Guenevere has a half-sister who looks just like her. The queen's father, King Leodagan, conceived this *doppelgänger* with the wife of his seneschal, Cleodalis. On the night of the queen's wedding, the kinsmen of the false Guenevere try to abduct the queen and substitute the look-alike in her place. However, the plot is foiled by Merlin through the knights Ulfin and Bretel, who kill the abductors, rescue the Queen, and capture the imposter.]

37. The False Guenevere and Bertelay[2]

Then Ulfin and Bretel took the queen and led her away very frightened to her bedroom, and they told her not to be afraid anymore. Afterwards they took the false Guenevere and led her off to their lodging, for they did not want anyone to find out about their secret.

Just as you have heard, the traitors were dealt with according to Merlin's advice, and the queen was rescued by the two worthy men. And as soon as they had left, Merlin knew it, and he came straight to King Leodagan and told him to send three of his young ladies to the queen's room to put her to bed. And the king asked him, "Why? Can't her nurse do it?"

And Merlin told him the whole truth just as it had happened. When the king heard it, he was deeply amazed about it, and he said that he could never rest until he had spoken to her. Then King Leodagan left and came straight to the bedroom where his daughter Guenevere was, and he took three young ladies with him to get her ready for bed. When she saw him, she began to weep mightily, and the king took her by the hand, drew her to one side, and spoke to her all alone. And she told him the truth just as it had happened, from beginning

---

1   From *Lancelot-Grail: The Old French Arthurian Vulgate and Post-Vulgate in Translation*, gen. ed. Norris J. Lacy, 5 vols. (New York and London: Garland Publishing, 1992-96). Reprinted with permission of the Taylor and Francis Group, LLC.

2   Chapters 37 and 38 are reprinted from *The Story of Merlin*, trans. Rupert T. Pickens, pp. 339-42.

to end, and the king told her that she had nothing to fear, for she need worry no more. And the king ordered the three ladies to get her ready for bed, and they did as they were told; nor did King Leodagan want to leave the room before they had put her to bed. After that, he came to his daughter's bed, raised the cover, and turned it down until he saw the mark of the crown on her back. Then he knew indeed that she was his daughter, whom he had had by his wife. After that, he put the cover back over her and went out of the room without saying a word, and the ladies wondered why he had done that.

Just then King Arthur came back from reveling with his companions. When he came into the hall, Merlin and King Leodagan came to meet him, and they told him to go to bed with his wife, for it was high time; he said that he would do so very gladly. So he went into the room where the three maidens were who had helped her get ready for bed, and as soon as the king was in bed, the ladies left the room. No one was left there but the king and queen, and all night they spent a most happy time together, for they loved each other deeply, and they did not stop until daybreak, when they fell asleep arm in arm.

Thus was Queen Guenevere to have been deceived by the traitors—by the ones because of whom she later had very great sorrow, which happened a long time afterwards, just as the story will relate it to you, if there is anyone to tell it to you. For the king lost her for a good three years, when he never had her with him. Galehaut, a wealthy prince in the kingdom of Sorelois, took her away for love of Lancelot. And the king kept the false Guenevere as his concubine until one day when, as it happened, he was taken ill. And this was because of Bertelay, a traitor who brought it about that King Arthur was unwilling to give her up for anyone's sake; in the end, everything on earth rotted. And the land and kingdom were under interdict for nearly three years, when no man's or woman's body was buried in consecrated ground except secretly and under threat of excommunication. And Our Lord allowed such hardship to befall them for the breech of faith in their sins, and they were sinful indeed. And all of this happened through a knight who afterwards died a dreadful death because of it, as the story will tell you later. But it is right and fitting that the story should tell you why this happened, for this is the place for it, and reason accords with this.

It was true that King Leodagan, who was a good ruler and lawgiver, had a knight who was most worthy and shrewd; he was a good knight who had served him well, and he was of noble stock. This knight's name was Bertelay, and he hated another knight with deadly hatred because the latter had slain one of his first cousins to have his wife because he loved her. When Bertelay found out that he had killed his cousin, and knew that his wife had shamed him, he never bothered to complain to the king. Rather, he went to him, broke faith with him, and threatened him with death, and he kept watching him many a day and many a night. At last, on the night that King Arthur wed his wife, when the knights left the court and went to their lodgings to rest, Bertelay happened to see his enemy. He ran him down and killed him with a short word he had with him. As soon as he had killed him, he went straight to his lodging, and the two squires who had been with the slain knight raised the cry, and people came pouring out everywhere with lanterns and torches aflame and found the slain knight. They asked the two squires, who were mourning sorrowfully, who had killed him, and they said that it was Bertelay the Red. After the squires had wept and wailed over their lord for a long time, they picked him up and carried him to his lodging, and they did to him what was fitting for a dead knight. They watched over him until daybreak and carried him to the church, and they had the service said and then buried him.

And in the morning, Ulfin and Bretel together sent for Cleodalis the Seneschal, and they ordered him to come speak to them at their lodging. He came there very willingly, for he was well-bred and noble. When they saw him, they drew him aside and told him what had happened just as it had occurred and how his daughter had behaved.

And when he heard the high treason she had done, he said that she could never be his daughter, "for if she were my daughter, she would never have done it no matter who might have begged her to."

While the three of them were talking in this way, King Leodagan had arisen very early, for he was very frightened by the strange things that had happened to his daughter that night. And Merlin was already out of bed, and he went straight to the king and bade him good day, and when the king saw him he turned a cheerful face to him and said God bless him. Then they took each other by the hand and came out of the hall talking of several things, and they walked until they came before the lodging of Ulfin and Bretel. Then they went inside so stealthily that those within did not know they were there until they were almost on top of them, but when they caught sight of them they sprang up to greet them, for they were not awkward at honoring worthy gentlemen. Then all five of them[1] went into a room by themselves, and Ulfin left and brought Guenevere in, and he told them what she and the traitors had done, although they already knew about it because Merlin had told the king.

Then King Leodagan spoke and said, "Seneschal, sir seneschal, I love you very much indeed, and I would gladly do anything for the sake of your honor; I would willingly increase that honor, and so I shall, if I live long enough, for you have served me faithfully and well. And I would do nothing or strive for nothing that could bring you shame or dishonor if I could shield you from them. Do you know why I say this? Look, this is your daughter, who has surely deserved to be condemned by the law. But you have been so faithful to me that, for love of you, I would have to forgive her for an even greater misdeed than this. But, as it would nevertheless be fitting for me to take vengeance in some way, you must take her out of this kingdom so that no man or woman who sees her will know who she is; for that is my pleasure and my will."

But the seneschal answered that she was never his daughter, "but because it is your will, I will do it. And God help me," he went on, "I would rather she were burned, or buried alive, in sight of all the townsfolk, for she does not belong to me in any way." .

"Now, right now," said the king, "let it lie! Take care that everything is done so that I may never again hear tell of her—and take as much of what is mine as you will."

---

1 That is, Ulfin, Bretel, Guenevere, Merlin, and Cleodalis.

This is what the barons decided, and right away, without a break, Cleodalis got himself and his stepdaughter ready to ride, and they took to the road and made their way until in time they came into another kingdom,[1] to an abbey that was in a wild, lonely place, where he put her. And there she stayed, so says the story, until Bertelay the Red found her; through his craft and trickery he set her free. Then many times he had his way with her and lay with her openly.

But with that, the story falls silent from talking about them right here, and it will tell you about Cleodalis the Seneschal, who came back to Carhaix, where King Arthur was.

38. Bertelay Condemned; Arthur to Hold Court

Here the story says that after King Leodagan had ordered his seneschal to take his daughter out of the kingdom of Carmelide, he left Ulfin and Bretel's lodging with Merlin, and they came back to his hall hand in hand. There they found the barons all out of bed and dressed; the bells had already been rung for Mass, and they were going to the church. When Mass had been sung, they came back to the hall. There the kinsmen of the knight whom Bertelay had slain came to bring their suit to the king. King Leodagan sent for him at his lodging, and he came right away, wearing armor beneath his clothing and carrying hidden weapons. And he had with him a great many knights, for he was full of great courtliness; he had always had a good tongue in his head, and he was always beautifully dressed.

And when King Leodagan saw him, he asked him why he had slain the knight unlawfully.

He answered that he would indeed defend himself against anyone who called him a criminal: "I do not say that I did not kill him, but I did break faith with him first. And I did not kill him without reason, for many know for a fact that he had slain a first cousin of mine to have his wife, whom he was shaming. So, as I see it, a man should harm his deadly enemy in all the ways he can—after he has broken faith with him."

And the king answered that he was mistaken, "but if you had come to me and brought suit against him, I would not have ruled against you; then you could have taken vengeance. But you did not find me worthy enough to seek justice from me."

"Sir," he said, "say what you will, but I have never done you any wrong, nor will I ever, God willing."

"It is my will," said the king, "that a rightful judgment will be pronounced."

"Sir," said Bertelay the Red, "I see clearly that it must be as you will."

Then the king ordered the decision to be reached in full sight of his barons.

At that trial were King Arthur, King Ban, King Bors, Sir Gawainet, Sir Yvain, Sagremor, Nascien, Adragain, Hervi of Rivel, and Guiomar. These ten were to make the judgment, so they talked together about many things until at

---

1 The source text here says "into the kingdom of Carmelide," but this must be a mistake, since Cleodalis has just been ordered to remove her from Carmelide. One could either read "into another kingdom," as here, or "away from the kingdom of Carmelide."

last they agreed that Bertelay should be stripped of his holdings and put out of King Leodagan's land forever. And King Ban made the speech, for he was wonderfully well-spoken, just as it had been entrusted to him:

"Sir, these barons gathered here have judged that Bertelay the Red should be stripped of all the land he holds from you as his overlord, and then he must forsake the kingdom forever. The reason is that he took it upon himself to judge the knight he killed, and at night, but justice was not his to mete out. Moreover, you hold high court, which should guarantee that all who have ever been there may come and go freely."

With that, King Ban sat down and said no more. And when Bertelay saw that it could not be otherwise, that he had been forsaken, he turned around without saying a word. He did not dare argue against the judgment, for the highest men in the world—and the mightiest—had made it; but if any others had made it, he would have done all he could to dispute it.

So Bertelay left, but he took along a most handsome following of knights to whom he had many times given fine gifts, for he had been a good and strong knight. And he made his way, little by little, hour by hour, until at last he came to the place where the false Guenevere was. There he lingered for quite a long time, and he brooded very darkly, like a man who had known every sorrow, about how he could take vengeance against King Leodagan and King Arthur, who had forsaken him. From this such great ordeals befell King Arthur, and such great strife arose between him and his wife, that he cast her aside for a long time, just as the story will relate it to you later.

74. Guenevere Is Accused of Imposture[1]

Now the story says that King Arthur was at that time staying at Camelot.... [A] young lady arrived at court and walked boldly up to the king as he was sitting with his knights; and there was a great escort behind her, more than thirty knights and men-at-arms making up her party. The damsel was very beautiful; she came before the king smartly dressed in tunic and cloak of rich silk cloth and wearing her hair in one long, thick braid, lustrous and light. Seeing her come along, the knights made way, and no baron, however noble, failed to leap to his feet; everyone who saw her was sure that she was the most noble lady in the world.

When she came before the king, she pulled off the wimple still covering her head and threw it to the ground, and there was no dearth of men to pick it up, since she was surrounded by the people in her large retinue and others as well. The wimple removed, they were all amazed by her great beauty, and she spoke loudly enough for them all to hear as she said boldly, "God save King Arthur and his knights (saving the honor and the rights of my lady)—King Arthur, worthiest man in the world if not for just one thing!"

"My lady," said the king, "whatever I am, God grant you good fortune! As for the honor and the rights of your lady, I want them to be safe, wherever she

---

1 Chapters 74, 77, and 80 are reprinted from *Lancelot Part III*, trans. Samuel N. Rosenberg, pp. 245-47, 262, and 275.

may be. Now, though, I would be grateful to you for telling me what failing I have that keeps me from being the worthiest man in the world. After that, you can tell me who your lady is and how I may have wronged her, though I don't think I have ever misbehaved toward any lady young or old, nor would I ever want to."

"King," she said, "if I were not able to make you see both my lady's rights and the failing that keeps you from perfection, I would have had no reason to come to your court. But I have not come without a reason. Indeed, I am here because of the strangest and most extraordinary thing ever to have happened in your household. Like you, your people will be more shocked by it, once they've learned the truth, than by anything else they have ever heard. First, let me tell you that the name of the lady who has sent me to you is Queen Guenevere, daughter of King Leodagan. But before I disclose what rights she claims, I must give you a letter I have here, sealed with her seal; it is meant to be read aloud in front of all your barons."

The young lady looked around, and an old, white-haired knight sprang forward. He handed her a very handsome box sparkling with gold and precious stones. She took the box and opened it, then took out a letter hung with a gold seal and said, "My lord, have this letter read aloud as I have stated, but with the understanding that it will be heard by every lady and maiden at this court; I have a right to ask that. A letter as important as this must not be read in private. You see, even if the largest court that you have ever held were brought together here, there would be no person too insensitive to be shocked by it. You would do well, then, to take up this extraordinary matter with a large group of worthy men."

The king stared dumbfounded at the young woman speaking so boldly, and all those with him were just as stunned.

He sent right away for the queen and all the ladies and maidens scattered through the rooms, and sent a crier through all quarters to make sure that every knight and man-at-arms came to court forthwith to hear the strange news. Once they were all gathered, the young lady spoke and asked the king to have her letter read. He handed it to the clerk whom he knew to be the best spoken and the most learned of all. The man unfolded the parchment and, scanning the letter from top to bottom, was so alarmed that the tears of his eyes ran down his face and fell onto his chest. The king stared at him with greater wonder than he had felt before, and everyone there was frightened by the sight.

"Speak!" said the king. "I am more eager to hear this letter than I've ever been."

The clerk looked at the queen, who was leaning against the shoulder of Sir Gawain, and when he saw her, his whole heart turned cold with anguish and locked so tight inside his chest that even to save his life he could not have uttered a word; and he began to totter.

Sir Yvain, who was very kind and gracious, saw what was happening and thought he had detected some threat to the king in the letter; he jumped forward to catch him, and the man fainted in his arms. That astonished the king and made him wonder what the news could possibly be. He sent at once for another reader and handed him the letter. This one scanned it too and broke into sighs and bitter tears; he dropped the letter onto the king's lap and turned away in utter grief. Walking past the queen, he said, "Ah, my lady! my lady! It's such woeful news!"

Thereupon he flung himself into another room and grieved more bitterly than he had ever done. The queen was dumbfounded.

The king could hardly take the matter lightly. He sent for his chaplain and, as soon as he appeared, said to him, "Sir chaplain, read me this letter. I urge you, by the faith you owe me and by the Mass that you have sung today, to tell me whatever you find in it and not hide a thing."

The chaplain took the letter and, when he had scanned it all, sighed deeply and said to the king, "My lord, am I to read this letter aloud?"

"Yes," said the king, "you are."

"The truth is," said the chaplain, "I am very sorry, because what I have to say will grieve and anger all the members of your court. If it were possible, I would ask you to please have someone else read the letter, but you have called on me to do it and I mustn't stand back."

"My lord," said the king, "you have no choice."

The chaplain, speaking loudly enough for the whole court to hear him, began. "My lord," he said, "Queen Guenevere, daughter of King Leodagan, greets King Arthur, as is proper for her to do, together with his whole company of barons and knights. King Arthur, I am hereby lodging a complaint first against you and then against all your barons. I want everyone to know that you have behaved disloyally toward me, while I have behaved loyally toward you. Indeed, you do not deserve to be king, for it is not proper that a king should live with a concubine, as you do. The truth is plain: I was joined to you as wife in true wedlock, anointed and crowned as queen and consort of the kingdom of Logres in the church of Saint Stephen the Martyr in the city of Logres, the head city of your realm.

"But that high honor lasted only a short while, for I was queen but a day and a night and was then taken away and cast out, either by your doing or someone else's. Then in my place was put the woman who was my maid and servant, the very Guenevere you hold to be your wife and queen. She sought my death and destitution, whereas she should have been ready to sacrifice her own self in order to save me. But God, who never once forgets those who wait upon His mercy, sent me a deliverer to whom I owe greater love than anyone else in the world. And though once banished and disinherited, I am now, by God's mercy, restored to my position and my inheritance. So I ask you, out of loyalty and for the sake of right, that, by the judgment and finding of your court, this act of disloyalty be avenged and the woman who has kept you so long in mortal sin be made to suffer torment and die, just as she wanted to make me die.

"That is what I want my letter to make known to you. But inasmuch as in the writing I could not recall every single thing that might have some bearing, I am sending you my first cousin, Clice, the bearer of the letter, to be my heart and my tongue. I urge you to trust whatever she tells you in my behalf, since she knows as much about my troubles as I do, and what she knows she knows properly. Together with her is a man who is even more to be trusted than she is or I: Bertelay the Old, the staunchest knight of his age in all the islands of the sea."[1]

With that, the chaplain stopped speaking; he handed the letter to the king and walked away downcast and dismayed. The king was dumbfounded by the news; all the others present were stunned and mute. Then the king looked at the young lady who stood before him, and said, "My lady, I have now heard your mistress's message, and if the letter was not read well, you can now make clear whatever is not so, for it seems you bear the heart and tongue of your lady. As for the knight, I would gladly meet the knight who is the staunchest and the most renowned in the world."

At that, the damsel stepped back, took the hand of the knight who had given her the letter, and led him up to the king, saying, "My lord, here is the knight whom my lady sends you to bear witness and to defend her cause."

The king looked at the knight, who struck him as quite old, for his hair was grey and white, and his face pale and lined and covered with scars, and his beard hung down onto his chest. Yet he had long arms and well-shaped shoulders; all his limbs were in fact so well made that you could not have imagined better. He was remarkably tall and robust and stood bolt upright and was more impressive than you could have expected such an old man to be.

"I must say, my lady," said the king, "this man is so remarkably advanced in age that he could surely never be involved in anything disloyal or treacherous."

"My lord," said the young lady, "you would say that even if you knew him well. But there is no need here for any proof of his worthiness, for God can tell easily enough who is a good man. But let me tell you what the letter doesn't speak of: the message that my lady sends through me. I believe you have understood that my lady's complaint is that you should be a loyal husband but are not. It is well known that, when you were crowned king of Britain, news came to you of King Leodagan of Carmelide, who was at that time the most valorous man in the world; he was at home on all the islands of the West and best maintained his knights in high esteem and in great honor.

"My lord the king's renown was great, but it was surpassed by what you heard of the great beauty and virtue of my lady his daughter, who was rightly the most esteemed of all young women. You said that you would not rest until you had seen why the king and his daughter were so admired in all lands. You left your land in the care of others and traveled to the kingdom of Carmelide disguised as a squire, as were the knights traveling with you. There you served my lord the king from Christmas to Pentecost, and that day you carved the peacock at the Round Table and earned the praise of the hundred fifty knights who sat there. Each was served his fill, and you thereby gained the most worthy lady alive, my lady the queen. And my lord the king gave you the noblest wedding gift ever given, the Round Table, which is honored by so many men of valor.

"After that, you took my lady to Logres, your city, and there she was wed, as the letter recounts, and that night you went to bed with her. But when you rose to go to the privy, my lady was betrayed and tricked and thrown out by

---

1 Presumably, the British isles.

the very people she trusted the most, and from then on you were coupled with that lady I see there for whom I have such dislike, that Guenevere who betrayed her mistress and threw her into prison and thinks she was killed there! But inasmuch as God was unwilling that the betrayal remain hidden, it has now come out in front of her. My lady, you see, escaped from prison by the will of God and with the help of this knight here; he became a robber for her sake and risked death to carry her out of the tower on his shoulders, which was very dangerous.

"Thus my lady was a long while in captivity, together with her attendants, until, thank God, her barons freed her and gave her back her land and her inheritance. If my lady wished, she could be married very handsomely, as no man under heaven, however highborn, would be stopped by birth or office from accepting her. But her feeling is that, if she loses you who are meant to be her true husband, she will give up wedlock altogether, for it seems to her that she would make no man a good wife but you, and you no woman a good husband but her; and if you were together, you would be a couple without peer, you the most worthy king and she the most worthy queen. That is why my lady urges you to acknowledge the faithful bond that you promised when you wed her, and to satisfy her claim against the woman who sought her doom and whom you have kept against God's will.

"If you do not agree, my lady forbids you, in God's name as in her own and her clan's, to keep from this time forward the noble gift that you received with her hand, that is, the Round Table. Send it back to her as well endowed with knights as when you received it, and take care that no Round Table ever again stand in your house, because it is such a lofty thing that there must not be more than one in all the world.

"To you, my lords called Knights of the Round Table, I say that you must give up that name until it is rightfully conferred on those who deserve the honor, for you might well come to such a pass that the proudest among you would be hard pressed to merit it.

"And you, my lord," she said to the king, "if you or any other person in your house should claim that my lady was not betrayed as you have just heard, I am ready to prove it either in your court or in another, right now or at some fixed time. The evidence will not be a bundle of lies or furnished without a trustworthy witness, but presented by a knight who heard and saw the whole affair. And whoever wants to gainsay him will have to know equally well the cause he tries to defend, for in so important a matter as this, that is how evidence and challenge must be treated."

When the young lady finished speaking, no one uttered a word, and the king was dumbfounded. He gazed upward and crossed himself again and again, astonished at what he had just heard. He was so distressed and so shamed by the damsel's charge that he almost took leave of his senses, and the look on his face made it plain that his heart was in turmoil.

"My lady," he said to the queen, "come forward. It is only right that we should hear you speak. Clear yourself! So help me God, if this young woman's accusation is true, you are more deserving of death than all other women who have ever sinned, and you have gulled us all into thinking you the most valiant lady in the world. You would be the falsest and the most disloyal, if it turned out true!"

At that, the queen stood up, showing no hint of fear, and the king and counts and other lords started toward her. But Sir Gawain stepped in front of her, his switch in hand and so overwrought with anger that it seemed red blood was about to gush from his face.

As the queen remained standing before the king, Sir Gawain took it upon himself to speak, saying to the young woman who had brought the news, "My lady, we want to know if your charge is made against my lady the queen, here present."

She answered, "Not against the queen, as I see no queen here—but against that lady over there, who betrayed her mistress and mine!"

"My lady is innocent, so help me God, of any betrayal," said Sir Gawain, "and she will be proven so! And I want you to know that you have almost driven me to behave as no other woman has ever made me do! If not for the shame it would bring to my lord even more than to me, I would make you realize that you have committed the greatest folly that you could have ever undertaken, for even if your story were sworn to by all the people in your country, it would still not be true!"

Sir Gawain went on, "My lord, here I am, ready to be my lady's champion against one knight or more, as you decide, and I am prepared to prove that she is not guilty of the betrayal she has been charged with, and that she is your wife and consort, rightly anointed and crowned as queen."

"That indeed sounds like a challenge, sir knight," said the young woman, "so it is only right that we should now be told your name."

He answered that his name was never hidden from any knight and certainly not from any maiden, and he said he was named Gawain.

That made the lady smile and say God keep him. "Now I feel better than before, knowing your name, because I know you to be such a noble knight and so loyal that you would not take the oath for the whole kingdom of Logres; and I know too that you would not for the whole world do battle after the oath. Still, many men receive more praise than they deserve, which is what I will soon see in whoever takes up the defense. Let anyone who does it beware! And even if you had more skill in battle than you have, you will soon be in hand-to-hand combat, if you dare take up the defense!"

Then the young lady took the hand of the knight named Bertelay the Old and led him up to the king, saying, "Bertelay, for your sake and your lady's, settle this matter in combat with Sir Gawain or another knight, if any there be bold enough to champion the accused against you!"

[King Arthur postpones the matter until Candlemas (2 February) when he will hold court at Bredigan, on the border between Ireland and Carmelide.]

77. Guenevere Is Confronted by Her Accusers; Arthur Is Captured and Succumbs to the Wiles of the False Guenevere

The truth is that King Leodagan of Carmelide had a seneschal whom he was very fond of and who was married to one of the most beautiful women in the world. The king fell in love with her, and the story tells that she had a beautiful daughter with him, the very woman who was now claiming the Round Table from Queen Guenevere and who was also named Guenevere. The two half-sisters looked so much alike that the people who brought them up could hardly tell them apart; and when Queen Guenevere left home to become King Arthur's bride, the other traveled with her and planned the very kind of betrayal now taking place.

She was stopped in time, however. People who became aware of her plan accused her of treason, but she ran away lest she be put to death and spent a long while in foreign lands. Then, urged on by Bertelay, the old knight who came to King Arthur's court, she undertook the deed after all, since he promised to help her in whatever ways he could, even putting his own life at risk. And so he took her back to the kingdom of Carmelide and gave everyone there to believe that she was Guenevere, the daughter of King Leodagan, and that the king had thrown her out in favor of the seneschal's daughter. The barons believed the story and, on the advice of the old man, acknowledged her as their lady. Bertelay had worked toward this end because of his bitterness toward King Arthur, who had once stripped him of his inheritance after a murder he had committed; King Arthur, though, did not remember it and knew nothing about it.

On Candlemas Day, once the king had heard Mass, which was fittingly high for this day that celebrates Our Lady, the young woman arrived with all the knights and advisors she could gather. This was not the one who had come earlier, but rather the woman who had sent that messenger to the king. She was gowned splendidly and had thirty young ladies with her who were dressed as elegantly as she. She came up to the king and spoke loudly enough to be heard by everyone.

"God save Guenevere, daughter of King Leodagan of Carmelide," she said, "and God confound all the foes of either sex that I have in this hall! King," she said, "I am called here today to denounce and prove to you the betrayal that I have suffered, as you know from my letter and my messenger; and I am ready to prove my case, as you will decide, either by a knight defending me in single combat or by all the people of my land, the land you stripped me of and drove me from, though I was your true wife and the daughter of the most noble king of Carmelide!"

At these words, Galehaut stood up and, with the king's leave, spoke in behalf of the queen, who had asked him to do so. "My lord," he said to the king, "we have heard what this lady asks; but it would be right for her to tell us in so many words whether she herself was the victim of the betrayal and who was the agent of it."

"Sir knight," said the lady, "I am the person who suffered the betrayal, and I add that the Guenevere whom King Arthur has until now considered his wife, was the agent of the betrayal. I am sure, moreover, that she is the woman whom I see over there!"

At that, the queen stood up and, coming before the king, stated that she had never had anything to do with such a scheme, "and I am ready," she said, "to defend myself before your court either by a knight engaged in single combat or by ordeal."

Then Galehaut called upon King Badermagu; he came up, and Galehaut asked him what he thought of the matter.

He answered, "My lord, this matter is so grave and so important that it must not be handled without thought and deliberation. And however the proof may be had, whether by battle or by ordeal, the question must first be judged by the present company. It is perfectly reasonable to look into this matter and be sure that this young lady will abide by the judgment of this court whatever it may bring her, whether honor or disgrace."

At that, the knight who had earlier offered to do battle stepped forward and said to the king, "My lord, my lady will ponder whether to accept or reject your judgment."

The king answered that he agreed.

Then the accuser withdrew with her advisors, and they spoke together at length. When they came back from their talks, the knight said to the king, "My lord, my lady asks you for a postponement until tomorrow. That is not too long a delay."

The king, with the approval of his barons, granted it, and the lady left the court with her retinue and rode as far away as she could that day.

That night, she took counsel with her barons, and the old knight Bertelay said to her, "My lady, if you accept the judgment of King Arthur, you may soon have grounds to regret it, because he would like to be sure tomorrow that you will abide by whatever his judgment entails. And I am sure that the judgment will be that, if the queen wants the ordeal, she may have it. If she goes through with it and is proved innocent, you will be put to death, because you are subject, if she is innocent of the betrayal, to the same punishment that would be meted out to her if she were shown to be guilty. And the judgment of the court will be in favor of the ordeal, even if it is not the right thing to do. Nor is it an easy thing to overturn a judgment handed down in front of all the barons; you would have to proceed by way of a champion in battle, and if a battle were granted you, you would not do too well.

"For these reasons, you need to think of another way out; and if you take any advice into account, I would like you to listen to mine more than any other, because once such an important project has been undertaken it must not be abandoned for fear of sin."

[Bertelay advises capturing King Arthur while he is out hunting, and this plan is put into action. They keep Arthur locked up, but the false Guenevere sleeps with him every night. Eventually, the king comes to believe that she is his wife. He returns to court and declares the queen to be an imposter. Bertelay tries to have her punished, but Lancelot intercedes. King Arthur hands the queen over to Lancelot and Galehaut. The three depart from the court, and Lancelot and the queen live together for two years in Galehaut's kingdom, Soirelois.]

80. The Imposture Is Revealed; the False Guenevere Dies; Arthur Repents and Is Reconciled First with Guenevere, Then with Lancelot

... Things reached the point where the pope who was then on the throne in Rome learned about it. He held it a grave offense that so important a man as the king of Britain should have cast aside his wife in disregard of the Holy Church. He ordered then that the vengeance of Our Lord make itself felt throughout the land where he had taken his first wife, until such time as they should be brought back together by the Church. In this way King Arthur's land was placed under interdiction for twenty-one months.

During that time, it happened that the king was at one of his castles in Britain together with a great number of knights as well as the queen and Bertelay the Old, who held considerable sway over the royal pair. The queen had so worked on the king with drugs that he could not oppose any wish of hers, and things had already gone so far that all the barons hated her. At the beginning of Advent, the king had held court at Caerleon, and the queen was there, since he took her along wherever he went, whether military marches, sieges, or tournaments, but he never slept with her except when he was staying in his own room. One time, after a quarrel with the barons, the queen withdrew to her quarters, and that night she lost all the strength in her limbs, so that she became paralyzed, except for her eyes, and her flesh began to rot from the feet up.

[Bertelay soon falls ill as well. To take his mind off his wife's sickness, King Arthur decides to go hunting. During the hunt he becomes hungry and finds a hermitage, where he is well received. After his meal, he gets so ill that he believes himself to be dying. He asks the hermit to hear his confession. The hermit refuses, saying that his soul is in a state of mortal sin, and will continue to be so until he takes back his true wife. About to die, the false Guinevere confesses the details of the substitution ploy to King Arthur and a group of witnesses. Bertelay confesses as well. Arthur is then reconciled with the queen.]

Appendix C: From The Knight with the Sword[1]

[*The Knight with the Sword* is an anonymous Old French verse romance of the late twelfth or early thirteenth century. The prologue cites Chrétien de Troyes's failure to write a romance devoted to Gawain and proposes to fill this void. Chrétien describes Gawain as a perfect knight but also pokes gentle fun at him, and the author of *The Knight with the Sword* writes in the same vein. Though the roles of knight and lady are reversed, the poem offers a number of interesting parallels to the bedroom scenes in fitt 3 of *Sir Gawain and the Green Knight*.]

If anyone loves entertainment and joy, let him come forward: listen, and hear an adventure which came to the Good Knight,[2] who upheld loyalty, prowess, and honor and never loved any cowardly, false or churlish man. I tell of Sir Gawain, who was more well bred and prized for his deeds of arms than anyone could describe. If someone wanted to relate all his good qualities and set them down briefly, he would never reach the end of it. Although I can't relate them all, still I shouldn't keep silent on that account, and not at least have my say. One may not reasonably reproach Chrétien de Troyes, in my opinion, who could tell stories of King Arthur and his court and retinue, which was praised and honored so much: he recounts the deeds of the others but never took any account of Gawain. He was too fine a man to forget. For this reason, I am pleased to be first to recount an adventure which happened to the Good Knight.

King Arthur was in his city of Cardueil one summer; he had with him the Queen and Gawain, Kay the Seneschal and Yvain, and only twenty of the others. Gawain was always moved by the desire to go out to entertain and amuse himself. He had his horse made ready, and dressed himself in courtly fashion: he fastened on spurs of gold over his cutaway hose of well-embroidered silken cloth. He had put on his breeches, extremely white and very delicate, and a short but ample shirt of finely pleated linen, and was wrapped in a fur-trimmed cloak: he was most elegantly attired.

Then he set out from the town, traveling straight along the road until he entered the forest. He heard the song of the birds which were singing very sweetly, listening to them for so long—there were plenty of them to hear—that he began to think about an adventure that had once come to him. He stayed that way for such a long time that he went astray in the forest and lost his way completely. The sun was setting and he began to get worried. It was starting to get dark when he finally emerged from this musing, and he had no idea where

---

1 From *Three Arthurian Romances: Poems from Medieval France*, trans. Ross G. Arthur, Everyman Library (London: J.M. Dent; Clarendon, VT: C.E. Tuttle, 1996), pp. 87–98, 104–05. Reprinted with permission of The Orion Publishing Group, London.
2 That is, Gawain.

he was: so he decided to turn back. He started along a cart-track which led him ever forward: the night was growing darker and darker, and he had no idea where to go.

Then he began to scan the road that lay before him and, through a clearing, he saw a large fire burning. He proceeded in that direction, expecting to find some man who would send him on his way, a woodcutter or a charcoal-maker. Next to the fire he saw a charger which had been tied to a tree. He drew nearer to the fire and saw a knight sitting by it; he greeted him at once: "May God who made the world and put the souls into our bodies, grant you His mercy, my dear lord."

"My friend," he replied, "may God protect you as well! But tell me where you are coming from, traveling alone at such an hour."

Gawain told him everything, the whole truth from beginning to end: how he had set out for entertainment, and then how he had gone astray in the forest because he had been so absorbed in his thoughts that he lost his way. The knight then offered to set him back on his road the next morning, quite willingly, provided he would stay with him and keep him company until that night had passed; this request was granted.

Gawain put down his lance and shield, dismounted from his horse, tied it to a little tree, and wrapped it in his mantle; then he sat down next to the fire. Then they asked each other how they had fared that day: Gawain told him everything and never stooped to lie to him, but the knight was false with him; he didn't tell him a single word of truth—you'll hear fully why he did so. When they had stayed awake a while, conversing about many different things, they fell asleep beside the fire.

At daybreak Sir Gawain woke first; then the knight woke up and said, "My house is very near here, two leagues away and no more; come there, I pray you, and you may be sure that you will soon receive friendly hospitality."

Then they mounted their chargers and took up their shields, lances, and swords; then they set out at once on a paved road. They hadn't traveled very far when they came out of the forest and were in open country. The knight spoke to him: "Listen to this, my lord," he said; "it is always proper and accepted behavior for a prudent and courtly knight who is bringing another along with him to send word ahead that his lodgings should be prepared, for if their arrival is not expected he might easily find something which might displease him. I have no one I can send there, as you can clearly see, except for myself. I hope it doesn't displease you if I ask you to travel along at your leisure while I ride on ahead in haste. Near an enclosure, straight ahead down in a valley, you will see my house." Gawain realized that what he said was reasonable and polite, so he traveled on quite slowly and the other man galloped quickly ahead.

[Gawain meets four shepherds who warn him that the knight has taken many men to his castle, but none have ever returned. Anyone who contradicts the knight's wishes is killed. Gawain refuses to be deterred from his journey.]

He saw a beautiful castle beside a large enclosure, up on a hillock, which had recently been refortified. He noticed that the moat was wide and deep, and in the courtyard in front of the bridge there were many rich outbuildings: never in all his life had Gawain ever seen anything more impressive, unless it belonged to a king or a prince. But I have no wish to linger over a description of these buildings, except to say they were very beautiful and fine. He came up to the tournament yard, but went right through the gate, passed right through the courtyard and arrived at the end of the bridge.

The lord of the castle rushed up to meet him, making a great show of pleasure at his arrival. A squire received his weapons, another took Gringalet, and a third removed his spurs. Then his host took him by the hand and led him across the bridge. They found a very beautiful fire in the hall in front of the tower with lovely couches around it, all covered in purple silk. They stabled his horse for him off to one side, where he could see it, and oats and hay were brought to it in great abundance. Gawain thanked him for all of this, for he didn't want to contradict him in anything.

"My dear lord," said the host, "your dinner is being prepared and you may be sure that the servants are hurrying to make it ready. Meanwhile you may amuse yourself: relax, and take things easy. If there is anything that displeases you, be sure to say so." Gawain said that the lodging was all arranged exactly to his wishes.

The lord went into the chamber to look for a daughter of his—in all the land there was no other young lady as worthy as she. I couldn't ever tell you all the beauty, or even half of it, with which she was endowed; but I do not wish to pass it over, so I will describe her in just a few words: Nature had gathered around her all the beauty and courtesy which ought to be pleasing for a human body. The host, who was no churl, took her by the right hand and led her into the hall.

As Gawain gazed upon her great beauty, he was almost overwhelmed, but nevertheless he jumped up. When she looked at Gawain, the young lady was even more amazed at his great beauty and his good manners. Nevertheless, most courteously and in a few brief words, he greeted her. Right away, the host offered her to Sir Gawain by the hand, and said to him, "May I present to you my daughter, if it doesn't displease you, for I have no more beautiful diversion to entertain and amuse you. If she is willing, she will surely be able to provide you with pleasing companionship. It is my will that she not be unwilling: there is such worth and discretion in you that if she were to fall in love with you she would have nothing but honor from it. As for myself, I grant you a gift, that I won't be a hindrance to you; rather, I command her, in your hearing, not to contradict you in anything."

Gawain thanked him politely for this, for he did not want to contradict him; the host then went to the kitchen at once to ask if they might dine soon.

Gawain sat down beside the maiden, most concerned about his host, for he feared him greatly. Nevertheless, he began to talk with the fair-haired young lady most courteously, and without a trace of incivility, saying neither too much nor too little to her. He conversed with her most discreetly, offering her his service politely and telling her about his feelings until she, who was both wise and worthy, recognized and understood that if it was agreeable to her he would love her more than anything. She did not know which to choose, whether to refuse him or accept him. She heard him speaking so courteously, and she saw that he was so well mannered, that she would have fallen in love with him if only she dared to open up to him. Yet not for anything would she consent to lead him on, since he wouldn't be able to take any more. She knew that she would be acting basely if she made him feel the pangs of love which she would never bring to a conclusion; but it was hard for her to refuse him because her heart was so drawn to him.

Then she spoke courteously to him. "My lord," she said, "I have heard my father forbid me to contradict you in anything. Now I do not know what to say to you, except that if I should consent to do what you desire, I would never bring it to a conclusion, and so I would have betrayed and killed you. I must warn you of one thing, and I tell you this in all good faith: you must be careful not to act basely. Whatever my father may say to you, good or bad, it would be disastrous for you to contradict him, for you would be killed on the spot: you'd be doomed if you give any sign that you know anything at all about this."

Now the host, who had gone to the kitchen, came back; the food was all ready, and he called for the water—but I don't want to dwell on all that. When they had washed, they sat down, and the servants spread the cloths over the beautiful white tablecloths, laid out the salt-cellars and the knives, then the bread, and then the wine, in cups of silver and pure gold. But I do not wish to linger over a description of every single course: they had plenty of meat and fish, roasted birds and venison, and they ate their fill most happily. The host was most insistent that Gawain and the maiden should drink, and so he told the young lady that she should urge the knight and said, "You may think very well of yourself that I should wish her to be your sweetheart." Gawain thanked him for this politely.

When they had eaten enough, the servants were prepared; some took away all the tablecloths and others brought them the water and the towel for drying. After dinner, the host said that he wanted to go out to inspect his woods, and asked Gawain to stay seated and amuse himself with the young lady. At the same time, he addressed Gawain, and told him—commanded him—not to go away before he returned. He gave orders to a servant that, if Gawain showed any indication, they should be ready to act at once.

Gawain, who was worthy and courtly, recognized that he had to remain, and that it could not be otherwise; so he told him at once that he had no desire to go, if he was willing to give him lodgings. The host mounted his charger and set out at top speed, going out to seek another adventure: he was quite certain about this one, for he had it closed up inside his wall!

Then the young lady took Gawain by the hand, and they sat down off to one side, in order to discuss how he might protect himself. She reassured him, sweetly and prettily, but she was distressed and undone because she did not know what plans her father had in mind. If she had known, she would have shown him some device by which he might escape: but her father would never tell her anything. He must take care not to contradict him, and so in that way he might be able to escape.

"Let it be," he said; "he won't do me any harm. He brought me into his house, and he has been very pleasant to me here. Since he has treated me well and honorably, I will never have any fear of him from now on, unless I see or learn some reason why I ought to be afraid of him."

"Then it's no use," she said. "The common man has a proverb and many people still repeat it: 'Praise the day in the evening when you see that it has ended well, and praise your host in the morning.' I hope that God will grant that you may take leave of your host joyfully and with no ill-will."

When they had conversed for a long time, chatting about this and that, the host returned to the castle. Gawain jumped up to meet him, hand in hand with the maiden, and they greeted him most politely. He told them that he had hurried back because he feared that if he delayed Gawain would have left already: that was why he didn't want to tarry.

It was growing dark, and the host asked the servants if he could have supper. "At your pleasure," said his daughter, "you may ask for wine and fruit, but nothing else would be proper, for you've already eaten plenty."

He ordered it at once. First they washed, and then the fruit was placed before them. The servants brought out an abundance of different kinds of wine. "Be of good cheer, my lord," he said to Sir Gawain, "and be certain of one thing: it often grieves and troubles me when I have a guest who doesn't enjoy himself and who doesn't say what he wants."

"My lord, you may be sure," said Gawain, "that I am delighted."

When they had eaten the fruit, the host ordered the beds to be made ready, and said, "I will lie in this room and this knight will lie in my bed. Don't make it up too narrow, though, for my daughter will lie with him. He is such a good knight that I think she will be well placed with him. She ought to be delighted with what has been granted to them." Both of them thanked him for it, and acted as if it pleased them greatly.

Now Gawain was very uncomfortable, for he was afraid that if he went to bed there, the host would have him cut to pieces, but he knew that if he contradicted him in his own house, he would kill him.

The host was eager to go to bed; he took Gawain by the hand and led him straight into the bedroom. The young lady with the fair complexion went in with him. The room was arrayed with tapestries, and twelve candles were burning there, set up all around the bed and shining very brilliantly. The bed was beautifully covered with costly quilts and pure white sheets. But I do not wish to linger over a description of all the splendor of the silken cloth from the Orient, from Palermo, and from Romagna[1] which decorated the room, or all the sables and furs, so I'll tell you everything in a word: anything that might be proper for a knight or to adorn the body of a lady, either in winter or in summer, all of it was there in profusion: there were many costly furnishings. Gawain was astonished at the wealth he saw.

The knight addressed him: "My lord," he said, "this room is very beautiful. You and this maiden will lie in it together, and there won't be anyone else. Close the door, young lady, and do his bidding; I know well that such folk have no need of a crowd. But I want to warn you about one thing: do not put out

---

1 Palermo and the Romagna were famous centers of silk production.

the candles, for I would be very angry at that. I have ordered this because I want him to see your great beauty when you are lying in his arms, so that he will have greater comfort, and I want you to see his fine body." Then he withdrew from the bedroom, and the maiden closed the door.

Sir Gawain lay down, and she came back to the bed and lay down beside him, naked: she didn't need to be asked. All night long she lay sweetly in his arms; he kissed and embraced her often, and he progressed so far that he was about to have his way with her when she said, "Please, my lord! It can't go any farther: I'm not here with you without a guard."

Gawain looked all around, but saw no living creature there. "My beauty," he said, "I ask you to tell me who is forbidding me to do what I desire with you."

"I'll tell you," she answered, "most willingly, all that I know. Do you see that sword hanging there, the one with the silver sword-knot and the pure gold hilt and pommel? This isn't just conjecture that you're about to hear me tell you, but something I've seen tested very well. My father loves it very much, for it has killed many good and worthy knights for him. You may be sure that it has killed more than twenty of them here alone—but I don't know where he got it from. No knight will ever come through this door and pull out alive. My father treats them most politely, but if he catches one in even the smallest fault he's sure to kill him. It is necessary to be on guard against baseness and to stick to the straight and narrow. He exacts his justice instantly if he catches him in any error: if a man acts so cautiously that he isn't caught in any wrong, he's sent to spend the night with me. Then he has come to his death. Do you know why no one gets out? If he gives any sign of the desire that has come upon him to do it to me, all at once that sword strikes him through the body. If he tries to go and grab it to get rid of it, it jumps out of the scabbard all by itself and strikes him right through the body. You may be certain that the sword is enchanted in some fashion, so that it always protects me in this way. You would never have been warned by me, but you are so courtly and wise that it would be a great pity and would cause me grief forever if you were killed on my account."

Now Gawain did not know what to do. Never before in all his life had he heard tell of such a threat, and he suspected that she might be saying this in order to protect herself, so that he would not take his pleasure with her. But on the other hand he considered that it could not be concealed or be kept from being known everywhere that he had alone lain beside her in her bed, with both of them naked, and just because of something she said, he had failed to take his pleasure: it's better to die with honor than to live a long time in shame.

"That's nothing, my beauty," he said. "Since I have come this far, I want to be your sweetheart now, and you really can't avoid it."

"Then you can't blame me," she said, "from now on."

He drew so close to her that she uttered a cry. The sword leaped out of its scabbard and struck a glancing blow to his side, cutting away a piece of his skin but not wounding him very much. It pierced right through the bedspread and all the sheets, as far as the mattress, and then it shot back into its scabbard.

Gawain was left quite stunned, and had lost his desire completely: he lay there beside her, totally amazed. "Stop, my lord!" she said, "By God! You thought that I said it because I wished to protect myself against you with such a pretext. I have certainly never said anything about this to any knight but you, and you may be sure that I'm astonished that you were not inevitably killed, right at the first stroke. By God, now lie in peace and from now on be careful not to touch me again in such a fashion! Even a wise man can readily undertake a thing which turns out badly for him."

Gawain was left there pensive and mournful, for he didn't know how to behave. If God should grant that he ever return to his own country, it could never be concealed, but would be known everywhere that he had lain all alone all night long with such a charming and beautiful maiden and he still had done nothing to her, though she had opposed him with nothing but the threat of a sword which was wielded by no one at all! He would be shamed forever if he escaped from her in that way!

Now the candles which he saw around him caused him great annoyance; they spread a great brightness by which he saw her great beauty: blonde hair and a broad forehead, delicate eyebrows, sparkling eyes, well-shaped nose, bright and fresh complexion, a small and laughing mouth, long and graceful neck, long arms and white hands, soft, full sides, and under the sheets, white and tender flesh! Her body was so graceful and well fashioned that no one could have found any cause for complaint in her.

He was no churl, and he drew closer to her very softly. He would have already been playing a certain game with her when the sword leaped out of the scabbard and attacked him once again: the flat of the sword struck his neck and he almost felt like a fool. But the sword wavered a little, turned towards his right shoulder, and cut off a slice of skin three fingers wide; it pierced the silken quilt, sliced off a piece of it, and then thrust itself back in its scabbard.

When Gawain realized he was wounded in the shoulder and the side, he saw that he couldn't bring it to the finish. He was very sad and didn't know what to do, frustrated that he had been checked.

"My lord," she said, "are you dead?"

"Young lady," he said, "I am not; but I grant you this gift for the rest of the night: you have a truce from me."

"My lord," she said, "by my faith, if it had been granted when it was first requested, things would be much better for you now."

Gawain was extremely disconcerted, and the young lady was too. Neither of them slept, but rather they stayed awake, in such sorrow, all that night until the dawn.

As soon as it was day the host rose quickly and promptly went to the bedroom. He was neither silent nor dumb, but called out very loudly, and the young lady hurriedly opened the door and then came back and lay down naked next to Gawain, and the knight followed along behind. He saw them both lying together peacefully, and asked them how they were.

Sir Gawain replied: "Very well, my lord, thank you."

When the knight heard him speaking so clearly, you may be sure that he was very sad, for he was very wicked and ill-tempered. "What!" he said, "Are you still alive?"

"By my faith," said Sir Gawain, "I am perfectly safe and sound. You may be sure that I've done nothing for which I ought to be put to death. If you should do me any harm or mischief in your own home for no reason, it would be wrong."

"What," he said, "so you're not dead? It disturbs me very much that you're alive."

Then he drew a little closer and saw clearly that the bedspread had been cut and the linens were stained with blood. "Vassal," he said, "tell me at once where this blood came from!"

Sir Gawain kept still, for he did not want to lie to him and he had no excuse by which he could conceal himself so that his host would not catch on. The host spoke again at once, saying, "Listen to this, vassal. It's pointless trying to hide it from me. You were trying to have your way with this young lady, but you could not bring it to the finish because of the sword which prevented it."

Sir Gawain said to him, "My lord, you are speaking the truth. The sword wounded me in two places but it didn't hurt me very much."

When the knight understood that Gawain had not been mortally wounded, he said, "My dear lord, you have arrived in a safe harbor. But tell me now, if you want to escape scot-free, your country and your name. You may well be of such a family, of such reputation and rank, that it will be necessary for me to fulfil your wishes: but I have to be completely sure."

"My lord," he said, "my name is Gawain and I am the nephew of good King Arthur. You may be certain of this, for I have never changed my name."

"By my faith," said the host, "I know well that in you the King has a fine knight; I wouldn't expect to hear of a better one! You have no peer from here to Majorca, nor could your equal be found in all the kingdom of Logres.[1] Do you know how I have tested all the knights in the world who go out in search of adventures? They could all have lain in this bed and they all would have had to die, one by one, until it happened that the best man of all should come. The sword was to make the choice for me, for it wasn't supposed to kill the best man when he came here. And now it has proven itself, for it has chosen you as the best. Since God has granted such honor to you, I don't know how I could find or select anyone more deserving of having my daughter. I give and grant her to you, and from now on you would be wrong to be on guard against me. And I grant to you, in all good faith and for all the days of your life, the lord-ship of this castle: do with it whatever you desire."

Gawain was delighted and joyful, and thanked him for it. "My lord," he said, "I am well rewarded with just the maiden: I am not interested in your gold or your silver or this castle."

[Gawain marries the maiden. After some time, the couple sets out for King Arthur's court; as they are about to leave, Gawain's wife asks that he bring along her favorite dogs, two beautiful greyhounds, which he does.

After traveling for a while in the woods, the couple is accosted by a fully armed knight who wishes to take away Gawain's wife. Since Gawain is wearing no armor, he asks that the other take off his mail. The knight refuses, instead proposing to let the

---

1 *From here to Majorca* means "anywhere"; Majorca is an island in the Mediterranean Sea. Logres is the conventional name for Arthur's kingdom (see note to line 691).

lady make the choice. Gawain, certain of his wife's love and loyalty, agrees. She, however, chooses the other knight. Upset at this betrayal, Gawain agrees to let her go. He sets off toward Arthur's court with the dogs.

Gawain's wife, however, refuses to go anywhere without her favorite dogs. Gawain now proposes a similar bargain to the earlier one, namely that the dogs should make the choice. When they choose Gawain, the knight attacks. Gawain kills him. His wife then protests that she only chose the other knight for fear that he would harm Gawain if she did not go along with him. Gawain refuses to believe her, and adds the following statement.]

"Such faith, such love, such nature one can often find in a woman: anyone who hopes to reap a different crop than he has sown in his land and anyone who hopes to find in a woman something other than her nature is a fool! They have always been this way, ever since God made the first one. The more a man takes pains to serve them, and treats them well and honors them, the more he repents at the end; the more he respects and serves them, the more he is vexed and the more he loses. This concern of yours did not arise to preserve my honor or my life, but came to you from quite another thing. The common man has a saying: 'At the end one sees how everything turns out.' If anyone finds woman false and deceitful and still cherishes, guards, and loves her, then may God never protect him! Now you can look after yourself."

He abandoned her there, all alone, and he never knew what happened to her.

He returned to his proper road, and thought a lot about his adventure. He traveled through the forest until at dusk he arrived in his country. His friends were delighted to see him, for they thought that they had lost him. He recounted his adventure, just as it happened, from beginning to end—and they were willing listeners—how at first it was fine and dangerous, and afterwards ugly and vexing because of the sweetheart he had lost, and then how he fought at great risk for the greyhounds: and so it all came to an end.

Appendix D: From Edward of Norwich, Second Duke of York, The Master of Game[1]

[Edward of Norwich (1373-1415) was the grandson of King Edward III and master of game for King Henry IV. Sometime before 1413, when the latter died, Edward wrote a treatise about hunting, dedicating it to the future Henry V. While largely a translation of the immensely popular *Livre de Chasse* (1387-89) by Gaston III, count of Foix, *The Master of Game* changes many passages, omits others, and adds several chapters that give evidence for distinctively English hunting practices. With its emphasis on proper terminology, arcane rituals, and proscribed practices, *The Master of Game* describes hunting as the quintessential aristocratic pastime. *Sir Gawain and the Green Knight* showcases its intimate acquaintance with the hunting lore; though the poem was almost certainly written some time before *The Master of Game*, the latter still serves as an excellent guide to the world of hunting as depicted in its verses.]

Chapter I: The Prologue

... Furthermore I will prove by sundry reasons in this little prologue, that the life of no man that useth gentle game and disport be less displeasable unto God than the life of a perfect and skilful hunter, or from which more good cometh. The first reason is that hunting causeth a man to eschew the seven deadly sins. Secondly men are better when riding, more just and more understanding, and more alert and more at ease and more undertaking, and better knowing of all countries and all passages; in short and long all good customs and manners cometh thereof, and the health of man and of his soul. For he that fleeth the seven deadly sins as we believe, he shall be saved, therefore a good hunter shall be saved, and in this world have joy enough and of gladness and of solace, so that he keep himself from two things. One is that he leave not the knowledge nor the service of God, from whom all good cometh, for his hunting. The second that he lose not the service of his master for his hunting, nor his own duties which might profit him most. Now shall I prove how a hunter may not fall into any of the seven deadly sins. When a man is idle and reckless without work, and be not occupied in doing some thing, he abides in his bed or in his chamber, a thing which draweth men to imaginations of fleshly lust and pleasure. For such men have no wish but always to abide in one place, and think in pride, or in avarice, or in wrath, or in sloth, or in gluttony, or in lechery, or in envy. For the imagination of men rather turns to evil than to good, for the three

---

1 From Edward, Duke of York, *The Master of Game*, ed. William Adolf Baillie-Grohman and Florence Baillie-Grohman (London: Chatto & Windus, 1909), pp. 4-13, 35, 46-53, 64-67, and 188-95. The Baillie-Grohmans's edition modernizes the Middle English spelling. The editors' italics, used to indicate where the English text diverges from the French original, have been omitted.

enemies which mankind hath, are the devil, the world and the flesh, and this is proved enough.

Nevertheless there be many other reasons which are too long to tell, and also every man that hath good reason knoweth well that idleness is the foundation of all evil imaginations. Now shall I prove how imagination is lord and master of all works, good or evil, that man's body or his limbs do. You know well, good or evil works small or great never were done but that beforehand they were imagined or thought of. Now shall you prove how imagination is the mistress of all deeds, for imagination biddeth a man do good or evil works, whichever it be, as before is said. And if a man notwithstanding that he were wise should imagine always that he were a fool, or that he hath other sickness, it would be so, for since he would think steadfastly that he were a fool, he would do foolish deeds as his imagination would command, and he would believe it steadfastly. Wherefore methinks I have proved enough of imagination, notwithstanding that there be many other reasons the which I leave to avoid long writing. Every man that hath good sense knoweth well that this is the truth.

Now I will prove how a good hunter may not be idle, and in dreaming may not have any evil imaginations nor afterwards any evil works. For the day before he goes out to his office, the night before he shall lay him down in his bed, and shall not think but for to sleep, and do his office well and busily, as a good hunter should. And he shall have nothing to do, but think about all that which he has been ordered to do. And he is not idle, for he has enough to do to think about rising early and to do his office without thinking of sins or of evil deeds....

[The various aspects of his craft keep the hunter too busy to be idle.]

... Wherefore I say that such an hunter is not idle, he can have no evil thoughts, nor can he do evil works, wherefore he must go into paradise. For by many other reasons which are too long to write can I prove these things, but it sufficeth that every man that hath good sense knoweth well that I speak the real truth.

Now shall I prove how hunters live in this world more joyfully than any other men. For when the hunter riseth in the morning, and he sees a sweet and fair morn and clear weather and bright, and he heareth the song of the small birds, the which sing so sweetly with great melody and full of love, each in its own language in the best wise that it can according that it learneth of its own kind. And when the sun is arisen, he shall see fresh dew upon the small twigs and grasses, and the sun by his virtue shall make them shine. And that is great joy and liking to the hunter's heart. ...

[The different aspects of hunting give great pleasure to those who practice it.]

... Wherefore I counsel to all manner of folk of what estate or condition that they be, that they love hounds and hunting and the pleasure of hunting beasts of one kind or another, or hawking. For to be idle and to have no pleasure in either hounds or hawks is no good token. For as saith in his book Phœbus the Earl of Foix that noble hunter, he saw never a good man that had not pleasure in some of these things, were he ever so great and rich. For if he had need to go to war he would not know what war is, for he would not be accustomed to travail, and so another man would have to do that which he should. For men say in old saws: "The lord is worth what his lands are worth." And also he saith in the aforesaid book, that he never saw a man that loved the work and pleasure of hounds and hawks, that had not many good qualities in him; for that comes to him of great nobleness and gentleness of heart of whatever estate the man may be, whether he be a great lord, or a little one, or a poor man or a rich one.

Chapter III: Of the Hart and His Nature

... As of the hinds some be barren and some bear calves, of those that be barren their season beginneth when the season of the hart faileth and lasteth till Lent. And they which bear calves, in the morning when she shall go to her lair she will not remain with her calf, but she will hold (keep)[1] him and leave him a great way from her, and smiteth him with the foot and maketh him to lie down, and there the calf shall remain always while the hind goeth to feed. And then she shall call her calf in her language and he shall come to her. And that she doeth so that if she were hunted her calf might be saved and that he should not be found near her....

Chapter VI: Of the Wild Boar and His Nature

A wild boar is a common beast enough and therefore it needeth not to tell of his making,[2] for there be few gentlemen that have not seen some of them. It is the beast of this world that is strongest armed, and can sooner slay a man than any other. Neither is there any beast that he could not slay if they were alone sooner than that other beast could slay him, be they lion or leopard, unless they should leap upon his back, so that he could not turn on them with his teeth. And there is neither lion nor leopard that slayeth a man at one stroke as a boar doth, for they mostly kill with the raising of their claws and through biting, but the wild boar slayeth a man with one stroke as with a knife, and therefore he can slay any other beast sooner than they could slay him. It is a proud beast and fierce and perilous, for many times have men seen much harm that he hath done. For some men have seen him slit a man from knee up to the breast and slay him all stark dead at one stroke so that he never spake thereafter.

They go in their love to the brimming[3] as sows do about the feast of St. Andrew,[4] and are in their brimming love three weeks, and when the sows are cool the boar does not leave them.

---

1 These parenthetical insertions were added by the editors.
2 Form, appearance.
3 State of being in rut or heat.
4 30 November.

He stays with them till the twelfth day after Christmas, and then the boar leaves the sows and goeth to take his covert, and to seek his livelihood alone, and thus he stays until the next year when he goeth again to the sows. They abide not in one place one night as they do in another, but they find their pasture for (till) all pastures fail them as hawthorns[1] and other things. Sometimes a great boar has another with him but this happens but seldom. They farrow[2] in March, and once in the year they go in their love. And there are few wild sows that farrow more than once in the year, nevertheless men have seen them farrow twice in the year.

Sometimes they go far to their feeding between night and day, and return to their covert[3] and den ere it be day. But if the day overtakes them on the way ere they can get to their covert they will abide in some little thicket all that day until it be night. They wind[4] a man as far as any other beast or farther. They live on herbs and flowers especially in May, which maketh them renew their hair and their flesh. And some good hunters of beyond the sea say that in that time they bear medicine on account of the good herbs and the good flowers that they eat, but thereupon I make no affirmation. They eat all manner of fruits and all manner of corn,[5] and when these fail them they root in the ground with the rowel of their snouts which is right hard; they root deep in the ground till they find the roots of the ferns and of the spurge and other roots of which they have the savour (scent) in the earth. And therefore have I said they wind wonderfully far and marvellously well. And also they eat all the vermin and carrion and other foul things. They have a hard skin and strong flesh, especially upon their shoulders which is called the shield. Their season begins from the Holy Cross day in September[6] to the feast of St. Andrew for then they go to the brimming of the sows. For they are in grease[7] when they be withdrawn from the sows. The sows are in season from the brimming time which is to say the twelfth day after Christmas till the time when they have farrowed. The boars turn commonly to bay on leaving their dens for the pride that is in them, and they run upon some hounds and at men also. But when the boar is heated,[8] or wrathful, or hurt, then he runneth upon all things that he sees before him. He dwelleth in the strong wood and the thickest that he can find and generally runneth in the most covered and thickest way so that he may not be seen as he trusteth not much in his running, but only in his defence and in his desperate deeds. He often stops and turns to bay, and especially when he is at the brimming and hath a little advantage before the hounds of the first

---

1   As the editors note, the meaning of this phrase is unclear; the source has "acorns and beachmast" instead of hawthorns.
2   Give birth.
3   Lair, den.
4   Detect by scent.
5   Grains.
6   14 September.
7   Well fattened.
8   Inflamed.

running, and these will never overtake him unless other new hounds be uncoupled to[1] him.

He will well run and fly from the sun rising to the going down of the sun, if he be a young boar of three years old. In the third March counting that in which he was farrowed, he parteth from his mother and may well engender at the year's end.

They have four tusks, two in the jaw above and two in the nether jaw; of small teeth speak not I, the which are like other boar's teeth. The two tusks above serve for nothing except to sharpen his two nether tusks and make them cut well and men beyond the sea call the nether tusks of the boar his arms or his files, with these they do great harm, and also they call the tusks above gres[2] for they only serve to make the others sharp as I have said, and when they are at bay they keep smiting their tusks together to make them sharp and cut better. When men hunt the boar they commonly go to soil and soil in the dirt and if they be hurt the soil is their medicine. The boar that is in his third year or a little more is more perilous and more swift and doth more harm than an old boar, as a young man more than an old man. An old boar will be sooner dead than a young one for he is proud and heavier and deigneth not to fly, and sooner he will run upon a man than fly, and smiteth great strokes but not so perilously as a young boar.

A boar heareth wonderfully well and clearly, and when he is hunted and cometh out of the forest or bush or when he is so hunted that he is compelled to leave the country, he sorely dreads to take to the open country and to leave the forest, and therefore he puts his head out of the wood before he puts out his body, then he abideth there and harkeneth and looketh about and taketh the wind on every side. And if that time he seeth anything that he thinks might hinder him in the way he would go, then he turneth again into the wood. Then will he never more come out though all the horns and all the holloaing of the world were there. But when he has undertaken the way to go out he will spare for nothing but will hold his way throughout. When he fleeth he maketh but few turnings, but when he turneth to bay, and then he runneth upon the hounds and upon the man. And for no stroke or wound that men do him will he complain or cry, but when he runneth upon the men he menaceth, strongly groaning. But while he can defend himself he defendeth himself without complaint, and when he can no longer defend himself there be few boars that will not complain or cry out when they are overcome to the death.

They drop their lesses (excrements) as other swine do, according to their pasture being hard or soft.

But men do not take them to the curée[3] nor are they judged as of the hart or other beasts of venery.

A boar can with great pain live twenty years; he never casts his teeth nor his tusks nor loses them unless by a stroke. The boar's grease is good as that of other tame swine, and their flesh also. Some men say that by the foreleg of a

---

1   Unleashed upon.
2   French *grés*, grinders.
3   The ceremonial rewarding of the hounds.

boar one can know how old he is, for he will have as many small pits in the forelegs as he has years, but of this I make no affirmation. The sows lead about their pigs with them till they have farrowed twice and no longer, and then they chase their first pigs away from them for by that time they be two years old and three Marches counting the March in which they were farrowed. In short they are like tame sows, excepting that they farrow but once in a year and the tame sows farrow twice. When they be wroth they run at both men and hounds and other beasts as (does) the wild boar and if they cast down a man they abide longer upon him than doeth a boar, but she cannot slay a man as soon as a boar for she has not such tusks as the boar, but sometimes they do much harm by biting. Boars and sows go to soil gladly when they go to their pasture, all day and when they return they sharpen their tusks and cut against trees when they rub themselves on coming from the soil. What men call a trip of tame swine is called of wild swine a sounder, that is to say if there he passed a five or six together.

Chapter VIII: Of the Fox and His Nature

The fox is a common beast and therefore I need not tell of his making and there be but few gentlemen that have not seen some. He hath many such conditions as the wolf, for the vixen of the fox bears as long as the bitch of the wolf bears her whelps, sometimes more sometimes less, save that the vixen fox whelpeth under the earth deeper than doth the bitch of the wolf. The vixen of the fox is a saute (in heat) once in the year. She has a venomous biting like a wolf and their life is no longer than a wolf's life. With great trouble men can take a fox, especially the vixen when she is with whelps, for when she is with whelps and is heavy, she always keeps near her hole, for sometimes she whelpeth in a false hole and sometimes in great burrows and sometimes in hollow trees, and therefore she draweth always near her burrow, and if she hears anything anon she goeth therein before the hounds can get to her. She is a false beast and as malicious as a wolf. The hunting for a fox is fair for the good cry of the hounds that follow him so nigh and with so good a will. Always they scent of him, for he flies through the thick wood and also he stinketh evermore. And he will scarcely leave a covert when he is therein, he taketh not to the plain (open) country for he trusteth not in his running neither in his defence, for he is too feeble, and if he does, it is because he is (forced to) by the strength of men and hounds. And he will always hold to covert, and if he can only find a briar to cover himself with, he will cover himself with that. When he sees that he cannot last, then he goeth to earth the nearest he can find which he knoweth well and then men may dig him out and take him, if it is easy digging, but not among the rocks. If greyhounds give him many touches and overset[1] him, his last remedy, if he is in an open country, will be that he vishiteth gladly (the act of voiding excrements) so that the greyhounds should leave him for the stink of the dirt, and also for the fear that he hath.

---

1 Assail, overcome.

A little greyhound is very hardy when (if) he takes a fox by himself, for men have seen great greyhounds which might well take a hart and a wild boar and a wolf and would let the fox go. And when the vixen is assaute,[1] and goeth in her love to seek the dog fox she crieth with a hoarse voice as a mad hound doth, and also when she calleth her whelps when she misses any of them, she calleth in the same way. The fox does not complain (cry) when men slay him, but he defendeth himself with all his power while he is alive. He liveth on all vermin and all carrion and on foul worms. His best meat that he most loveth are hens, capons, duck and young geese and other wild fowls when he can get them, also butterflies and grasshoppers, milk and butter. They do great harm in warrens of coneys and of hares which they eat, and take them so gynnously (cunningly) and with great malice and not by running. There be some that hunt as a wolf and some that go nowhere but to villages to seek the prey for their feeding. As I have said they are so cunning and subtle that neither men nor hounds can find a remedy to keep themselves from their false turns. Also foxes commonly dwell in great hedges or in great coverts or in burrows near some towns or villages for to evermore harm hens and other things as I have said. The foxes' skins be wonderfully warm to make cuffs and furs, but they stink evermore if they are not well tawed.[2] The grease of the fox and the marrow are good for the hardening of sinews. Of the other manners of the fox and of his cunning I will speak more openly hereafter. Men take them with hounds, with greyhounds, with hayes[3] and with purse-nets, but he cutteth them with his teeth, as the male of the wolf doth but not so soon (quickly).

Chapter XXXVI: Of the Ordinance and the Manner of Hunting when the King Will Hunt in Forests or in Parks for the Hart with Bows and Greyhounds and Stable

The Master of the Game should be in accordance with the master forester or parker where it should be that the King should hunt such a day, and if the tract be wide, the aforesaid forester or parker should warn the sheriff of the shire where the hunting shall be, for to order sufficient stable,[4] and carts, also to bring the deer that should be slain to the place where the curées at huntings have been usually held. And thence he should warn the hunters and fewterers[5] whither they should come, and the forester should have men ready there to meet them, that they go no farther, nor straggle about for fear of frightening the game, before the King comes. And if the hunting shall be in a park all men should remain at the park gate, save the stable that ought to be set ere the King comes, and they should be set by the foresters or parkers. And early in the morning the Master of the Game should be at the wood to see that all be ready,

---

1 In heat.
2 Cured.
3 Nets.
4 The station supplied with both hunters and dogs, usually situated on the periphery of the hunting ground.
5 Huntsmen who care for hounds and manage them in the hunt.

and he or his lieutenant or such hunters that he wishes, ought to set the greyhounds and who so be teasers[1] to the King or to the Queen, or to their attendants. As often as any hart cometh out he should when he passes blow a mote[2] and recheat,[3] and let slip to tease it forth, and if it be a stag, he should let him pass as I said and rally to warn the fewterers what is coming out. And to lesser deer should no wight let run, and if he hath seen the stag, not unless he were commanded. And then the master forester or parker ought to show him the King's standing if the King would stand with his bow, and where all the remnant of the bows would stand. And the yeoman for the King's bows ought to be there to keep and make the King's standing, and remain there without noise, till the King comes. And the grooms that keep the king's dogs and broken greyhounds should be there with him, for they belong to the yeomen's office, and also the Master of the Game should be informed by the forester or parker what game the king should find within the set,[4] and when all this is done, then should the Master of the Game worthe (mount) upon (his) horse and meet the King and bring him to his standing and tell him what game is within the set, and how the greyhounds be set, and also the stable, and also tell him where it is best for him to stand with his bow or with his greyhounds, for it is to be known that the attendants of his chamber and of the queen's should be best placed, and the two fewterers ought to make fair lodges of green boughs at the tryste[5] to keep the King and Queen and ladies, and gentlewomen and also the greyhounds from the sun and bad weather. And when the King is at his standing or at his tryste, whichever he prefers, and the Master of the Game or his lieutenant have set the bows and assigned who shall lead the Queen to her tryste, then he should blow the three long motes for the uncoupling. And the hart hounds and the harriers that before have been led by some forester or parker thither where they should uncouple, and all the hounds that belong to both the mutes (packs) waiting for the Master of the Game's blowing. Then should the sergeant of the mute of the hart-hounds, if there be much rascal[6] within the set, make all them of office, save the yeomen of the horse, hardel[7] their hounds, and in every hardel two or three couple of hounds at the most suffice. And then to stand abroad in the woods for relays, and then blow three motes to the uncoupling. And then should the harrier uncouple his hounds and blow three motes and seek forth saying loud and long, "hoo sto ho sto, mon amy, ho sto"[8] and if they draw far from him in any unruly manner he should speak to them in that case as when he seeketh for the hare. And as oft as he passes within the set from one quarter to another, he should blow drawing, and when he is passed the boundary of the quarter, and entered into

---

1 Light greyhounds used to rouse deer.
2 Note or series of notes blown on hunting horn.
3 Hunting call on a horn that summons together, or calls back, the hounds.
4 The area of the forest or park wherein the hunt takes place.
5 The place where the hunter awaits the game to be shot.
6 Deer too small or young to be hunted.
7 Tie the couples of hounds together.
8 *Ho sto, mon amy*: "ho now, my friend."

a new quarter, he should blow three motes and seek forth, but if so be, that his hounds enchace anything as he wishes, and if any hound happen to find of the King's (game), he should hue to him by his name and say loud: "Oyez a Bemond,[1] oyez-oyez, assemble, assemble," or what the hound is named, "assemble, assemble" and jopey[2] and rally. And if it be an hart and any of the hart hounds meet with it they should blow a mote and rechace[3] and relay,[4] and go forth therewith all rechacing among. And if it come to the bows or to grey-hounds and be dead, he should blow the death when he is come thither, and reward his hounds a little, and couple them up and go again to his place. And if the hart has escaped he should no longer rechace, but blow drawing and draw in again, and in the best way that he can, take up his hounds and get in front of them. And after that the harriers have well run and well made the rascal void,[5] then should the sergeant and the berners[6] of the hart hounds blow three motes, the one after the other and uncouple there where they suppose the best ligging (lair) is for a hart, and seek as before is said; unless it be the season when the hart's head is tender, then he shall use some of the aforesaid words of seeking to the hounds: "Le doulez, mon amy, le doulez, le doules,"[7] and if his hounds find anything do as before is said, and if it be a hart, do as above is said, as he may know by his fues[8] or by men that meet with him. And if it be ought else, the berner ought to blow drawing, and who meeleth with him (the hart), call to them, and the berner should say "Sto arere[9] so how, so how." And if the lymerer[10] meet withal, or see by the fues that it is an hart, he should sue thereto till he be dead. If it go to the greyhounds and if it go to the bows, and be smitten anon, as he findeth blood he should take up his hounds and lead them thence and reward them a little, and then if he escape out of the set, he should reward his hounds, and take them up and go again to the wood and look if he may meet with anything. And as often as he meeteth and findeth, or his hounds run on a fresh scent, do as before is said. And one thing is to be known, that the hart-hounds should never be uncoupled before any other, unless a hart be readily harboured, and that he may be sued to and moved with the lymer, or else that they be uncoupled to a herd of great male deer at the view, namely within a set in a forest or in a park, there where there is a great change of rascal. And that is the cause why the other hounds shall be first uncoupled to make the rascal void, for small deer will sooner leave their covert than will a great hart, unless it be a hind that hath her calf in the wood, and hath lately calved. And when the rascal is thus voided then the hart hounds are

---

1   Listen to Bemond.
2   Shout, cry.
3   Call to summon back the hounds.
4   Summon fresh dogs to replace hounds grown weary in the hunt.
5   Leave the area of the hunt.
6   The attendants in charge of hounds.
7   *Le doulez, mon amy*: "Softly, my friend."
8   Tracks, spoor.
9   *Sto arere*: "Draw back."
10   The attendant in charge of scent hounds.

uncoupled and they find the great old wily deer that will not lightly void, and they enchace him well and lustily and make him void both to bows and to greyhounds, so that they fully do their duty. And all the while that the hunting lasteth should the carts go about from place to place for to bring the deer to the curée. And there should the server of the hall be to arrange the curées, and to lay the game in a row, all the heads one way—and every deer's feet to the other's back. The harts should be laid in two or three rows (by themselves) according to whether there be many or few, and the rascal in the same way by themselves, and they should take care that no man come within the curées till the King come, save the Master of the Game. And when the covert is well hunted and cleared, then should the Master of the Game come to the King to know if he would hunt any more. And if the King say yea, then shall the Master of the Game if the greyhounds or bows or stable need not to be removed, blow two long motes for the hounds, and forthwith blow drawing with three long motes that men should stand still, and the hunters may know that they should come to a new seeking with their hounds. And when the hounds be come there where they should uncouple blow three long motes and do and seek and blow, as is before said. And if the bows and greyhounds and stable should be removed, then should he blow a mote and stroke, without the mote in the middle, for to draw men together, and thereby may men know that the king will hunt more ere he go home. And when men come together, then should the Master of the Game see to the placing of the King and of the Queen and of the bows and of the greyhounds and of the stable, as I have said here before, and the hunters to their seeking, and of all other things do in the same manner as I have said. And if the king will hunt no more, then should the Master of his Game, if the King will not blow, blow a mote and stroke with a mote in the middle and the sergeant or whoso bloweth next him, and no man else, should blow the first mote but only the middle, and so every man as oft as he likes to stroke, if they have obtained that which they hunted for. And the middle mote should not be blown save by him that bloweth next the master. And thereby may men know as they hear men stroke homeward whether they have well sped or not. And this way of stroking should serve in the manner I have rehearsed for all hunting save when the hart is slain with strength.

Glossary

[Words are listed under the form that occurs most commonly in the *Gawain* manuscript. Variant spellings have been recorded where they are likely to trouble the reader; *i/y* variation (*abide*, *abyde*), doubled consonants (*after*, *aftter*), and final *-e* (*als*, *alse*) are generally not indicated.

Where it is relevant, the reader is referred to notes; e.g., "(793n)" references the note to line 793 in this Broadview text.

When a word has a range of possible meanings that would fit the context, I have listed some of these. Readers are encouraged to further explore word meanings by looking them up in the *Middle English Dictionary* (*MED*), available online at <http://quod.lib.umich.edu/m/mec/>; to facilitate this, corresponding *MED* headwords are listed in brackets when words are spelled significantly differently in the poem.]

Abbreviations

adj.	adjective	*n.*	noun
adv.	adverb	*num.*	numeral
arch.	architecture	*obl.*	oblique
art.	article	*pa. t.*	past tense
aux.	auxiliary	*phr.*	phrase
compar.	comparative	*pl.*	plural
conj.	conjunction	*pp.*	past participle
def.	definite	*pres. p.*	present participle
indef.	indefinite	*refl.*	reflexive
inform.	informal	*sing.*	singular
interj.	interjection	*superl.*	superlative
iron.	ironic, ironically		

a *interj.* ah.
a, an *art.* a, an, one.
abataylment *n.* battlement (790n).
abelef *adv.* obliquely, slantwise (2487n).
abide *v.* endure, await, stop.
abloy *pp.* carried away (with joy), reckless (for joy).
abode *n.* delay.
abof *see* **above(n)**
aboute *adv.* and *prep.* around, on every side, about, attendant upon.
above(n) *adv.* and *prep.* above, overhead, higher up.
absolucioun *n.* absolution.
achaufed *v. pa. t.* warmed.
acheve *v.* gain, finish, accomplish; succeed in reaching, find.
acole *v.* embrace.
acorde *v.* agree to or with; reconcile; make common cause with; be suitable for, match.
adoun *adv.* down.
after *adv.* and *prep.* after; later; behind; in the same manner, likewise; along.

afyaunce *n.* faith, trust, reliance [affīaunce].

agayn *adv.* and *prep.* in return, back, again.

age *n.* age; **first age** young adulthood (54n).

aghlich *adj.* terrifying, terrible [ei(e)slīch].

aght, aghte *see* **oghe**

agreved *pp.* aggrieved, distressed, incensed.

al *see* **all**

alce *see* **als**

alder *adj. compar.* older; **the alder** the older one.

alder-truest *adj. superl.* most true, the soundest of all.

alder *n.* prince.

algate *adv.* nevertheless.

Al-hal-day *n.* All Saints' Day (536n).

all *adj., adv., pron.* and *conj.* all, everyone, everything; entirely, wholly; although.

aloft *adv.* and *prep.* up, up high, on top; **stryde alofte** mount; **halde alofte** keep up.

alone *adv.* alone.

alosed *pp.*, esteemed, valued, praised.

als *adv.* also; as.

also *adv.* also, likewise.

alther-grattest *adj. superl.* the very largest [alder-].

alvisch *adj.* elvish, supernatural, otherworldly [elvish].

alway *adv.* always.

alyve *adj.* living, in existence.

am *v.* am.

amende *v.* improve.

among *prep.* among.

amount *v.* signify, mean, amount to.

an *see* **a, an**

anamayld *pp.* enameled [ameled].

and *conj.* and; but, yet; if (1009n).

anele *v.* pursue.

angard *n.* arrogance; **angardes pryde** overweening pride.

anger *n.* harm.

ani *see* **any**

anious *adj.* difficult, troublesome, dangerous.

answare *v.* answer.

any *pron.* and *adj.* any, anyone, any at all, any whatever.

anyskynnes *adj.* any kind [anī-kin(nes)].

apende *v.* belong, be fitting or appropriate to.

apere *v.* present oneself.

apert *adj.* plain, obvious, clearly visible.

apparayl *n.* (martial) gear, furnishing, adornment.

aproche *v.* approach.

aquoyntaunce *n.* intimate acquaintance, familiarity; **kallen hym of aquoyntaunce** ask to get to know him (better), seek to be better acquainted with him [aqueinta(u)nce].

ar *v.* are.

aray *n.* array, outfit, garments.

arayde *pp.* prepared, organized; **wel arayed** well-built.

are *v. see* **ar**

are *adv.* before [ēr].

arered *pp.* retreated, fled, drawn back [arrēren].

arewes *see* **arwes**

arme *n.* arm.

armed *pp.* armed, equipped for battle.

armes *n. pl.* weapons and (esp.) armor; the practice of arms, chivalry; coat of arms.

arn *see* **ar**

arounde *adv.* at the edges.

arsoun *n.* saddlebow, the uptilted front or back of a saddle.

art *n.* art.

art *v.* (you, *sing.*) are.

arwe *adj.* afraid [argh].

arwe *n.* arrow.

arwe *v.* be afraid, grow faint, be intimidated [arghen].

aryght *adv.* correctly, properly, as is fitting.

as *adv.* and *conj.* as, like; as if; as far as; since, because; when; **as help me** so help me.

as-swythe *adv.* at once [swīth(e)].

as-tyt *adv.* quickly, right away [tīte].

asaute *see* **assaut**

asay *n.* assay, testing of quality of meat (1328n).

asay *v. see* **assay**

ascrye *v.* shout.

ask *v.* ask, ask for, ask of, demand, request.

aske *n.* ash [asshe].

askyng *n.* request, demand.

asoyle *v.* absolve.

aspye *v.* find out, discover.

assaut *n.* armed attack, assault (upon).

assay *v.* test, tempt, learn through testing.

asyngne *v.* assign [assīgnen].

at *prep.* and *adv.* at, in, next to, near; from; with; according to.

athel *adj.* noble, excellent, famous.

atle *v.* intend; aim (a blow) at.

atwaped *pp.* escaped.

atyred *pp.* attired, dressed.

aumayl *n.* enamel [amal].

auncian *adj.* aged, old; wise, venerable (2463n).

aune *see* **awen**

aunt *n.* aunt.

aunter *n. see* **aventure**

aunter *v.* venture, dare.

auter *n.* altar; **the heghe auter** altar on which Eucharist is offered.

auther *see* **other**

avanters *n. pl.* neck entrails.

ave *n.* Ave Maria prayer.

aven *see* **awen**

aventayle *n.* mail neck and shoulder guard, attached to helmet (608n).

aventure *n.* adventure, knightly exploit, marvel.

aventurus *adj.* adventurous, bold, daring, marvelous.

avinant *adj.* agreeable, seemly, worthy, proper [avenaunt].

avyse *v.* look at; contrive, devise.

away *adv.* away [awei].

awen *adj.* and *pron.* own [ouen].

awenture *see* **aventure**

awharf *v. pa. t.* turned away.

awles *adj.* fearless.

awyse *see* **avyse**

ax *n.* axe (289n, 477n).

ay *adv.* always, every time, in each instance.

ayayn *see* **agayn**

ayaynes *prep.* against, toward.

ayle *v.* ail [eilen].

ayther *pron.* each one, both, either (of two); **ayther other** one another, each the other [either].

aywhere *adv.* everywhere, on all occasions [iwhēr].

bade *see* **bid**

bak *n.* back.

bak-bon *n.* back-bone, spinal column.

baken *pp.* backed.

bald(e)ly *adj.* boldly, vigorously.

bale *n.* death, sorrow, torment, misery.

balé *n.* belly, abdomen [belī].

balw *adj.* big, stout, bulging, rounded [balgh].

bande *n.* band [bōnd].

baner *n.* pennant hanging from trumpet.

barayne *adj.* barren, unpregnant.

barbe *n.* barb of arrow; cutting edge of axe.

barbican *n.* fortified outer enclosure or bailey (793n).

bare *adj.* and *adv.* open, uncovered, unarmed; mere, just; firmly, unqualifiedly; **thre bare mote** three single long notes (1143n) [bār].

barely *adv.* without fail, without exception [bārlī].

baret *n.* battle, conflict; trouble, misery, woe [barat(e)].

bargayn *n.* bargain, business transaction, agreement.

barlay *interj.* used to confirm a pledge (296n).

barre *n.* ornamental strip or bar.

barred *pp.* ornamented with bars.

bastel *n.* turret.

batayl *n.* battle, single combat (277n).

bate *n.* battle, fighting.

bathed *pp.* soaked, steeped.

bauderyk *n.* baldric; sash, girdle, or shield-strap worn over shoulder.

bawemen *n. pl.* bowmen, hunters with bows [boue].

bay *n.* bay; **byde at the bay** stand at bay, face pursuing dogs or hunters.

bay *v.* bark at, bring animal to bay, hold at bay (1603n).

bayn *adj.* obedient, submissive, accommodating.

bayst *v. pa. t.* be dismayed [baishen].

baythe *v.* agree; grant.

be *prep. see* **bi**

be *v.* be.

beau *adj.* good, fair, fine.

becom *see* **bicome**

bed, bedde *n.* bed.

bedde *see* **bid**

beddyng *n.* bedding.

bede *v.* offer, bid, command; *see also* **bid**

bed-syde *n.* bedside.

befalle *see* **bifalle**

beholde *see* **biholde**

belde *n.* courage, strength.

bele *adj.* fair, fine, good; **bele cher** good company.

belle *n.* bell.

belt *n.* belt.

belted *pp.* belted on.

beme *n.* beam.

ben *see* **be**

bench *n.* bench.

bende *n.* band, stripe (2506n).

bende *v. pa. t.* and *pp.* bent; caused.

bene *adj.* and *adv.* good, fine; pleasantly.

bene *v.* see **be**

bent *n.* field, tract of uncultivated ground, battle-field (1599n).

bent-felde *n.* battle-field.

ber *n.* beer.

berd *n.* beard.

berdles *adj.* beardless.

bere *n.* bear.

bere *v.* bear, carry, lift up; cast; **bere lyf** be alive; **bere on** urge on, thrust upon; **born open** thrown open.

berw *n.* mound, barrow [bergh].

beseche *v.* beseech, entreat, request, ask for, pray for [bisēchen].

best *adj.* and *adv. superl.* best; finest, greatest, highest ranking; most valuable, most excellent, most desirable; **the best** the best (knights); **of the best** of the best sort, kind, or quality, in the best way.

best *n.* beast.

bete *v.* beat, ornament, decorate, embroider.

bette *pp.* kindled [bēten].

better *adj.* and *adv. compar.* better; **the better** the better, all the better; **lere other better** better or worse.

bever-hued *adj.* beaver-colored, reddish-brown.

beverage *n.* drink, esp. one used to seal a bargain (1112n).

bewté *n.* beauty, handsomeness [beautē].

bi *prep.* by, near, beside, when, with, (near) to; **bi that** *adv.* by that time, by the time that, when, after.

bicause *prep.* because.

bicome *v.* become; come to; be fitting, suitable, becoming for.

bid *v.* bid, command, urge, offer, ask, request.

bide *v.* abide, endure, await, remain ; **bydes the (his) baye** stands at bay.

bifalle *v.* befall, happen.

bifor(n)e *adv.* and *prep.* before, in front of, ahead of, in preference to; in front, earlier.

big *adj.* strong; **bigger** *compar.* bigger.

big(g)e *v.* build, settle, establish.

bigines *see* **bigynne**

bigly *adv.* vigorously, fiercely.

bigog *interj.* by God [Gog].

bigraven *pp.* engraved.

bigyled *pp.* beguiled, tricked, deceived, led astray.

bigynne *v.* begin, found, establish, start.

bihalden *see* biholde

bihinde *adv.* behind, in back, worse.

biholde *v.* behold, look at; **biholde** indebted; **bihalden** obliged, duty-bound.

bihove *v.* behoove, be obligated, be inescapable; **me bihoves** I must, I am compelled to.

bihynde *see* **bihinde**

biknowe *v.* confess, reveal; **beknowen of** absolved from (2385n).

bilyve *adv.* quickly, immediately, at once.

bischop *n.* bishop.

biseme *v.* be becoming, suited to, fitting for; appear, seem to be (2035n).

bisides *adv. see* **bisyde(s)**

bisied *see* **busy**

bisinesse *see* **busynes**

bisoght *see* **beseche**

bisyde *adv.* and *prep.* beside, near, next to.

bisydes *adv.* on the sides, around.

bit *n.* bit, blade, cutting edge.

bite *v.* bite, pierce.

bitte *see* **bit**

bitwene *adv.* and *prep.* between, among.

bityde *v.* happen, befall, come to.

biwyled *pp.* deluded, tricked.

biyonde *prep.* beyond, across.

blake *adj.* black.

blame *n.* blame, offense; **for blame** as reproof.

blame *v.* blame.

blande *n.* mixture, mingling; **in blande** side-by-side [in-bland].

blande *pp.* adorned.

blasoun *n.* shield.

blaste *n.* gust of wind; blowing of trumpet.

blaunmer, blaunner *n.* ermine, expensive fur that is white with black spots.

blawyng *n.* blowing.

ble(e)aunt *n.* costly silk fabric; tunic made of costly silk.

blede *v.* bleed.

blenche *v.* turn, dodge, retreat; **blenched ayayn** turned around, dodged aside.

blende *v. pa. t.* and *pp.* mixed; **blode ... blende in his face** blood suffused his face.

blended *pp.* blinded by, led astray by (2419n).

blenk *v.* blink, shine, glisten [blenchen].

blent *see* **blende**

blered *pp.* bleary, watery or rheumy (eyes).

blessed *v. pa. t.* blessed; **blessed hym** crossed himself.

blessyng *n.* blessing.

blew *see* **blowe**

blis *see* **blys**

blithe *see* **blythe**

blod *n.* blood (89n).

blodhound *n.* blood-hound.

blonk *n.* horse, steed [blank(e)].

blossum *n.* blossom [blosme].

blowe *v.* blow; bloom (1362n) [blouen].

blubred *v. pa. t.* seethed, bubbled, foamed [bloberen].

blue *adj.* blue (1928n) [bleu].

bluk *n.* torso, trunk [blok(ke)].

blunder *n.* strife, trouble [blõnder].

blusch *n.* gleam [blish].

blusche *v.* look at, glance at, behold; **blusschande** shining [blishen].

blyce, blykke *v.* shine, gleam, glitter, glisten.

blynne *v.* cease, stop.

blys *n.* joy, happiness, prosperity, pleasure.

blysful *adj.* joyful, glad, pleasing.

blythe *adj.* and *adv.* happy, merry, lovely, shining; graciously.

blythely *adv.* cheerfully, happily, merrily; with pomp, splendidly.

bobbaunce *n.* pride, ostentation, arrogance.

bobbe *n.* branch, twig, cluster.

bode *n.* command; offer.

bode *v. see* **bide**

bodé, bodi, body *n.* body.

boerne *see* **borne**

boffet *see* **buffet**

boghe *n.* bow, branch.

bok *n.* book; **Brutus bokes** chronicles or histories of Britain, named after Brutus (2523n).

bold *adj.* and *adv.* bold, brave, fearless; as *n.* bold men; boldly.

bole *n.* tree.

bolne *v.* swell.

bonchef *n.* cheerfulness, happiness, gaiety.

bone *adj.* good.

bone *n.¹* boon, request.

bone *n.²* bone.

bonk *n.* hill, ridge, mountain; slope, hill-side; bank, shore, coast [bank(e)].

bor *n.* boar.

borde *n.¹* band, strip of embroidered stuff.

borde *n.²* table.

borde *n.³ see* **bourde**

borelych *adj.* large, huge, stout, excellent.

borgh *see* **burgh**

born, borne *see* **bere** *v.*

borne, boerne *n.* stream.

bornyst *see* **burnyst**

bost *n.* clamor.

bot *adv.*, *conj.*, and *prep.* but, except, except that; nothing but, only, merely; but rather, however [but].

bot, bote *v. see* **bite**

both *adj.*, *pron.*, and *conj.* both; also, as well.

bothem *n.* bottom [botme].

botoun *n.* button.

boun *adj.* ready, prepared, dressed; bound.

bounden *see* **bynde**

bounté, bountee *n.* virtue, merit.

bourde *n.* jest; **in bourde** in a jesting manner.

bourded *pa. t.* jested, joked, spoke wittily.

bourdyng *n.* jesting.

boure *n.* bower, bedroom, chamber, a lady's chamber.

bout *prep.* without.

bowe *v.* go, move, travel, depart; turn (to); come together [bŏuen].

boweles *n. pl.* bowels, intestines, internal organs [bŏuel].

boyle *v.* boil, bubble; **byled** boiled.

brace *n.* arm-plates, pieces of armor covering arms.

brache, brachete *n.* hunting dog, hound, small scenting hound (1143n).

brad *pp.* roasted [brēden].

bradde *v. pa. t.* reached [brēden].

brath *adj.* fierce, violent, angry [brōth].

braunch *n.* branch.

brawden *see* **brayde**

brawen, brawne *n.* flesh, meat.

brayde *v.* pull, draw out; take; throw; **brayde doun** lowered; **brayden, brawden** *pp.* linked, embroidered, embellished [breiden].

braye *v.* bray.

brayn *adj.* mad, insane.

brayn *n.* brain (89n).

braynwod *adj.* fierce, maddened, frenzied [brain].

bred *n.* bread.

bredden *v. pa. t.* lived, dwelled [brēden].

bredes *n. pl.* planks, boards.

breke *v. pa. t.* broke; cut open; passed, was disclosed; foamed.

brem *adj.* and *adv.* fierce, big, loud, rugged; quickly, fiercely, completely.

bremely, bremly, bremlych *adv.* fiercely, quickly, loudly, gloriously.

brenne *v.* burn; cook; **brende golde** pure gold, gold refined by fire.

brent *adj.* steep, high [brant]; *see also* **brenne**

bresed *pp.* shaggy.

brest *n.* breast (955n).

brether *n. pl.* brothers [brōther].

breve *v.* declare, say, tell; announce (the presence of game); record in writing.

britne, britten *v.* cut, divide; smash; kill.

brod *adj.* and *adv.* broad, wide, large; with eyes wide open, staringly.

broght *see* **bryng**

broke *n.* brook, stream.

bronde *n.* sword; cinder [brānd].

brothe *adj.* eager, angry, fierce.

brothely *adv.* angrily, fiercely.

brotherhede *n.* brotherhood.

broun *adj.* bright, shining; brown (618n).

browe *n.* brow.

bruny *n.* byrnie, coat of mail [brinie].

brusten *pp.* burst, shattered [bresten].

bryd *n.* bird.

brydel *n.* bridle.

bryge, brygge *n.* drawbridge.

bryght *adj.* bright, brilliant, vivid in color; **bryghter** *compar.* brighter; **bryghtest** *superl.* most beautiful.

brymme *n.* water.

bryné *see* **bruny**

bryng *v.* bring.

buffet *n.* blow, stroke.

bugle *n.* bugle.

bukk *n.* buck (1159n).

bull *n.* wild bull.

bult *see* **bylde**

bur *n.* blow; strength.

burde *n.* lady, maid, woman; the Virgin Mary (1283n) [bīrde].

burde *v.* should, ought, must, deserve.

burgh *n.* castle, city.

burn *n.* man, knight [bērn].

burnyst *adj.* burnished.

burthe *n.* birth.

busk *n.* bush.

busk *v.* hurry, hasten, prepare, dress, make.
busy *v.* (make, get) busy [bisī].
busyly *adv.* busily, intently, zealously [bisīlī].
busynes *n.* exertion, insistence, solicitude [bisīnesse].
buttoks *n. pl.* buttocks.
buurne *see* **burn**
by- *see also* **bi-**
bye *v.* buy.
byght *n.* fork of the hind legs.
byhode *see* **bihove**
bykenne *v. in* **bykennen to Kryst** commend to Christ.
bylde *v.* build, dwell.
byled *see* **boyle**
bynde *v.* bind, tie, fasten.
bysily *see* **busyly**
bytoknyng *n.* sign, symbol.

cace *n.* case; situation, circumstance; suggestion, question [cās].
cach *v.* catch, take, seize, get, receive, acquire; lift; urge on; **kaght to** caught hold of (2508n) [cacchen].
cacher *n.* hunter (1139n) [caccher].
cakled *pp.* clucked, cackled.
calle *v.* call; invite; bay; **kallen ... of aquoyntaunce** ask to get to know.
can *see* **con** *v.²* *aux.*
capados *n.* hooded cape.
caple *n.* horse (capel).
care *n.* care, anxiety, hardship, sadness, fear.
care *v.* care, be concerned or anxious about.
carnel *n.* battlement.
carole *n.* ring-dance accompanied by song (43n).
carp, karp *n.* speech, words, mention, report.
carpe, karpe *v.* say, speak.
caryes *see* **cayre**
case *see* **cace**
cast *n.* manner; scheme; belt; blow.
cast *v.* cast; strike; pull on; hold up; establish; consider; **kest of** raised by; **cast unto** reply to; **of kest** untied.
castel *n.* castle.
cause *n.* reason.
cave *n.* cave.
cavelacioun *n.* caviling, quibbling, pretend argument.
cayre *v.* go, travel, depart, return.
cemmed *pp.* combed [kēmben].
cercle *n.* metal band encircling a helmet.
chace *n.* hunt.
chace *v.* hunt.
chaffer *n.* business transaction, trading, deal, bargain [chaffāre].
chalkwhyt *adj.* chalk-white.
chamber, chambre *n.* private room; chamber, bedroom [chaumbre].
chamberlayn *n.* attendant, valet [chaumberlein].
chapayle, chapel(le) *n.* chapel.
chaplayn *n.* chaplain, priest officiating in a chapel [chapelein].

charcole *n.* charcoal.

charg *n.* importance; **no charg** never mind, it does not matter.

charge *v.* charge, demand; put on.

chargeaunt *adj.* troublesome, burdensome.

charre *v.* take, turn back, return.

charre *n.* task, matter, chore [chār].

charyté *n.* charity, benevolence, beneficence.

chastyse *v.* curb, bring under control, restrain (1143n).

chasyng *n.* hunting, the hunt.

chaunce *n.* something that happens, event; fortune, fate; adventure, errand.

chauncely *adv.* luckily, by good fortune.

chaunge *v.* change; exchange.

chaunsel *n.* chancel (946n).

chauntré *n.* singing or chanting of mass.

chef *adj.* chief, main.

chefly *adj.* promptly, quickly; mainly, first of all.

chek(ke) *n.* gain, success; blow; ruin, ill fortune.

cheke *n.* cheek.

cheldes *see* **scheld**

chemné *see* **chymné**

chepe *n.* bargain, price, purchase; **goud chepes** good price, favorable purchase (1939n).

chepe *v.* obtain (1277n).

cher, scher *n.* expression, behavior, mood, good spirits, show of affection; **bele chere** good company; **chaunged his cher** changed his position, turned his body.

cheryche, cheryse *v.* greet, welcome, entertain.

ches *see* **chose**

chesly *adv.* solicitously (850n) [chīslī].

chevalrous *adj.* chivalrous.

chevalry *n.* knighthood, knightly conduct, code of chivalry.

cheve *v.* get, win, bring about, end; **cheve to** reach.

chevely *see* **chefly**

chevicaunce, chevisaunce *n.* winnings; fulfillment, completion.

cheyer *n.* chair.

childgered *adj.* boyish, light-hearted; childish (89n) [chīld].

chorle *n.* peasant; one who does not belong to nobility or clergy [chērl].

chose *v.* choose, select; choose or take one's way, go; venture [chēsen].

chylde (*pl.* **chylder**) *n.* child.

chymbled *pp.* wrapped up.

chymné *n.* fireplace, chimney.

chyn, chynne *n.* chin.

chyne *n.* backbone.

clad *v. pa. t.* and *pp.* dressed, covered.

clamberande *pres. p.* clustering; **clambred** *pp.* clustered.

clanly *adv.* exactly, completely [clēnlī].

clannes *n.* moral purity, integrity, sinlessness; sexual purity, chastity, celibacy (653n).

clater *v.* clatter, crash, splash, fall with a loud noise.

clayme *v.* claim.

clene *adj.* and *adv.* clean, pure, bright, elegant; morally clean; brightly, neatly, handsomely, properly, flawlessly, perfectly, fully, wholly (146n).

clenge *v.* cling, remain; **clenges adoun** shrinks away.

clepe *v.* call.

cler *adj.* bright, pure, beautiful, fair, sparkling; **the clere** the beauty, the beautiful woman.

clergye *n.* clergy.

clerk, klerk *n.* cleric; scholar, master (of magic).

cleve *v.* crack, split open.

clomben *v. pa. t.* climbed.

close *v.* close, enclose, contain; **closed fro** devoid of.

closet *n.* private pew.

clothe *n.* cloth, tablecloth, bedcover, cloth cover.

cloud, clowd *n.* cloud.

cloyster *n.* enclosure, castle.

cluster *n.* cluster.

clyff *n.* cliff, hill, large rock.

cnokes *v.* deliver a blow, knock [knokken].

cofly *adv.* quickly.

coghed *v. pa. t.* coughed, cleared his throat.

coke *n.* cock.

colde *adj.* cold; disconsolate; the cold; the (cold) ground; **in hot and colde** whatever the circumstance.

cole *v.* relieve, cool.

colour *n.* color; complexion.

com *v.* come.

comaunde *v.* command; commend [commaunden].

comaundement *n.* command, order [commaundement].

comfort *n.* delight, pleasure, assurance.

comfort *v.* amuse, entertain; comfort.

comly, comlych *adj.* and *adv.* comly, fair, elegant, beautiful; beautiful woman; beautifully, courteously, gracefully; **comloker** *compar.* more comely; **comlokest** *superl.* comeliest, most handsome, fairest.

comlyly *adv.* courteously, gracefully, graciously.

comme *see* **com**

compas *n.* figure.

compast *v. pa. t.* considered.

compayny, compeyny *n.* company, companionship, retinue.

con *v.¹* know, know how, be able, be versed in.

con *v.² aux.* do, begin to do [can].

conable *adj.* excellent, accomplished [cŏvenāble].

concience *n.* mind, conscience.

confessed *pp.* absolved by having made confession.

conquest *n.* conquest, victory.

constrayne *v.* compel, force [constreinen].

contray *n.* country, open country, territory [cŏntrē(e)].

conveyed *v. pa. t.* accompanied, escorted.

conysaunce *n.* heraldic device, emblem.

coolde *see* **colde**

coproun *n.* capital, top.

corbel *n.* raven.

corner *n.* corner.

cors *n.¹* course of a meal [cŏurs].

cors *n.²* person, body (1237n).

corsed *pp.* cursed.

corsedest *superl. adj.* most accursed.

corsour *n.* steed [cŏursēr].

cort *see* **court**

cort-fere *n.* companion at court.

cortays *adj.* courteous, refined, graceful [cŏurteis].

cortaysly *adv.* graciously, courteously (775n).

cortaysye, courtaysye *n.* courtesy, politeness; manners and refinement appropriate to "court."

cortyn *n.* curtain [curtīn(e)].

cortyned *pp.* curtained.

corvon *pp.* carved.

cosse *n.* kiss.

cost *n.*[1] quality, condition, state, cirumstance; conduct, behavior; terms of bargain; *pl.* manners, virtues.

cost *n.*[2] coast.

cosyn *n.* cousin, kinsman (372n).

cote *n.* tunic; surcoat (see next); coat, skin.

cote-armure *n.* surcoat, garment displaying heraldic arms worn over armor (586n).

cothe *see* **quoth**

coundue *v.* lead [conduiten].

coundut *n.* carol [cŏndūt].

counse(y)l *n.* counsel, advice, help.

countenaunce *n.* behavior; custom; mien, expression, glance.

couple *n.* leash.

cource *see* **cors**

court *n.* court.

courtaysye *see* **cortaysye**

couthe *adj.* shown, revealed, manifest.

couthe *v. see* **con** *v.*[1]

couthly *adv.* familiarly.

covardise *see* **cowardise**

covenaunt *n.* covenant, contract, agreement, promise (393n).

coverto(u)r *n.* blanket, cover, quilt; horse-cloth.

covetyse *n.* covetousness, greed, avarice (2374n) [cŏveitīse].

cowardise *n.* cowardice [cŏuardīse].

cowpled *v. pa. t.* leashed together.

cowter *n.* elbow armor [cŏutēr].

cowthe *see* **con** *v.*[1]

coynt, koynt *adj.* exact, precise; skillfully made; marvelous, excellent, wonderful.

coyntly, coyntlych, koyntly *adv.* neatly, gracefully; cunningly.

crabbed *adj.* disagreeable, wicked.

craft *n.* skill; purpose, business; way, conduct; events, affairs.

crafty *adj.* well-made.

craftyly *adv.* expertly, skillfully.

cragge *n.* crag, steeply projecting mass of rock (1421n).

crakkande *pres. p.* thundering, crashing.

crakkyng *n.* blaring.

crathayn *n.* knave, base and contemptible person [crachŏun].

crave *v.* crave, desire, ask for, claim.

crede *n.* creed.

creped *v. pa. t.* crept.

cresped *pp.* curled.

crest *n.* mountaintop.

crevisse *n.* hollow, crevice.

criande *see* **crye**

Cristmasse *n.* Christmas.

croked *adj.* crooked, defective.

cropore, cropure *n.* crupper, cover for haunches of horse [crŏupēr].

cros *n.* cross; **cros Kryst** Christ's cross.

croun *n.* crown, top of head, head [coroune].

crowe *v.* crow.

croys *n.* cross.

crue *see* **crowe**

cry, kry *n.* cry, call, shout.

crye, krye *v.* lament, cry, call out, shout; **criande** crying, calling out (64n).

Crystemas, Crystenmas *see* **Cristmasse**

cum, cum(m)en *see* **com**

cumaundes *see* **comaunde**

cumly *see* **comly**

curious *adj.* exquisite, finely made, costly.

dabate *see* **debate** *n.*

dale *n.* dale, valley.

dalt, dalten *see* **dele**

daly *v.* converse, flirt (1253n).

dalyaunce *n.* conversation (1012n).

dame *n.* lady.

dar *v.* dare [durren].

dare *v.* tremble, be afraid.

daunsed *v. pa. t.* danced.

daunsyng *n.* dancing.

dawed *v. pa. t.* would be worth.

day *n.* day.

daylyeden *see* **daly**

daylyght *n.* daylight.

daynté *adj.* agreeable, pleasing [deinté].

daynté, dayntye *n.* dainty, delicacy; worth, praise; **hit were littel daynté** it would reflect poorly on me; **al in daynté** politely; **hade daynté of him** admired him (1890n) [deinté].

debate *n.* debate, argument, resistance.

debate *v.* debate, argue.

debonerté *n.* humility, kindness, courtesy, graciousness.

dece *n.* dais, raised platform [deis].

ded *adj.* dead.

dede *n.* deed, action, behavior, task, pursuit.

defence *n.* defense, defend by fighting; **ferde with defence** resisted, proceeded defensively.

defende *v.* defend, protect; prohibit.

degré *n.* rank.

dele *n.* see **devele**

dele *v.* deal, mete out, give, accord; receive; hold; talk; **dalten untyghtel** reveled; **dalt drury with** had a love-affair with.

delful *adj.* cruel, grievous, sorrowful [dolful].

deliver *adj.* full; **iif I deliver had bene** if I had exerted all my strength.

deliverly *adv.* quickly.

delyver *v.* bring; complete.

demay *see* **dismay**

deme *v.* deem, judge, believe, decree; agree, decide; describe (1082n).

denes *adj.* Danish (2223n) [Dānish].

dep *see* **depe**

depart *v.* depart; separate.

departyng *n.* parting.

depaynt(ed) *pp.* depicted [dēpeinten].

depe *adj.* and *adv.* deep.

deprece *v.¹* subjugate, conquer; press [dēpressen].

deprece *v.²* release [dēprecen].

deprese *see* **deprece** *v.¹*

der, dere *n.* deer.

dere *adj.* dear, splendid, noble, great, excellent, pleasant, festive, precious; **the dere** the dear man (Gawain); **derrest** *superl.* noblest.

dered *pp.* hurt.

derely *adv.* dearly, graciously, courteously, pleasantly, splendidly, in courtly fashion.

derf *adj.* noble, strong; severe, painful.

derfly *adv.* promptly.

derk *adj.* dark.

derk *n.* darkness.

derne *adj.* intimate (1012n).

derrest *see* **dere**

derve *see* **derf**

dervely *see* **derfly**

derworthly *adv.* sumptuously, honorably, reverently [dēre-wŏrthlī].

des *see* **dece**

deserve *v.* deserve.

destiné, destyné *n.* destiny, fate.

desyre *v.* desire.

dethe *n.* death.

devaye *v.* refuse.

deve *v.* overcome, strike down.

devele, dele *n.* devil.

devised *pp.* told.

devocioun *n.* worship.

devys *n.* in *phr.* **a devys** of the best.

dewe *n.* dew.

deye *v.* die [dīen].

diamaunt *n.* diamond.

dich *n.* ditch, trench, moat (786n).

did, didden *see* **do**

dight *v.* prepare, make ready; dress; ornament, array; decree, appoint, grant; go.

dille *adj.* stupid, foolish, dull [dil].

diner *n.* first big meal of the day; a feast.

dint *see* **dynt**

discever, discover *v.* uncover, reveal.

disch *n.* dish.

discrye *v.* see; describe [dēscrīven].

disert *n.* merit, worthiness [dēsert].

dismay, demay *v.* become alarmed, be frightened, dismayed; **demay yow never** never be dismayed, don't be frightened.

displayed *pp.* displayed, revealed.

displese *v.* displease, be displeased, offend.

disport *n.* conduct, behavior; entertainment, relaxation, amusement, pastime.

dispoyled *pp.* undressed.

disserve *see* **deserve**

disstrye *v.* destroy [dēstroien].

dit *pp.* locked [ditten].

do *v.* do; make; cause; give; **do way** do away with, stop.

doel *n.* grief, expression of grief, lamenting [dōl].

does *n. pl.* does, female fallow deer (1159n).

dogges *n. pl.* dogs.

doghter *n.* daughter.

doghty *adj.* bold, brave, valiant, strong in battle [doughtī].

dok *n.* trimmed hair (of tail and forelock).

dole *n.* part [dōl].

dom *n.* judgment; judicial decision, right.

domesday *n.* Last Judgment.

don, done *see* **do**

donkande *pres. p.* moistening [danken].

dor *n.* door.

dos *n. see* **does**

dos *v. see* **do**

doser *n.* ornamental cloth used as wall hanging.

dote *v.* be out of one's mind; grow silly, upset, deranged, crazed.

doub(b)le *adv.* doubly, twice, with twice the amount.

double *adj.* double (786n).

double-felde *adv.* two servings, twice the normal portion [dŏuble-fōld].

doun *adv.* down; **up and doun** up and down, back and forth.

dounes *n. pl.* hills.

doute *n.* fear, doubt, perplexity.

douteles *adv.* without doubt, certainly.

douth *n.* company of people, nobleman's retinue.

dowelle *v.* remain, linger, tarry [dwellen].

downes *see* **dounes**

draght *n.* drawbridge.

draveled *v. pa. t.* muttered.

drawe *v.* draw, pull, shut; draw back; **drawen on dryye** hold back, keep from leaving; **draw chaffer** do trading, strike a bargain.

drechch *n.* trouble; delay [drecch(e)].

drede *n.* fear, dread.

dredles *adj.* fearless.

dreme *n.* dream.

dreped *pp.* killed.

dres(se) *v.* arrange, put in place, ornament, adorn, dress; prepare; serve, attend to; go, get up.

drey *see* **dryye** *adj.* and *adv.*

dreyly *adv.* without pause [drīlī].

drive *see* **dryve**

droght *n.* dry weather [drŏught(e)].

dronken *see* **drynk** *v.*

drope *v.* drop, fall in drops [droppen].

droupyng, drowping *n.* uneasy sleep; grief, anxiety.

drow, drowen *see* **drawe**

drury *n.* love, flirtation, love-making; **dalt drury** had a love-affair [drūerīe].

dryftes *n. pl.* snowdrifts.

Dryghtyn *n.* Lord, God, Christ [Drihten].

drynk *n.* drink.

drynk *v.* drink.

dryve *v.* pursue, press forward, drive, drive away; to bring, lead toward; enclose; pass (time); **drive doel** voice grief, make lament.

dryye *adj.* and *adv.* heavy, severe; hardy; impassive; fiercely [drī(e)].

dryye *n.* length of time; **drawen on dryye** hold back, keep from leaving [drī(e)].

dryye *v.* endure, suffer, abide.

dubbed *pp.* adorned, clad.

dublet *n.* doublet, man's tight-fitting garment covering body from neck to hips or thighs [dŏublet].

duches *n.* duchess.

dughty *see* **doghty**

duk *n.* duke.

dulful *see* **delful**

dunt *see* **dynt**

durst *see* **dar**

dust *n.* dust.

dut *n.* joy; **drive dut** make merry.

dut(te) *v.* fear, be afraid.

dyght *see* **dight**

dyn *n.* din, clamor, noise, sound [dine].

dynge *v.* strike, beat; **dynge to dethe** beat to death, kill.

dyngne *adj.* noble, worthy of great reverence [digne].

dynt, dyntt *n.* blow.

dyye *see* **deye**

eft *adv.* again, once more; later, thereafter; then.

eft(er)sones *adv.* thereafter; immediately after.

egge *n.* edge, blade.

eke *adv.* likewise.

elbowe *n.* elbow.

elde(e) *n.* age; generation (844n).

elles *adv.* and *conj.* else; also; other; provided that.

elnyerde *n.* ell (45 inches).

em, eme *n.* uncle.

enbaned *pp.* fortified with projecting masonry (790n).

enbelyse *v.* adorn [embelishen].

enbrauded, enbrawded, enbrawden *pp.* embroidered [embrouden].

enclyne *v.* bow, bend head or body forward.

ende *n.* end, ending, outcome.

endeles *adj.* endless.

endite *v.* consign, indict, prosecute; **to dethe endite** consigned him to death.

endured *pp.* endured.

enfoubled *pp.* covered, veiled.

Englych *n.* the English.

enker-grene *adj.* vivid green.

enmy *n.* enemy, adversary [enemī].

enn(o)urned *pp.* endowed with; worked upon [enŏurnen].

enquest *n.* question.

entayled *pp.* embroidered, ornamented [entaillen].

enterlude *n.* interlude, dramatic entertainment (472n).

entre *v.* enter.

entyse *v.* allure or attract (a blemish) [entīcen].

er(e) *adv.*, *prep.*, and *conj.* before.

erande *see* **ernd**

erber *n.* esophagus.

erbes *n. pl.* plants, vegetation [hērbe].

erde *n.* earth, world; **in erde** indeed, in truth.

ere *see* **er**

erly *adv.* early (in the morning).

ermyn *n.* ermine, expensive fur that is white with black spots.

ernd *n.* mission, task, errand; request [ērend(e)].

erraunt *adj.* questing; **knyght erraunt** knight on a quest.

erthe *n.* earth, ground.

ese *n.* ease, comfort, joy.

etayn *n.* giant, ogre [ēten].

ete *v.* eat.

ethe *adj.* easy.

ethe *v.* ask, entreat.

ette *see* **ete**

evel *n.* wickedness, sinfulness [ivel].

even *adj.* and *adv.* even; levelly; directly, straight (toward); exactly; indeed.

even *n.* evening, eve of a festival.

evenden *v. pa. t.* trim, make even (1345n).

evensong *n.* vespers, evening service.

eventide *n.* evening.

ever *adv.* ever, always, continually.

evermore *adv.* henceforth, always.

eves *n.* edge of a forest.

evesed *pp.* clipped, trimmed.

excused *pp.* excused.

exellently *adv.* surpassingly, without equal [excellentlī].

expoun *v.* explain, describe, expound; **speche expoun** talk about.

face *n.* face.

fade *adj.* fierce, bold, eager for battle; inimical, hostile; supernatural, endowed with magic powers, elvish (149n).

fader *n.* father.

fage *n.* falsehood; **no fage** no falsehood, this is the truth, indeed.

falce *adj.* false, disloyal, guilty of breach of trust.

fale *adj.* pale [falwe].

falle *v.* fall; hasten, rush; happen, befall; be fitting for (1588n).

falssyng *n.* something that deceives or misleads [falsing].

faltered *v. pa. t.* faltered, staggered, tottered.

fange *see* **fonge**

fannand *pres. p.* flowing, spreading out like fan.

fantoum *n.* apparition, illusion [fantōm].

farand *pres. p.* splendid, excellent.

fare *n.* track; behavior, conduct, manners; food, feasting (694n).

fare *v.* go, proceed, travel; **fares wel** farewell.

fast(e) *adj.* and *adv.* firm, binding; firmly, tightly, securely; earnestly, tenaciously; quickly; loudly.

faut *n.* flaw, blemish.

fautles *adj.* flawless, without blemish; **fautlest** *superl.* most flawless; **on the fautlest** the most flawless.

fawne *v.* pat [faunen].

fawty *adj.* faulty, flawed, guilty of sin [fautī].

fax *n.* hair.

fay *n.* faith; **ma fay** by my faith, assuredly, certainly [feith].

faye *n.* person of magical powers.

fayle, fayly *v.* fail; end.

fayn *adj.* glad, pleased, happy.

fayntyse *n.* frailty, lack of spirit, cowardice [feintīse].

fayr, fayre *adj.* and *adv.* fair, beautiful, attractive; courteous; good; well, gracefully, courteously; **fayrer** *compar.* better; **the fayrer to have** to have the better luck; **fayrest** *superl.* most beautiful, best (99n).

fayryye *n.* magic, enchantment, illusion; supernatural being.

fayth *n.* faith; honesty; honor; **bi my fayth, in (god) fayth** in truth, indeed, assuredly [feith].

faythely *adv.* truly, in fact, indeed [feithlī].

faythful *adj.* faithful, loyal, true, truthful [feithful].

feblest *adj. superl.* feeblest, weakest.

fech *v.* fetch, bring; receive [fecchen].

fede *v.* feed.

fee *n.* payment, portion, share; **corbeles fee** raven's share of deer carcass [fē].

feersly *see* **fersly**

feght *see* **fyght**

feghtyng *n.* fighting; **in feghtyng wyse** equipped for battle.

fel *see* **falle**

felawes *n. pl.* other members of the pack.

felawschyp *n.* friendship, companionship; **bere felawschyp** keep company.

felde *n.* field, battle-field.

felde *v. pa. t.* fold, clasp; **in armes felde** embrace [fōlden].

fele *adj.* many, much; **feler** *compar.* more.

fele *v.* feel; perceive.

felefolde *adj.* in many ways, many times over; **a folé felefolde** a great folly.

felix *adj.* happy (13n).

felle *adj.* bold, fierce, terrible [fel]; see also **fele**

felle *n.¹* skin, complexion; fur, animal hide [fel].

felle *n.²* hill, cliff [fel].

felle *v. see* **falle**

felly *adv.* fiercely [fellī(che)].

femed *v. pa. t.* foamed.

fende *n.* fiend, devil (2193n).

feng *see* **fonge**

fer, ferre *adv.* far, far away; **fire, firre, fyrre** *compar.* further, also.

ferde, ferden *see* **fare** *v.*

fere *adj.* bold, proud.

fere *n.¹* group, company; **in fere** with others, with an army (267n).

fere *n.²* companion, fellow, neighbor; wife; equal.

ferk *v.* go, travel, ride; flow; **ferkes hym up** gets up.

ferly *adj.* and *adv.* surprising, marvelous; marvelously, exceedingly, extremely.

ferly *n.* marvel, wonder, adventure.

ferlyly *adv.* wondrously; **ferlyly he telles** he tells of marvels, of his adventure.

fermed *pp.* made, established, confirmed (2329n).

fermysoun *n.* closed season on male deer.

ferre *see* **fer**

fersly *adv.* proudly, fiercely, vigorously.

fest *n.* feast, religious festival.

fest *v. pa. t.* made, established, pledged [fasten].

festned *pp.* committed, attached [fastnen].

fete *see* **fot(e)**

feted *v. pa. t.* behaved, conducted himself.

fetled *pp.* bestowed, fixed.

fetly *adv.* elegantly, prettily.

fette *see* **fech**

fetures *n. pl.* features (of body or face).

feye *adj.* dead.

fiften *adj.* fifteen.

figure *n.* figure, image, symbol.

fildore *n.* gold thread.

finde *see* **fynde**

fire *see* **fyr(e)**

fire, firre *compar. adv. see* **fer**

first *see* **fyrst**

fische *n.* fish.

flagh *see* **fle**

flat *n.* field, plain.

flaw *see* **flyye** *v.*

fle *v.* flee, flinch, give way.

flesch *n.* flesh, body, meat; sensual bodily appetites.

flet, flette *n.* paved floor of room or hall.

flete *v.* fall; **fer floten** having wandered far.

flod *n.* flowing body of water, stream, river; **French flod** English channel.

flokked *v. pa. t.* flocked together, assembled.

flone *n.* arrow.

flor *n.* floor.

flosche *n.* pool, marsh, swamp (1421n) [flashe].

floten *see* **flete**

flowre *n.* flower [flōur].

flynt *n.* cobblestone pavement.

flyye *n.* butterfly.

flyye *v.* fly, fly out, fall down.

fnast *v.* snort, pant.

foch *v.* fetch, receive, take [fecchen].

fode *n.* food.

folde *n.* the earth, world; ground; land, country.

folde *v.* fold, braid; turn back; pledge, promise; match, correspond; **foldes hit to me** it falls to me.

fole *n.^{1}* horse.

fole *n.^{2}* fool.

folé *see* **foly**

folk *n. inform.* people, persons, crowd.

folwe *v.* follow, hunt; be connected or associated with; **folwande** similar, of the same kind (2422n).

foly *n.* folly.

fonde *v.* test, tempt; try, attempt; *see also* **fynde**

fondet *see* **founde**

fonge *v.* take, receive; get, derive from; receive as guest, welcome.

foo *adj.* and *adv.* perilous; fiercely.

foo *n.* foe, enemy.

for *conj.* and *prep.* for, because, through; on account of, for the sake of; for the purpose of, in order to; for fear of, to guard against, to prevent; **for sothe** indeed.

forbe *prep.* above, beyond, surpassing [fōrbī].

force *n.* strength, force; **fyne force** sheer necessity, main force.

ford *n.* ford, a shallow place where one may pass through water.

forest *n.* woodland, wilderness, forest; wooded area set apart for hunting.

forfaren *pp.* intercepted, headed off (1895n).

forferde *v. pa. t.* killed [forfāren].

forfeted *pp.* transgressed, sinned.

forgat *v. pa. t.* forgot.

forgoo *v.* lose, forfeit.

forlond *n.* headland, promontory; land between sea and hills (699n) [fōre-land].

forme *adj.* first.

forme *n.¹* beginning.

forme *n.²* (bodily) shape, figure; form; manner, fashion.

forne *adv.* of old, previously.

forred *see* **furred**

forsake *v.* forsake, reject, refuse.

forse *see* **force**

forsnes *n.* strength [forceness(e)].

forsoke *see* **forsake**

forst *n.* frost [frost].

forth *adv.* forth, onward, forward, out, away.

forth *n.* see **ford**

forthi, forthy *adv.* therefore, thus.

fortune *n.* chance, fate, fortune.

forw *n.* course (lit. furrow, trench).

forward *n.* agreement, contract, promise; terms of agreement or contract [fōre-wārd].

forwondered *pp.* astonished, amazed.

foryate *see* **foryete**

foryelde *v.* repay, reward; **God (Kryst) yow foryelde** may God (Christ) reward you, God (Christ) bless you.

foryete *v.* forget.

fot(e) *n.* foot.

fotte *v.* come get, receive [fetten].

foule *adj.* foul, ugly, wicked, evil; **fowlest** *superl.* poorest, least well-grown (1944n).

founde *v.* come, proceed, go, walk; *see also* **fonde, fynde**

fourche *n.* fork formed by legs and trunk of body.

foure *adj.* four.

fourme *see* **forme** *n.*

fourty *adj.* forty.

fowlest *see* **foule**

fowre *see* **foure**

fox *n.* fox.

foyned *v. pa. t.* kicked.

foysoun *n.* abundance, plenty, profusion.

fraunchis *n.* generosity, liberality.

frayn *v.* ask, inquire, question; attempt, seek.

frayst *v.* seek, search; find out, experience; test, tempt, put to trial.

fre *adj.* noble, courteous; frank, free; **freest** *superl.* best, most excellent, noblest.

freke *n.* knight, warrior, lord; man, person.

frely *adv.* freely; courteously.

fremedly *adv.* as a stranger, in a foreign land.

French *adj.* French (1116n) [Frēnsh].

frend *n.* friend.

frenges *n. pl.* fringes, ornamental borders.

Frenkysch *see* **French**

fres *v. pa. t.* froze.

fresch *adj.* fresh, new [frēsh].

freschly *adv.* quickly, sharply, eagerly.

fro, from *prep.* and *conj.* from, away from; from the time that, when, after [from].

frote *v.* caress.

frothe *n.* froth, foaming saliva.

frounse *v.* purse (lips), wrinkle (brows) [frǒuncen].

frount *n.* forehead.

fryth *n.* forest, wood, wilderness.

ful *adj.* full.

ful *adv.* very, quite; full.

fulsun *v.* assist, help [fils(t)nen].

funde(n) *see* **fynde**

furred *pp.* lined with fur.

fust *n.* hand, fist [fīst].

fute, fuyt *n.* trail of game animal.

fyched *pp.* attached, fixed, fastened.

fyft *adj.* fifth.

fyght *n.* fight.

fyght *v.* fight.

fyked *v. pa. t.* flinched.

fyled *pp.* sharpened.

fylle *v.* fulfill, carry out, keep (an agreement).

fylor *n.* sharpener or contrivance for holding weapon being sharpened [fīlǒur].

fylter *v.* contend.

fylthe *n.* sordidness, corruption, sin, lust.

fylyoles *n. pl.* pinnacles, turrets.

fyn *adj.* fine, excellent, superior; binding; **fyne force** sheer necessity, main force.

fyn *adv.* completely; superbly.

fynde *v.* find.

fyndyng *n.* trailing game with dogs to rouse it (1433n).

fyngeres, fyngres *n. pl.* fingers (641n, 1329n).

fynisment *n.* end, outcome [finishment].

fynly *adv.* fully, completely [fīnelī].

fyr(e) *n.* fire.

fyrre *see* **fer**

fyrst *adj.* and *adv.* first; **upon fyrst** in the beginning.

fysche *see* **fische**

fyske *v.* scamper.

fyve *adj.* and *n.* five, set of five.

fyyed *pp.* matched in style, went together [feien].

gafe *see* **gif**

game, gamne *see* **gomen**

gargulun *n.* throat, gullet of deer.

gart *v. pa. t.* caused, brought about [gēren].

garysoun *n.* treasure; keepsake, token of remembrance, gift.

garyte *n.* watchtower, turret.

gast *adj.* afraid.

gate *n.* way, road, path; **bi gate** on the way; **let ... haf the gate** allow to pass freely, let escape.

gaudi *n.* ornamentation.

gay *adj.* and *adv.* gay, merry; beautiful; excellent; noble; gaily, merrily, cheerfully; *superl.* **gayest** best attired.

gayly *adv.* beautifully, splendidly, richly.

gayn *adj.* and *adv.* helpful, obedient; pleasing, agreeable; directly; **gaynest** *superl.* by the shortest or quickest route.

gayn *n.* gains, profit [gein].

gayn *v.* help, benefit, profit [geinen].

gaynly *adv.* properly; courteously [geinlī].

geder *v.* gather, assemble; **geder up**, **geder on hyght** raise up high, over one's head; **geder to** put spurs to; **geder the rake** follow the path [gaderen].

gef *see* **gif**

gemme *n.* gem, precious stone.

gentyle *adj.* noble, of the nobility; having traits befitting the nobility; polite, kind, courteous, well-bred; **gentylest** *superl.* noblest (774n).

gere *n.* clothes, dress; gear, equipment; bedclothes.

gere *v.* prepare, equip, dress; place; make.

geserne *see* **giserne**

gest *n.* guest, stranger, traveler.

get *n.* gains, that which one has gotten.

gete *v.* get, receive, gather.

geven *see* **gif**

gif *v.* give; convey, say; **gef hym god day**, said "good day" to him, wished him a good day; **geven** given.

gift *n.* gift.

gile *n.* guile.

gilt *adj.* gold, golden, gilded.

girdel *n.* belt worn around waist.

giserne *n.* long-handled battle-axe [gisarme].

glad *adj.* glad, happy, cheerful.

glade *v.* gladden.

gladly *adv.* gladly; **gladloker** *compar.* more gladly.

glam, glaum *n.* loud noise, din; revelry.

glaver *n.* clamor, din.

gle *n.* joy, mirth; joyous din, entertainment, music.

glede *n.* fire, hot charcoal.

glem *n.* gleam.

glemed *v. pa. t.* gleamed, shone.

glemered *v. pa. t.* gleamed.

glent *n.* a glance.

glent *v. pa. t.* moved, flinched; looked, glanced at; shone, glittered, glinted; **glent up** arose.

glod *see* **glyde**

glode *n.* glade, clearing, open space; patch [glāde].

glopnyng *n.* fright, terror.

glorious *adj.* glorious.

glove *n.* glove; **gloves of plate** plate-mail gauntlets.

glowande *pres. p.* glowing, shining.

glyde *v.* walk, travel, move quietly; fall, descend.

glyfte *v. pa. t.* glanced.

glyght *v. pa. t.* looked at, glanced at [glīen].

glyter *v.* glitter, shine.

go *v.* go; **go myn ernde** take my request; **hit gos not in mynde** it is impossible to believe (1293n).

god(e), good(e), goud(e), guod *adj.* good, excellent, worthy, fine; seemly, decorous; **no howe goud** no good coif.

God(e), Godde *n.* God; **upon Godes halve** in God's name; **gef hym God** commended him to God.

god *n.* goodness, virtue, righteousness.

goddes *n.* goddess.

godemon, godmon *n.* master of the house, head of household.

godly *adv.* graciously, kindly; in good faith (920n).

godlych *adj.* fine, excellent.

gold *adj.* gold.

gold *n.* gold.

golde-hemmed *adj.* fringed with gold.

gome *n.* man, warrior, knight.

gomen *n.* game, sport, pleasure, jest (277n) [gāme].

gomenly *adv.* joyfully.

gon *see* **go**

good(e) *see* **god(e)** *adj.*

gorde *see* **gurde**

gordel *see* **girdel**

gordes *see* **gyrde**

gorger *n.* wimple covering neck and bosom.

gos *see* **go**

gost *n.* soul, spirit, life.

gostlych *adv.* like a spirit or demon.

goud *see* **god(e)** *adj.*

goudly *see* **godly**

goules *n.* gules (heraldic: red).

goune *n.* garment, gown.

governour *n.* lord, military commander.

gowles *see* **goules**

grace *n.* grace, gift, favor, mercy.

gracios *n.* beautiful, fair.

graciously *adv.* graciously, benevolently, beautifully.

grame *n.* remorse, vexation.

grant *see* **graunt**

gra(u)nt mercy *n.* and *interj.* many thanks, thank you [gramercī].

grattest *see* **gret**

graunt *v.* grant, permit, agree to.

gray *adj.* grey [grei].

grayes *v.* wither, become gray [greien].

grayn *n.* spike [grein].

grayth *adj.* ready, available [greith].

graythe *v.* prepare; dress; place, arrange [greithen].

graythely *adv.* readily, quickly; properly; pleasantly; willingly.

grece *n.* fat (1378n) [gres(e)].

gref *n.* grief, sorrow, distress.

grehound *n.* greyhound.

grem *n.* anger, grimness; harm, shame, grief.

grene *adj.* green; **grener** *compar.* greener (2193n).

grenne *v.* grin.

gres *n. see* **grece**

gres(se) *n.* grass.

gret, grett *adj.* large, big, great; splendid; proud, arrogant; *superl.* **grattest** most intense.

gret *v. pa. t.* greeted.

greve *n.* grove, thicket, wood.

greve *v.* grieve, trouble; frighten; become angry.

greves *n. pl.* greaves, armor for shins.

gripped *see* **grype**

grome *n.* servant, attendant, retainer; man.

grone *v.* groan.

gronyed *v. pa. t.* grunted [groinen].

grounde *n.* ground; area; the earth.

grounden *pp.* ground, sharpened [grīnden].

growe *v.* grow.

gruch *v.* resist, protest, withstand; dispute, disagree with.

gruchyng *adj.* annoyed, angry.

grue *n.* bit, whit; **no grue** not a bit, not at all.

gryed *pp.* shuddered.

grymme *adj.* grim, frightening, savage.

gryndel *adj.* fierce, angry.

gryndellayk *n.* fierceness (312n).

gryndelly *adv.* fiercely.

gryndelston *n.* grindstone.

grype *v.* grip, hold, grasp; **gryp to** take.

guod *see* **god(e)** *adj.*

gurde *pp.* girded [gīrden].

gurdel *see* **girdel**

guttes *n. pl.* guts, entrails.

gyft *see* **gift**

gyld *see* **gilt**

gyng *n.* band of warriors, retinue, company.

gyrde *v.* spur; **gyrde to** put spurs to.

habbe, had *see* **have**

hadet *pp.* beheaded.

haf *see* **have**

hagher *adj.* noble, skillfully wrought; **hagherer** *compar.* readier, more eager [hauer].

hal, hale *n. see* **halle**

halawed *see* **halowe**

halce *see* **hals**

halche *v.* enclose; loop; fasten, join; embrace, salute (939n).

halde *v.* hold, contain, keep, maintain, rule.

hale *v.* draw, pull; loose; rush, hasten; thrust (788n).

half, halve *adj. and adv.* half.

half, halve *n.* half, part, side; direction; on behalf of, in the name of.

half-suster *n.* half-sister.

haliday *see* **halyday**

halle *n.* hall, esp. of a castle.

halle *v. see* **hale**

halme *n.* handle.

halowe *v.* call out, shout.

hals *n.* neck.

halve *see* **half**

halwe *n.* saint.

halydam *n.* sacred relics [hālī-dōm].

halyday *n.* holiday, Christian festival.

hame *see* **home**

han *see* **have**

hande *see* **hond(e)**

hanselle, hondeselle *n.* gift given (esp. in New Year) for good luck (66n).

hap *n.* happiness.

hapnest *adj. superl.* happiest [happī].

happe *v.* cover, enclose, imprison with a covering; attach by wrapping, make fast; clothe.

hard *adj. and adv.* hard, difficult; firm, firmly; rough; **harder** *compar.* more firmly.

harden *v.* harden; encourage, make bold.

hardi, hardy *adj.* hardy, bold, fearless.

hardily *adv.* fully, firmly, certainly.

harled *pp.* intertwined.

harme *n.* harm; wrong-doing.

harnays *n.* fighting equipment, armor, gear [harneis].

harnayst *pp.* equipped with armor [harneisen].

has *see* **have**

hasel *n.* hazel tree.

haspe *n.* latch, door fastening.

haspe, hasppe *v.* fasten, enclose (in clothes or armor), embrace.

hast(e) *n.* haste, speed, hurrying.

hasted, hastid *v. pa. t.* hastened, hurried; **hasted hym** *refl.* (they) were hurrying.

hastily *adv.* quickly, hurriedly; eagerly, readily.

hastlettes *n. pl.* entrails (1612n) [hastelet].

hasty *adj.* urgent.

hastyly *see* **hastily**

hat, hatte *v.* am (is) called.

hathel *n.* man, knight; fellow, servant.

hatte *n.* hat.

hatte *v. see* **hat**

hauberghe *see* **hawbergh**

haunche *n.* haunch, hips.

have *v.* have.

haviloune *v.* double back.

hawbergh *n.* coat of mail [hauberk].

hawtesse *n.* haughtiness, pride.

hawthorne *n.* hawthorn.

hay *interj.* hey!

haylce, haylse *v.* greet, salute.

he *pron.* he; **him, hym** (to, for) him, *refl.* (for) himself; **his** his; **himself, hymselven, hisselven** *refl.* himself, the very one.

hed *n.* head; lord; **mawgref his hed** despite his resistance.

hedles *adj.* headless.

hef *see* **heve**

hegge *n.* hedge.

hegh- *see* **high-, hygh-**

helde *v.* go, proceed, come, follow; set; **helden to** made for; **heldet hym fro** kept back from him; **heldande** bowing; *see also* **halde**

helder *adv. comp. in* **never the helder** none the more (376n).

heles *n. pl.* heels; spurs; **gilt heles** gold (gilded) spurs.

helme *n.* helmet.

help *n.* help, assistance.

help, helppe *v.* help.

hem, him, hom *pron.* (to, for) them, *refl.* (for) themselves; **her, hor** their; **hemself** *refl.* themselves.

heme *adj.* neat, suitable, fitting.

hemely *adv.* neatly.

hemme *n.* border, edge.

hemself *see* **hem**

hende *adj.* and *adv.* courteous, gracious, noble; courteously, graciously, freely; **hendest** *superl.* most courteous.

hendelayk *n.* courtesy, nobility, courtliness.

hendely, hendly *adv.* courteously; quickly.

heng *v.* hang.

henne *adv.* from here, hence.

hent *v.* take, catch, receive.

hepe *n.* large number, group, heap; **on hepes** together; **upon hepes** into masses (of shattered rock).

her *see* **hem, ho**

herande *see* **here** *v.*[1]

herber *n.* lodging, shelter [herberwe].

herber *v.* lodge, take shelter [herberwen].

herd, herde *see* **here** *v.*[1]

here *adv.* here, now, at this time [hēr].

here *n.*[1] armed company, army.

here *n.*[2] hair [hēr].

here *v.*[1] hear.

here *v.*[2] praise [herien].

heredmen *n. pl.* retainers.

herinne *adv.* herein, in this place.

herk(k)en *v.* hear, listen to, harken.

herle *n.* strand.

herre *see* **hygh**

hersum *adj.* devout; noble, festive (932n).

hert *n.* heart [herte].

hertt *n.* stag (1159n) [hert].

hervest *n.* harvest, autumn, fall.

hes *n.* promise [hēst(e)].

hest *n.* command, bidding.

hete *n.* vow [hōt].

hete *v.* promise.

het(t)erly *adv.* quickly, vigorously, fiercely, violently, viciously.

hethe *n.* heath.

hethen *adv.* hence, away (from here).

hetterly *see* **heterly**

heve *v.* raise, lift; raise words, utter.

hevé *see* **hevy**

heven *n.* heaven, the heavens.

heven-quene *n.* queen of heaven, Virgin Mary.

heven-ryche *n.* kingdom of heaven; **under hevenryche** under the heavens, on earth.

hevy *adj.* heavy [hēvī].

hewe *n. see* **hue**

hewe *v.* hew, cut; shape, fashion, make [heuen].

hid *see* **hyden**

hider *adv.* hither, here.

high- *see also* **hygh-**

highlich *adj.* splendid.

hightly *adv.* entirely [hightlī(che)].

hil(le) *n.* hill.

him *see* **he, hem**

himself, himselven *see* **he**

hind *n.* hind (1159n).

hir *see* **ho**

his, hisselven *see* **he**

hit *pron.* it; **hitself** *refl.* itself.

hit(te) *v.* hit, strike.

hiyed *see* **hyye**

ho, scho *pron.* she; **hir, her** (to, for) her; **her** *refl.* herself.

hod(e) *n.* hood.

hode *n.* order of knighthood.

hoge *see* **huge**

hogh *n.* hock, joint in the hind leg of deer [hough].

holde *adv.* faithfully.

holde *n.* possession, control; castle.

holde *v.* see **halde**

holdely *adv.* faithfully, carefully.

hole *n.* hole.

hol(l)e *adj.* whole, intact; healed, amended.

holly *adv.* wholly, entirely.

holsumly *adv.* soundly.

holt *n.* wood.

holtwod *n.* grove, forest; **holtwodes under** underneath groves (of trees) (742n).

holw *adj.* hollow.

holyn *n.* holly (206n).

hom *pron.* see **hem**

hom(e) *n.* home, dwelling.

homered *v. pa. t.* struck [hameren].

hond *n.* hand; **halden ... in honde** maintain.

hondele *v.* handle, touch, take hold of, wield [hōndlen].

hondeselle *see* **hanselle**

hone *n.* delay.

honour *n.* honor, worship, fame; **not your honour** below your honor.

honour, honowr *v.* honor, worship, celebrate.

hoo *v.* stop, cease.

hope *v.* believe, know; **hope of** expect, hope for.

hor *see* **hem**

horce *see* **hors(se)**

hore *adj.* ancient, gray.

horne *n.* horn.

hors(se) *n.* horse.

hose *n. pl.* tights, hose.

hostel *n.* dwelling; lodging, accommodation, entertainment.

hot *adj.* hot; **in hot and colde** whatever the circumstance.

hound *n.* hound, hunting dog.

hous *n.* house.

hove *v.* wait, halt, stop.

hoves *n. pl.* hoofs.

how *adv.* how.

how-se-ever *adv.* however.

howe *n.* head-dress, coif (1738n).

howndes *see* **hound**

hue *n.* hue, color, complexion; **alle on hues** in all its colors.

huge *adj.* huge, great.

hult *n.* hilt.

hundreth *num.* a hundred; a countless number (743n) [hundred].

hunt *v.* hunt.

hunte *n.* hunter.

hunter *n.* hunter (1139n).

huntyng *n.* hunting.

hurt *n.* hurt, wound.

hurt *v.* hurt; **hurtes of** drives off (1452n).

hyde *n.* hide, skin.

hyde *v.* hide, conceal.

hygh *adj.* and *adv.* high, tall, large; great, important, noble; loud; highly, loudly; **upon heghe** of the highest degree; **He that on hyghe syttes** God; **hegh wede** complete gear, armor; **of hyghe eldee** full in years; **hyghe tyde** festive occasion, solemn feast; **the hyghe** high ground, heights; **herre** *compar.* taller; **hyghest, heghest** *superl.* noblest, highest (831n, 844n) [heigh].

hyghly, heghly, *adv.* high, highly, greatly; solemnly, devoutly; cheerfully [heighlī].

hyght, heght *n.* height.

hyght *v. see* **hete**

hylle *see* **hil(le)**

hym- *see* **he-, hem-**

hyndes *see* **hind**

hypped *v. pa. t.* hopped, bounced; **hypped ayayn** rebounded, bounced back.

hys *see* **he**

hyt *see* **hit** *pron.*

hyye *n.* haste; **in hyye** at once, quickly [hī(e)].

hyye *v.* hurry, hasten [hīen].

I *pron.* I; **me** (to, for) me; **my, myn** my, mine; **myself, myselven** *refl.* myself.

iche *see* **uche**

i(i)f *conj.* if, if only; **bot if** unless.

iisse-ikkle *n.* icicle [īs-ikle].

ile *n.* island; **the west iles** Europe (7n).

ilk *adj.* and *pron.* same, the same thing.

ille *adv.* with displeasure; **lyke ille** displease.

ille *n.* harm, injury; **tas it to non ille** take it not ill, do not regard it as insult.

ilyche *adj.* continual, constant, unchanging.

in, inn(e) *prep.* and *adv.* in; on; into; within.

inmyddes *prep.* and *adv.* in the middle, in the center.

innermore *adv.* farther within.

in(n)ogh, innowe *adj.* and *adv.* enough, many; **hevé (fayr, etc.) innogh** very heavy (beautiful).

inore *adj. comp.* inner, inside [inner(e)].

into *prep.* into.

inwith *adv.* and *prep.* within.

irked *v. pa. t.* grew weary.

is *v.* is.

iwys(s)e *adv.* indeed, in fact, certainly.

jape *n.* jest, amusement, joke, banter.

jentyle *see* **gentyle**

jolilé *adv.* vigorously, stoutly.

joly *adj.* happy, cheerful.

jopardé *n.* danger, hazard, risk [jūpartī(e)].

joy *n.* joy; **mynne upon joye** be joyful (646n).

joyfnes *n.* youth [junesse].

joyles *adj.* joyless.

joyne *v.* meet, come together.

juel *n.* treasure, valuable thing.

jugged *pp.* ordained, fated, assigned.

justed *v. pa. t.* jousted.

justyng *n.* jousting.

kach, kachande, kaght *see* **cach**

kallen *see* **calle**

kanel *n.* neck [canēl].

karp *see* **carp**

kastel *see* **castel**

kavelacion *see* **cavelacioun**

kay *adj.* left.

kayre *see* **cayre**

kende *see* **kenne**

kene *adj.* brave, fierce.

kenel *n.* kennel.

kenet *n.* small hunting dog.

kenly *adv.* keenly, fiercely, daringly.

kenne *v.* teach; commend.

kepe *v.* keep; guard, defend, protect; pursue, practice; care, want; care for, attend to; await **kepe hym with carp** speak with him; **kepe thee** take care.

ker(re) *n.* marsh, bog; **ker syde** side of a marsh (1421n).

kerchofe *n.* woman's headcloth, worn to cover hair, sides of face, and back of neck [cŏver-chēf].

kest *see* **cast**

kever *v.* shield, protect; recover; manage, succeed; obtain; give; proceed [cŏveren].

klerk *see* **clerk**

klyf *see* **clyff**

knaged *pp.* fastened.

knape *n.* fellow, man.

knarre *n.* crag.

knawen *see* **know**

kne *n.* knee.

kneled *v. pa. t.* kneeled.

knew *see* **know**

knightes *see* **knyght**

knit *v.* tie, knot up; bind, fix, join; make (a bargain).

knokke *n.* blow, strike.

knokled *adj.* rugged, craggy.

knorned *adj.* gnarled.

knot(t) *n.* knot; tassel; thicket; **endeles knot** pentangle (630n).

know *v.* know; acknowledge, recognize; discover.

knyf(fe) *n.* knife.

knyght *n.* knight.

knyghtly *adv.* as proper for a knight; honorably, courteously.

knyghtyly *adj.* knightly, honorable, brave [knightlī].

knyt *see* **knit**

knyves *see* **knyf(fe)**

kok *see* **coke**

kort, kourt *see* **court**

kowarde *n.* coward [cŏuard].

koynt see **coynt**

koyntly see **coyntly**

koyntyse n. knowledge, wisdom, magic [queintīs(e)].

kry see **cry**

kryes see **crye**

krystmasse see **Cristmasse**

kyd(de) pp. and adj. known; made known, displayed, revealed; behaved (toward), treated (someone); famous (775n) [kīthen].

kylled pp. killed.

kyn(ne) n. kind.

kynde adj. pleasing.

kynde n. nature, essential character; kind; **highe kynde** great descendants, noble offspring; **bi kynde** properly, normally.

kyndely adv. courteously.

kyng n. king.

kynnes see **kyn(ne)**

kyrf n. blow, cut, wound.

kyrk n. church [chirche].

kyrtel n. gown.

kysse v. kiss.

kyssyng n. kissing.

kyth n. land, place [kitthe].

lace n. lace, cord, belt [lās].

lach(ch) v. take, grasp, seize, catch, take hold of; take on; find; accept.

lachet n. strap, loop.

lad, ladde see **lede** v.

ladi, lady n. lady.

laft see **leve** v.[1]

laghe v. laugh; **laghande** laughing [laughen].

laght see **lach(ch)**

laghter n. laughter [laughter].

laghyng n. laughing [laughing(e)].

lagmon n. last or hindmost person; **lad hem bi lagmon** led them astray, led them to come out last (1729n).

lakked v. be lacking; scorn, disparage; **yow lakked** you were lacking.

lampe n. lamp.

lance v. see **launce**

lante v. pa. t. lent, gave [lēnen].

lappe n. sleeve; loose end or flap of flesh.

lappe v. encase, wrap around, embrace.

large adj. large, long, huge.

larges(se) n. bulk, great size; generosity.

lasse adj. and adv. less; **lest** superl. least.

lassen v. lessen.

last adj. superl. last; **at the last** at last, finally.

laste v. last, endure, live; reach, extend to.

late adj. late.

later adv. compar. later; **never the lece ne the later** nevertheless [nēver-the-lāter].

lathe n. see **lothe**

lathed v. pa. t. invited.

laucyng see **lause**

launce n. lance.

la(u)nce *v.* gallop; fly; speak, tell, utter (words); detach, cut.

launde *n.* clearing, glade; (lightly) wooded area, forest.

lause *v.* loosen, untie, undo [lōsen].

lawe *n.¹* law; manner [laue].

lawe *n.²* mound, hill [loue].

lawses *see* **lause**

lay *v.* lay, place, put; **layde hym doun** lay down; **layd hym bysyde** turned aside [leien].

laye *n.* narrative poem, usu. sung and accompanied on instrument (30n).

layk *n.* sport, game, amusement, festival; **the lel layk** the true practice [leik].

layke *v.* play; **laykyng of enterludes** performing of interludes.

layne *v.* hide, conceal, keep secret [leinen].

layt *n.* lightning [leit].

layte *v.* seek; **who laytes the sothe** whoever wants to know the truth [leiten].

lece *adv.* less; **never the lece ne the later** nevertheless [nēver-the-lēs].

lede *n. see* **le(u)de**

lede *v.* lead; make (joy).

leder *n.* leader.

lee *n.* shelter; castle [lē].

lef *adj.* dear, pleasant, agreeable; **lever** *compar.* dearer; **that lever wer** whom it would please more; **levest** *superl.* most desirable, best, dearest (1719n).

leg(g)e *adj.* liege, sovereign, entitled to subject's allegiance.

leg(g)e *n.* leg.

leghten *see* **lach(ch)**

leke *see* **louke**

lel *adj.* true, loyal, correct (35n).

lelly *adv.* faithfully, loyally.

leme *v.* shine, gleam.

lemman *n.* sweetheart, lover.

lende *v.* come to, arrive, approach; live in, stay, remain, sit; **is lent on** is engaged in.

lened *v. pa. t.* leaned; **he lened with the nek** he stuck out his neck.

lenge *v.* stay, remain, reside, abide.

lenger *see* **long**

lenkthe *see* **lenthe**

lent *see* **lende**

lenthe *n.* length; **on lenthe** for a long time; **on lenthe faren** gone far away [length(e)].

Lentoun *n.* Lent (502n).

lepe *v.* leap.

lere *adj.* useless, worthless; **lere other better** worse or better.

lere *n. see* **lyre**

lern *v.* learn; instruct.

lese *v.* lose.

lest *comp. see* **lasse**

lest *conj.* lest, for fear that, that not.

lested *see* **laste**

let(te) *v.* let; pretend, act as though; **let ... lotes** let out words; **the lady ... let not to slepe** the lady did not allow herself to sleep (248n).

lethe *v.* humble.

lether *n.* skin; **lether of the paunches** covering of the stomachs of deer.

lette *v.* prevent, hinder, dissuade; *see also* **let(te)**

letteres *n. pl.* letters; alliterating sounds (35n).

lettrure *n.* knowledge; **lettrure of armes** essence of knighthood (1513n).

le(u)de *n.* person, man, knight.

leudles *adj.* without companion, alone.

leve *adj. see* **lef**

leve *n.* leave, permission, permission to go.

leve *v.¹* leave; leave off; spare (someone); give; dismount.

leve *v.²* believe, trust.

leve *v.³* live [liven].

lever, levest *see* **lef**

leves *n. pl.* leaves [lēf].

lewed *adj.* ignorant, uneducated, lacking in refinement [leued].

lewté *n.* loyalty, faithfulness; fidelity to one's oath; honesty (2374n) [leauté].

ley *see* **ly**

liddes *n. pl.* eye-lids.

lif *n.* life; **upon lyve** alive, in this world.

liflode *n.* food and drink, nourishment.

light *see* **lyght**

like *see* **lyk**

lis *see* **ly**

list *n.* the ear, hearing; **lof upon list** pleasing to the ear (1719n).

lithernes *n.* ferocity, viciousness.

lit(t)el *adj.* little, small, slight.

lo *interj.* see, behold; **we loo** woe, alas.

lode *n.* load, baggage; **on lode** leading; **in his lode** in his tow, he has with him.

lodly *adv.* harshly; cowardly; **let lodly therat** pretended to be scared of it [lōthlī].

lof *see* **lef**

lofden *see* **luf** *v.*

loflyest *see* **lufly**

lofte *n.* (upstairs) chamber; high place; **(up)on lofte** aloft, up high.

loghe *n.* low place; **on loghe to lyght** to come down [loue].

loghe *v.* see **laghe**

loke *n.* look, glance.

loke *v.* look, see, stare at; **God thee mot loke** may God protect you.

loken *see* **louke**

lokkes *n. pl.* locks of hair.

lokyng *n.* looking, staring.

lome *n.* weapon.

londe *n.* land, country; **in londe** in the world.

long *adj.* and *adv.* long; **lenger** *compar.* longer.

longe *v.* belong to, pertain to, be fitting for.

longynge *n.* distress, anxiety, sorrow.

loo *see* **lo**

lopen *see* **lepe**

lorde *n.* lord.

lore *n.* learning.

lortschyp *n.* lordship; household of a lord [lōrdship(e)].

los *n.* praise, renown, reputation.

losse *n.* loss [lōs].

lost *see* **lese**

lote *n.* bearing, conduct, demeanor; words, speech, cry; noise, din.

lothe *adj.* unpleasant, disagreeable.

lothe *n.* offense, harm.

loude *adj.* and *adv.* loud.

louke *v.* close, fasten, join (35n).

loupe *n.* loop; loophole, embrasure in wall (792n).

loute *v.* bow, bow to, honor; descend.

louve v. praise [lōven].

love see **luf**

lovely, lovelych, loveloker, lovelokkest see **lufly**

lovie, lovy see **luf**

lowande pres. p. brilliant, shining [louen].

lowde see **loude** adv.

lowe adj. and adv. low [loue].

lowe v. see **louve**

lowkes see **louke**

lowly adv. humbly, deferentially.

lude see **le(u)de**

luf n. love, affection, friendship, joy [lŏve].

luf v. love, be in love [lŏven].

luf-lace n. love-lace, belt given as token of love [lŏve].

luf-laghyng n. friendly laughter [lŏve].

luf-talkyng n. love-talking, conversing about love [lŏve].

lufly(ch) adj. and adv. beautiful, fair, handsome; worthy, noble, gracious, excellent; graciously, gracefully, courteously, cheerfully; skillfully; **loveloker** compar. more lovely; **loflyest, lovelokkest** superl. loveliest [lŏvelī].

luflyly adv. graciously, gracefully, amiably [lŏvelīlī].

lufsum adj. lovely; **that lufsum** that lovely one [lŏfsŏm].

lur n. loss, harm, sorrow [lire].

lurk(k)e v. lie concealed, hidden; be covered (1180n).

lut(te) see **loute**

ly, lyye, lyge v. lie; dwell, sojourn [līen].

lyf see **lif**

lyft adj. left [lift].

lyft n. sky, heaven [lift].

lyft v. lift, raise [liften].

lyges see **ly**

lyght adj.[1] bright [light].

lyght adj.[2] light, light-hearted; merry; eager; **set at lyght** undervalue [light].

lyght n. light; dawn (992n) [light].

lyght v. alight; dismount; come down [lighten].

lyghtes n. pl. lungs [lightes].

lyghtly adj. and adv. made of light material; easily, quickly, swiftly, gracefully [lightlī].

lyk v. lick, taste (968n) [likken].

lyke adj. and adv. like, similar; **lyk as** as if [līke].

lyke v. like, desire, please, love, esteem; **as hym lykes** as he wishes, as pleases him; **lyke ille** displease, distress [līken].

lykkerwys adj. delicious, delightful (968n) [likerŏus].

lym(m)es n. pl. limbs [lim].

lymp v. happen, befall, turn out [limpen].

lynde n.[1] lime tree; tree [līnd(e)].

lynde n.[2] loin [lēnd(e)].

lynde-wode n. forest [līnd(e)].

lyne n.[1] line [līne].

lyne n.[2] linen; **under lyne** clothed in linen, well-dressed (1814n) [līnen].

lyppe n. lip.

lyre n.[1] cheek, face, neck; coat (of horse) [lēr].

lyre n.[2] flesh, body; coat (of horse) [līre].

lyst(e) v. desire, want, like; **hym lyst** he wanted [listen].

lyste v. hear; lyste his lyf hear his confession [listen].

lysten *v.* listen to, pay heed to [listenen].

lystily *adv.* craftily, cunningly; carefully [listelī].

lyt(e) *adj.* little, brief, few [līt(e)].

lyte *n.* delay, postponement; **on lyte drowen** hesitated (in fear) [līte].

lytel *see* **littel**

lythen *v.* hear, listen to [līthen].

lyttel *see* **littel**

lyve *see* **lif**

lyver *n.* liver.

lyye *see* **ly**

ma fay *phr.* by my faith, certainly [feith].

mace *see* **make**

mach *v.* match, equal, rival.

mad, madee, maden *see* **make**

madame *n.* my lady; respectful form of address, usually to women of upper class.

madde *v.* behave madly, be mad.

maghtyly *adv.* mightily.

make *v.* make; do, commit; give.

male *adj.* male.

male *n.* bag.

malt *v. pa. t.* melted [melten].

mane *n.* mane.

maner *n.* manner; kind; consideration.

manerly *adj.* seemly.

mansed *v. pa. t.* menaced.

mantile *n.* mantle, cloak, robe.

marre *v.* kill [merren].

mas *see* **make**

masse *n.* mass [messe].

masse-prest *n.* priest ordained to celebrate mass [messe].

mat *adj.* daunted; tired.

matyn(n)es *n.* matins (canonical hour, recited in early morning).

mawgref *prep.* in spite of; **mawgref his hed** despite his resistance [maugrē].

may *n.* woman.

may *v.* can, may, might [mouen].

mayme *v.* maim.

mayn *adj.* great; strong; forceful.

maynteine *v.* command, rule.

mayster *n.* master; huge man (136n).

maystres *n.* mistress; woman in charge or control, sovereign lady, ruler; sexual partner other than wife (2448n).

me *see* **I**

Meghelmas *n.* Michaelmas (532n) [Mīghel-mes(se)].

mekely *adv.* meekly.

mele *n.* meal, feast; **at mes and at mele** at small and large meals.

mele *v.* say, speak.

melle *in* **inn melle** *adv.* completely [emel(le)].

melle *v.* blend, mix; **the blod in his face con melle** blood rushed to his face, he reddened [medlen].

melly *n.* battle, fight, single combat [medlē].

membre *n.* limb.

men(ne) *see* **mon** *n.*

mended v. pa. t. improved.

mene v. mean.

menged pp. joined, mixed, mingled.

mensk adj. beautiful (iron.).

menske n. honor, fame; courtesy.

mensked pp. adorned.

menskful adj. beautiful, noble; **the menskful** the noble (knight, woman).

menskly adv. courteously, fittingly.

meny see **meyny**

menyng n. understanding, knowledge.

merci n. mercy; **gra(u)nt mercy** many thanks.

mere adj. fine, good.

meré adj. see **mery**

mere n. landmark.

merk n. place, locale [mark(e)].

merkke v. mark, observe, take note [marken]

merthe n. mirth, joy, pleasure, happiness [mirth(e)].

mervayl n. marvel; **to mervayle hym thoght** it seemed strange (to him) [merveille].

mery adj. merry, joyful, cheerful, festive; delightful, pleasing to the ear; fine; **myriest** superl. most handsome, most delightful [mirīe].

meryly merrily, cheerfully; in jest; briskly (740n) [mirīlī].

mes see **messe**

meschaunce n. ill fortune, bad luck, mishap; wrongdoing, wicked behavior [mischaunce].

meschef n. wickedness [mischēf].

messe n. food, meal, dish; **at mes and at mele** at small and large meals [mēs]; see also **masse**

messewhyle n. time at which mass is sung [messe].

mesure n. measure, size, height.

met see **mete** v.

metail n. metal.

mete adj. equal; **mete to the erthe** even with the earth (extending to the ground).

mete n. food, meal.

mete v. meet; **mete with** welcome, receive.

metely adv. rightly, fittingly.

methles adj. violent, unrestrained.

mette(n) see **mete**

meve, mewe v. move, go, set out; make, create; mean; **meve to** hunt, attack.

me(y)ny n. household, retinue, company [meinē].

miche see **much**

mirthe see **merthe**

miry see **mery**

mislyke see **myslyke**

mist n. mist.

misy n. swamp, bog.

miyry see **mery**

mo adj. and adv. more.

mode n. mind, intent, will, purpose.

moder n. mother.

moght, moghten see **may**

molayne n. stud on bit of bridle.

molde n. earth, world; **on (the) molde, upon molde** in the world (anywhere).

mon n. man, person.

mon pron. indef. one, anyone (1682n).

mon *v.* must [mŏnen].

mone *n.[1]* prayer, request, entreaty.

mone *n.[2]* moon.

moni *see* **mony**

monk *n.* monk.

mony *adj.* and *pron.* many [manī].

mor *n.* moor.

more *adj. comp.* and *adv.* more, greater, larger, further; **lasse ne more** at all; **most** *superl.* largest, greatest, most.

morn *n.* morning.

morning *n.* morning; *see also* **mournyng**

moroun *see* **morn**

morsel *n.* morsel, small meal.

mosse *n.* moss.

most *superl. see* **more**

most *v. see* **mot**

mot *v.* may, might, must [mōten].

mote *n.[1]* gathering of people; **in mote** among people [mōt].

mote *n.[2]* moat; castle.

mote *n.[3]* note sounded on hunting horn (1143n) [mōt].

mote *n.[4]* whit [mōt].

mount *n.* mountain, hill.

mounture *n.* mount, horse.

mourne *v.* grieve [mŏrnen].

mournyng *n.* mourning, sadness, sorrow [mŏrning(e)].

mouth *n.* mouth, voice.

mowe *see* **may** *v.*

much *adj.* and *adv.* much, many, abundant, large, great; extremely, greatly, fully.

much *n.* much, a great deal.

muchwhat *pron.* various things, many things.

muckel *n.* size [muchel].

muged *v. pa. t.* drizzled.

mulne *n.* mill [milne].

munt *see* **mynt**

muryly *see* **meryly**

mused *v. pa. t.* were capable of thought, lived.

mute *n.* pack of hunting dogs; baying of pack.

muthe *see* **mouth**

my *see* **I**

mych *see* **much**

myd-over-under *n.* mid-afternoon (1730n).

myddel-erde *n.* earth, world.

myddes *n.* middle, center.

mydmorn *n.* mid-morning, about 9 AM

mydnyght *n.* midnight.

myerthe *see* **merthe**

myght *n.* might, power, ability.

myght *v. see* **may**

myldest *adj. superl.* most gracious, most merciful.

myle *n. pl.* miles.

myn(e) *see* **I**

mynde *n.* mind, thought, memory; **hit gos not in mynde** it is impossible to believe (1293n).

myne *v. see* **mynne**

mynged *v. pa. t.* called out, directed attention to.

mynne *adj.* lesser, smaller, less significant; **the more and the mynne** greater and lesser.

myn(ne) *v.* remember, be mindful of, think about, consider; report, declare; call for.

mynstralcie, mynstralsye *n.* entertainment, esp. music, singing, dancing or story-telling.

mynt *n.* feint, attempt or aim to strike.

mynt *v.* aim, swing, strike.

myre *n.* mire.

myrthe *see* **merthe**

myry, myriest *see* **mery**

mysboden *pp.* mistreated, abused [misbēden].

mysdede *n.* wrongdoing, sin.

myself, myselven *see* **I**

myslyke *v.* displease; **hym myslyke** he was perturbed.

mysses *n. pl.* errors [mis].

myst-hakel *n.* mantle of mist.

myyn *see* **I**

nade *v. pa. t.* (*ne hade*) had not.

naf *v.* (*ne haf*) have not.

naght *see* **nyght**

naked *adj.* and *adv.* naked, bare; barren; plain, unconcealed.

naked *n.* bare skin.

naker *n.* kettledrum; **nakryn** *gen. pl.* or *adj.* of kettledrums.

name *see* **nome**

nar *v.* (*ne ar*) are not.

nas *v.* (*ne was*) was not.

nase *n.* nose.

nauther, nawther *adj., conj.* and *pron.* neither; either; or.

nay *adv.* and *interj.* no.

nay *v.* refuse.

nayles *n. pl.* ornamental studs, nails.

naylet *pp.* decorated with studs.

nayted *v. pa. t.* repeated, recited.

ne *adv.* and *conj.* not; nor; or.

nec *see* **nek**

nede *adv.* of necessity.

nedes *n.* desires, needs, purposes.

nedes *v.* be needed, be necessary; **hit nedes no more** there is no need for more.

negh, niegh *adv.* and *prep.* near, close (to), almost.

negh *v.* draw near; reach; touch.

nek *n.* neck (2498n).

neked *n.* small amount, bit.

neme *v.* name [nāmen].

ner(re) *adj., adv.,* and *prep.* near(er); nearly.

neven *v.* name; call out by name; speak about.

never *adv.* never; not; **never the helder** nevertheless.

New Yer *n.* New Year, season of the New Year.

newe *adj.* and *adv.* new, novel; newly; **what newes** whatever new (spoils) (636n) [neue].

nexte *prep.* nearest or closest to.

niegh *see* **negh** *adv.*

nif *conj.* (*ne if*) if not.

night *see* **nyght**

nikked *v. pa. t.* denied; **nikked hym (with) naye** gave a negative reply, refused his offer.

nirt *n.* scar; nick, slight cut.

niyght *see* **nyght**

no *adj.* and *adv.* no.

nobelay *n.* nobility of conduct or morals; **thurgh nobelay** as point of honor [nōbelei(e)].

nob(e)le *adj.* noble, splendid, admirable; excellent, fine, pleasing.

nobot *conj.* nothing but, merely [nō-but].

noght *adv. see* **not**

noght *n.* and *pron.* nothing [nought].

noke *n.* point, angle formed by meeting of two lines.

nolde (*ne wolde*) would not, did not wish to.

nome *n.* name [nāme].

nome(n) *v. see* **nyme**

non(e) *pron.* none, no one.

non *see also* **no**

nones *in phr.* **for the nones** indeed.

norne *v.* state, declare; **norne on the same note** propose the same conditions; **nurne ayaynes** rebuke, refuse.

northe *n.* north.

not *adv.* not.

note *n.*[1] undertaking, business, affair; battle; **to the note** ready for the occasion.

note *n.*[2] musical note.

note *pp.* noted, notorious.

nothyng *adv.* not at all.

noumbles *n. pl.* numbles, entrails.

nouthe, nowthe *adv.* now.

nouther *see* **nauther**

now *adv.* and *conj.* now; now that.

nowel *n.* cry of joy at the birth of Christ [nouel].

nowhere *adv.* nowhere; not at all.

nowthe *see* **nouthe**

noyce, noyse *n.* noise.

nurne *see* **norne**

nurture *n.* breeding, manners, courtesy.

nye *n.* harm; difficulty [noi].

nye *v.* injure, harrass [noien].

nyght *n.* night.

nykked *see* **nikked**

nyme *v.* take, obtain.

nys *adj.* foolish, absurd [nīce].

nys *v.* (*ne is*) is not.

nyye *see* **nye** *n.*

o, of *prep.* of; in; about; by; with.

of *adv.* off.

offred *v. pa. t.* made an offering.

oft *adv.* often.

oghe *v.* own, possess, rule; ought, should [ouen].

oght *n.* anything.

oke *n.* oak.

olde *adj.* old.

on *adj.* one.

on *adv.* and *prep.* on, upon, about.

on-ferum *adv.* from afar, at a distance [aferrom].

on-stray *adv.* away [astrai].

on(e) *pron.* one, someone.

one *adj.* and *adv.* alone, only.

ones *adv.* once; before; **at thys ones** right now.

onewe *adv.* anew, once again [aneue].

only *adv.* only.

onsware *see* **answare**

open *adj.* open.

or *conj.* or; than.

oritore *n.* oratory, place for prayer.

orpedly *adv.* boldly, vigorously.

oryght *see* **aryght**

ostel *see* **hostel**

other *adj.* and *pron.* other, another; next, second.

other *adv.* and *conj.* or; also; otherwise.

otherwhyle *adv.* at other times.

othes *n. pl.* oaths.

oure *see* **we**

out *adv.* out; far and wide.

outtrage *adj.* extraordinary, marvelous [ŏutrāğe].

over *adv.* and *prep.* over; upon, above; across.

overal *adv.* everywhere, wholly, entirely.

overclambe *v. pa. t.* climbed over [overclīmben].

overgrowen *pp.* overgrown.

overtake *v.* catch, seize; **overtake your wylle** (re)gain your good will, understand your will (2387n).

overthwert *adv.* angrily, furiously.

overwalt *pp.* overcome, overwhelmed, overthrown.

overyede *v. pa. t.* passed.

owen *see* **awen**

owhere *adv.* anywhere.

palays *n.* palisade; **pyked palays** palisade of spiked poles [palis].

pane *n.* edging, lining.

papiayes *n. pl.* parrots [papejai(e)].

papure *n.* paper (802n) [papīr(e)].

paradise *n.* paradise.

paraunter, paraventure *adv.* perhaps, maybe; indeed; as it happens.

pared *pp.* cut.

park *n.* enclosed tract of land bordering a castle; game preserve (768n).

parte *v.* part.

passage *n.* journey.

passe *v.* come, go, pass; proceed, go further; depart; surpass; **was passande** surpassed.

pater *n.* Pater Noster prayer.

patrounes *n. pl.* lords.

paumes *n.* antlers.

paunce *n.* armor covering the abdomen (2017n).

paunches *n. pl.* stomachs.

pay *n.* payment.

paye *v.* pay, repay; please (1379n).

payne *n.* suffering, hardship, danger [pein(e)].

payne *v.* strive, attempt; **can hym payne** did exert himself.

paynted, payntet *pp.* painted; depicted [peinten].

payre *v.* fail; weaken, diminish [peiren].

payttrure *n.* decorative breast-armor of horse [paitrūre].

pece *n.* piece.

pelure *n.* fur.

penaunce *n.* penance; meager meal, penitential fare (897n).

pendaund, pendaunt hanging end of belt, often richly ornamented; pendant (2038n).

penta(u)ngel *n.* five-pointed star, pentagram (620n).

pented *v. pa. t.* pertained to [penden].

penyes *n. pl.* silver pennies, money.

peple *n.* people.

pere *n.* peer, equal.

perelous *adj.* perilous.

perile, peryl *n.* peril, danger; spiritual peril (1768n).

perle *n.* pearl.

persoun *n.* person, individual; **hys persoun** himself.

pertly *adv.* clearly, openly.

pervyng *n.* periwinkle (611n) [pervink(e)].

peryl *see* **perile**

pes *n.* peace.

pese *n.* pea.

piched *see* **pyche**

piked *pp.* polished.

pine *see* **pyne**

piped *v. pa. t.* cheeped, chirped.

pipes *n. pl.* pipes.

pité *n.* compassion, pity; piety, righteousness (654n).

pitosly *adv.* pitifully, miserably [pitŏusli].

place *n.* place; home; space, room.

plate *n.* plate armor (2017n).

play *n.* play, merriment.

play *v.* play.

playnes *n. pl.* fields.

plede *v.* plead, argue, debate; **plede hit** argue your case.

plesaunce *n.* pleasure, gratification.

plesaunt *adj.* pleasant.

plese *v.* please.

plyght *n.* fight, battle, strife; sin, offense.

plytes *n. pl.* troubles; conditions [plight].

polaynes *n. pl.* knee-plates [polein(e)].

policed, polysed, polyst *pp.* polished; cleansed.

pore, pover *adj.* poor [povre].

porter *n.* gate-keeper.

poudred *pp.* scattered, ornamented in random pattern.

pover *see* **pore**

poynt *n.* point; arrow point; angular point of star; virtue; **bryng me to the poynt** get to the point (627n).

poynte *v.* detail, record item-by-item (1009n).

praunce *v.* prance.

pray *v.* pray, ask, request [preien].

prayere *n.*[1] prayer [preiēr(e)].

prayere *n.*[2] meadow [praiere].

prayse *v.* praise; value, prize, esteem.

prece, prese *v.* press forward; hasten, push ahead [prēssen].

presense *n.* presence.

prest *n.* priest.

prestly *adv.* eagerly, promptly.

preve *adj.* brave.

prevé *adj.* discreet [privē].

preved *see* **proved**

prevély *adv.* privately; alone; discreetly [privēlī(e)].

prik *see* **pryk**

pris *see* **prys** *n.¹*

profered *v. pa. t.* proffered, offered, gave; asked [profren].

proude *adj.* proud; rich, splendid; spirited.

proved *pp.* proven; shown, displayed; proven by testing [prēven].

provinces *n. pl.* nations, lands, realms.

prowde *see* **proude**

prowes *n.* prowess, martial might or skill, valor [prŏues(se)].

pryde *n.* pride; **with pryde** splendidly.

pryk, prik *v.* prick; tempt, provoke; gallop.

pryme *n.* prime (canonical hour, 6-9 AM) (1675n).

prynce *n.* prince; **the Prynce of paradise** Christ.

prynces *n.* princess.

prys *adj.* valuable; excellent.

prys *n.¹* worth, value; honor, praise; prize; prowess; nobility (1277n, 1379n).

prys *n.²* hunting call blown when game is taken (1362n).

prysoun *n.* prisoner.

pure *adj.* and *adv.* pure; true; noble; completely.

pured *pp.* purified, refined; (of fur) trimmed to show one color only (633n).

purely *adv.* fully, entirely.

purpose *n.* purpose, intention, plan.

put *v.* put.

pyche *v.* embed, fasten, attach; build, erect; **that pyght in hir hert** that was fixed in her heart, that her heart was set on.

pyked *adj.* provided with spikes; **pyked palays** palisade of spiked poles.

pynakle *n.* pinnacle.

pyne *n.* affliction, trouble, difficulty; grief.

pyne *v.* take pains, trouble oneself, exert oneself.

pyned *pp.* enclosed [pīnden].

pypyng *n.* sound of pipes.

pysan *n.* breast and neck armor.

pyth *n.* toughness.

quaked *v. pa. t.* quaked, trembled.

quaynt *see* **coynt**

queldepoyntes *n. pl.* quilted coverlets [quilt(e)].

quelle *v.* kill; end.

queme *adj.* fine, pleasing, agreeable.

quene *n.* queen.

querré *n.* collection of game killed in hunt [quirrē].

quest *n.* searching of hounds for prey, or barking upon having scented it.

quethe *n.* speech, talk; **quethe of the quest** sound of dogs barking.

quik *see* **quyk**

quikly *see* **quykly**

quit-clayme *v.* relinquish entirely (293n).

quoth *v. pa. t.* said.

quyk *adj.* and *adv.* alive; lively; quickly.

quykly *adv.* quickly.

quyssewes *n. pl.* armor covering the thighs, consisting of front and back plates [quisseu].

quyssyn *n.* cushion [quishin].

quyte *v.* requite, repay; get even, punish.

rabel *n.* pack (of dogs), rabble.

race *n.* forward movement, race; stroke [rās(e)].

rach(ch) *n.* running dog that hunts by scent (1142) [racch(e)].

rad *adj.* afraid, fearful, frightened.

rad *adv.* quickly, promptly.

radly *adv.* quickly, swiftly.

raged *adj.* shaggy [ragged(e)].

raght *see* **reche**

rak *n.* cloud, rain or storm cloud.

rake *n.* path, track.

ran *see* **renne**

rande *n.* strip of land.

rape *v.* hurry, rush.

rapely *adv.* urgently.

rase *v.¹* charge, rush.

rase *v.²* snatch, pull away.

rasor *n.* rasor [rāsŏur(e)].

rasse *n.* ledge (1421n).

ratheled *pp.* rooted.

rawes *n. pl.* hedge-rows [reue].

rawthe *n.* sorrow, grief; **rawthe to here** horrible to hear [reuth(e)].

rayke *v.* go, proceed; rush; **rayked hir** betook herself.

rayled *pp.* arrayed, adorned, placed; strewn.

rayn *n.* rain [rein].

rayne *n.* rein [rein(e)].

raysed *v.* raise; ask to rise.

raysoun *see* **resoun**

rechate *v.* recheat, call back and summon together dogs (1446n).

reche *v.* reach; give, offer; **reche to** merit.

rechles *adj.* carefree.

recorded *v. pa. t.* repeated, recalled.

recreaunt *adj.* defeated; cowardly.

red *adj.* red.

rede *v.* advise; deal with; perceive (2111n).

redé *adv.* readily, willingly.

red(i)ly *adv.* readily, promptly; fully.

refourme *v.* restate, renew, re-create [refōrmen].

refuse *v.* refuse.

rehayted *v.* encourage, urge on; greet cheerfully, speak kindly to [rehēten].

reherce, reherse *v.* restate; describe.

rekenly *adv.* worthily, nobly, courteously; readily, promptly.

rele *v.* roll; double back, turn around; do, act (229n).

relece *v.* release (2342n) [relēsen].

remene *v.* recount, relate.

remewe *v.* change [remēven].

remnaunt *n.* remnant, remainder [remenaunt].

remorde *v.* recall with remorse.

renay *v.* refuse, reject [reneien].

rende *v.* tear apart, cut apart, strip off.

renk(k) *n.* man, knight [rink].

renne *v.* run.

renoun *n.* renown, fame, distinction; **of renoun** esteemed, honored; **riden in renoun** to be honored wherever one travels (2434n).

rent *see* **rende**

repayre *v.* arrive.

repreved *v. pa. t.* reproved.

require *v.* ask, inquire about [requēren].

rere *v.* come about, break out.

res *n.* rush.

resayt *n.* station where "receiving" dogs are kept (1168n) [receit(e)].

resayve *v.* receive [receiven].

rescowe *n.* rescue [rescŏue].

resette *n.* dwelling [recet].

resoun *n.* speech, discourse, words; **by resoun** correctly; by rights.

respite *n.* respite, temporary postponement.

rest *n.* rest.

restayed *see* **resteyed**

rested *v. pa. t.* rested.

resteye *v.* turn back; hold back, restrain.

restore *v.* restore; make restoration; revive, cure, make whole.

reve *v.* take away.

revel *n.* revelry; joy, happiness.

revel *v.* make merry.

reverence *n.* honor, respect.

reverenced *v. pa. t.* honored.

rewarde *n.* reward.

rewarde *v.* reward.

rich- *see* **rych-**

ride *see* **ryde**

right *see* **ryght**

rime *v. refl.* draw oneself up, sit up straight.

ringe *v.* ring.

rise *see* **ryse**

robe *n.* robe.

roche *n.* rock, crag.

roché *adj.* rocky.

rocher *n.* rocky hillside, cliff.

rod, rode *v. see* **ryde**

rode *n.* (Christ's) cross.

rof-sore *n.* gash, cut.

roffe *n.* roof [rōf].

rogh, rugh *adj.* rough; rugged; thick, dense; unflayed (1608n) [roughe].

rokk *n.* rock.

rokked *pp.* burnished (2018n).

rol(l)e *v.* roll; overhang in rolls or loose folds.

romaunce *n.* romance.

rome *v.* walk.

rone *n.* thicket.

ronge *see* **ringe**

ronk *adj.* full, thickly grown, abundant [rank].

ronkled *pp.* wrinkled [runklen].

rope *n.* cord, rope.

ros *see* **ryse**

rote *n.[1]* habit, custom (2207n).

rote *n.[2]* root.

rote *v.* rot.

roun *v.* confer, consult, deliberate.

rouncé *n.* horse, steed.

rounde *adj.* round.

roungen *see* **ringe**

rous *n.* fame, praise [rōs].

roust *n.* rust [rūst].

rout *n.* jerk, sharp pull.

rove *see* **ryve**

roves *see* **roffe**

ruch(ch)ed *see* **ryche** *v.*

rudede *pp.* reddened, fiery [rēden].

rudele *n.* bed-curtain [ridel].

ruful *adj.* dreadful, fearful [reuful].

rugh, rughe *see* **rogh**

rungen *see* **ringe**

runisch *adj.* violent, rough, vigorous [rūnish].

runischly *adv.* fiercely, roughly, harshly [rūnishlī].

runnen *see* **renne**

runyschly *see* **runischly**

rurd *n.* noise, clamor; voice.

rusched *v. pa. t.* made loud rushing noise; kept up (loud noise).

ruthe *v.* awaken; **ruthes hym** he gets up.

ryal *adj.* royal, kingly, glorious [roial].

ryally *adv.* royally [roiallī].

ryalme *n.* kingdom, realm [rēaume].

rybbe *n.* rib.

rych, ryche *adj.* and *adv.* rich, noble, mighty; great; valuable, precious; flourishing; richly; **rychest** *superl.* most nobly (360n).

ryche *v.* arrange; prepare; adorn; dress, clothe; proceed; turn.

rychely, richly *adv.* richly; lordly, masterfully, boldly; ceremoniously.

ryd(de) *v.* rid, relieve, free; separate; **ryde of** clear out internal organs.

ryde *v.* ride (2434n).

rydyng *n.* riding.

rygge *n.* back.

ryght *adj.* and *adv.* right; exact; correct, true; precisely, exactly.

ryght *n.* right, justice, law; **bi ryght** rightly.

ryght *v. pa. t.* straightened; **ryght hym to speke** straightened himself and said.

ryme *n.* membrane.

ryne *v.* touch, strike.

rynk (*pl.* **rynges**) ring.

rynkande *see* **ringe**

ryol *see* **ryal**

rype *adj.* ripe.

rype *v.* ripen.

rys *n.* thicket, brush.

ryse *v.* rise; arise; grow.

rytte *v.* cut off.

ryve *adv.* amply, greatly.

ryve *v.* cut.

sabatoun *n.* steel shoe.

sadel *n.* saddle.

sadel *v.* saddle.

sadly *adv.* firmly, vigorously; long enough.

saf *see* **save** *prep.*; **wowche hit saf** *see* **wowche**

sake *n.* sake.

sale *n.* hall.

salue *v.* greet.

salure *n.* dish for salt [salēr(e)].

same *adj.* same.

same(n) *adv.* together.

samen *v.* gather, assemble; **samned** came together [samnen].

sanap *n.* cloth runner placed on table-cloth [sāve-nāp(e)].

sate *see* **sitte**

saule, sawle *n.* soul [soul(e)].

save, saf *prep.* except.

save *v.* save, preserve, protect, deliver (from danger or sin), bring salvation.

saver *adj. compar.* safer [sauf].

savered *pp.* flavored.

saverly *adv.* safely; confidently (1937n).

sawe *n.* speech, words; prayer.

sawes *n.* sauce.

sawle *see* **saule**

say *v.* say.

saylande *pres. p.* flowing [seilen].

sayn *see* **saynt**

sayned *v. pa. t.* crossed, made sign of the cross [sīgnen]

saynt *n.*[1] saint [seint(e)].

saynt *n.*[2] belt, sash, girdle [ceint].

scathe *n.* harm, injury, loss; **hit is scathe** it is a pity.

schadde, schade *see* **schede**

schaft *n.* shaft, handle; spear [shaft(e)].

schafted *v. pa. t.* set [shaften].

schal *v.* shall, will, ought, must; **schuld** *pa. t.* should, would [shulen].

schalk *n.* man; knight; servant [shalk(e)].

schame *n.* shame [shāme].

schamed *v. pa. t.* was embarrassed [shāmen].

schankes *see* **schonkes**

schape *v.* arrange; design; depict; tell (a tale); specify; agree upon [shāpen].

scharp *adj.* sharp [sharp].

schaterande *pres. p.* breaking (upon shores) [scateren].

schave *v.* scrape; **schaven** smoothed [shāven].

schawe *see* **schewe**

schede *v.* fall; **schade** sliced, cut [shēden].

schelde *n.* shield; **scheldes** tough hide at shoulders and neck of wild boar; slabs of boar meat [shēld].

schemered *v. pa. t.* shimmered [shimeren].

schende *v.* kill [shēnden].

schene *adj.* splendid, fair; bright [shēne].

scher *n. see* **cher**

schere *v.* cut [shēren].

schewe, schawe *v.* show; bring; offer; reveal; appear; look at [sheuen].

schinande *pres. p.* [shīnen].

scho *see* **ho**

scholes *adj.* shoe-less (160n) [shōles].

schome *see* **schame**

schon *v. pa. t.* shone [shīnen].

schonkes *n. pl.* legs [shank(e)].

schop *see* **schape**

schore *n.* shore; cliff; ground [shōre].

schorne *see* **schere**

schort *adj.* short [short].

schote *v.* shoot; **schot with** tossed from [shēten].

schow(v)e *v.* shove; press; flow [shŏuven].

schowres *n. pl.* showers [shŏur].

schrank *v. pa. t.* shrank, flinched; cut [shrinken].

schrewe *n.* villain, evil-doer, rascal [shreue].

schrof *v. pa. t.* confessed [shrīven].

schuld *see* **schal**

schulder *n.* shoulder [shulder].

schunt *n.* jerk [shunt].

schunt *v.* flinch, dodge [shunten].

schuve *see* **schowe**

schyire *see* **schyr**

schylde *v.* prevent; **God schylde** God forbid [shēlden].

schyn *see* **schal**

schyndered *v. pa. t.* shattered, burst, sundered.

schyr, schyre, schyree, schyire *adj.* bright, fair, white; **schyrer** *compar.* brighter [shīr(e)].

schyrly *adv.* completely, thoroughly [shīrlī].

scowte *n.* crag [scŏute].

scrape *v.* paw (the ground).

scurtes *see* **skyrt**

se *v.* see.

seche *adj. see* **such**

seche *v.* seek, find; **soght fro** set out from.

sedes *n. pl.* seeds.

seg(g)e *n.* siege.

segg *n.* man; knight; priest.

segh, seghe *see* **se**

seker *see* **siker**

selden *adv.* seldom.

sele *n.* good fortune, prosperity; happiness, bliss (2422n).

self, selven *adj.* same; self; **under Krystes selven** below Christ himself (i.e., anywhere, in the world); **Goddes self** God himself.

selly *adj.* wonderful, marvelous; **sellokest** hugest, most marvelous.

selly(ly) *adv.* very, extremely; **sellyly ofte** many times over.

selly *n.* wonder, marvel.

selure *n.* canopy [celūre].

selven *see* **self**

semb(e)launt *n.* semblance, appearance; manner, behavior, demeanor; look.

semblé *n.* throng, assembled hunting party.

seme *adj.* seemly, attractive, agreeable.

seme *v.* seem; be apparent; suit, be becoming for.

semes *n. pl.* seams; strips of embroidered material (610n).

semly *adj.* seemly, fair, attractive; **semloker** *compar.* more beautiful.

semly(ch), **semlyly** *adv.* excellently; beautifully; decorously.

sen *see* **se**

sendal *n.* kind of costly fabric [cendāl].

sende *v.* send.

sene *adj.* visible; plain, straightforward.

sene *v. see* **se**

sengel *adj.* alone.

serched *v. pa. t.* examined.

sere *adj.* and *adv.* various, several, many; **sere twyes** on two occasions, twice.

serlepes *adv.* separately, in turn [sēr(e)-lēpes].

sertayn *adv.* indeed.

servaunt *n.* servant.

serve *v.* serve.

served *pp.* deserved.

servise, **servyce** *n.* service; **at sawe other at servyce** in speech or action, in words or deeds.

sese *v.* seize, take, grasp [seisen].

sesed *pp.* ceased, stopped, ended [cēsen].

sesoun *n.* season; appointed time, particular time.

sesounde *pp.* seasoned.

set(te) *v.* set, set down, put, place; guide; set table; devise; attain; settle; **set at lyght** undervalue; **settes hym out** rushes out.

sete *adj.* tasty.

sete *n.* seat; act of sitting down.

sete(n) *v. see also* **sitte**

settel *n.* seat [setle].

seven *num.* seven.

sever *v.* cut; part, depart.

sewe *n.* sauce, gravy, broth; stew.

sey *see* **se**

seye *v.* go; come, arrive [sīen].

seye(n) *v. see also* **se**

sid-bordes *n. pl.* side-tables (73n).

side *see* **syde** *n.*

sight *see* **syght**

siker *adj.* and *adv.* safe; stout, doughty, strong in arms; trusty, faithful; sure, assured; completely; **in a siker wyse** securely.

silk *n.* silk.

sille *n.* paved floor of hall; **on sille** in hall.

sir, **syre** *n.* lord; as title, used of knights and nobility; also, a formal or respectful mode of address.

sister-sune *n.* sister's son, nephew (111n) [suster].

sithen *see* **sythen**

sitte *v.* sit.

skayned *pp.* grazed.

skere *adj.* faultless, innocent; sincere (1261n).

skete *adv.* rapidly, suddenly, quickly.

skewes *n. pl.* clouds, heavens [skeu].

skyfted *v. pa. t.* alternated.

skyl(le) *n.* reason.

skyrt *n.* lower part of gown or robe; saddle-skirt.

slade *n.* valley; glade, clearing.

slaked *v. pa. t.* grew still, dimished.

slayn *pp.* slain [slēn].

sleght *see* **slyght**

slentyng *n.* shooting.

slepe *n.* sleep.

slepe *v.* sleep.

sleper *n.* sleeper.

slete *n.* sleet.

sleye *adj.* well-crafted; subtly seasoned [sleigh].

sleyly *adv.* quietly, imperceptibly.

slode *see* **slyde**

sloke *v.* cease, stop; **slokes** enough!

slomeryng *n.* slumbering, sleep [slŏmbering(e)].

slot *n.* hollow at base of throat above breast-bone.

slowe *v. pa. t.* slew, killed [slēn].

slyde *v.* enter, come, move; **as in slomeryng he slode** as he was emerging from sleep.

slyght *n.* skill; stratagem, trick, device; subtlety [sleight].

slyp *v.* slip; **slypped upon slepe** fallen asleep; **slyp unslayn** escape alive.

slyt *v. pa. t.* slit.

smal *adj.* small; slim; fine, light (fabric).

smartly *adv.* quickly, promptly [smertlī].

smeten *see* **smyte**

smethely *adv.* politely, sweetly, pleasantly.

smolt *adj.* gentle.

smothe *adj.* pleasant.

smothely *adv.* deftly.

smyle *v.* smile.

smylyng *n.* smiling.

smyte *v.* smite; **thay smeten into merthe** they fell into merriment.

snart *adv.* bitterly.

snawe *n.* snow.

snayped *v. pa. t.* nipped, afflicted.

snitered *v. pa. t.* fell.

snyrt *v. pa. t.* nicked, grazed.

so *adv.* and *conj.* so; as; thus; any, whatsoever; in this way, in this manner; in the same way as.

soberly *adv.* solemnly, earnestly, with appropriate dignity.

softe *adj.* and *adv.* soft; softly; comfortably; **softer** *compar.* less martial.

softly *adv.* quietly.

soght *see* **seche**

sojorne *n.* stay, visit.

sojo(u)rne *v.* stay; **hade ben sojourned** had been stabled.

solace *n.* joy, amusement, mirth, pleasure; assistance [sōlās].

somer *n.* summer; the warm half of the year (510n).

son *n.* son.

sone *adv.* soon, quickly, at once, without delay.

songes *n. pl.* songs.

sop *n.* piece of bread dipped in wine, water, milk, etc.; **ete a sop** had a light meal [sop(pe)].

soper *n.* supper, evening meal.

sore *adj.* grievous.

soré *adj.* sorry, sad.

sorwe *n.* sorrow, grief.

sostnaunce *n.* sustenance, nourishment, food [sustenaunce].

soth(e) *adj.* and *adv.* true, truly, truthfully.

sothe *n.* truth; **for sothe** truly, indeed.

sothen *pp.* boiled [sēthen].

sothly *adv.* truly; quietly (673n).

sounde *n.* safety; **in sounde** in good health.

sounder *n.* herd of wild swine (1440n) [sŏundre].

soundyly *adv.* soundly.

soure *adj.* unpleasant, unattractive.

sourquydrye *see* **surquidré**

soverayn *n.* sovereign; mistress, liege lady.

sowme *n.* number [somme].

space *n.* space, period of time; **in space** shortly; in (due) time.

spare *adj.* brief, scant; **upon spare wyse** tactfully.

spared *pp.* spared.

sparlyr *n.* calf.

sparred *v. pa. t.* rushed, darted, sprang.

sparthe *n.* long-shafted battle-axe.

spech *n.* speech; **speches** words.

specially *adv.* particularly.

specialté *n.* love.

sped *n.* power; speed; **good sped** quickly.

spede *v.* succeed, fulfill (desires); help, aid, bless; fare; hasten.

spedly *adv.* readily.

speke *v.* speak.

spelle *n.* speech, words.

spelle *v.* say.

spend *see* **spenne** *v.*

spende *v.* spend, expend.

spenet *see* **spenne** *v.*

spenne *n.* fence; hedge; **in spenne** there.

spenne *v.* fasten.

spenne-fote *adv.* with feet together.

spere *n.* spear.

sperred *v. pa. t.* struck (horse with spurs), spurred on.

spetos *adj.* cruel [spītŏus].

spied *see* **spye**

spoken *see* **speke**

spon *n.* spoon.

spores *see* **spures**

sprange *see* **sprong**

sprenged *v. pa. t.* (of day) dawned, broke.

sprent *v. pa. t.* sprang.

sprit *v. pa. t.* leaped.

sprong *v. pa. t.* sprang [springen].

spured *pp.* asked [spiren].

spures *n. pl.* spurs [spore].

spuryed *see* **spured**

spyces *n. pl.* spices; spiced cakes, delicacies.

spye *v.* inquire; find, find out.

spyt *n.* injury; **boute spyt more** without inflicting more injuries.

stabeled *v. pa. t.* stabeled [stāblen].

stabled *pp.* established.

stablye *n.* group of hunters and hounds stationed around perimeter of wood during hunt to prevent escape of game (1149n) [stāblīe].

stad *pp.* placed, set down, fixed; hard pressed, assailed; equipped with, furnished with (31n) [steden].

staf *n.* staff; club.

staf-ful *adj.* stuffed; full to utmost degree.

stale *n.* place.

stalked *v. pa. t.* moved, walked (237n).

stalle *see* **stale**

stalworth *adj.* powerful, valiant.

stange *n.* pole.

stapled *pp.* equipped with staples (606n).

starande *pres. p.* glittering.

start *v.* move quickly; bound forward; flinch; draw back [sterten].

statut *n.* contract, compact, agreement.

stave *see* **staf**

stayned *pp.* colored, dyed [steinen].

sted(de) *n.* place.

sted(e) *n.* steed.

stek *v. pa. t.* clung to.

stel-bawe *n.* stirrup [stēl(e)].

stel-gere *n.* (steel) armor [stēl(e)].

stele *n.¹* handle.

stele *n.²* steel.

stele *v.* steal; **stollen** furtive, secret.

stem(m)e *v. pa. t.* lingered, tarried; stopped (talking).

steppe *v.* step.

steropes *see* **stirop**

steven *n.¹* speech, words, voice.

steven *n.²* time; appointed time, appointment; meeting.

stif(fe) *adj.* firm; unmoving; bold, brave, resolute; strong; stout; loud; **stif to strayne** diffi-cult to restrain; **stif(f)est** *superl.* boldest, bravest.

stif, stifly *adv.* securely; stoutly; forcefully; swiftly, quickly.

stightel, stightle *v.* govern, rule, give orders; **stightles in stalle** stands in place.

stille *adj. and adv.* still, silent, noiseless; furtive; meekly; quietly; privately, in private; **stiller** *compar.* more silent.

stilly *adv.* quietly, silently.

stirop *n.* stirrup.

stod, stoden *see* **stonde**

stoffed *pp.* padded [stuffen].

stoken *pp.* fixed, set down; appointed; **stoken of** stocked with, fully provided with (31n) [stēken].

stollen *see* **stele** *v.*

ston stone; gem; stone pavement.

ston-fyr *n.* sparks struck from stone [stōn].

ston-stil *adj.* stone-still; perfectly silent and motionless.

stonde *v.* stand; withstand; exist, loom; **stondande alofte** mounted prominently, set so as to stand out.

stonyed *see* **stoune**

stor *adj.* strong; loud; harsh, severe; reproving, rebuking.

stori *n.* story.

stounde *n.* short period of time; time of trial or suffering, hardship; **bi stoundes** in turn, at various times.

stoune *v.* astonish, amaze, surprise; be astonished [stŏnen].

stoutly *adv.* vigorously, loudly; securely.

stowned *see* **stoune**

strakande *pres. p.* sounding prolonged hunting call on horn (1364n).

straunge *adj.* foreign, unfamiliar, unknown.

strayne *v.* restrain [streinen].

strayt *adj.* tight-fitting [streit].

streght *adj.* straight [streight].

strenkthe *n.* strength [strength(e)].

strike *v.* strike; **stroke** was struck.

strok *n.* stroke, blow.

stroke *v.* stroke; *see also* **strike**

stronge *adj.* strong, powerful.

stronge *see also* **straunge**

strothe *n.* marshy land.

stryde *v.* stride; **stryde alofte** mount (horse).

strye *v.* kill, slaughter [stroien].

stryf *n.* strife, resistance, opposition.

stryke *see* **strike**

stryth(th)e *n.* stance.

stubbe *n.* tree stump.

studie *v.* strive, endeavor; try to find out; think about, reflect upon; be perplexed by, wonder about.

study *n.* being lost in thought, perplexed, amazed.

stuffe *n.* cloth, fabric.

sture *v.* brandish, swing [stiren].

sturn *adj.* stern, grim; serious; bold; cruel; tough; massive [stern(e)].

sturnely *adv.* forcefully, violently; fiercely, sternly, grimly [sternlī].

styf, styffest *see* **stif**

styghtel *see* **stightel**

stylle, stylly *see* **stille**

stythly *adv.* forcefully, steadfastly.

suande *see* **sue**

such *adj.* and *pron.* such.

sue *v.* follow, pursue.

suffer *v.* suffer; allow; **suffer hym byhoved** he was compelled, he was forced (2040n).

sum(me) *adj.* and *pron.* some (247n) [sŏm].

sumned *pp.* summoned [somnen].

sumtyme *adv.* in the past [sŏm-tīme].

sumwhat *adv.* and *pron.* somewhat; something.

sumwhyle *adv.* sometimes; in the past [sŏm-whīle].

sun *see* **son**

sunder *adv.* asunder, apart [sŏnder].

sunder *v.* sunder, separate, break apart [sŏnderen].

sunne *n.* sun.

sure *adj.* trusty, dependable, good [seur].

surely *adv.* completely (1884n) [seurlī].

surfet *n.* fault, misdeed, sin.

surkot *n.* emblazoned tunic worn over armor [surcōt(e)].

surquidré *n.* arrogance, pride, presumption.

sute *n.* suit; **of his hors swete** of his horse matched (the Green Knight's color); **of a sute** alike; **of folwande sute** of the same kind; **in swete** all together, all alike.

swange *n.* waist.

swap *v.* make an agreement, bargain (1108n).

sware *adj.* strongly built, thick-set [squār(e)].

sware *v.* answer.

swenge *v.* rush, hurry, start.

swere *v.* swear.

swete *adj.* and *adv.* sweet, dear (man, lady); sweetly.

swete *n. see* **sute**

swetely *adv.* eagerly, willingly, happily, well.

swethled *v. pa. t.* wound, tied [swāthelen].

sweven *n.* dream.

sweye *v.* rush, hasten; **sweye doun** lean down.

swoghe *adj.* swooning, faint, unconscious; **in a swoghe sylence** in deadly silence [swŏu(e)].

sworde *n.* sword.

swyeres *n. pl.* squires.

swyft(e) *adv.* swiftly.

swyn *n.* boar, swine.

swynge *v.* rush.

swyre *n.* neck.

swythe, swythely *adv.* quickly; eagerly; earnestly; diligently; greatly.

syde *adj.* long.

syde *n.* side; waist; edge.

syfle *v.* blow gently, breathe.

syght *n.* sight.

syke *v.* sigh.

syker *see* **siker**

sykyng *see* **syke**

sykynges *n.* sighing.

sylence *n.* silence.

sylk *see* **silk**

sylkyn *adj.* silken, made of silk [silken].

sylveren, sylverin *adj.* silver.

symple *adj.* plain; modest.

syn *conj.* since.

syng *v.* sing.

syngne *n.* sign, symbol, token.

synne *adv.* since then [sin].

synne *n.* sin.

syre *see* **sir**

sythe *n.[1]* way; turn; time; set, group, unit.

sythe *n.[2]* scythe.

sythen *adv.* and *conj.* then, from that time on, afterwards; since [sitthen].

sytte *see* **sitte**

syy *see* **se**

ta *see* **take**

table, tabil *n.* table; *arch.* cornice.

tacche, tach(ch)e *v.* attach [tachen].

taght, taghtte *see* **teche** *v.*

take *v.* take; accept; give, assign; overcome, vanquish, defeat; discover; **take at** receive from; **as he is tan** according to his circumstances, as he finds himself.

takle *n.* gear, equipment [takel].

tale *n.* tale; word; conversation; report, account.

talenttyf *adj.* eager [talentīf].

talk *n.* talking, speaking.

talk(k) *v.* talk, speak.

talkyng *n.* talking, conversation, speech.

tame *adj.* tame; **make ful tame** subdue thoroughly, control completely.

tan *see* **take**

tape *see* **tap(p)e**

tapit *n.* decorative fabric; carpet; tapestry, wall-hanging [tapēt(e)].

tap(p)e *n.* tap, light blow (2357n).

tapytes *see* **tapit**

tars *n.* fine Tharsian fabric (77n).

tary *v.* tarry, delay.

tas *see* **take**

tasseles *n. pl.* tassels.

tayl *n.* tail.

taysed *pp.* driven.

tayt *adj.* merry; well-grown.

teccheles *adj.* faultless.

teche *n.* characteristic; feature of disposition; (moral) blemish, fault; token, sign, symbol [tach(e)].

teche *v.* teach, show, guide, inform.

tel *see* **til(le)**

telde *n.* building, dwelling, house.

telde *v.* set (up); build, erect.

telle *v.* tell, say, state, report, recite.

temes *n. pl.* themes; **temes of tyxt** subject matter.

tender *adj.* eager; morally weak, unable to resist temptation.

tene *adj.* perilous; tedious; dense, rough.

tene *n.* strife; harm; difficulty.

tene *v.* distress; beset, harass; grow vexed, become angry.

tent *n.* intention, purpose; **I am in tent** I intend, it is my purpose.

tented *v. pa. t.* tended (to), attended.

tenthe *num.* tenth.

terme *n.* term, vocabulary, expression; appointed place or time.

tevelyng *n.* toiling, struggling.

thad *see* **that** *def. art.* and *adj.*

thagh *conj.* though; if [though].

thanne *see* **then** *conj.*

thar *adv.* there.

that *conj.* that, so that (912n).

that *def. art.* and *adj.* that; the.

that *pron.* that, what, which, who(m).

thay *pron.* they; **thayr** their; **thayres** theirs, their own [thei, their(e), theires].

the *adv. with comp. adj.* or *adv.* the, so much the.

the *def. art.* the.

thede *n.* land, country, realm.

theder *adv.* thither, to that place, there [thider].

thee *pron. see* **thou**

thef *n.* thief.

then(ne) *adv.* and *conj.* then; there; when [thenne].

then *conj.* than [than].

thenk(k) *v.* think, think about, be mindful of, practice; **hym thoght** it seemed to him (them) [thinken].

thenn, thenne *see* **then(ne)**

ther *adv.* there, where, when; in heaven (839n).

ther-aboute *adv.* near it, (at work) on it.

ther-amonges *adv.* among it, mixed with it.

ther-as *conj.* where.

ther-at *adv.* at that, of it.

ther-bi *adv.* from them.

ther-byside *adv.* next to it, beside it.

ther-on *adv.* on it.

ther-oute *adv.* out of it; outside.

ther-ryght *adv.* right there.

ther-to *adv.* to it, there, to this, on it.

ther-tylle *adv.* to that.

ther-under *adv.* under it, underneath.

ther-with *adv.* with it, with this, with them.

therafter *adv.* thereafter, afterward, after it.

therfor(n)e *adv.* therefore; for it.

therinne *adv.* therein, in it.

therof *adv.* thereof, of it, about it.

thes *see* **this**

thewes *n. pl.* manners, conduct [theu].

thi *see* **thou**

thider *see* **theder**

thiderwarde *adv.* in that direction.

thik(ke) *adj.* and *adv.* thick, burly, stout, large; thickly, densely, close-set; hard; **trochet ful thik** embellished with many pinnacles.

thin *see* **thou**

thing *see* **thyng**

think *see* **thynk(k)**

this *adj.* and *pron.* this; **thes(e)** *pl.* these.

thiself *see* **thou**

tho *def. art.* and *adj.* those; that, the.

thof, thogh *conj.* though [though].

thoght *n.* thought [thought].

thoght, thoghten *v. see* **thenk(k)** *and* **thynk(k)**

tholed *v. pa. t.* allowed; suffered.

thonk *n.* thanks [thank].

thonk(ke) *v.* thank [thanken].

thore *see* **thar**

thorne *n.* thorn.

those *adj.* and *pron.* those.

thou, thow *pron.* you (*inform.* and *sing.*); **thee** you (*obl.*), to you; **thy, thyn** your; **thiself, thyselven** yourself (272n).

thrast *n.* thrust [threst(e)].

thrat *see* **threte**

thrawe *v.* throw; lay (bare); bind; **thrawen** burly; **thrid tyme throwe best** third time's the charm, third time's lucky (*lit.* "third time throw best") (1680n) [throuen].

thre *num.* three.

thred *n.* thread; **neghe the thred** near the limit (1771n).

threpe *n.* contest; insistence, importunate request, pressing entreaty.

threpe *v.* struggle with, fight against, contend with.

thresch *v.* strike, attack [threshen].

threte *n.* force, compulsion.

threte *v.* threaten; attack; curse; urge.

thrich *n.* rush, charge.

thrid *num.* third.

thro *adj.* and *adv.* bold, fearless; savage, angry, threatening; steadfast; eager, willing; fair, delightful, good; eagerly; firmly.

throly *adv.* warmly.

thronge *see* **thrynge**

throte *n.* throat.

throwe *n.* while, short time [throu].

throwe(n) *v. see* **thrawe**

thryd *see* **thrid**

thrye(s), thryse *adv.* thrice, three times [thrīce].

thryght *v. pa. t.* threw, shoved; *pp.* pressed [thricchen].

thrynge *v.* gather in crowd, throng together; go, move, rush.

thrynne *num.* third.

thryse *see* **thrye(s)**

thryvande *adj.* hearty [thrīven *v.*].

thryvandely *adv.* heartily; abundantly [thrīvinglī]

thryve *v.* thrive, live, prosper; **so mot I thryve** as I may thrive, upon my life.

thryven *adj.* lovely, fair [thrīven *v.*].

thught *see* **thynk(k)**

thulged *v. pa. t.* bore, endured, was patient with [thilgen].

thurgh *adv.* and *prep.* through; throughout; above, beyond; because of.

thurled *v. pa. t.* pierced [thirlen].

thus *adv.* thus, so, in this manner, therefore.

thwarle *adj.* intricate, tight.

thwong *n.* thong [thong].

thy *see* **thou**

thygh *n.* thigh.

thyk *see* **thik(ke)**

thyn *see* **thou**

thyng, thynk *n.* thing; affair, event, matter; person, creature.

thynk(k) *v.* think; like, desire; appear, seem; **me (him, etc.) thynkes** it seems to me (him); · **me thynk hit an other** I believe otherwise, I see it differently.

thys *see* **this**

thyselven *see* **thou**

til(le) *prep.* and *conj.* to; until.

tit *adv.* quickly; **as tit** at once, immediately.

titleres *n. pl.* hounds kept at hunting station until game approaches.

to *adv.* too.

to *prep.* and *adv.* to; into; toward; at; for; as; **to tachched** attached to them.

today *adv.* today.

tofylched *v. pa. t.* seized.

togeder *adv.* together.

toght *adj.* strong [tought, tough].

tohewe *v.* cut down.

tok *see* **take**

token *n.* token, sign, symbol; lesson; title.

token *v. see* **take**

tokenyng *n.* sign; **in tokenyng** signifying (that), as a sign (that).

tolde *see* **telle**

tole *n.* tool; weapon.

tolke *see* **tulk**

tolouse *n.* fine fabric from Toulouse (77n).

tomorn *adv.* tomorrow.

tone *see* **take**

tonge *n.* tongue; **with tonge** by words, orally.

toppyng *n.* forelock.

tor *adj.* hard, difficult.

toraced *pp.* mutilated, torn to pieces [tōrāsen].

torch *n.* torch.

toret *adj.* edged, ornamented.

tornaye *v.* take part in tournament, joust; double back [tŏurneien].

torne *pp.* torn.

torne *v.* turn, return; **turned tyme** turbulent, changeful, or destructive time; **tourne to** reach [turnen].

tortor *n.* turtledove [turtur].

torvayle *n.* trouble, effort, labor.

tote *v.* peer, gaze, look.

toun *n.* town; **as I in toun herde** as I have heard it told; **halet out of toun** over and done (31n).

tournayed *see* **tornaye**

tourne *see* **torne**

toward *prep.* toward; **to hir warde** toward her.

towch *n.* touch; sound produced by instrument; hint, impression; **halde the towches** keep the covenant [tŏuch(e)].

towche *v.* touch; describe, mention [tŏuchen].

towen *pp.* come, traveled, journeyed [tēn].

towrast *pp.* distorted, gone awry.

towres *n. pl.* towers, turrets [tŏur].

trammes *n. pl.* schemes, plots, machinations.

trante *v.* double back.

trased *pp.* entwined, interwoven, braided (1739n) [trācen].

traunt *n.* cunning, trickery, caginess (1700n) [trant(e)].

trauthe *see* **trawthe**

travayl *n.* journey.

travayled *v. pa. t.* traveled, journeyed.

trawe *see* **trow(o)e**

trawthe, trauthe *n.* truth; word (of honor); fidelity, faithfulness; honor, integrity, adherence to one's word; knightly honor, adherence to chivalric ideal (394n) [treuth].

trayle *v.* trail (game); cross a trail.

trayst *adj.* assured, certain; **that be ye trayst** be assured of this.

trayteres *n. pl.* tricks, turns; **a trayteres** by tricks or turns (1700n) [cf. a-traverse].

traytor *n.* traitor; one who betrays his lord, esp. by seducing his wife.

tre *n.* tree.

trecherye, tricherie *n.* treachery, treason; faithlessness, dishonesty, duplicity.

treleted *pp.* interlaced.

tresoun *n.* treason, treachery [treisŏun].

tressour *n.* hair-net, head-dress.

trestes *n. pl.* trestles, supports for tabletop [trestel].

trewest *see* **true(e)**

tricherie *see* **trecherye**

tried *see* **tryed**

trifel *see* **tryfle**

trochet *pp.* embellished with pinnacles or crenelations.

trow(o)e *v.* believe; expect; trust [trouen].

tru-luf *see* **true-luf**

true(e) *adj.* true; faithful, loyal; honest; accurate; **trewest** *superl.* most certain; most faithful, honest (4n) [treu(e)].

true-luf, tru-lof *n.* true love, devoted fidelity in love; true-love, herb paris (*Paris quadri-folia*); true-love knot [treu-lŏve].

tru(e)ly *adv.* truly, faithfully, devoutly, rightly, sincerely [treulī].

trump *n.* trumpet [tromp(e)].

trusse *v.* tie, fasten, pack.

tryed *pp.* tried (in court); fine, choice, excellent (4n).

tryfle *n.* trifle; trifling or playful reference; ornamental or decorative detail [trufle].

tryst *v.* trust, count on, rely on [trusten].

tryster, trystor *n.* station where hunters await game (1149n) [trist(e)].

trystyly *adv.* faithfully [trustīlī].

tulé *see* **tuly**

tulk *n.* man; **iche tolke** every man, everyone.

tuly *adj.* deep red, crimson; *as n.* red silk fabric from Toulouse.

turned *see* **torne**

tusch *n.* tusk [tush].

twayne, tweyne *num.* two [twein].

twelmonyth *n.* period of twelve months, year (298n) [twelve-mōnth].

twelve *num.* twelve.

twenty *num.* twenty.

tweyne *see* **twayne**

two *num.* two.

twy(e)s *adv.* twice.

twyg *n.* twig, small branch.

twynne *num.* two.

twynne *v.* depart, separate, part from.

twynnen *pp.* braided, plaited [twīnen].

twys *see* **twy(e)s**

tyde *n.* time, season; feast; **hyghe tyde** festive occasion, solemn feast; holiday season.

tyde *v.* be one's lot or fate; happen, befall; **that yow tydes** that which is your due [tīden, bitīden].

tyffe *v.* prepare, make ready.

tyght *v.¹* spread, hang.

tyght *v.²* intend.

tyl *see* **til(le)**

tyme *n.* time.

tymed *pp.* timed.

tyrve *v.* strip, flay.

tyt *see* **tit**

tytel *see* **tytle**

tytelet *pp.* inscribed [tītlen].

tytle *n.* proof; authorization, warrant, right; **bi tytle that hit habbes** as it is entitled to do.

tyxt *n.* text, narrative, tale, romance [text(e)].

uch *adj.* each, every, all, every kind of.

uchon *adj.* each one, everyone, all (of them).

ugly *adj.* and *adv.* dreadful, terrifying; loathsome, repulsive; threateningly.

umbe *prep.* around.

umbeclypped *v. pa. t.* clasped, encircled.

umbefolde *v.* enclose.

umbekesten *v. pa. t.* searched, explored [umbecasten].

umbelappe *v.* overlap, interlace.

umbeteye *v. pa. t.* encircled, enclosed.

umbetorne *adv.* all around.

umbeweved *v. pa. t.* enclosed.

unbarred *pp.* unbarred.

unbene *adj.* cheerless, inhospitable.

unblythe *adj.* joyless.

unbynde *v.* cut apart.

uncely *adj.* vicious, dangerous [unsēlī].

unclosed *v. pa. t.* opened.

uncoupled *pp.* unleashed.

uncouthe *adj.* foreign; unfamiliar.

under *prep.* and *adv.* under; underneath, below (742n).

undertake *v.* understand, perceive.

undo *v.* carve up, dismember, cut open.

unethe *adv.* scarcely.

unfayre *adv.* profusely; horribly.

unhap *n.* mishap.

unhap *v.* come undone (2511n).

unhardeled *v.* unleashed (dogs).

unlace *v.* carve up, cut apart, dismember [unlāsen].

unleuté *n.* dishonesty, lack of loyalty [leautē].

unlouked *v. pa. t.* opened.

unlyke *adj.* unlike, dissimilar.

unmanerly *adv.* rudely, uncivilly.

unmete *adj.* extremely heavy or large.

unrydely *adv.* disorderly, confusedly.

unslayn *adj.* alive, not slain.

unslyye *adj.* unwary, incautious.

unsoundyly *adv.* in deadly fashion.

unsparely *adv.* without stinting, unsparingly.

unspurd *pp.* without asking.

unthryvande *adj.* ignoble, unseemly.

unto *prep.* to.

untrawthe *n.* dishonesty, disloyalty, oath-breaking, faithlessness, shameful conduct [untreuth].

untyghtel *n.* lack of restraint; **dalten untyghtel** reveled.

unworthy *adj.* unworthy; of little worth.

up *adv.* up; open.

upbrayde *pp.* drawn up.

uphalde *v.* hold up.

uphalt *pp.* (raised) high [uphālen].

uplyfte *v.* rise.

upon *prep.* and *adv.* upon; on; in; into; from.

upon *v.* open.

upryse *v.* arise; come out.

urysoun *n.* silk mantling (608n).

us *see* **we**

use *v.* practice, follow, perform, do; give (mercy); have dealings with, associate with.

utter *adv.* out.
uus *see* **we**

valay *n.* valley [valei(e)].
vale *n.* vale, dale; **by hylle ne be vale** anywhere.
vayles *n. pl.* veils [veil].
vayres *adv.* truly; **in vayres** in truth.
velvet *n.* velvet.
venquyst *v. pa. t.* defeated (foes), triumphed (in combat).
venysoun *n.* venison.
ver *n.* Spring.
verayly *adv.* truly; indeed; correctly.
verdure *n.* green.
vertue *n.* virtue, moral excellence, goodness; fortitude, endurance.
vertuus *adj.* having beneficial properties; possessing magical powers (2027n).
vesture *n.* clothing, garments.
vewter *n.* huntsman who cares for dogs and manages them in hunt [feut(e)rer].
vilanous *adj.* ill-bred, unrefined [vileinŏus].
visage *n.* appearance, looks.
voyde *v.* empty, clear out; remove; leave (table); **voyded of** devoid of.
vyage *n.* journey.
vylany *n.* rudeness; baseness; sinfulness.
vyse *n.* vice, flaw, failing.

wade *v.* wade; go, go down (788n).
wage *n.* wage; **wynter wage** promise of winter, foretaste of winter.
wake *v.* feast, celebrate (into the night).
wakened *v. pa. t.* awakened, woke up; arose.
wakkest *adj. superl.* weakest, least distinguished, least deserving of consideration (person) [wŏk].
wakned *see* **wakened**
wal(le) *n.* wall.
wal(l)e *adj.* good; pleasant; lovely.
wale *v.* choose; find; take.
walke *v.* walk; **your worchip walkes aywhere** your worth is known everywhere.
wallande *adj.* surging, gushing; abundant.
walle *see* **wal(le)** *n.* and **wal(l)e** *adj.*
walour *n.* valour, bravery, courage; strength, might[valŏur].
walt *see* **welde**
waltered *v. pa. t.* welled out, surged forth [waltren].
wan *see* **wynne** *v.*
wande *n.* staff; tree.
wane *adj.* entirely lacking.
wap *n.* blow, stroke.
wapped *v. pa. t.* flew; rushed.
war *adj.* aware; on guard.
war *interj.* beware.
warde *see* **toward**
ware *v.* use; deal (a blow).
warly *adv.* warily; stealthily; **warloker** *compar.* more wisely [wārelī].
warme *adj.* warm.
warmed *v. pa. t.* warmed.
warne *v.* warn.

warp *v.* throw; utter, shout; offer [werpen].

warthe *n.* ford.

waryst *pp.* recovered (from exertions) [warishen].

was *v.* was; **wer(e)** *pa. t.* were (*sing.*); **weren** *pa. t.* were (*pl.*).

wasche *v.* wash.

wast *n.* waist.

waste *n.* wasteland, wilderness, deserted or desolate land.

wat *see* **what**

wathe *see* **wothe**

wat(t)er *n.* water.

wax *v.* grow; become.

waxen *adj.* made of wax.

way *adv.* away; **do way** cease, enough of that [wei].

way *n.* way; path, road; direction; **bi non way** there is no way, by no means.

wayke *adj.* feeble, weak [weik].

wayne *v.* send; bring; challenge (to a game).

wayte *v.* wait; look, see.

wayth *n.* spoils of hunt, game killed in hunt.

wayve *v.* wave; show; **wayve up** swing open [weiven].

we *interj.* alas; **we loo** woe, alas.

we *pron.* we; **u(u)s** (*obl.*) us, to us; **oure** our.

wede *n.* garment, item of clothing; armor.

weder *n.* weather; good weather; violent, stormy weather.

weghed *v. pa. t.* brought, served (wine) [weien].

wel *adv.* well; fully, completely, totally; truly, accurately; sincerely, genuinely; clearly, conclusively; amply, copiously, richly; **thenk wel** be mindful; **wyt ye wel** be assured; **fares wel** farewell.

wel-haled *adj.* well pulled-up, drawn tightly [hālen].

wela *adv.* very [wellā].

welcom, welcum *adj.* welcome; **welcomest** *superl.* most welcome.

welcum *v.* welcome [welcŏmen].

welde *v.* wield; enjoy, make use of; have, own, possess; wear; **walt out** cast out.

wele *n.* wealth, riches; worth, value; joy, happiness; **worthe hit wele other wo** for better or worse.

welkyn *n.* sky; cloud.

welnegh *adv.* almost [wel-neigh].

wende *n.* turn.

wende *v.* go; turn; *see also* **wene**

wene *v.* know, believe, think.

wener *adj. comp.* fairer, more lovely.

wenged *v. pa. t.* avenged [venğen].

went *see* **wende** *and* **wene**

weppen *n.* weapon [wēpen].

wer *see* **was**

werbelande *adj.* whistling, blowing fiercely [werblen].

werbles *n. pl.* notes, melody.

were *v.¹* protect, defend; resist, ward off, keep away.

were *v.²* wear.

were *see also* **was**

were-so-ever *see* **where-so-ever**

weren *see* **was**

werk(k) *n.* work; artistic design, ornamentation; embroidery; **of red golde werkes** made of red gold (1515n, 2367n).

werne *v.* refuse, reject.

wernyng *n.* resistance, obstruction, refusal.

werre *n.* war, fighting.

werre *v.* fight.

wesaunt *n.* esophagus.

wesche *see* **wasche**

west *adj.* western; **the west iles** Europe (7n).

weterly *adv.* clearly, fully, utterly [witterlī].

weve *v.* give; show (honor).

wex *see* **wax**

wharred *v. pa. t.* whirred.

what *interj.* exclamation emphasizing speaker's emotional involvement: See! Look! Listen! etc.

what *pron.* and *adj.* what; whatever.

what-so *pron.* whatever.

what-so-ever *pron.* whatever at all.

whederwarde *adv.* where, in what direction [whiderward].

whel *see* **whyle** *conj.*

when *adv.* and *conj.* when [whanne].

when-so *conj.* whenever [whanne-sō].

where *adv.* and *conj.* where; wherever.

where-ever *conj.* wherever.

where-so *adv.* wherever.

where-so-ever *adv.* and *conj.* wherever.

wherfore *adv.* therefore; why.

whethen *adv.* whence, from where, from whatever.

whether *adv.* and *pron.* yet, however; whether; **whether this be** can this be, is this.

whette *v.* whet; make a grinding noise.

whettyng *n.* sharpening edge with grindstone.

whiderwarde-so-ever *conj.* in whatever direction.

whil *see* **whyle** *conj.*

white *see* **whyte**

who *pron.* who; whoever; if someone.

who-so *pron.* whoever.

why *adv.* and *interj.* why.

whyle *conj.* while; as long as; until.

whyle *n.* while, time, period of time; opportunity; **the servise whyle** during the service, throughout the service.

whyrlande *pres. p.* whirling.

whyte *adj.* white.

wich *adj.* what.

wight *see* **wyght**

wil *see* **wyl**

wille *see* **wylle**

wit *see* **wyt**

with *see* **wyth**

withalle *adv.* indeed.

withhelde *see* **wythhalde**

withinne *see* **wythinne**

withoute(n) *prep.* without.

wlonk *adj.* beautiful; fine; rich; noble; **wlonkest** *superl.* most splendid.

wo *n.* woe.

wod *n.* wood, forest.

wod *v. see* **wade**

wodcraftes *n. pl.* art of hunting [wōde].

wode *adj.* insane.

wode *n. see* **wod**

wodwos *n. pl.* wild men of woods (721n) [wōde-wōse].

woghe *n.* sin, sinful act (1550n) [wough].

woke *see* **wake**

wol, wolde, woled *see* **wyl**

wolves *n. pl.* wolves.

wombe *n.* stomach.

won, wone *v.* dwell; stay; live.

wonde *v.* delay, hesitate (for fear).

wonder *adv.* extraordinarily.

wonder *n.* marvel, wondrous thing; wonder, amazement.

wondered *v. pa. t.* **wondered** was surprised [wŏndren].

wonderly *adv.* wondrously; greatly.

wone *n.¹* dwelling; place.

wone *n.²* pleasure, desire, inclination.

wone *n.³* multitude, large number; **al the wone** all the multitude, the sum total.

wone *v. see* **won**

wonnen *see* **wynne** *v.*

wont *n.* lack, shortage [want].

wont *v.* lack, be lacking; **er me wont** before I lose.

wonyd, wonyes *see* **won**

worche *v.* work, make, create; do; carry out; bring about; **let God worche** let God exercise His power, let God do as He intends.

worchip *n.* honor, fame, renown; worth; prize [worship(e)].

worchipe *v.* honor [worshipen].

worde *n.* word; fame; **grete wordes** boasting, blustering.

woried *v. pa. t.* worried, shook (fox) by throat (1905n) [wirīen].

worlde *n.* world.

wormes *n. pl.* dragons.

worre *adj. comp.* worse [wer].

wors *adj. comp.* worse; **worst** *superl.* worst [werse, werste].

worschip, worschyp *see* **worchip**

worst *see* **wors**

wort *n.* plant.

worth *adj.* worth.

worth, worthe *v.* be; become; turn out; be fitting for; **wel worth thee** I wish you well, may you be well.

worthé, worthy *adj. and adv.* worthy; noble; of worth; fitting, appropriate; courteously; **worthyest** *superl.* most honored.

worthily(ch) *adv.* worthily; properly; appropriately; honorably.

wot *see* **wyt**

wothe *n.* danger, peril, harm, injury.

wound *n.* wound (642n).

wounded *pp.* wounded.

wounden *see* **wynde** *v.*

woven *adj.* woven.

wowche *v.* vouch; **wowche saf** give, grant, bestow, provide [vŏuchen sauf].

wowe *n.* wall [wough].

wowyng *n.* wooing, love-making, seduction [wouing].

wrake *n.* destruction, ruin; distress, woe; vengeance.

wrang *adj.* wrong [wrong].

wrast *adj.* loud [wrest].

wrast *pp.* disposed toward [wresten].

wrastele *v.* wrestle, contend with [wrestlen].

wrathe *v.* anger, offend, vex; become angry; harm [wratthen].

wreyande *pres. p.* making location known, revealing [wreien].

wro *n.* nook, corner.

wroght, wroghten *see* **worche**

wroth *adj.* wroth, angry, enraged, vexed; loud, furious (1660n).

wrothely *adj.* and *adv.* enraged, furious; violently, ferociously; **wrotheloker** *compar.* more harshly [wrōthlī].

wruxled *pp.* clad [wrixlen].

wy *interj.* well, well then, why.

wyde *adv.* wide.

wyf *n.* wife; woman.

wyghe *see* **wyy(e)**

wyght *adj.* and *adv.* brave; swift; loud; **wyghtest** *superl.* most valiant; swiftest.

wyght *n.* creature; person; lady.

wyghtly *adv.* swiftly.

wykes *n. pl.* corners.

wyl *v.* will; intend; want, desire.

wylde *adj.* wild; unruly, headstrong, reckless; distracted, restless (89n).

wylde *n.* wild beast, animal; game; wild boar.

wyldrenesse wild, uninhabited region; **wyldrenesse of Wyrale** forest of Wirral [wīldernes(se)].

wyle *see* **whyle**

wylé *see* **wyly**

wyles *n. pl.* wiles, tricks, deceitful actions, clever maneuvers (1700n).

wylle *n.* will, desire; intention; character; **at (your, his, etc.) wylle** as (or when) you desire.

wylnyng *n.* request, desire.

wylsum *adj.* desolate, wild, pathless.

wylt *pp.* stolen away (through trickery) [wīlen].

wylt *v. see* **wyl**

wyly *n.* wily, guileful, cunning.

wylyde *adj.* skillful, intricate (2367n).

wymmen *n. pl.* women [wŏmman].

wyn *n.* wine.

wynde *n.* wind.

wynde *v.* wind, turn; progress; **wynde ayayn** return.

wyndow *n.* window [windou(e)].

wyne *see* **wyn**

wynne *adj.* delightful; lovely, beautiful; goodly; precious [win].

wynne *n.*[1] joy, happiness; strife, conflict (15n).

wynne *n.*[2] gain, benefit, advantage.

wynne *v.* win; go, come, make one's way to.

wynnelych *adj.* delightful.

wynt-hole *n.* wind-pipe.

wynter *n.* winter; **seven wynter** (for) seven years.

wyppe *v.*[1] whip; **wypped of** struck off, cut off [whippen].

wyppe *v.*[2] wipe, burnish, polish [wīpen].

wyrde *n.* fate, destiny (2134n) [wērd].

wys *adj.* wise, skilled in.

wyse *n.* manner, fashion; **in feghtyng wyse** equipped for battle; **in a siker wyse** securely.

wysse *v.* guide.

wyst(en) *see* **wyt**

wysty *adj.* desolate, deserted [wēstī].

wyt *v.* know, discover, be aware of, learn.

wyte *n. see* **wytte**

wyte *v.* look at [witīen].

wyth *prep.* with; from; by; against; within (1660n).

wythhalde *v.* restrain, check, stop [withhōlden].

wythinne *adv.* within, on the inside, in.

wythoute *see* **withoute(n)**

wytte, wyte *n.* wit, sense, reason, understanding (640n).

wyttenesse *n.* witness; **bere wyttenesse** bear witness, testify, corroborate [witnes(se)].

wyy(e), wyghe *n.* knight; man; person.

yarande *see* **yar(r)ande**

yare *adv.* fully, well, thoroughly.

yarkke *v.* give, bestow, grant; **yarked up** opened.

yar(r)ande *adj.* snarling; raucous, strident, loud [yerren].

yate *n.* gate.

yaule *v.* yowl, howl, yelp [youlen].

yayned *pp.* greeted, met [yeinen].

ye *adv.* and *interj.* yes; indeed.

ye *pron.* you (*pl.* and/or *form.*); **yow** you (*obl.*), to you; **your, yowre** your; **youres, yowres** yours; **yourself, yowreself, yorselven, yourselven** (you) yourself.

yede *v. pa. t.* went; **yedoun** (= **yede doun**) went down.

yederly *adv.* promptly, quickly, without delay; readily.

yedoun *see* **yede**

yef *see* **gif**

yelde *v.* yield; give; thank, reward, requite; return; **yelde ayayn** yield an answer, answer back.

yelle *v.* cry out.

yelpyng *n.* challenge, boast (492n).

yep *adj.* young, youthful; dashing, vigorous, daring.

yeply *adv.* at once, quickly.

yer(e) *n.* year.

yeres-yiftes *n. pl.* New Year's gifts [yēr, yēres yēve].

yerne *adv.* eagerly; quickly, at once.

yerne *v.¹* yearn, be eager.

yerne *v.²* pass by; hasten.

yet(te) *adv.* yet; then; yet again, once more; **bot yet** but even.

yeye *v.* announce, cry out; **yeye after grace** sue for grace, ask for mercy [yeien].

yif *see* **i(i)f**

yirnes *see* **yerne** *v.²*

yisterday *n.* yesterday.

ymage *n.* image, likeness.

yod *see* **yede**

Yol *n.* Yule, Christmas (season).

yolden *see* **yelde**

yolwe *adj.* yellow of complexion, sallow.

yomerly *adv.* pitifully.

yon *adj.* yonder, that one (over there).

yonder *adj.* the one, yonder, that one (over there).

yonge, yonke *adj.* young.

yore *adv.* for a long time.

yor-, your-, yow, yowr- *see* **ye**

yrn *n.* iron, armor [īren].

yye *n.* eye [eie].

yye-lyddes *n. pl.* eye-lids [eie-lid].

Select Bibliography and Works Cited

Sir Gawain and the Green Knight has been the subject of much excellent scholarship, and, while it has proven impossible to note every contribution, I have tried to incorporate enough to give the reader a start in pursuing topics of interest. A more thorough treatment of the scholarship up to 1993 is available through the following works: Malcom Andrew, *The* Gawain *Poet: An Annotated Bibliography, 1839-1977* (New York: Garland, 1979); Meg Stainsby, *Sir Gawain and the Green Knight: An Annotated Bibliography, 1978-1989* (New York: Garland, 1992); and Robert J. Blanch, *The* Gawain *Poems: A Reference Guide, 1978-1993* (Albany, NY: Whitson, 2000).

Abbreviations

Archiv	*Archiv für das Studium der neueren Sprachen und Literaturen*
ChR	*Chaucer Review*
EETS	Early English Text Society
ELN	*English Language Notes*
JEGP	*Journal of English and Germanic Philology*
LSE	*Leeds Studies in English*
MÆ	*Medium Ævum*
MIP	Medieval Institute Publications
MLN	*Modern Language Notes*
MLR	*Modern Language Review*
MP	*Modern Philology*
MS	*Mediaeval Studies*
Neophil	*Neophilologus*
NM	*Neuphilologische Mitteilungen*
N&Q	*Notes and Queries*
OS	Original Series
PMLA	*Publications of the Modern Language Society of America*
PQ	*Philological Quarterly*
RES	*Review of English Studies*
SAC	*Studies in the Age of Chaucer*
SP	*Studies in Philology*
UP	University Press

Ackerman, Robert W. (1944). "The Knighting Ceremonies in the Middle English Romances." *Speculum* 19: 285-313.

——. (1957). "'Pared out of Paper': *Gawain* 802 and *Purity* 1408." *JEGP* 56: 410-17.

——. (1958). "Gawain's Shield: Penitential Doctrine in *Gawain and the Green Knight*." *Anglia* 76: 254-65.

Aers, David. (1988). *Community, Gender, and Individual Identity: English writing, 1360-1430*. London: Routledge.

——. (2000). *Faith, Ethics, and Church: Writing in England, 1360-1409*. Cambridge: D.S. Brewer.

Allen, Valerie. (1992). "'Sir Gawain,' Cowardyse, and the 4th Pentad." *RES* new series 43: 181-93.

[*Alliterative Morte Arthure.*] (1994). *King Arthur's Death: The Middle English Stanzaic* Morte Arthur *and Alliterative* Morte Arthure. Ed. Larry D. Benson. Rev. Edward E. Foster. Kalamazoo, MI: MIP.

Ancrene Wisse. (2000). Ed. Robert Hasenfratz. Kalamazoo, MI: MIP.

Anderson, J.J. (1990). "The Three Judgments and the Ethos of Chivalry in *Sir Gawain and the Green Knight*." *ChR* 24.4: 337-55.

——. (1994). "*Sir Gawain and the Green Knight*, 1008-1009." *N&Q* 41: 443-43.

——, ed. (1996). Sir Gawain and the Green Knight; Pearl; Cleanness; Patience. London: Everyman.

——. (2005). *Language and Imagination in the* Gawain-*Poems*. Manchester: Manchester UP.

Andreas Capellanus. (1990). *The Art of Courtly Love*. Trans. John Jay Parry. New York: Columbia UP.

Andrew, Malcolm. (1997). "Theories of Authorship." In Brewer and Gibson 23-33.

——, and Ronald Waldron, eds. (2002). *The Poems of the* Pearl *Manuscript*: Pearl, Cleanness, Patience, Sir Gawain and the Green Knight. 4th ed. Exeter Medieval English Texts and Studies. Exeter: U of Exeter P.

Arthur, Ross G. (1987). *Medieval Sign Theory and* Sir Gawain and the Green Knight. Toronto: U of Toronto P.

Astell, Ann W. (1999). "Penitential Politics in *Sir Gawain and the Green Knight*: Richard II, Richard of Arundel, and Robert de Vere." In *Political Allegory in Late Medieval England*. Ithaca, NY, and London: Cornell UP. 117-37.

Barrett, Robert W., Jr. (2009). *Against all England: Regional Identity and Cheshire Writing, 1195-1656*. Notre Dame, IN: U of Notre Dame P.

Barron, W.R.J. (1980). Trawthe *and Treason: The Sin of Gawain Reconsidered*. Manchester: Manchester UP.

——, ed. (1998). *Sir Gawain and the Green Knight*. 2nd ed. Manchester : Manchester UP.

Batt, Catherine. (1992). "Gawain's Antifeminist Rant, the Pentangle, and Narrative Space." *Yearbook of English Studies* 22: 117-39.

The Battle of Maldon. (2001). *Eight Old English Poems*. Ed. John C. Pope. 3rd ed. rev. by R.D. Fulk. New York: W.W. Norton.

Battles, Dominique. (Forthcoming in 2013). *Cultural Difference and Material Culture in Middle English Literature: Normans and Saxons*. New York: Routledge.

Battles, Paul. (2007). "Sir Gawain's *bry t and broun* Diamonds (*SGGK*, 1. 618)." *N&Q* 54: 370-71.

——. (2008). "*Sir Gawain and the Green Knight*, Stanzas 32-34 (lines 740-810)." *Explicator* 67: 22-24.

——. (2010a). "Amended Texts, Emended Ladies: Female Agency and the Textual Editing of *Sir Gawain and the Green Knight*." *ChR* 44: 323-43.

——. (2010b). "*May the kny t rede: Sir Gawain and the Green Knight*, 1. 2111." *N&Q* 57: 29-31.

Bennett, Michael J. (1983). *Community, Class, and Careerism: Cheshire and Lancashire Society in the Age of* Sir Gawain and the Green Knight. Cambridge Studies in Medieval Life and Thought, 3rd series, 18. Cambridge and New York: Cambridge UP.

——. (1997). "The Historical Background." In Brewer and Gibson 71-90.

Benson, Larry D. (1961). "The Sources of the Beheading Episode in *Sir Gawain and the Green Knight*." *MP* 59: 1-12.

——. (1965). *Art and Tradition in* Sir Gawain and the Green Knight. New Brunswick, NJ: Rutgers UP.

Bernheimer, Richard. (1952). *Wild Men in the Middle Ages: A Study in Art, Sentiment, and Demonology*. New York: Octagon Books.

Blackwell, Alice. (2008). "Gawain's Five Senses: Technical Difficulties in the Endless Knot." *Quidditas* 29: 8-25.

Blanch, Robert J. (1983). "The Legal Framework of *A Twelvemonyth and a Day* in *SGGK*." *NM* 84: 347-52.

Blanch, Robert J., and Julian N. Wasserman. (1984). "Medieval Contracts and Covenants: The Legal Coloring of *Sir Gawain and the Green Knight*." *Neophil* 68: 598-610.

——. (1986). "To 'ouertake your wylle': Volition and Agreement in *Sir Gawain and the Green Knight*." *Neophil* 70: 119-29.

——. (1993). "The Current State of *Sir Gawain and the Green Knight* Criticism." *ChR* 27: 401-12.

——. (1995). *From* Pearl *to* Gawain: *Forme to Fynisment*. Gainesville: UP of Florida.

Borroff, Marie. (1962). Sir Gawain and the Green Knight: *A Stylistic and Metrical Study*. New Haven, CT: Yale UP.

Boulton, D'Arcy Jonathan Dacre. (1987). *Knights of the Crown: The Monarchical Orders of Knighthood in Later Medieval Europe, 1325-1520*. New York: St. Martin's.

Bowers, John M. (2001). *The Politics of* Pearl: *Court Poetry in the Age of Richard II*. Cambridge: D.S. Brewer.

Bredehoft, Thomas A. (2005). *Early English Metre*. Toronto Old English Series. Toronto: U of Toronto P.

Breeze, Andrew. (1996). "The *Gawain*-Poet and Toulouse." *N&Q* 43: 266-68.

——. (2007). "The *Gawain*-Poet and Hautdesert." *LSE* 38: 135-41.

Brewer, Derek. (1997a). "Armour II: The Arming Topos as Literature." In Brewer and Gibson 175-79.

——. (1997b). "The Color Green." In Brewer and Gibson 181-90.

——. (1997c). "Feasts." In Brewer and Gibson 131-42.

Brewer, Derek, and Jonathan Gibson, eds. (1997). *A Companion to the* Gawain-*Poet*. Woodbridge, Suffolk, and Rochester, NY: D.S. Brewer.

Brewer, Elisabeth. (1992). Sir Gawain and the Green Knight: *Sources and Analogues*. Arthurian Studies 21. 2nd ed. Woodbridge, Suffolk, and Rochester, NY: D.S. Brewer.

——. (1997). "Sources I: The Sources of *Sir Gawain and the Green Knight*." In Brewer and Gibson 243-55.

Burrow, J(ohn) A. (1959). "The Two Confession Scenes in *Sir Gawain and the Green Knight*." *MP* 57: 73-79.

——. (1965). *A Reading of* Sir Gawain and the Green Knight. London: Routledge & Kegan Paul.

——. (1971). *Ricardian Poetry: Chaucer, Gower, Langland, and the* Gawain *Poet*. New Haven, CT: Yale UP.

——. (1972). "Two Notes on *Sir Gawain and the Green Knight*." *N&Q* 19: 43-45.

——, ed. (1987). *Sir Gawain and the Green Knight*. Harmondsworth, Middlesex: Penguin.

Capellanus. *See* Andreas Capellanus.

Carruthers, Leo. (2001). "The Duke of Clarence and the Earls of March: Garter Knights and *Sir Gawain and the Green Knight*." *MÆ* 70: 65-78.

Chaucer, Geoffrey. (1987). *The Riverside Chaucer*. Ed. Larry D. Benson. Boston: Houghton Mifflin.

Cherewatuk, Karen. (1993). "Echoes of the Knighting Ceremony in *Sir Gawain and the Green Knight*." *Neophil* 77.1: 135-47.

——. (2009). "Becoming Male, Medieval Mothering, and Incarnational Theology in *Sir Gawain and the Green Knight* and the *Book of Margery Kempe*." *Arthuriana* 19.3: 15-24.

Chickering, Howell. (1997). "Stanzaic Closure and Linkage in *Sir Gawain and the Green Knight*." *ChR* 32.1: 1-31.

Christophersen, Paul. (1971). "The Englishness of *Sir Gawain and the Green Knight*." In *On the Novel: A Present for Walter Allen on His 60th Birthday from His Friends and Colleagues*. Ed. B.S. Benedikz. London: Dent. 46-56.

Clark, Cecily. (1966). "*Sir Gawain and the Green Knight*: Characterization by Syntax." *Essays in Criticism* 16: 361-74.

Cleanness. In Andrew and Waldron 2002.

Clein, Wendy. (1987). *Concepts of Chivalry in* Sir Gawain and the Green Knight. Norman, OK: Pilgrim Books.

Clough, Andrea. (1985). "The French Element in *Sir Gawain and the Green Knight*." *NM* 86: 187-96.

Cockcroft, Robert. (1978). "Castle Hautdesert: Portrait or Patchwork?" *Neophil* 62: 459-77.

Condren, Edward I. (2002). *The Numerical Universe of the* Gawain-Pearl *Poet: Beyond* Phi. Gainesville: UP of Florida.

Conquergood, Dwight. (1981). "Boasting and Performance in Anglo-Saxon England: Performance and the Heroic Ethos." *Literature in Performance* 2: 24-35.

Cooke, Jessica. (1998). "The Lady's 'Blushing' Ring in *Sir Gawain and the Green Knight*." *RES* 49: 1-8.

Cooke, W.G. (1989). "*Sir Gawain and the Green Knight*—A Restored Dating." *MÆ* 58: 34-48.

Cooke, W.G., and D'A. J.D. Boulton. (1999). "*Sir Gawain and the Green Knight*: A Poem for Henry of Grosmont?" *MÆ* 68: 42-54.

Cox, Catherine S. (2001). "Genesis and Gender in *Sir Gawain and the Green Knight*." *ChR* 35: 378-91.

——. (2005). *The Judaic Other in Dante, the* Gawain *Poet, and Chaucer*. Gainesville: UP of Florida.

——. (2007). "Eastward of the Garden: The Biblical Landscape of *Sir Gawain and the Green Knight*." In *Place, Space, and Landscape in Medieval Narrative*. Ed. Laura L. Howes. Knoxville: U of Tennessee P. 155-70.

Davenport, W.A. (1978). *The Art of the* Gawain-*Poet*. London: Athlone P.

David, Alfred. (1968). "Gawain and Aeneas." *English Studies* 49: 402-09.

Davis, Norman. (1970). "*Sir Gawain and the Green Knight* 2073." *N&Q* 17: 163-64.

——, ed. (1967). Sir Gawain and the Green Knight. 2nd rev. ed. of Tolkien and Gordon 1930. Oxford: Clarendon.

Delany, Paul. (1965). "The Role of the Guide in *Sir Gawain and the Green Knight*." *Neophil* 49: 250-55.

De Roo, Harvey. (1997). "What's in a Name? Power Dynamics in *Sir Gawain and the Green Knight*." *ChR* 31.3: 232-55.

Derrickson, Ann. (1980). "The Pentangle: Guiding Star for the *Gawain*-Poet." *Comitatus* 11: 10-19.

[*Destruction of Troy*.] (1869-74). *The "Gest Hystoriale" of the Destruction of Troy: An Alliterative Romance Translated from Guido de Colonna's "Hystoria Troiana"*. Ed. G.A. Panton and D. Donaldson. EETS OS 39, 56 (1869, 1874). London: Pub. for EETS by N. Trübner & Co.

Diamond, Arlyn. (1976). "*Sir Gawain and the Green Knight*: An Alliterative Romance," *PQ* 55: 10-29.

Dodman, Trevor. (2005). "Hunting to Teach: Class, Pedagogy, and Maleness in *The Master of Game* and *Sir Gawain and the Green Knight*." *Exemplaria* 17: 413-44.

Dove, Mary. (1986). *The Perfect Age of Man's Life*. Cambridge: Cambridge UP.

Duggan, Hoyt N. (1997). "Meter, Stanza, Vocabulary, Dialect." In Brewer and Gibson 221-42.

Eadie, John. (1981). "Sir Gawain and the Ladies of Ill-Repute." *Annuale Mediaevale* 20: 52-66.

Edward, Duke of York. (1909). *The Master of Game*. Ed. William Adolf Baillie-Grohman and Florence Baillie-Grohman. London: Chatto & Windus.

Elliott, Ralph W.V. (1974). "Some Northern Features of Landscape in *Sir Gawain and the Green Knight*." In *Iceland and the Mediaeval World: Studies in Honour of Ian Maxwell*. Ed. Gabriel Turville-Petre and John Stanley Martin. Melbourne: U of Melbourne P. 132-43.

——. *The Gawain Country*. (1984). Leeds Texts and Monographs 8. Leeds: University of Leeds, School of English.

——. (1997). "Landscape and Geography." In Brewer and Gibson 105-17.

Evans, W.O. (1968). "Gawain's New Pentangle." *Trivium* 3: 92-94.

Farley-Hills, David. (1996). "'Largesse' in *Sir Gawain and the Green Knight*." *N&Q* 43: 136-38.

Federico, Sylvia. (2007). "The Place of Chivalry in the New Trojan Court: Gawain, Troilus, and Richard II." In *Place, Space, and Landscape in Medieval Narrative*. Ed. Laura L. Howes. Knoxville: U of Tennessee P. 171-79.

Feinstein, Sandy. (2001). "Sounding the Hunt in *Sir Gawain and the Green Knight*." *Dalhousie Review* 82.1: 35-53.

Field, P.J.C. (1971). "A Rereading of *Sir Gawain and the Green Knight*." *SP* 68: 255-69.

Finley, C. Stephen. (1990). "'*Endeles Knot*': Closure and Indeterminacy in *Sir Gawain and the Green Knight*." *Papers in Language and Literature* 26: 445-58.

Fisher, Sheila. (1996). "Leaving Morgan Aside: Women, History, and Revisionism in *Sir Gawain and the Green Knight*." In *Arthurian Women: A Casebook*. Ed. Thelma S. Fenster. New York: Garland. 77-95.

Frankis, P.J. (1961). "*Sir Gawain and the Green Knight*, line 35: *with lel letters loken*." *N&Q* 8: 329-30.

Friedman, Albert B. (1960). "Morgan le Fay in *Sir Gawain and the Green Knight*." *Speculum* 35: 260-74.

Friedman, Albert B., and Richard H. Osberg. (1977). "Gawain's Girdle as Traditional Symbol." *Journal of American Folklore* 90: 301-15.

Fries, Maureen. (1994). "From the Lady to the Tramp: The Decline of Morgan le Fay in Medieval Romance." *Arthuriana* 4: 1-18.

Gee, Elizabeth. (1984). "The Lists of Knights in *Sir Gawain and the Green Knight*." *Australasian Universities Modern Language Association* 62: 171-78.

Geoffrey of Monmouth. (1966). *History of the Kings of Britain*. Trans. Lewis Thorpe. London: Penguin.

Goldhurst, William. (1958). "The Green and the Gold: The Major Theme of *Gawain and the Green Knight*." *College English* 20: 61-65.

Gollancz, Sir Israel. (1923). Pearl, Cleanness, Patience *and* Sir Gawain *Reproduced in Facsimile from the Unique MS. Cotton Nero A.x in the British Museum*. London: Oxford UP for EETS.

——, ed. (1940). *Sir Gawain and the Green Knight*. With Mabel Day and Mary S. Serjeantson. EETS OS 210. London: Pub. for EETS by H. Milford, Oxford UP.

Green, Richard Firth. (1999). *A Crisis of Truth: Literature and Law in Ricardian England*. Philadelphia: U of Pennsylvania P.

Green, Richard Hamilton. (1962). "Gawain's Shield and the Quest for Perfection." *Journal of English Literary History* 29: 121-39.

The Green Knight. (1985). In *Sir Gawain: Eleven Romances and Tales*. Ed. Thomas Hahn. Kalamazoo, MI: MIP.

Griffith, Richard R. (1978). "Bertilak's Lady: The French Background of *Sir Gawain and the Green Knight.*" In *Machaut's World: Science and Art in the Fourteenth Century.* Ed. Madeleine Pelner Cosman and Bruce Chandler. New York: New York Academy of Sciences. 249-66.

Hanna, Ralph, III. (1983). "Unlocking What's Locked: Gawain's Green Girdle." *Viator* 14: 289-302.

Hardman, Phillipa. (1999). "Gawain's Practice of Piety in *Sir Gawain and the Green Knight.*" *MÆ* 68: 247-67.

Haydock, Nicholas. (2006). "Treasonous Founders and Pious Seducers: Aeneas, Gawain, and Aporetic Romance." In Risden 112-20.

Heng, Geraldine. (1991). "Feminine Knots and the Other *Sir Gawain and the Green Knight.*" *PMLA* 106: 500-14.

———. (1992). "A Woman Wants: The Lady, *Gawain*, and the Forms of Seduction." *Yale Journal of Criticism* 5: 110-15.

Herman, Jason M. (2010). "'With Lel Letteres Loken': *Sir Gawain and the Green Knight* Line 35." *N&Q* 57: 311-13.

Hill, Ordelle G. (2009). *Looking Westward: Poetry, Landscape, and Politics in* Sir Gawain and the Green Knight. Newark: U of Delaware P.

Holthausen, F. (1974). *Altenglisches etymologisches Wörterbuch.* 3rd ed. Germanische Bibliothek, 2. Reihe. Heidelberg: Carl Winter.

Hornstein, Lilian Herlands. (1941). "The Historical Background of the *King of Tars.*" *Speculum* 16: 404-14.

Ingledew, Francis. (2006). Sir Gawain and the Green Knight *and the Order of the Garter.* Notre Dame, IN: U of Notre Dame P.

Jonassen, Frederick B. (1986). "Elements from the Traditional Drama of England in *Sir Gawain and the Green Knight.*" *Viator* 17: 221-54.

Keen, Maurice. (1984). *Chivalry.* New Haven, CT and London: Yale UP.

Kelley, Robert L. (1982). "Allusions to the Vulgate Cycle in *Sir Gawain and the Green Knight.*" In *Literary and Historical Perspectives of the Middle Ages: Proceedings of the SEMA Meetings.* Ed. Patricia W. Cummins et al. Morgantown: West Virginia UP. 183-99.

Kennedy, Edward Donald. (2007). "Gawain's Family and Friends: *Sir Gawain and the Green Knight* and Its Allusions to French Prose Romances." In *People and Texts: Relationships in Medieval Literature.* Ed. Thea Summerfield and Keith Busby. Amsterdam: Rodopi. 143-60.

Kitson, P.R. (1998). "The Name of the Green Knight." *NM* 99: 39-52.

Knight, Rhonda. (2003). "All Dressed Up with Someplace to Go: Regional Identity in *Sir Gawain and the Green Knight.*" *SAC* 25: 259-84.

Kottler, Barnet, and Alan M. Markman. (1966). *A Concordance of Five Middle English Poems:* Cleanness, St. Erkenwald, Sir Gawain and the Green Knight, Patience, *and* Pearl. Pittsburgh: U of Pittsburgh P.

Kropp, Josefa. (1992). "On the Translation of Middle English *Hastlettez.*" *N&Q* 39: 438-41.

Lacy, Michael. (1997). "Armour I." In Brewer and Gibson 165-73.

Lacy, Norris J., and Geoffrey Ashe. (1997). *The Arthurian Handbook.* 2nd ed. New York and London: Garland.

Lancelot-Grail: The Old French Arthurian Vulgate and Post-Vulgate in Translation. (1992-96). Ed. Norris J. Lacy. Garland Reference Library of the Humanities. 6 vols. New York: Garland.

Lass, Roger. (1966). "Man's Heaven: The Symbolism of Gawain's Shield." *MS* 28: 354-60.

Lehmann, Winfred P. (1956). *The Development of Germanic Verse Form*. Austin: U of Texas P and Linguistic Society of America.

Longo, Joseph H. (1967). "*Sir Gawain and the Green Knight*: The Christian Quest for Perfection." *Nottingham Medieval Studies* 11: 57-85

Lucas, P.J. (1968). "Gawain's Anti-Feminism." *N&Q* 15: 324-25.

Machan, Tim William. (2012). "Chaucer and the History of English." *Speculum* 87: 147-75.

Malarkey, Stoddard, and J. Barre Toelken. (1964). "Gawain and the Green Girdle." *JEGP* 63: 14-20.

Malory, Sir Thomas. (2004). *Le Morte Darthur*. Ed. Stephen H.A. Shepherd. New York: W.W. Norton.

Mann, Jill. (1986). "Price and Value in 'Sir Gawain and the Green Knight.'" *Essays in Criticism* 36.4: 294-318.

——. (2009). "Courtly Aesthetics and Courtly Ethics in *Sir Gawain and the Green Knight*." *SAC* 31: 231-65.

Markus, Manfred. (1974). "Some Examples of Ambiguity in *Sir Gawain and the Green Knight*." *NM* 75: 625-29.

Martin, Carl Grey. (2008). "The Cipher of Chivalry: Violence as Courtly Play in the World of *Sir Gawain and the Green Knight*." *ChR* 43: 311-29.

Martin, John W. (1973). "The Knight Who Stayed Silent Through Courtesy." *Archiv* 210: 53-57.

Marvin, William Perry. (2006). *Hunting Law and Ritual in Medieval English Literature*. Cambridge: D.S. Brewer.

Mathew, Gervase. (1968). *The Court of Richard II*. New York: W.W. Norton.

Matthews, William. (1975). "*bi lag mon*: A Crux in *Sir Gawain and the Green Knight*." *Medievalia et Humanistica* 6: 151-55.

McCarthy, Conor. (2008). "*Luf-talkyng* in *Sir Gawain and the Green Knight*." *Neophil* 92.1: 155-62.

McIntosh, Angus, M.L. Samuels, and Michael Benskin. (1986). *A Linguistic Atlas of Late Medieval English*. 4 vols. Aberdeen: Aberdeen UP.

Metcalf, Allan A. (1976). "Silent Knight: 'Sum for Cortaysye?'" *Archiv* 213: 338-42.

Meyer, Ann A. (2001). "The Despensers and the *Gawain* Poet: A Gloucestershire Link to the Alliterative Master of the Northwest Midlands." *ChR* 35: 413-29.

Meyer, Heinz, and Rudolf Suntrup. (1987). "Fünf." In *Lexikon der mittelalterlichen Zahlenbedeutungen*. Münsterische Mittelalter-Schriften 56. Munich: Wilhelm Fink. 403-42.

Middle English Dictionary. (1952-2001). Ed. Hans Kurath, Sherman M. Kuhn, and Robert E. Lewis. Ann Arbor: U of Michigan P.

Miller, Mark. (2010). "The Ends of Excitement in *Sir Gawain and the Green Knight*: Teleology, Ethics, and the Death Drive." *SAC* 32: 215-56.

Mills, David. (1968). "An Analysis of the Temptation Scenes in *Sir Gawain and the Green Knight*." *JEGP* 67: 612-30.

Monmouth, Geoffrey of. *See* Geoffrey of Monmouth.

Moody, Patricia A. (1976). "The Childgered Arthur of *Sir Gawain and the Green Knight*." *Studies in Medieval Culture* 8-9: 173-80.

Moorman, Charles, ed. (1977). *The Works of the Gawain-Poet*. Jackson: U of Mississippi P.

Morgan, Gerald R. (1979). "The Significance of the Pentangle Symbolism in 'Sir Gawain and the Green Knight.'" *MLR* 74: 769-90.

——. (1985). "The Validity of Gawain's Confession in *Sir Gawain and the Green Knight*." *RES* 36: 1-18.

——. (1991). Sir Gawain and the Green Knight *and the Idea of Righteousness.* Dublin Studies in Medieval and Renaissance Literature. Blackrock, Co. Dublin: Irish Academic P.

——. (1997). "The Perfection of the Pentangle and of Sir Gawain in *Sir Gawain and the Green Knight.*" In *Essays on Ricardian Literature in Honour of J.A. Burrow,* ed. A.J. Minnis, Charlotte C. Morse, and Thorlac Turville-Petre. Oxford: Clarendon; New York: Oxford UP. 252-75.

——. (2002). "Medieval Misogyny and Gawain's Outburst Against Women in *Sir Gawain and the Green Knight.*" *MLR* 97: 265-79.

Myer, Thomas. (1995). "*Sir Gawain and the Green Knight,* line 1771." *Explicator* 53: 188-89.

Neaman, Judith S. (1976). "Sir Gawain's Covenant: Troth and *Timor Mortis.*" *PQ* 55: 30-42.

Newhauser, Richard. (1990). "The Meaning of Gawain's Greed." *SP* 87: 410-26.

Ng, Su Fang, and Kenneth Hodges. (2010). "Saint George, Islam, and Regional Audiences in *Sir Gawain and the Green Knight.*" *SAC* 32: 257-94.

Nicholls, Jonathan. (1985). *The Matter of Courtesy: Medieval Courtesy Books and the Gawain-Poet.* Woodbridge, Suffolk and Dover, NH: D.S. Brewer.

Noah's Flood. (1974). In *The Chester Mystery Cycle.* Ed. R.M. Lumiansky and David Mills. Vol. 1. EETS Second Series 3. London: Oxford UP for EETS.

Nolan, Barbara, and David Farley-Hills. (1971). "The Authorship of *Pearl*: Two Notes." *RES* 22: 295-302.

Ong, Walter J. (1950). "The Green Knight's Harts and Bucks." *MLN* 65.8: 536-39.

Ovid. (1982). *The Art of Love.* In *The Erotic Poems.* Trans. Peter Green. London: Penguin.

Oxford English Dictionary. (2008). 3rd ed.

Pace, George B. (1969). "Sir Gawain and Michaelmas." *Traditio* 25: 404-11.

Patience. (2002). In Andrew and Waldron.

Pearsall, Derek. (2011). "*Sir Gawain and the Green Knight*: An Essay in Enigma." *ChR* 46: 248-58.

Perryman, Judith. (1978). "Decapitating Drama in *Sir Gawain and the Green Knight.*" *Dutch Quarterly Review of Anglo-American Letters* 8: 283-300.

Plummer, John. (1991). "Signifying the Self: Language and Identity in *Sir Gawain and the Green Knight.*" In *Text and Matter: New Critical Perspectives on the Pearl-Poet.* Ed. Robert J. Blanch, Miriam Youngerman Miller, and Julian N. Wasserman. Troy, NY: Whitston Publishing Co. 195-212.

Prior, Sandra Pierson. (1994). *The Pearl Poet Revisited.* New York: Twayne.

——. (1996). *The Fayre Formez of the* Pearl *Poet.* Medieval Texts and Studies 18. East Lansing: Michigan State UP.

Prose Merlin. (1998). Ed. John Conlee. Kalamazoo, MI: MIP.

Putter, Ad. (1995). Sir Gawain and the Green Knight *and French Arthurian Romance.* Oxford and New York: Clarendon.

——. (1996). *An Introduction to the* Gawain *Poet.* London: Longman.

——. (2006). "The Ways and Words of the Hunt: Notes on S*ir Gawain and the Green Knight, The Master of the Game, Sir Tristrem, Pearl,* and *Saint Erkenwald.*" *ChR* 40: 354-85.

Putter, Ad, and Myra Stokes. (2007). "The *Linguistic Atlas* and the Dialect of the *Gawain* Poems." *JEGP* 106: 468-91.

Putter, Ad, Judith Jefferson, and Myra Stokes. (2007). *Studies in the Metre of Alliterative Verse.* Medium Ævum Monographs, new series 25. Oxford: Society for the Study of Medieval Languages and Literature.

Reichardt, Paul F. (1984). "Gawain and the Image of the Wound." *PMLA* 99: 154-61.

Renoir, Alain. (1960). "The Progressive Magnification: An Instance of Psychological Description in *Sir Gawain and the Green Knight.*" *Moderna Språk* 54: 245-53.

Revard, Carter. (2001-02). "Was the Pearl Poet in Aquitaine with Chaucer? A Note on *Fade*, L. 149 of Sir Gawain." *SELIM: Journal of the Spanish Society for Medieval English Language and Literature* 11: 5-26.

Risden, E.L., ed. (2006a). Sir Gawain *and the Classical Tradition.* Jefferson, NC, and London: McFarland.

——. (2006b). "The 'Tresounous Tulk' in *Sir Gawain and the Green Knight.*" In Risden 112-20.

Roberts, Stephen J. (2002). *A History of Wirral.* Chichester: Phillimore.

Robertson, D.W., Jr. (1954). "Why the Devil Wears Green." *MLN* 69: 470-72.

Rooney, Anne. (1993). *Hunting in Middle English Literature.* Woodbridge, Suffolk, and Rochester, NY: Boydell P.

Rowley, Sharon M. (2003). "Textual Studies, Feminism, and Performance in *Sir Gawain and the Green Knight.*" *ChR* 38: 158-77.

Rudd, Gillian. (2007). *Greenery: Ecocritical Readings of Late Medieval Literature.* Manchester: Manchester UP.

——. (2010). "'Substituting Earth for God?': Ethics and the Recognition of Specific Place in *Sir Gawain and the Green Knight* and *The Secret Garden.*" In *Literature and Ethics: From the Green Knight to the Dark Knight.* Ed. Steve Brie and William T. Rossiter. Newcastle upon Tyne: Cambridge Scholars. 17-30.

Russom, Geoffrey. (2004). "The Evolution of Middle English Alliterative Meter." In *Studies in the History of the English Language II: Unfolding Conversations.* Ed. Anne Kurzan and Kimberly Emmons. Berlin: Mouton de Gruyter. 279-304.

Rutter, Russell. (2006). "The Treason of Aeneas and the Mythographers of Vergil: The Classical Tradition in *Sir Gawain and the Green Knight.*" In Risden 30-48.

Sadowski, Piotr. (1996). *The Knight on His Quest : Symbolic Patterns of Transition in* Sir Gawain and the Green Knight. Newark: U of Delaware P.

Sanderlin, George. (1973). "'Thagh I Were Burde Bryghtest.'" *ChR* 8: 60-64.

Savage, Henry L. (1931). "A Note on Sir Gawain and the Green Knight 700-2." *MLN* 46: 455-57.

——. (1944). Review of Gollancz 1940. *MLN* 59: 342-50.

——. (1952). "The Feast of Fools in *Sir Gawain and the Green Knight.*" *JEGP* 51: 537-44.

——. (1956). *The* Gawain-*Poet: Studies in His Personality and Background.* Chapel Hill: U of North Carolina P.

Schmidt, A.V.C. (1987). "'Latent Content' and 'The Testimony of the Text': Symbolic Meaning in *Sir Gawain and the Green Knight.*" *RES* 38: 145-68.

Scott, Joanna. (2010). "Betraying Origins: The Many Faces of Aeneas in Medieval English Literature." *LATCH: A Journal for the Study of the Literary Artifact in Theory, Culture, or History* 3: 64-84.

Scott-Macnab, David. (2010). "The Medieval Boar and Its Haslets." *NM* 111: 355-66.

Shaw, Ian. (1980). "Sir Gawain Lurking: A Note on *Sir Gawain and the Green Knight,* l. 1180 and l. 1195." *ELN* 18: 1-8.

Shoaf, R.A. (1984). *The Poem as Green Girdle:* Commercium *in* Sir Gawain and the Green Knight. University of Florida Monographs 55. Gainesville: UP of Florida.

Silverstein, Theodore. (1965). "*Sir Gawain,* Dear Brutus, and Britain's Fortunate Founding: A Study in Comedy and Convention." *MP* 62: 189-206.

——, ed. (1984). Sir Gawain & the Green Knight: *A New Critical Edition.* Chicago: U of Chicago P.

Smithers, G.V. (1953). "Story-Patterns in Some Breton Lays." *MÆ* 22: 61-92.

Southwood, Paul. (1997). "Gawain's Helmet." *N&Q* 44: 164-68.

Spearing, A.C. (1964). "*Sir Gawain and the Green Knight*." In *Criticism and Medieval Poetry*. London: Arnold; New York: Barnes and Noble. 26-45.

——. (1970). *The Gawain-Poet: A Critical Study*. Cambridge: Cambridge UP.

Speirs, John. (1957). "*Sir Gawain and the Green Knight*." In *Medieval English Poetry: The Non-Chaucerian Tradition*. London: Faber. 215-51. Orig. publ. in *Scrutiny* 16 (1949): 274-300.

Sprunger, David A. (1993). "Wild Folk and Lunatics in Medieval Romance." In *The Medieval World of Nature: A Book of Essays*. Ed. Joyce E. Salisbury. Garland Medieval Casebooks 5. New York: Garland. 145-63.

Stanbury, Sarah. (1991). *Seeing the Gawain-Poet: Description and the Act of Perception*. Philadelphia: U of Pennsylvania P.

Stephens, Carolyn King. (2006). "The 'Pentangle Hypothesis': A Dating History and Resetting of *Sir Gawain and the Green Knight*." *Fifteenth-Century Studies* 31: 174-202.

Stevens, John. (1986). *Words and Music in the Middle Ages: Song, Narrative, Dance and Drama, 1050-1350*. Cambridge: Cambridge UP.

Stewart-Brown, Ronald. (1907). *The Wapentake of Wirral*. Liverpool: Henry Young and Sons.

Suzuki, Eiichi. (1969). "Two Notes on Sir Gawain." *Essays and Studies in English Language and Literature* 55: 63-80.

——. (1977). "A Note on the Age of the Green Knight." *NM* 78: 27-30.

——. (1981). "Another Note on Hyghe in Sir Gawain." *Mediaeval English Studies Newsletter* 5: 1-2.

Sykes, Naomi Jane. (2007). *The Norman Conquest: A Zoological Perspective*. Oxford: Archaeopress.

Tamplin, Ronald. (1969). "The Saints in *Sir Gawain and the Green Knight*." *Speculum* 44: 403-20.

Thompson, Michael. (1997). "Castles." In Brewer and Gibson 119-30.

Thompson, Raymond H., and Keith Busby, eds. (2006). *Gawain: A Casebook*. Arthurian Characters and Themes 8. New York: Routledge.

Tolkien, J.R.R., and E.V. Gordon, eds. (1930). Sir Gawain and the Green Knight. Corrected Impression. Oxford: Clarendon.

Tracey, Larissa. (2007). "A Knight of God or the Goddess? Rethinking Religious Syncretism in *Sir Gawain and the Green Knight*." *Arthuriana* 17: 31-55.

Twomey, Michael W. (2001). "Morgan le Fay at Hautdesert." In *On Arthurian Women: Essays in Memory of Maureen Fries*. Ed. Bonnie Wheeler and Fiona Tolhurst. Dallas, TX: Scriptorium P. 103-19.

Vantuono, William. (1975). "A Name in the Cotton MS Nero A.X. Article 3." *MS* 37: 537-42.

——. (1981). "John de Mascy of Sale and the *Pearl* Poems." *Manuscripta* 25: 77-88.

——, ed. (1999). *Sir Gawain and the Green Knight*. Notre Dame, IN: U of Notre Dame P.

Veck, Sonya. (2010). "Quat Is This Fairy Burial Mound? The Gawain-Poet's Green Moment in Sir Gawain and the Green Knight." In *Standing in the Shadow of the Master? Chaucerian Influences and Interpretations*. Ed. Kathleen A. Bishop. Newcastle upon Tyne: Cambridge Scholars. 113-22.

Veldhoen, Bart. (1990). "Psychology and the Middle English Romances." In *Companion to Middle English Romance*. Ed. Henk Aertsen and Alistair A. MacDonald. Amsterdam: VU UP. 101-27.

Wade, Sidney. (1986). "An Analysis of the Similes and Their Function in the Characterization of the Green Knight." *NM* 87: 375-81.

Walls, Kathryn. (2003). "The Axe in *Sir Gawain and the Green Knight*." *American Notes and Queries* 16.1: 13-18.

Watson, Elizabeth Porges. (1987). "The Arming of Gawain: *Vrysoun* and *Cercle*." *LSE* 18: 31-44.

Watson, Melvin R. (1949). "The Chronology of *Sir Gawain and the Green Knight*." *MLN* 64.2: 85-86.

Weiss, Victoria L. (1977). "The Medieval Knighting Ceremony in *Sir Gawain and the Green Knight*." *ChR* 12: 183-89.

——. (1991). "*Sir Gawain and the Green Knight* and the Fourteenth-Century Interlude." In *Text and Matter: New Critical Perspectives on the* Pearl-*Poet*. Ed. Robert J. Blanch, Miriam Youngerman Miller, and Julian N. Wasserman. Troy, NY: Whitston. 229-41.

White, Robert B., Jr. (1965). "A Note on the Green Knight's Red Eyes (GGK, 304)." *ELN* 2: 250-52.

Whiteford, Peter. (2004). "Rereading Gawain's Five Wits." *MÆ* 73: 225-34.

Whiting, B.J. (2006). "Gawain: His Reputation, His Courtesy, and His Appearance in Chaucer's *Squire's Tale*." In Thompson and Busby 45-94. Orig. publ. in *MS* 9 (1947): 189-234.

Williams, Edith Whitehurst. (1985). "Morgan La Fee as Trickster in *Sir Gawain and the Green Knight*." *Folklore* 96: 38-56.

Wilson, Edward. (1979). "*Sir Gawain and the Green Knight* and the Stanley Family of Stanley, Storeton, and Hooton." *RES* 30 308-16.

Woods, William F. (2002). "Nature and the Inner Man in *Sir Gawain and the Green Knight*." *ChR* 36: 209-27.

from the publisher

A name never says it all, but the word "broadview" expresses a good deal of the philosophy behind our company. We are open to a broad range of academic approaches and political viewpoints. We pay attention to the broad impact book publishing and book printing has in the wider world; we began using recycled stock more than a decade ago, and for some years now we have used 100% recycled paper for most titles. As a Canadian-based company we naturally publish a number of titles with a Canadian emphasis, but our publishing program overall is internationally oriented and broad-ranging. Our individual titles often appeal to a broad readership too; many are of interest as much to general readers as to academics and students.

Founded in 1985, Broadview remains a fully independent company owned by its shareholders—not an imprint or subsidiary of a larger multinational.

If you would like to find out more about Broadview and about the books we publish, please visit us at **www.broadviewpress.com**. And if you'd like to place an order through the site, we'd like to show our appreciation by extending a special discount to you: by entering the code below you will receive a 20% discount on purchases made through the Broadview website.

Discount code: **broadview20%**

Thank you for choosing Broadview.

Please note: this offer applies only to sales of bound books within the United States or Canada.